SERMONS
TOO HOT TO
PREACH

*To Mary Brau & Jour—
It was great to see
you at the
coming Clergy Clambake,
October, 2010
John*

John M. Miller

SERMONS TOO HOT TO PREACH

John M. Miller

Copyright © 2004
All Rights Reserved

PUBLISHED BY:
BRENTWOOD CHRISTIAN PRESS
4000 BEALLWOOD AVENUE
COLUMBUS, GEORGIA 31904

FOREWORD

This book of sermons was completed in the early summer of 2002. Being the sometimes optimistic soul that I am, I began sending a summary of its contents and a few sample sermons to various publishers, in the hope that some adventurous company would decide to publish the complete collection of sermons.

Being also the realist that I am, I decided after nearly a year of rejection letters that no one seemed to have discovered what a veritable treasure-trove of homiletical gems were contained herein, nor was anyone likely to do so in the future. Then, in my nihilistic mode, for an additional year I did nothing with the manuscript for the book.

However, hope springs eternal in the human breast, as Alexander Pope once wrote, and I finally decided to have my book of sermons printed privately. This is the sixth book that has appeared with my moniker attached to the cover, and five of them have been privately printed. Ah well, some day I may become a serious writer, recognized by people beyond the list of my kindly acquaintances who are willing to pay their hard-earned cash for my authored efforts.

Well-known authors have a great advantage over the multitude of us who are would-be authors. They, or their literary agents, can get a manuscript to a publisher and get a quick response. And that is enormously helpful to a writer, even if the response is negative.

The issue of a quick response impacts upon these sermons, because a good bit of water has gone over the homiletical dam since the summer of 2002. A war was waged in Iraq, and it is still going on. A national election in the USA is rapidly approaching, and it will affect our common life greatly, no matter who wins. The world is changing more rapidly than is our usual pace of change. I might have written about some of these events if I had just finished writing these sermons, but I didn't, so I didn't. I decided to leave them in their 2002 completed state.

Perhaps there is some value for you, as well as for me, to observe what was coursing through my cranium two years ago as compared to what might be coursing through now. Some of the politically-oriented perorations are a bit dated. Some things I wrote were more prescient than I ever could have imagined. But it was interesting to me as I re-read the manuscript to see how things have or have not changed in the passage of two years, and perhaps you will find that of interest as well.

One factor struck me in particular in reviewing these sermons. Up until two years ago, I had always capitalized "**He**" when referring to Jesus by the male personal pronoun, just as I had always capitalized "He" when referring to God by means of the male personal pronoun. Several years ago I admitted to myself that I no longer consider Jesus divine, so I now call God "**Him**," but Jesus "**him**." But Jesus remained "Him" until I started writing sermons again as the organizing pastor of The Chapel Without Walls on Hilton Head Island, South Carolina. However, since 2002 was then and 2004 is now, I decided to leave the spelling regarding Jesus the way it was in my head when these sermons were first completed. A lengthy rationale for this change in thinking is recorded in the last book I had printed, which was called *The Irony of Christianity: A Pastor's Appeal for a Higher Theology and a Lower Christology.* But even there I continued to use the evangelical writer's convention of the "He" Jesus. Go figure.

In advance, I want to thank you for showing sufficient confidence and faith in me that you actually purchased a copy of this tome. Truly I am grateful to you. I think the sermons are worth reading, or else I would not paid to have them printed. But I am honored that you feel sufficiently motivated to buy a copy of the book, and it helps affirm me in choosing to go ahead with the publication of *Sermons Too Hot to Preach.*

I also want to thank Jerry Luquire, who heads the Brentwood Publishers Group in Columbus, Georgia. Brentwood has published five of my six books. Most of their authors are far, far more conservative than I. It is a sign of Jerry Luquire's Christian grace that he is willing to allow such a collection of sermons as these to be foisted upon the innocent reading public, especially considering that most Brentwood readers would be mildly miffed or exceedingly enraged by what I have said in these pages.

Since you paid for the book, obviously you can read it by any method you choose. However, I suggest that you read only one sermon at a time, and then put the book down. Certainly you should not try to read the whole book in one "fell swoop," as Mr. Shakespeare would say. It is simply too **too** for you to try doing that.

Put the book in a convenient place, and pick it up to read a sermon whenever it is convenient. If you tend to spend a long time in the bathroom, this could be a good Bathroom Book. If you travel a lot, it could be a good Boeing Book. If you have to sit around frequently waiting to see someone or other (most likely your doctor), or if you have increments of twenty to thirty minutes on your hands on a regular basis, this could be a good Between-Times Book.

One final suggestion. At the beginning of each sermon there is a scripture passage listed. It is upon that biblical reading that each sermon is purportedly based. (Some purport to stick with the text far better than others, as you shall see.) Please read the whole scripture passage **before** you read the sermon. That way you will derive the greatest benefit from your efforts.

All that preliminary palaver having been stated for you, dear reader, read on!

John M. Miller
Bluffton, South Carolina
August 21, 2004

TABLE OF CONTENTS

PREFACE

or:
why I wrote a spate of sermons
I never intended orally to deliver

For 36 years, I was a parish minister. For 31 of those years, I was either the pastor or interim pastor of congregations, and for 5 years I was an assistant minister.

Of all the responsibilities and duties of a parish parson, the one I much preferred was that of writing sermons. Not **delivering** sermons, particularly, but **writing** them. For me, preaching sermons was the second-best part of the ministry; composing them was *Numero Uno*.

Until the late Eighties, I used to start writing a sermon, in pencil, longhand, early Thursday afternoon, right after lunch. Barring a lengthy late-in-the-week pastoral emergency, I would make my revisions in longhand, and then type the manuscript with my two index digits, finishing up by late Friday afternoon. I wish they had required typing class in junior high school rather than shop class. Everything I made in shop class looked as though it had been put together by a quadriplegic arthritic munchkin. But typing is a skill which would have come in handy for somebody who has spent his entire adult life in the word business. Now, millions of words later, I am still flailing away at the keyboard with two index fingers, which now are worn shorter than my two little toes.

Once I began to use a word processor, I could do a whole sermon from stem to gudgeon (as my mother used to say) from 8:00 AM to 5:00 PM on a Friday. Some Fridays God and/or the muses sped up the process, so that I could completely finish a sermon in five hours or so. Even I was astonished by that.

Word processors are the greatest invention since night baseball, in my opinion. Computers, as such, are another issue altogether. And the Internet has become The Primary Waster of Free Time (Or Office Time) the world has ever known. But word processors: ah, what a great leap forward they are! Further, as my horrendous scrawl became more and more illegible, I found it more and more difficult to read what I had written, let alone revise it, even though it was I who had inscribed those words on that shamefully-smudged paper. (I am left-handed, and write upside down and backwards, if you know what I mean. It is not a pretty sight.) Thus these penciled pages looked increasingly like ancient Egyptian hieroglyphics which had been written by a heavy-handed, palsied blind man.

Thank God for the word processor! Once its klutzy user learns the proper commands, deletions, additions, or corrections can be made in a skinny second. What a scribal godsend it was when I started writing my sermons on my trusty w.p.!

Many clergy never actually write out a sermon. Others initially write out their sermon completely, and then distill them into an outline or mere notes, casting aside the original written version. Of those who initially never originally write a complete manuscript, some begin with notes or an outline, some scribble down an idea or two, and some seem never to have given a single thought to what they were going to say on Sunday morning before they said it on Sunday morning. You may have encountered one or two such preachers in your lifetime.

I started preaching sermons on a very infrequent basis when I was just a student in high school. I was the sort of strange youth who, as long as I had thought about "being" anything, thought I'd be a minister. There was no bolt from the blue, no Damascus Road experience. Nobody, clergy or otherwise, slapped a portentous paw upon my quavering shoulder and said, "Boy-o, you should become a parson." From at least fifth grade on, I was going to be a minister, and that was that. I have always been convinced that God was behind that decision, but He never sharply or gently tapped me on the rotator cuff, either. In my experience, God is distinctly not a shoulder-tapping type of deity. I am convinced it is just as well. Better, really.

From the first such-as-it-was sermon I ever preached, which was thrust upon the innocent membership of Christ Presbyterian

Church in Madison, Wisconsin, on Youth Sunday, I wrote out every word I would speak before going into the pulpit. Since then, I have tried to follow every word in my written manuscript, but very deliberately without appearing to be reading each of them. However it is that any preacher prepares a sermon, I am persuaded that most sermons are meant to be **delivered**, not **read**, which is probably why the Outline-, Notes-, or No-Notes-type preachers never write out their sermons. They want them to sound fresh and unrehearsed, which is understandable, acceptable, and even commendable.

Well, I was always the type of preacher who wanted to say exactly what I wanted to say, because I knew that I would get into enough trouble intending to say what I said, instead of saying something I didn't intend to say. Therefore, from my homiletical git-go in the mid-Fifties to the last sermon I shall ever preach upon this earth (and heaven knows nobody in heaven will need to hear any of my sermons, or anyone else's), a completely written manuscript is what I have always used and will continue to use. That way nobody can ever accuse me of proclaiming something I did not mean to proclaim. Small or large parts of my sermons may have been incautious, incorrect, or unabashedly unorthodox, but when I wrote what I wrote, I truly meant to say what I said. (Looking back over some of my early or later sermons, I have had a bone or two to pick with myself, and have wondered how such cockamamie notions ever emerged from my crenellated cranium. But that's another story altogether, as any long-of-tooth preacher can tell you.)

I was mentally and vocationally in gear for the ministry for a dozen years before I ever went to seminary, so I was pleased that when at last I entered the preaching classes of McCormick Theological Seminary in Chicago, my homiletics professors urged all of us would-be preachers to write out every word of our sermons. I being I, I would have done it anyway, whether or not they told us to do so. But it was edifying to know that their prejudice and mine were synonymous.

The man who has influenced the style and content of my sermons more than any other minister, more than all other ministers put together, is Elam Davies. Dr. Davies was also known as "The Boss" by me and other assistant ministers who had the singular and sobering experience of working on his staff at the Fourth Presbyterian Church in Chicago. He was a visiting professor of homiletics at McCormick when I was there in the Sixties, so he gleefully seized the opportunity to take broad, sweeping whacks at me in those tender and formative circumstances. Then, when I served on the staff at Fourth Church for five years, he relished being able to lace into me again. That I survived his altruistic assaults is a testimony both to his ability to victimize his victims without utterly slaying them and to my ability to be thus victimized without being slain. He didn't need me at all, but I desperately needed him. Without his therapeutically surgical slicings of my sermons in the early years of my preaching career, it is hard to imagine what my later sermons would have been like. If, as the letter to the Hebrews says, "It is a fearful thing to fall into the hands of the living God," for me it was almost as fearful to fall into the hands of Elam Davies. But I trust both falls have benefitted me in ways far too numerous to tally.

Earlier, I offered the opinion (of which I have an endless supply, as you shall see) that most sermons are meant to be heard, not read. I mean that in two ways.

First, a sermon is an exercise in public speaking, in what the British used to call elocution, or what might prosaically be referred to simply as speech. That is to say, countless sermons are reproduced on paper, and therefore may later be read. But originally, **in their original intent**, they were spoken out loud by some preacher in some worship context somewhere within a reasonably religious setting. For this reason, especially in these days of too much television, too many videos, too much e-mail, and too much of nearly everything else, books of sermons don't sell well. Therefore, initially it is important to observe that sermons are first meant to be **heard;** they are not meant to be **read.** Books, journals, and magazines we read, but sermons we listen to, if this statement is a sentence I may end with a preposition, which somehow I did end it with.

However —— and here is the second part —— a sermon should truly be **delivered** by the preacher, and not merely **read**. This means that the personality of the preacher must inevitably become evident in what the preacher says and how she/he says it, even though preaching ought not to be about personality. Some famous preacher (alas, I know not who beyond a doubt, so I am only saying "some famous preacher") said that "Preaching is truth mediated through personality." By no means does that say everything there is to say about preaching, but it does say an important something. No one who has ever attempted to proclaim the truths of God did so without having his or her personality enter into the homiletical stew. It simply can't be done. Personality is in preaching as surely as oxygen is in air.

Clearly some preachers preach too much of their own personalities or life experiences, some do it too little, and some use just the right amount, at least some of the time. But nobody can preach without the "-body" of anybody who is preaching coming through.

Members of the historically liturgical churches (Roman Catholics, Orthodox, Episcopalians, and to a lesser extent Lutherans) tend not to assess their clergy first on their preaching abilities. In those denominations, sermons are to be snappy, short, and preferably insipid. (Perhaps you detect a note of skepticism here. It is not accidental; it is intentional.) But in the homiletical churches (Presbyterian, Baptist, Methodist, United Church of Christ, Pentecostal, etc.), preachers pontificate for at least 12 to 15 minutes (too short, says I) to 45 to 50 minutes (too long, says I). The person-ness of any person who yacks for at least fifteen minutes is bound to emerge, whether she/he likes it or not. No one can speak for more than ten minutes whose personal being does not manage to manifest itself in some discernible manner.

Thus pet phrases, or gestures inappropriately small or grandiosely large, or little quirky pauses, or fitful movements, or inexplicable or irritating or infuriating bits of *dramatis personnae ecclesiasticae* present themselves every time every preacher presents whatever he/she presents to those present. The more *personae* the better, according to some listeners, and the less the better, according to others. But personality there is and necessarily must be in preaching, which is why sermons need to be delivered, and nor read. "I'd rather be dead than red," said the conservative anti-commies of the Sixties. Any sermon that is only read *is* dead.

Nevertheless, the sermons which follow herein are meant to be read, and not heard. Never would I go into any pulpit anywhere and attempt to preach these sermons. In the first place, they are far too long. Were they actually to be delivered, they would average 45 to 60 minutes in length. As I have said, in my judgment that is too lengthy for all but the most masochistic of listeners. "The mind can absorb only what the tuckus will allow," as they say. Well, that's more or less what they say anyway.

In each of the sermons that follow, I wanted to say more than time would allow in a normal worship setting. Most Protestants, and Catholics and Orthodox too, I guess, want their service finished within an hour. A 45-minute sermon leaves time for little else if the service is to end in an hour. But you will be reading these sermons; you won't be listening to them. And if you get tired of a particular sermon in the middle of things, you can put the book down. In a church setting, you have no such luxury. You're stuck with continuing to try to listen, or giving up listening altogether. But unless you want to make a nuisance of yourself, and embarrass your spouse and children, you have to stay put till the preacher stops preaching.

Any of you who actually have heard me preach may conclude that I have already preached far too many sermons that were already far too hot to preach. Quite not. Those were just short, tepid, cautious perorations about this and that. **These** are the genuine sermons which are too hot to preach.

Further, the content of these sermons is meant to be so confrontational, even so inflammatory, that I hope you will stop and cogitate or ruminate or infuriate over whatever lunatic idea you are reading. In a "heard sermon," you can't stop to think about what the preacher is saying, because the preacher inevitably

13

moves on. Here, you can stop. **You** are the one who decides when to move on in these *Sermons Too Hot to Preach*, not the **preacher**.

In addition, the "style" of these sermons would not harmoniously lend itself to worship. It simply is too confrontational, too in-your-face for the acceptable worship of God.

In that sense, the "sermons" in this book of sermons are technically not sermons at all. They are more like theological essays or biblical soliloquies. Thus they are *sersays* or maybe *esmons*. I want you clearly to understand that I would **never** deliver any of these so-called sermons in any church anywhere, because I know it would severely rile far too many people who would essentially be members of a captive audience. Besides being grossly unfair, it would also be grossly unwise.

But **you** are not a captive. You chose to read this group of sermons, assuming you go ahead with the reading of this tome of hard-edged homilies. Whatever is the correct terminology for each of the following entities, they are much more **like** sermons than they actually **are** sermons, and I want you to know that I know that. I want you to know it too.

The novelist John Updike is one of the most gifted Christian critics of our time. He wrote, "To be Christian in this day and age is to be unorthodox, and readers should look elsewhere for the consolations of conventional sentiment and the popular, necessary religion of optimism." With Mr. Updike I could not be in greater concord. What the world needs now is not sweetness and optimism; it needs sharpness and reproof. What follows is a long-time preacher's attempt to provide just that.

* * * * * *

All that introduction having been properly prefaced, then why on earth would a retired preacher ever start writing a book called *Sermons Too Hot to Preach*? If sermons are meant to be preached instead of perused, is a book of sermons that were never preached, whether too hot or otherwise, doomed from the start?

That prompts us to ponder another of the roles of the clergy, namely, the role of **pastor**. There are oodles of things preachers would like to say which pastors know they could never say. **Prophets** can get away with saying some pretty outlandish stuff, but what prophet would ever last long as the pastor of dear old First Church or Lambsblood Tabernacle or St. Swithin's-by-the-Swamp? Truly prophetic preaching, on a regular basis, is the kind of preaching that regularly gets the clergy chucked out of churches. If all members of the clergy always said in sermons what they wanted to say in sermons, there would be no clergy left standing to say anything. It is not conscience that doth make cowards of the clergy. Quite the contrary. Fear makes the clergy cowards, fear of upsetting people, fear of offending. Like most people, the clergy like to be liked. Of far greater significance, they realize they have a very serious institutional responsibility which lies more heavily on their shoulders than on anyone else's shoulders. The sheer weight of that undeniable and unavoidable responsibility is what usually turns the clergy into quaking protectors of the status quo.

But, what the hell, on Oct. 16, 2001, I retired. Up till that date I couldn't **get** another job, anywhere, try as I might. In light of what has already been said, or in light of what you imagine shall yet be said, it may not surprise you I couldn't find another job, but it certainly surprised me. As cantankerous as I might have been, I also had done reasonably well in the pastorate. In truth, however, the governing board of one of the churches I served as interim pastor did not think so, and I was unceremoniously ushered off, stage left. Other than that, though, I had been quite well received everywhere else I had been.

Nonetheless, when I was unable to **find** another job, hard-headedly I decided I didn't **need** another job. So I took my marbles, which because it all ended sooner than expected were fewer than expected, and I left. I packed it in. And to my utter astonishment, not for a fleeting instant I have I missed any aspect of the pastorate, including preaching, which I had anticipated I would feel devastated not to be doing.

To any active clergy who may decide to read this book, I am happy to report my primary perception of retirement. **It is so** *liberating*! **It is fantastic! They can't get me anymore! Free at last, free at last; praise God Almighty, I'm free at last! They can't fire me, because I am no longer hired! They can't call me onto the carpet, because there's no ecclesiastical carpet anymore to call me onto! They're THERE, and I'm HERE, and now I have this splendid superannuated immunity!**

Before Oct. 16, 2001, I never would written, let alone stated, "But, what the hell, on Oct. 16, 2001, I retired." I just wouldn't have done it. Some ministers would say that, but not I. But now, **now**, there is the blissful and comforting knowledge which only an out-to-pasture pastor can have: whatever I say or do cannot seriously harm anyone other than myself. And what a blessing is that wondrous awareness.

Thinking back over the years during which I was a paid preacher, I am struck by how fortunate I was to have been attacked as gently and as infrequently as I was. If I am honest with myself, I must admit I said more than my share of stuff in sermons which I knew would not repose comfortably in every ear into which that stuff was stuffed. Most of the people in the congregations I served were remarkably patient with my sometimes moderately strengthy homiletical broadsides. There may have been occasions when I said something which surprised me by causing offense, but they were quite infrequent. Normally I **knew** when I would offend, and I **intended** to offend. The Bible is an offensive collection of writings. Anybody who isn't offended by the Bible hasn't come to grips with what the Bible says. The Gospel of Jesus Christ is **really** offensive. Not for nothing did that man end up on a cross. He was not the lamb of God. He was the leopard of God, the lion of God, the fearsome feline of God.

Jesus was and is the great Head of the Church, and for all its faults, of which there are legion, the Church is still the Church. And **a** church is still **a** church. Pastors need to protect and defend and edify churches, because God knows every church needs protection and defense and edification. Therefore, as mad a March

16

hare as I may have been on many occasions in my preaching, I certainly never meant to damage any church in which I served. Maybe I prescribed some distasteful new medications every now and then, perhaps I thought a little preventive surgery would be useful here and there, but I never attempted a heart transplant, nor did I ever intentionally issue a death certificate. To do that would have been to negate my ordination vows. It is an obligation of pastors to care for the whole flock, and that's what I tried to do.

The Church is an institution. Every congregation is an institution. Institutions are both very fragile and very tenacious. Sometimes it seems they just won't take root, and sometimes you can't seem to eradicate them, no matter what anybody does intentionally or unintentionally to try to uproot them.

Congregational clergy are many things, but one role they cannot and must not cast off is to be institutional nurturers. Institutions require constant nurture, and whoever are the institutional leaders must, above all, provide nurture.

I have tried to do that. I hope that sometimes I did it well. Sadly I am keenly aware that sometimes I did it very poorly.

But I have done it. Now it is no longer my God-given vocation to do it. Now others, who are younger and more zestful and committed and eager, must do it.

I do not perceive myself recently to have entered my golden years. Rather I perceive that I have just started my red years, when the internal juices run more freely in hues of liberated crimson. My caution, never a long suit anyway, can now be flung to the winds. Now if someone takes offense at what I say, it is with **me** that the offense is taken, not with the church — or worse, The Church.

Would I do it differently, if I had it do all over again? Would I have packed it in sooner if I had been fiscally able so to pack? No, I don't think so. I served as a parish parson for over 35 years. I hope to serve as a "minister-at-large" for another 35 years. It's great, being at large. I was in a carefully-chosen institutional prison for three and a half decades. Now, I am responsible to no one other than to God and my family, or more precisely, only to God and my wife. The way I see it, by the grace of God I have suddenly been granted a second career. I might embarrass some people by what I say or do, I might cause a little uneasiness hither or yon. But I'm not really going to hurt anyone, least of the Church of Jesus Christ. Nobody was required to accept what I said before anyway, and for certain no one has to buy it now.

Still, there **are** these sermons I want to write… And there **are** those things I would have said to church people if I hadn't always had this abiding concern for Mother Church… But you, the reader, chose to read this book. Nobody put a gun to your head to do it. And if you get angry, which I certainly expect will happen, you can't hold it against your congregation, if you are a church member, or against The Church of Jesus Christ, or Christianity, or organized or unorganized or disorganized religion, or God, or anybody or anything else. Your beef is solely with me, and with no one else.

But before you start, be clear about this: I definitely intend to disturb you. And that is because God is disturbing. He who created us also makes it His business to disturb us. If in these pages I become one of His unfettered agents of disturbance, so much the better. And that's why I wrote this spate of sermons I never really intended orally to deliver.

A Spattering of Social/Political Sputterings

Scripture – Hosea 10:9-15; Amos 7:10-17; Micah 2:6-8, 3:9-12

Text – Hear this, you heads of the house of Jacob and rulers of the house of Israel, who abhor justice and pervert all equity, who build Zion with blood, and Jerusalem with wrong. Its heads give judgment for a bribe, its priests teach for hire, its prophets divine for money. Micah 3:9-11 (RSV)

WHY PROPHETIC SERMONS ARE A RELIGIOUS NECESSITY, EVEN IF YOU HATE TO HEAR THEM

The Hebrew prophets were the most remarkable political preachers who ever lived. The fact that almost all of them managed to continue to live is a testimony to how remarkable they were. They were, at once, highly revered and highly reviled. I suspect that the high mucky-mucks of Judah and Israel often would gladly have ordered them to be tarred and feathered, and then have them boiled in oil. They were relentless in their vitriolic attacks on the kings and the ruling class. Regular tortures of the tuckus they were.

Ahab, one of the most powerful of the kings of Israel, who built some of the most magnificent structures and fortresses of the ancient world, called the prophet Elijah "you troubler of Israel." Ahab terrified the divine courage straight out of Elijah, and he fled for his life, thinking that God had completely forsaken him. But God continued to be with Elijah, and the gloomy prophet lived to see Ahab and his wife Jezebel overthrown.

The prophet Amos described himself as "a herdsman and dresser of sycamore trees." Whatever that occupation was, the scholars all agree that it offered very low pay and no benefits at all. Yet this low-class seasonal worker stood up to the monarchs and the wealthy landowners of Israel again and again, ceaselessly excoriating them for their ruinous avarice and their uncaring attitudes toward the poor. Amos gave them so much holy what-for that he singed their lathered hides by the fiery bursts which issued from his ever-unbridled mouth.

20

"Power tends to corrupt, and absolute power corrupts absolutely," said Lord Acton, in the only statement I ever heard ascribed to Lord Acton, a.k.a. J.E.E. Dalberg, who, according to my trusty quotations book, was the first Baron Acton. Every society functions because certain people have certain kinds of power. No society can operate in a power vacuum. Thus there is political power, economic power, social power, ecclesiastical power, military power, academic power, judicial power, and so on and so on. Almost nobody, other than God, ever has absolute power over anything, so almost nobody ever gets absolutely corrupted, a' la' Lord Acton. Nevertheless, because power is required for the smooth operation of the social order, and because there always are people eager to acquire and to utilize power, whether or not they are able to do so wisely, there must be critics on the sidelines who deliver perorations about the power users. Every society requires squeaky wheels in order for the proper amount of grease to be properly administered.

Power *does* tend to corrupt whoever possesses it, and therefore society needs to have impartial observers who produce unofficial outside observations on the actions of those in power. In modern times, the press has fulfilled this necessary function more than any other social element. Newspapers, magazines, television, and radio all pay pundits to unburden themselves of broadsides against whatever suits their fancy. And because there are so many people with so many kinds of power, there is never a shortage of subjects about which the pundits of the so-called Fourth Estate may thus become unburdened.

In ancient Israel, of course there were no newspapers, magazines, television networks or radio stations. Thus, so far as we know, prophets fulfilled the social-commentary roles of all those other media for the Jewish nation. However, the prophets spoke from a distinctly different perspective as compared to our modern media commentators. Pundits say whatever they think because it is what they think. Prophets said what they said because they believed it was God who moved them to say it. It is one thing to have opinions on political and social issues, but it is

21

quite another to proclaim those opinions with the conviction that it is God who moves the divine spokesmen to speak as they do.

Obviously ancient Israelites could insist that the prophets were not truly speaking God's word, and frequently they did so insist. The prophets themselves occasionally report such instances. It is a very tricky business, this. Who can know for certain whether or not a prophet is declaring what God wants to be said — including the prophet himself? The prophets themselves not infrequently attacked other purported prophets for being frauds. Micah groused about the false prophets who declared, "'Do not preach' — thus they preach — 'one should not preach of such things; disgrace will not overtake us.'"

Public personages often make grandiloquent claims which turn out to be false. "I am not a crook!" said Richard M. Nixon — but in many ways he was. "Read my lips; no new taxes!" said George H.W. Bush, so we read his lips, and listened to what he said — and he raised taxes (which, for whatever it is worth, was okay by me). "I did not have sex with that woman, Monica Lewinsky!" William Jefferson Clinton righteously proclaimed, righteously pointing his crooked index finger at us — but he did, as later he himself admitted.

Now, no one would ever suggest that Messrs. Nixon, Bush I, or Clinton were prophets. They were, however, very public figures, as were the Hebrew prophets. The point is, anyone is free to declare that the prophet does not speak for God when he says he does, and all of us can disregard the prophet's words if we choose to do so, just as we might choose to disregard what our Presidents say, particularly if we are not especially enamored of them anyway. *Saying* that one is speaking in God's name does not, in itself, authenticate divine authority.

As a matter of fact, attempting to be a genuine prophet is a recipe for loneliness, abuse, and possibly even danger. In the twentieth century, Mohandas K. Gandhi, Martin Luther King, and Malcolm X all discovered that truth with the most lethal of results. The Hebrew prophets also experienced enormous social and political ostracism and animosity. Squeaky wheels get not only the grease, but they also can get figuratively or even literally "greased."

In the past couple of generations, denominations and other religious groups have engaged in what might be called "institutional prophecy" as compared to "individual prophecy." That is, church bodies, through an officially sanctioned ecclesiastical process, have made pronouncements about the kinds of issues which the biblical prophets addressed: social and political justice, economic fairness, social class equity, and so on.

For four decades I have served as a minister in a denomination which has reveled in taking public stands on nearly every matter which has confronted the human race in the past fifty years. The Presbyterian Church (USA), as we have come to be called in our latest updated moniker, has made declarations at every annual General Assembly with all the ecclesiastical gravitas it can muster. As time went on, fewer and fewer people, either outside or inside the Presbyterian Church (USA), paid any positive attention to what was said, and more and more were negatively affected by it. It peeved them, it irritated them, it infuriated them. Who the hell was the Church to be making pronouncements on matters about which it had no expertise, they wondered. And so they ignored what was said.

Why is that? Why is institutional prophecy so ineffectual? The answer, I think, lies in this: fundamentally it takes no real courage for a church body to attempt to be prophetic. Taking a stand as an institution may exact an institutional price, it may be wise or unwise, it may feel good to those who nurse the resolution through to an affirmative vote, but everybody knows that the very politics for achieving institutional political stands undermines the very effectiveness of those stands.

Not so for the individual prophet. Anyone who takes a public position on anything, knowing that many will strongly react negatively to that position, pays an immediate price. Such people evoke rancor, animosity, disgust, hatred, and seething opposition. The sober truth is that some have a hide that is sufficiently thick to withstand the resistance, and some don't.

23

One of the ministers I have most admired through the years has been consistently a prophetic preacher. He is a few years older than I, and managed to survive in the pastorate longer than I. He also is very pastoral. But the strength of his prophetic ministry has greatly overshadowed his pastoral ministry in the minds of many of his parishioners, and although he may generally have received grudging respect, he has not been warmly loved by many of the people in the congregations he has served.

His voice has been desperately needed among his people and among all the people in the communities in which he has served. But heaven knows it has not been easy for him. Heaven also knows how depressed he has become at times when he felt compelled to address issues head on, knowing how angry he would make some of the members of the church and community he served.

What kinds of things did he say? Things like this: "You have plowed iniquity, you have reaped injustice, you have eaten the fruit of lies. Because you have trusted in your chariots, and in the multitude of your warriors, therefore the tumult of war shall arise among your people, and all your fortresses shall be destroyed" (Hosea 10:13-14). Or like this: "Now therefore hear the word of the Lord. You say, 'Do not prophesy against Israel, and do not preach against the house of Isaac.' Therefore thus saith the Lord: 'Your wife shall be a harlot in the city, your sons and your daughters shall fall by the sword, and your land shall be parceled out by line; you yourself shall die in an unclean land, and Israel shall surely go into exile away from its land'" (Amos 7:16-17). Or this: "Hear this, you heads of the house of Jacob and rulers of the house of Israel, who abhor justice and pervert all equity, who build Zion with blood and Jerusalem with wrong" (Micah 3:9-10).

When a prophetic preacher makes statements like those, it is absolutely inevitable that she or he will encounter vehement resistance, especially when the prophetic preachments are addressed directly to the most powerful in the land. It all sounds so unpatriotic! It all sounds so moralistic, so judgmental, so negative! From whence cometh the brazen chutzpah that anybody should ever say anything like that?

Precisely because the downside of prophetic preaching is so evident, very, very few clergy, academics, politicians, or anyone else engage in such painful polemics. And thus the infection and corruption eats deeper and deeper into the social fabric. To avoid conscientiously dealing openly with our social ills is to guarantee that they will get worse. A society which refuses to give its prophets their vocal or literary freedom deserves the inevitable collapse which shall surely accompany such a prohibition. When the powerful prevent the treatment of decay, decay will run its inevitable course to destruction.

That last statement raises one of the major misunderstandings of the true nature of prophecy, however. Most people believe that the prophet's primary task is to predict the future. That is absolutely not so. The prophet always speaks primarily to the ills and injustices of the contemporary situation. What does God say to what is going on *now*? If the present is sufficiently bleak and irredeemable, then the future is bound to be even more bleak. Prophets don't predict collapse with any sense of joy or hope; they do it because they are in despair! By their very inner nature, prophets cannot be fundamentally optimistic people! Complete mental equanimity and effective prophecy do not go hand in hand! In order to produce, prophets must be pills! There is no other option!

Sometimes the biblical prophets predicted devastation and destruction, and sometimes they were correct in their predictions. But sometimes they also were wrong. The societal apple cart was not always overturned as they insisted would happen; the threatened defeat in war did not always occur. It isn't the correctness of the prediction which counts in prophecy; it is the validity of the castigation of current woes which matters.

So it is that all humans in all situations need prophets to point out their faults when they are unwilling or unable to perceive those faults themselves. All kinds of leaders need to be subjected to the voice of prophets on a regular but not too frequent basis: presidents and kings and senators, provosts and chancellors and professors, CEOs and COOs and CFOs, popes and priests, bishops and ministers, anybody who leads anybody in any endeavor.

We can all become blinded to whatever enables us to do "business as usual," and we must have prophets to tell us that our business has become too unusual, our accepted norms have become abnormal in the sight of Almighty God.

It might be inferred that ecclesiastical ordination is a requirement to becoming a prophet. God forbid! There are far more lay prophets than clergy prophets. Here is a suggestive, though by no means exhaustive, list of contemporary or recent prophets: Thomas Friedman, George Will, Garry Wills, Maureen Dowd, Saul Bellow, Molly Ivins, Charles Colson, Chaim Potok, William Sloane Coffin, Paul Wellstone, Pat Buchanan, Phyllis Schlafly, Dorothy Day, Pat Conroy, Flannery O'Connor, Joseph Lieberman, Rush Limbaugh, Norman Lear, H.L. Mencken, Pat Robertson, Walter Shapiro, Jerry Falwell, and Ellen Goodman.

Does anybody agree with every thought ever expressed by all those folks? If so, you can totally dismiss the thinking of such a person! Prophets come in all sizes and shapes, and their prophetic utterances range all over the map of human opinion and experience. In the churches, this means that prophetic preachers will come from both the left and the right, and that their proclamations will often conflict with one another. No prophet is correct all of the time, and none is wrong all of the time, but all are right some of the time. It behooves us to listen with the ears God gave each of us to what is said by the prophets of God.

Charles T. Matthewes teaches at the University of Virginia. In an article in *Theology Today* (January, 2002), he previewed some ideas which shall be expressed in a book soon to be published, called *The Quiet Voice of God: Faith-Based Activism and Mainline Protestantism*. The book is edited by Robert Wuthnow and John H. Evans. In the article Prof. Matthewes said, "Rather than direct intervention in the political process of elections and public-policy advocacy, the mainline churches are indirectly influential through their influence on the broader 'civic culture.' They preach a gospel of social involvement that encourages their congregants' participation in debates about the common good, albeit not always in Christianly indexed ways, but often as 'bare citizens.'" Later Prof. Matthewes says that "while the churches' preaching offers a sophisticated argument in favor of political participation by Christians, often it does so by asking congregants to participate not as Christians but as 'bare' or 'mere' citizens, stewards of civil society who steward it partly by leaving behind their particularistic identities when they enter the public square. This tradition has a long and honorable theological heritage, stretching back to Martin Luther (and, arguably through him to Saint Paul), with his 'two kingdoms' theology, encapsulated in his quip, 'Better to be ruled by a wise Turk than a stupid Christian.' Yet, it can go too far and ossify into a theologically principled refusal to let wise Christians be involved in politics as wise Christians."

I deduce from this that most of the prophetic voices currently being lifted by Christians or any other religious people belong to ordinary believers, not to the professionally trained and ordained. In truth, ordination may be the greatest impediment to prophecy among the clergy. They grow too timid once hands are laid upon their quavering heads, and they become too concerned about institutional wellbeing at the expense of societal wellbeing.

I want to come back to a theme introduced earlier. I stated that corporate prophecy is usually ineffective, but that individual prophecy can often be highly effective. In like manner, it is quite acceptable for individuals prophetically to try to influence the political or social process, but it is totally unacceptable for denominations or other church bodies to expend funds given for religious purposes to try prophetically to influence politics. Two bills currently being debated in the United States Congress would allow that. The first bill would give churches or denominations permission to endorse particular candidates without losing their tax exemption. Another bill would allow churches to spend up to 20% of their total budget on lobbying and an additional 5% campaigning for particular candidates.

In my judgment, both those proposed measures are examples of "corporate prophecy" gone absolutely amuck. If any church with which I was affiliated used money I had given to it to support the election of any political candidate, even ones I might personally support, I would stop giving that church another nickel in the non-stroke of my check-writing pen. Both of these particular bills happen to be supported by the Religious Right (what a surprise), but whether coming from the religious right or left, they are terribly flawed ideas which need to be given a rapid political *coup de grace*.

This sermon is called *Why Prophetic Sermons Are a Religious Necessity, Even If You Hate to Hear Them*. It might more appropriately be called *Why Political, Social, Economic, Ecclesiastical, Legal, Cultural, and Other Such Sermons Are a Religious Necessity, and Why Such Sermons Inevitably Slice Savagely in All Directions*. That, however, is too much of a mouthful, especially coming from one such as I who possesses such a big mouth. But it is true; individually and collectively, we all need to be exposed to the corrective influences which only prophetic statements can produce. However, much as we might like all such statements to go "our" way, to reflect "our" thoughts and feelings and prejudices, we too need to be smitten between the eyes every now and again, just to keep us straight, as well as humble.

It is little short of astonishing that the Jews allowed the prophetic books to make it into the canon of accepted Hebrew scripture. Some of the people voting in that conclave had to be mightily put off that anyone would seriously countenance adding the likes of Amos and Jeremiah to the collection of holy writ. Nevertheless, the prophetic books somehow were included, and the tradition of religiously oriented political-social-economic-ecclesiastical commentary has had an accepted, if uneasy, place in the religious life of the West.

Jesus of Nazareth was many things, but one of His most important roles was to be a prophet. When Jesus quoted scripture, more often than not He quoted the Hebrew prophets. He valued prophetic declarations, and so should we. If we refuse to listen to the prophets, we will slowly – or quickly – decline into oblivion.

Sister Joan Chittister is a Benedictine nun who has called the Roman Catholic Church to task over many, many issues. She was such a thorn in the side of the Bishop of Rome that John Paul II probably had a large picture of her hung on the walls of the Vatican, which decreed, "Wanted: Dead or Alive." Not long ago

I heard a man ask Joan Chittister in a Q&A session why she continues to remain a Roman Catholic. (The man himself, I deduced from other things he said, has also stayed Catholic.) She said she had been asked variations of that question several times before, and the more she was asked it, the more a word kept popping into her mind. It was the word "oyster."

Well why, she wondered, should an oyster leap into her cranium when she was asked this type of question? She said she took a time-out after the inquiry was made yet again, and she sat down to think about everything she knew about oysters, which wasn't much. She didn't like to eat them, she knew they preferred to live in rocky places near the shores of the sea, and whenever they got a grain of sand in them, they would secrete a certain kind of gel which enveloped the sand, thus preventing its shell from being damaged by the scouring action of the sand. And thus the oyster's life is saved. So, she said, she concluded that hers is "a ministry of irritation."

What a spectacular insight! And how necessary it is for all of us to have individuals who conduct the ministry of irritation! If there is a sufficient amount of poking at problems, then at least some of the problems will be more directly addressed, and some of them will even be solved! But unless and until somebody summons up the courage to do the poking, the dis-ease of whatever is wrong will continue to damage the body politic!

But precisely because somebody needs publicly to identify the issues which are being ignored by most people, most people will be put off when they hear the problems so pointedly and painfully identified. The proposed solutions to our social and political ills may come from the left, right, or center of the spectrum, and inevitably many people will not be located in whatever "camp" the prophet represents. Thus if the prophets will be popular at all (which is unlikely over the long haul), they will be popular with only a certain percentage of the population. It cannot be otherwise.

Other sermons in this irritating collection of homilies address specific issues. But this sermon is written in the attempt to provide a rationale for the existence, indeed the necessity, of prophetic sermons. Anybody who opposes the voices of prophecy automatically turns out to support decay and death. But they also oppose the voice of God uttered through the prophets. Once again, the prophets are not always correct in what they say, but they **are** correct when they try to be truly prophetic.

Tension and division follow the prophets as surely as the night follows the day. If, as Shakespeare said, "Uneasy lies the head that wears the crown," exceedingly uneasy lies the head that proclaims – or hears – the prophetic word.

But society and all religious institutions need to listen to the prophets, lest we become too smug in our behavior and traditions. "Where there is no vision, the people perish," decrees Proverbs 29:18. Prophecy provides a vision of that which we don't want to see from those we don't want to hear. Yet for our own good, we must look and listen. Thus, I believe, saith the Lord.

Scripture - Isaiah 5:18-23

Text – Woe to those who call evil good and good evil, and put darkness for light and light for darkness, who put bitter for sweet and sweet for bitter. Woe to those who are wise in their own eyes, and shrewd in their own sight! – Isaiah 5:20-21

THE GREATEST ENEMY OF
AMERICA IS AMERICAN ARROGANCE

Since September 11, 2001, the United States of America has acquired an awareness of a certain kind of reality which many other nations have known for generations or centuries. We Americans now realize in the deepest recesses of our being what the peoples of Asia and the Middle East and Europe and Africa have long taken for granted. It is this: terrorism is **always** a clear and present danger. Other people have long accepted that at any moment religious or political extremists might attack them personally, or the nations of which they are citizens. But for most Americans, that awareness was virtually non-existent. Terrorism might strike others with massive force, but no one would dare attack the USA. September 11, 2001 changed all that. Now we are convinced that two oceans can no longer guarantee relative safety to our shores.

American responses in the aftermath of those terrorist attacks have been quintessentially American. Never was our flag flown more widely or more proudly. Millions of cars suddenly became mobile paroxysms of patriotism. Our leaders engaged in indecorous chest-pounding. We declared a macho War on Terrorism, and our President proclaimed the existence of an "Axis of Evil," consisting of Iran, Iraq, and North Korea.

It is possible that the USA is the most admired and the most despised nation in the world, both at the same time, and often by the same people. That is, there are probably millions of citizens of other nations who think the United States is, on the one hand, the greatest country currently on the face of the earth, but on the other hand, as a nation we are also seen as being more arrogant than anyone else. Yet millions of Americans perceive only our greatness, and don't have a clue about how arrogant we are. American naivete regarding America is one of our most evident and mystifying of traits. We just don't get it about us! And sadly, we may never get it!

Back in 1989, several events inexorably illustrated that no longer were there two superpowers (the USA and the USSR), but there was only one superpower, the USA. It is highly unenviable to be the world's sole surviving national colossus. Such a nation is bound to become widely watched, with growing suspicion, if not disdain, if not outright hatred. Seldom in world history has any single nation dominated the world stage as the USA now dominates the globe. In fact, that has never before happened to the degree this unhappy circumstance has now befallen the US. As a nation, we did not ask for this role to be cast upon us, but it has thus been cast, nonetheless.

Arrogance is inevitable for a sole superpower. It could not be otherwise. When major events occur, most of our allies want to know what we intend to do before deciding what they intend to do. And obviously our enemies, actual or potential, try to forecast our response prior to launching any kind of attack on us. Anything we do or do not do will be perceived as arrogance by someone.

Still, in our arrogance we seem to go above and beyond the expected limits of arrogance. Look at a couple of peculiar examples. We are the only western nation which continues to practice capital punishment. Not even very many dictatorships or totalitarian states execute criminals or traitors. Nonetheless, for a mere $23.95, American children (or their parents) can buy a toy electric chair that electrocutes a doll, whose head and shoulders writhe when the "juice" is applied. More than 66,000 of these ghastly gadgets have been sold. If that does not illustrate American arrogance, what does? The US is now the only industrialized nation in the world which has a fertility rate at or above the replacement level of 2.4 children per woman. Might arrogance be concealed in that statistic? Have American parents decided that the world needs more little Americans than little British or Germans or Japanese or Australians?

The day before **the** September 11, Secretary of Defense Donald Rumsfeld was castigating the wasteful habits of the Pentagon. He called our defense establishment "one of the last bastions of central planning," the kind of institution where there is no competition, and thus there is also bound to be huge inefficiency. Yet within weeks of September 11, Mr. Rumsfeld was requesting, and the President was approving, a defense budget which rose the greatest percentage of any such budget in the past twenty years. It shows American arrogance at its glaring worst. We will now manufacture whatever technological whizbangs we think might be necessary to do whatever job needs to be done, against anybody, anywhere.

In our war with the Taliban in Afghanistan, we presumed that we represented good, and the Taliban were evil incarnate. But the Muslim press around the world did not see it that way. Even moderate Muslim journalists cast the US in harshly negative terms. They see our association with the Northern Alliance and with the new US-installed Afghan government to be both one-sided and short-sighted. We have punished Afghans of other factions or tribes who have grievances every bit as legitimate as the bitterness which is felt by "our" Afghans. "The US has lost the propaganda war," declared a Jordanian newspaper - - - and Jordan is one of our closest allies in the world of Islam. By attempting to portray ourselves as completely good and to depict Muslim extremists as completely evil, we have succeeded only in angering hundreds of millions of Muslim moderates.

Franklin Graham, Billy Graham's son, told a television interviewer shortly after September 11, "The God of Islam is not the same God [as that of Christianity.] It's a different God, and I believe it is a very wicked and evil religion." Jerry Falwell called the prophet Muhammad a murderer and a terrorist. Other Christians in other nations might think such inexcusable thoughts, but American Christians, tragically, are more likely to think it. It is a toss-up as to which is the more frightening: that many Americans actually believe such things, or that they have the arrogance brazenly to proclaim they believe such things.

Our patriotic zeal following 9/11 is problematic at best, and potentially disastrous at its worst. In his book *Making Patriots*, Walter Berns suggests a very interesting distinction between patriotism and nationalism. "It is said that what makes patriotism different from nationalism is that patriotism expresses itself as a love of one's own country, while nationalism manifests itself more as the dislike of other countries." That is a notion worth gnawing upon. If it is correct, how best can we characterize the post 9/11 American zeal: is it patriotism, or is it nationalism?

No doubt there is some of both in what many Americans are now feeling. But the more dangerous inclination is nationalism, because it feeds the kind of natural isolationism or xenophobia which have been prevalent in our nation since the mid-19th century. Once we stretched "from sea to shining sea," many Americans became convinced we were rendered geographically impregnable and invincible. Because only two nations have abutted our borders since 1850, many Americans ever since felt justified in thumbing their noses at all other nations anywhere on the globe, especially if they represented a different religion, culture, or political or economic system from our own. It is bad enough when ordinary countries become nationalistic in the early 21st century, but when the sole superpower flexes its nationalistic muscles, it is indescribably worse. And that is what seems to be happening since the attacks on the World Trade Center and the Pentagon. In a *Time* Magazine editorial (Feb. 18, 2002), Michael Elliott wrote, "If you lived through the horrors of Europe's last century, patriotic fervor is a dish that comes a little too highly seasoned with memories of nationalism, war and genocide."

No less an evangelical giant than Richard Mouw writes, "I am grateful to God for the privilege of being an American. There is much about my country that makes me proud. But we, too, fall short of God's standards of righteousness.... While I will continue to express affection for my country, I will always warn my fellow citizens not to take that kind of thing too literally. I will do this because I believe strongly in democracy. But even more important, I will do it because I worry about the ever-present threat of spiritual pridefulness – and even worse, of idolatry" (*beliefnet*, "Patriotism as Idolatry").

No one can know beyond dispute the circumstances around which the prophet Isaiah wrote the first several chapters of his prophecy. Many biblical scholars insist that Isaiah was an upper-crust member of the society of Judah in the middle of the 8th century BCE. Although his social status should have made him a supporter of the status quo, he was anything but that. He excoriated the monarchy and most of the monarchs during his long life, which no doubt prevented him from being named Man of the Year by *The Zion Times*. The editor of the *Times* might personally have considered Isaiah a noble chap, but he was not going to jeopardize the value of his journal's stock on the Jerusalem Stock Exchange by drawing the displeasure of the king. As is true of most newspaper editors, that anonymous (to us) figure did not just fall off the turnip truck.

So furious at his fellow Four Hundred was Isaiah that he declared, "Therefore my people go into exile for want of knowledge; their honored men are dying of hunger, and their multitude is parched with thirst. Therefore Sheol has enlarged its appetite and opened its mouth beyond measure, and the nobility of Jerusalem go down, her throng and he who exults in her" (Isa. 5:13-14).

Social swells are never thrilled to hear the prophets of God tell them that Hell had opened its gaping jaws to chew them up. Such observations generally do not elicit strong shouts of affirmation. Instead, they infuriate people, especially people who are not used to being challenged by anyone, let alone one of their own. Those who are to the manor born might expect the *hoi poloi* occasionally to attack them, but when an upper crust chap lays out the upper crust in lavender, they become a tad frothy at the corners of their slack-jawed maws.

However, Isaiah had not finished his jeremiad (two centuries before the time of Jeremiah, no less). "Woe to those who call evil good and good evil, who put darkness for light and light for darkness, who put bitter for sweet and sweet for bitter! Woes to those who are wise in their own eyes, and shrewd in their own sight!"

In the first years of the 21st century, the United States of America has both elected and appointed leaders who reflect the very behavior which Isaiah decried nearly three millennia earlier. We have high government officials who crow that what we are doing as a nation is good, when in fact much of it is evil, and they declare that what some other nations or people are doing is utterly evil, when in fact some of it is no doubt quite good. We go swooping into a distressed third-world country, drop a multitude of bombs, kill a few technologically targeted troublemakers, and decree that now all shall be well. We destroy what little order might have existed there, without replacing it with anything remotely appearing to be a new democratic government. Or if the new government we install **is** democratic, we refuse to pump in the huge amounts of money necessary to sustain it over the long haul, and we lack the necessary patience to await its widespread acceptance by the very people in those nations we arrogantly choose to "protect and defend." Just who the hell do we think we are, God Himself? Is the American "terrible swift sword" the only implement left to "make the world safe for democracy?"

Although Americans probably travel more widely than anyone else, clearly we don't get around enough! We don't listen to the mutterings and murmurings of others against us! We feel perfectly free to make unilateral American decisions with impunity which affect other nations, as though they have no legitimate say in their own internal affairs, or as though only the USA can be trusted to know what is truly good for the world and all its inhabitants! Any American who is incapable of hearing or understanding the accusations of other nationalities against us is the kind of American who is likely to call evil good and good evil! Our ignorance is almost as galling as our arrogance!

Are **all** Americans arrogant? Of course not. Are all **arrogant** Americans evil? No. But all Americans share in the allegations of American arrogance against us from other people, and we need to be aware of and concerned about that.

Columnist Molly Ivins was railing against our double standard with respect to so-called "prisoners of war." In our frequent mini-wars we expect any of our soldiers who are captured to be treated by the rules of the Geneva Convention. But the prisoners we flew out of Afghanistan to Guantanamo Bay, Cuba are not, so we declared, prisoners of war. They are, in words we ourselves coined especially for this made-to-order situation, "illegal combatants." **We** can go fight on someone else's territory, and it is AOK, but if someone else fights there whom we do not officially approve as adversaries, they become "illegal combatants." So the Unsinkable Molly writes, "This is why a lot of people hate us. For the sheer bloody arrogance of having it both ways all the time. For thinking that we are above the rules, that we can laugh at treaties, that we can do whatever we want.... Now among thoughtful world citizens this is not why they hate us, but why they consider us stupid."

Arrogance which morphs into stupidity is a uniquely dangerous kind of arrogance. It is one thing to be arrogant, but quite another to be stupidly arrogant. If our government were becoming merely the laughingstock of the world it would be bad enough. But we are becoming repulsive to a growing number of the world's population, and we don't even know it. Our power has blinded us. We have assumed our uniqueness as a nation has given us license to do as we please, giving little or no thought to how our actions affect others, or how those decisions are likely to affect even us over the inexorable march of time. We are committed only to the present, giving no thought at all to the future.

Precisely because we are so powerful, no nation or bloc of nations is likely to challenge us to a major war. But we are probably faced with an ongoing series of little wars, including our "war on terrorism," for many years to come. In the meantime, we carry out ill-conceived strikes against ill-perceived "enemies," and we boast that we are just crazy enough to take on anyone whom we deem to be a threat. In a letter to the editor of the *New York Times*, a Frenchman said, "Deterrence through calculated craziness is not really a novel doctrine; one need only to recall the doctrine of mutually assured destruction of the late cold war period. But if displays of ferocious nuttiness are the basis for the homeland and international security of the United States, everyone (not only terrorists) in the world has a great deal to worry about."

On October 22, 1939, C.S. Lewis preached at the evensong service in the church of St. Mary the Virgin in Oxford, England. Many of the undergraduates of Oxford University soon would be bearing arms against the Nazis of Germany. The magnificent Mr. Lewis said on that occasion, "If we had foolish unchristian hopes about human culture, they are now shattered. If we thought we were building up a heaven on earth, if we looked for something that would turn the present world from a place of pilgrimage into a permanent city satisfying the soul of man, we are disillusioned, and not a moment too soon."

An admirable and aggravating trait of Americans is our persistent belief that good old American ingenuity can solve any problem, fix any conflict, right any wrong. Too often we forget that here on earth have we no continuing place. God alone is our refuge and strength. No one, other than He, is our present help in time of trouble. That is not pious pap; it is permanent geopolitical reality. Americans need to repent of our American optimism that American action can rid the world of its multitude of troubles. Because we do so well in so many ways, we delude ourselves into believing that we can effect good in every situation. But we can't.

The USA is one nation among over two hundred nations. We are neither father nor mother to the others, nor are we God's chosen protector of all the others. The world got along without us before there was an "us" to get along with, and it could get along without us now. Nonetheless, for now, we **are** us, we are the US, we are the United States of America, and God expects great things of us, if for no other reason than simply because we are great.

In one of the several volumes of *Children's Letters to God*, there is this plaintive childish query of the Almighty: "Dear God, Who draws the lines around the countries?" Who, indeed? Not God. Not the USA either, try as we might to guarantee or abolish or alter certain of the lines. Our arrogance impels us to act, but it also often stymies our successful action.

We cannot opt out of having our role as the world's current sole superpower. Not to use power when any person or nation possesses power is to abandon the providential position in which one finds oneself. To give up power, especially when it can be used for great good, is to stoop to crass cowardice. On the other hand, to use power unwisely or thoughtlessly is to cast the strongest possible condemnation upon oneself.

In the 6th chapter of Isaiah, the prophet has his famous vision in the temple in Jerusalem, where he saw the Lord, high and lifted up. When Isaiah heard God's voice ask, "Whom shall I send, and who will go for us?", Isaiah proclaimed, "Here am I, Lord; send me."

Among all the nations of the earth now in existence, the decisions of the United States of America normally have more consequence and influence than the decisions of any other single nation in almost any conceivable political or international scenario. It would be folly for us to ask God for such an exalted position. But equally it would be folly to flee from such a position when providence places us in such a pivotal situation. We dare not imagine that what we choose to do will happen because we believe we are nobly doing it for God. But we must not do it in opposition to what we know to be the will of God either.

As the poem, and later the hymn, declared, "We are living, we are dwelling/ In a grand and awful time." Here we are. Let us see ourselves as being sent. But for God's sake, let us have some humility as we go about our national and international mission.

Scripture – I Corinthians 6:1-8

Text – To have lawsuits at all with one another is defeat for you. Why not suffer wrong? Why not rather be defrauded? – I Cor. 6:7 (RSV)

THE LANGUISHING LAND OF
LICENTIOUS LITIGATION

The first-century Christians in Corinth to whom the apostle Paul wrote his epistles were pistols. We have all known of fractious churches in our time, but that bumptious bunch were something else again. If every accusation Paul lodged against them was valid, by comparison they made Mike Tyson or Saddam Hussein look like Miss Manners or Little Lord Fauntleroy.

According to the Tarsus tentmaker, some of the Corinthian Christians were perverted sex maniacs. They slept around a lot. And the people they slept around with nobody was supposed to sleep with. They were brazen braggarts, said Paul, and if Paul thought that, they must have been off the charts in the boasting category, because Paul himself was no shrinking violet in the self-confidence department. They apparently worshipped idols. They were money-grubbers.

Furthermore, the Corinthians had a noted tendency to get drunk - - - in church. They were gluttons - - - at church pot luck dinners, no less. They tried to outdo one another in displaying spiritual gifts - - - in the worship of Almighty God, not-for-heaven's-sake. They engaged in egregious oneupsmanship of the most sordid sort.

Another thing the Corinthian Christians did was to haul one another into court on a far-too-frequent basis, at least far too frequently to suit Paul. As Jesus has earlier told His followers (see Matthew 18:15-20), Paul also told the Corinthians that when they had disputes with one another, they should resolve them among themselves, rather than subpoena one another to appear before a magistrate.

There is an important detail we need to note here, however. It is this: **believers were commanded not to go to court to seek justice from other** *believers*. Jesus assumed, as did Paul, that people who shared a common faith should be able, in common, to work out differences among themselves. Neither Jesus nor Paul said anything about whether believers were ethically entitled to go to court for recompense from non-believers.

Nobody can be certain of the degree to which the teachings of Jesus and Paul regarding litigation among the faithful were followed in the early Church. It takes an enormous amount of trust in an extra-legal ecclesiastical system to guarantee that justice will be served when Christians or other people of faith disagree in fiscal or other disputes. It's all well and good informally to try to work things out with Jack Jones, who is a member of your church. But what if Jack Jones is a jerk? Or what if Jack thinks you are a jerk (which you just might be, although you're likely not very aware of it)? How then shall the dispute be equitably resolved? And if the two of you can't agree, will the entire congregation be able to help overcome the disagreements?

The 21st century world is very different, legally and ethically, from the 1st century world. The contemporary United States of America is a far cry from ancient or classical Greece. If all the law books in all the law offices in the land were piled up on the Mall in Washington, D.C., the Mall would disappear in a wall of weighty tomes. The US has more laws than Carter has little liver pills. If it is true that "possession is nine-tenths of the law," then it follows that American courts are clogged with a myriad of cases involving lawsuits of somebody or other against somebody or other over something or other which somebody possesses, possessed, or wants to possess.

Nonetheless, there are still Christian communities in the 21st century where disputants attempt to overcome their disputes without resorting to suing one another. In the Anabaptist churches (Amish, Mennonite, Brethren, etc.), going to court is always perceived to be a last resort. The individuals who feel wronged by one another will first try to come to an agreement, and if that fails, they will take it to the congregation. Most congregations among the Anabaptists are fairly small, and are founded on a few key families. Thus it is fairly common for folks who act on the principle of "good faith" to settle things out of court, without ever having engaged attorneys or writing legal briefs or any such thing.

But what if you're something more outlandish than an Amish or a Mennonite, like maybe a Roman Catholic or Lutheran or Methodist, or — God forbid — a Presbyterian, or something equally peculiar? And if you and your adversary can't settle your dispute, who's going to trust a congregation of five hundred or a thousand or three thousand to thrust their oars into your particular personal wrangle? If they don't know you, and you don't know them, how in the 21st century world is justice ever going to come out of going to the brethren and sistern for justice? And what if your beef is not with another Christian at all, but it is a perfectly peaceful pagan with whom you strongly disagree, and you cannot come to terms with him?

Look, God wants us to live in peace and harmony with one another. He wants us to forgive one another for our inevitable offenses against each other. And He wants **everybody** to live peacefully together, not just those who believe in Him, but **everybody**. The Bible contains a plethora of advice of what to do when disagreements arise, but most of this advice is directed to insiders, not outsiders. A surprising percentage of the Old Testament law, the Torah, has to do with how to work out our problems with each other. Much of Jesus' Sermon on the Mount has to do with what today we call "conflict management."

Still, we all have conflicts. Most of us have relatively few conflicts with other people, some of us have more than a few, and a few of us have conflicts with many others most or all of the time.

Sadly, in "the Christian West" (whatever and wherever that is), it has become increasingly the vogue to go to court to settle personal or financial disputes. Nowhere is that more apparent than in the U.S. of A.. And no land has more lawyers to attend to more lawsuits than the U.S. of A.. Some years ago it was claimed that the United States graduates more attorneys per year than all the attorneys of all ages put together in the whole nation of Japan. The same is probably still true — only more so. As the old joke goes, "If all the attorneys in the land were laid end to end" — well, you know the options for ending the old joke. No profession produces more sardonic mirth than the legal profession. Everybody loves lawyer jokes, except for lawyers, most of whom are not at all amused by them.

The USA is the Languishing Land of Licentious Litigation. I doubt there are accurate statistics to support the following allegation, but I shall forthwith allege it anyway: More litigation, both legitimate and specious, is thrashed out in American courts than in the courts of all other nations combined. Americans are shameless litigators, boundless litigators, heartless litigators. Whatever anyone anyplace might ever sue anyone over, somebody in America has surely sued somebody over it. The hot coffee spilled in the lap of the McDonalds drive-in customer. The tooth the dentist tried to fix but didn't. The dog which added to the fecundity of the neighbor's garden. The eighteen-wheeler truck whose cardiac-arrested-and-shortly-to-be-cadaverous driver slowly rolled onto the newly-sodded immaculate lawn of a spectacular new suburban estate. The wacky widget whose errant whatchamacallit flew into the face of a beauty queen, causing a plastic surgeon to sew 95 stitches into her theretofore unsullied face, 4 of which left a small but permanent wrinkle, causing the queen, and especially the plastic surgeon, even greater legal and fiscal distress.

God and Jesus and Paul have some advice for us: Don't go to court over such stuff! Work it out! Settle it! Get over it! Stuff happens! It is a verity of existence! Get **over** it! Put it behind you! But **don't sue** one another over it!

As a society, we largely ignore the biblical advice. And when we try to institute legal limits on our own bad behavior for dragging one another to court, courts strike down the prudent limitations we seek to place on ourselves, because, they say ("they" being judges), it is unconstitutional to limit our litigiousness. What will courts and judges have to do if we greatly limit our litigiousness? There are already too many lawyers to go around anyway!

What a crowd of cowed ninnies we are! The Republicans, financially supported by big corporations, try to put limits on torts. The Democrats, supported by the trial lawyers, fight tort limits tort and claw. The politicians often do what they do for all the wrong reasons, allowing the people to continue doing what they often do for all the wrong reasons, and the body politic gets more and more corrupt and corrupted by our licentious litigiousness.

Consider the recent flood of lawsuits against the tobacco companies. Have the tobacco companies deliberately attempted to deceive the public about the dangers of addiction to nicotine? Is the sky blue, for heaven's sake? Of course they have; systematically they have! Ought the companies to be nailed for their decades of deceit? Undoubtedly. But how much? How much? And who, having become addicted to smoking for twenty or forty or sixty years, never once thought that smoking might not really be such a good idea? There shall always be smokers, so there shall always be tobacco companies. The issue here is not shall there, or shall there not, be justice. The issue is this: what constitutes justice when both cigarette makers and cigarette smokers are to blame? It is exceedingly difficult to engender any sympathy for tobacco companies, but where is the honest and genuine justice in some of the awards juries have given to smokers or the surviving members of their families?

A jury in Oregon gave the family of a Portland janitor $79,500,000 in their suit against a major tobacco producer. The trial judge reduced the award to $32,000,000. An Oregon Court of Appeals allowed the original award to stand, declaring that it fell within the guidelines established by a federal court. Seventy-nine-and-a-half million dollars. Nice work, if you can get it.

In Los Angeles, a longtime smoker won $100,000,000 in his suit against a tobacco company, but he died before he was able to take advantage of his litigious largesse. Presumably the award shall now be given to his survivors. The first time around, the jury granted him a nice round $3,000,000,000 (that is $3 **billion** for those who have trouble with multitudes of decimals), but it got chopped down to a mere $100,000,000 (a hundred mil).

The most absurd award a jury made occurred in Los Angeles in October of 2002. They gave a lady **$28 billion** in judgment against the lady's cigarette maker of choice. Her case was argued by the same trial lawyer who earlier had won $3 billion. It is obscene — not the fact that the tobacco company exists, nor the fact that the woman took up smoking at a young age, but the grotesque size of the punitive damages. The tobacco companies should long have been ashamed of themselves, but that woman also should be ashamed, and the members of the jury should be infinitely ashamed. They did not engaged in social engineering, much as they might suppose they did; they engaged in legal and social anarchy.

In Louisiana a retired judge named Joseph Grefer won $1.06 billion from the Alpha Technical Corporation. He convinced a jury they dumped radioactive waste on his property. That's a lot of nuked do-do, no matter how you slice it. Is anybody's personal piece of ground — or **person** — worth $1,060,000,000? And why are we not surprised to hear that the plaintiff in this case was a retired judge? Might a judge know better than your average John Q. Citizen how the litigation business operates?

Have you noticed, in the past ten or twenty years, that any kind of liability insurance you carry has risen dramatically in cost? Do you suppose there is any connection between these obscene awards and the cost of that insurance? Does it cost more to buy a better mousetrap now than it did two decades ago? It might even cost less to produce it, but the manufacturer charges much more to sell it because of the fear that somebody will bring suit against Mousetrap Manufacturers Ltd. when some klutz didn't follow directions and got his right index digit smartly snapped by incorrectly attempting to set the trap.

Laying aside the multitude of extra options you choose for your new car, does your basic new car now cost a lot, lot, **lot** more than your basic new car cost years ago? Did you ever stop to think why? Well, there are many reasons, but one of them is that Mr. GM or Mr. Ford or Mr. DaimlerChrysler or Messrs. Toyota, Honda, or Nissan have to charge you more to be able to buy the insurance to cover their losses and to build up a war chest for when you are automatically included in a class-action lawsuit against them because 54 cars in a particular model and year, out of a total of 546,192, had their brakes fail when the drivers were doing 92 MPH in 124 degree heat on a curvy road in a lonely desert in August, and now all those brakes in all those cars have to be replaced.

For centuries, there has been a legal precedent that artists of various kinds cannot defame dead people who actually lived, because when they're dead, their income can't be damaged by the defamation. Thus they could take a reasonable degree of artistic license by taking swipes at the dear departed. But a lady whose late husband was depicted as being somewhat imprudent in a blockbuster Hollywood movie brought suit against the studio. I saw the movie. The character wasn't portrayed as being evil or sinful or foolish. As it turned out, maybe he was shown to be a tad imprudent, if also a bit overly courageous as an entrepreneur. So the widow took the movie corporation to court. Her lawyer piously intoned, "This suit's not about money. The movie's about money. This is about accountability to the truth."

Accountability to the truth is important. We all ought to feel compelled to tell the truth. But unless a lawsuit is instituted with the expressed intention of winning $1.00 plus court costs and attorneys fees for "the principle of the thing," then it *is* about money; it *is* about the princi**pal** of the thing.

The events of 9/11, and especially the few months immediately afterward, awakened the nation to the issue of giving particular financial awards to the families of the victims of the terrorist attacks. One of the major concerns in these awards was the income and age of the people who were killed. Should everyone get the same amount, or should future earning power, based on the age of the people when they died, be taken into account?

In some cases, family members actually filed lawsuits against various institutions to attempt to gain some funds. But in most instances, with so much money having come from both private and public sources, including many millions of dollars given as charity, the question of equity naturally centered on the income and age of the victims.

But how does one determine equity in such awesome – and awful – matters? Or how does society or a court or government decide what is equitable? In the eyes of the law, one person's life is "worth" much more than another person's, but is that also true in the eyes of God? Without question certain people produce much more for the world than most other people, and some people use their lives to the fullest while others seem entirely to waste their lives. God alone is capable of ultimately placing a truly valid value on every human life, but courts must place such value in a temporal, limited sense. And what is the life of any of us worth? It is a **vital** question, obviously.

Pay close attention to this: **Life itself is a risk**. Courts are incapable of **mitigating** the risk, but constantly they find themselves in the position of **litigating** the risk. Legally, perhaps that can be done, but ethically, it is an impossibility, in terms of absolute justice.

If we are alive, at all, anywhere and at any time, we are at risk. If it were possible to have eliminated all risks altogether, somebody long ago would have done it, and most assuredly that person would have patented it. She also would have made a fortune. But somebody else would have tried to steal the patent. And the whole thing would have ended up in some court somewhere.

Americans may be the people who are the least likely of all nationalities to accept the risky nature of human existence. We have more safety measures built into more stuff we use on a daily basis than the US Patent Office can shake a law book at. Nonetheless, we continue to sue one another or to sue corporations in obscene excess, thus indirectly declaring that life ought not to be a risky business.

But it is! It always has been! And by the very lifestyles which most of us have chosen, it becomes increasingly more risky! Get a life, Christian people! Live the life you get in faith! And accept the fact that one day, by one means or another, your life will become threatened, if not by illness, then by accident, and if not by accident, then by violence, and if not by violence, then by a so-called "act of God." But we need to live with the constant awareness that not only shall we eventually die, but that until we do die, we shall certainly experience serious problems of our own making or the making of others. We can absolutely count on it.

Non Sequitur is one of my favorite comic strips. In mid-December one year there was a one-frame cartoon that showed a little house in the deep snow, in front of which stood a large empty sleigh. Above the small house was a sign which read, "Santa's Workshop." Beside the house was a huge, multistory building above whose door was the sign, "Santa's Legal Dept." From inside the small house came the verbalized caption — with no visible personage there to say it, but we all know who it is —, "This used to be such a simple time of year."

Somebody e-mailed me a long list of one-liners, one of which said, "99% of lawyers give the rest a bad name." By chance it was followed by another one-liner which declared, "42.7% of all statistics are made up on the spot."

Well, 99% of all lawyers are decent, honest, hard-working people who do their best to interpret, administer, and uphold the law. But 1% give the rest a bad name. And most of that 1% are probably avaricious litigators, avaricious for their clients, but most of all, avaricious for themselves. There is no difference in essence between the Democrats accepting multi-millions of dollars in contributions every year from the trial lawyers and the Republicans accepting their multi-millions from the energy companies. Much if not most of that money is already tainted from the git-go.

Many people tend to distrust all lawyers —- until they need one themselves. Then lawyers are perceived in quite a different light. Because there are fallible and sinful human beings, there have to be laws. But further, because there are laws, there have to be lawyers; because there are lawyers, there have to be laws. It is both that simple, and that complicated.

48

In 2002, and perhaps for the next several years, the major arena of litigation which will capture public attention is the money being awarded by the Roman Catholic Church to victims of pedophile priests. Restitution must be made, and the Church itself is the single most obvious institution to make the restitution. It is beyond refute that the damage done to thousands of victims is both incalculable and indescribable.

Nevertheless, for the good of the entire society, as well as the health of the Catholic Church, there must be lower limits set on these awards. When the damage to individuals who were victimized by the pedophiles is potentially without limit, there still is inevitably a limit to the punitive payments which must be paid out. As terrible as the crimes and sins of these priests are, it would be more terrible still if the American Roman Catholic Church were effectively to be literally as well as figuratively liquidated by these horrific judgments against it. Only in the USA would the Church already have paid out as much as it has, seeking to prevent more of the cases of abuse from going to trial. The fear of litigation in America is as great if not greater as the actuality of litigation in America. More money is paid outside of courtrooms by more individuals and corporations than this world dreams of. But again, I am not attempting to excuse or ignore the wrongdoing of the priests, or anyone else who is judged guilty in any litigation. I am just saying, with Gilbert and Sullivan, that the punishment in many of these instances does not fit the crime.

There is another major question here, which has long been a distinctly American problem. Are we going to be more concerned in this country about individual wellbeing, or about social wellbeing? Upon whom shall we focus more of our political, legal, and spiritual strength: **Me,** or **Us**? For much of our history, and in many of our actions, we have shown ourselves to be considerably more concerned about Me than about Us. As noble an organization as it is, the American Civil Liberties Union is, in my opinion, far too focussed on Me, almost to the total exclusion of Us.

Litigation generally benefits Me, or at most a limited number among Us. However, litigation usually damages Us more than it helps Us. I am well aware that trial lawyers would vehemently argue that they provide an absolutely necessary societal service, and to a very significant extent they do. As long as sinful humanity exists, litigation shall be necessary. But excessive litigation must be curtailed, and in the USA, it seems never to have been contained within reasonable boundaries.

Because of the ungodly increase in legal torts, the quality of American medical care is declining. Too many highly gifted people are either leaving medical practice or are not going into medical schools because they believe the likelihood of litigation does not make it worth the effort to learn the skills necessary to practice a medical specialty in the most litigious nation on earth. In Cleveland, where we live, the cost of malpractice insurance has forced many doctors out of their profession, a profession for which they are highly qualified, but in which they choose no longer to practice. Either they cannot get malpractice insurance at all, or if they are able to procure it, they have to charge their patients too much to be able to pay for it. As a nation, we cannot afford the costs of a medical system where litigation may well be the fastest increasing cost factor.

Even many of the clergy believe it has become necessary for them to obtain malpractice insurance. Heaven knows too many clergy abuse their clerical status. But the vast majority of the clergy do not abuse their position. Still, increasing numbers of clergy are being sued by irate parishioners who claim they were badly advised or mistreated by their priest, minister, or rabbi. In a congregational setting, the clergy don't charge for their services, so how can they be charged with malpractice, for crying out loud? If you get what you pay for, how can you get paid for what you don't pay for, for crying out loud? It is enough to make the clergy cry out loud, for crying out loud!

Forgiveness of one another is at the heart of biblical faith put into action. It behooves all of us, in the huge majority of instances, to work out our disagreements with one another in as amicable a fashion as we can. If we can't agree, then we must agree to disagree. But we must learn to do so agreeably.

If you get into a squabble with somebody over something, go to that person privately. Try to get him/her to resolve the issue informally. If it is a corporate entity with whom you disagree, go to an officer of the institution, and as calmly as you can, explain your grievance. If you think a monetary resolution is necessary, suggest what you think is a fair amount. For both of you, talking it out in private is ever so much less stressful and costly than duking it out in court.

And remember this: It is a greater sin to be overcompensated by a defeated adversary in court than was the sin which the adversary committed in the first place. A judicial process which results in too much recompense is justice thwarted. And every day, in courtrooms throughout our languishing land, justice is being grossly thwarted.

Is the process I am suggesting likely to work? Frankly, no. Not in the USA anyway, not in the early stages of the 21st century. But it certainly is worth a try.

But what if it doesn't work? What if, informally, you seek a resolution, and you fail? What then? Set it aside. Put it behind you. Accept the reality that you think a grave injustice was thrust upon you, and do everything you can to get over it. Forgive your adversary. We are not **requested** by God to forgive one another; we are **commanded** to do so. Litigation may benefit **me** if I am successful in it, but in the end, it is bound to damage **us**. It cannot be otherwise, because all of us ultimately pay whatever financial awards are made through litigation.

Finally, if you think justice demands that you go to court to right a wrong, then seek **justice**. For God's sake, your own sake, the sake of your adversary, and especially for the sake of the larger society, **do not seek retribution**. Punitive damages, even for egregious offenses, actually benefit no one, least of all the person or people to whom such damages are awarded. They end up by concluding they deserve something they don't deserve. Bad behavior should not go unpunished, but bad behavior should not result in large financial rewards for those who are wronged, either. When anyone is rewarded by someone else's wrongdoing, wrong compounds wrong.

"To have lawsuits at all with one another is defeat for you. Why not rather suffer wrong? Why not rather be defrauded?"

Paul is right, you know. It's hard to accept, hard to take, hard to swallow. But the apostolic pistol is right. Suffer the wrong. It's the right thing to do.

Scripture – Matthew 23:23-28

Text – You blind guides, straining out a gnat and swallowing a camel! – Matthew 23:24 (RSV)

THE PERVERSE RESULTS OF
POLITICAL CORRECTNESS

The most versatile language in the world is the English language. It contains far more words than any other language. We have tens of thousands or hundreds of thousands more words than any other language on the planet. And our English words are derived from a whole host of other languages. English is a veritable verbivore of languages, an eater-up of all etymological edibles.

From Chaucer to T.S. Eliot, from Beowulf to Saul Bellow, there has been a remarkable progression and evolution of the world's most flexible tongue. Now, a dozen centuries after the primary origins of our language, we have an almost limitless choice in how we express the realities we see around us. If, for example, someone wants to grumble, he can grumble. But he also can groan, moan, grouse, mutter, murmur, bitch, bellyache, beef, crab, fuss, gripe, complain, kick, kvetch, squawk, whine, or mumble. All those words mean more or less the same thing, but what a cornucopia of choices we have when we want to describe what happens when we want to express displeasure with somebody or something.

In this sermon, I am going to take issue with a linguistic pattern which, in the past twenty years or so, has quickly become an art form. I refer to what is now universally known as "politically correct language."

The proponents of politically correct language or behavior have a legitimate concern. Their concern is not to offend anyone unnecessarily by the words we use. Feminist sensitivities have produced many of the most obvious illustrations of PC language. Thus "mankind" is out, and "humankind" is in. **Man**kind presumably ignores half of humanity, but **human**kind includes

53

everybody. Why? I haven't a clue. I understand the objection to the first word, but I am unable to determine why the second word has become *au currant.*

Or there is the word "humanity" itself. You don't hear it used much anymore. I'm not positive why that has happened, but I will posit a theory. "HuMANity" puts an emphasis on **man**, which is not PC, whereas HUmankind puts the emphasis on **hu**. "Man" won't do, so go with "hu." Truly, I think that is why humankind is in and humanity is out. The syllabic emphasis has determined the correctness of usage. Very strange.

A similar bizarre result has occurred because of the use of the word "person." For example, no longer is it acceptable to say that a person can be **his** own worst enemy. Now we must say that a person can be his **or her** own worst enemy. We want to include the female half of the race in such statements.

In general, I agree with that change. For far too long were male pronouns used to describe the entire human race. But still, it has thrown the word "person" into a linguistic alphabet soup, and for no valid reason. No longer are there spokesmen; now there are spokespersons. Chairmen are a thing of the past; chairpersons presumably are a thing of the present and future. (The alternative "chair" is even more repulsive. Anybody who agrees to being **chair** of anything may as well **be** a chair, says I.) Firemen become firepersons (even if all of them are men), the ice man no longer cometh, now it is the ice person who shows up, etc., etc.

Strangely, because "person" has become the usual substitute for the former "man," "persons" has become the plural for a bunch of individuals, rather than "people." Have you noticed that? People don't say "people" much anymore! Now they say "persons!" Why? I can only guess it is because man in out and person is in, so people are out and persons are in. Go figure.

Politically correct language is, in essence, a sensitivity to sensitivity. That is, it is an attempt to take into consideration that some people might be sensitive (as compared to **in**sensitive) to how we use words. Do our words and expressions show that we understand the feelings of others? Are we aware how our use of language may hurt or offend or demean others?

These are excellent questions, and they deserve our attention. Nonetheless, a sensitivity to sensitivity does not necessarily express sensitivity. In other words, we may **say** all the right things, but **think** or **do** all the wrong things. People can be fastidious in their use of words who are horrible in their thought processes or in their actions.

Some of the most emotionally charged words in the English language are the words we use to describe or define black people. Whatever words we use, do we capitalize them, or use lower case? Is it Black, or black? And if "Black," then must it also be "White?"

From the time the first Africans were brought to these shores as slaves, there has been an evolution of terminology to describe black people. The word "negro" simply means "black" in Italian, Spanish, and Portugese. Those words come from the Latin *niger*. Over the centuries, blacks in the USA have been called Negroes (or negroes – curiously, the spell checker on my word processor rejected the lower-case possibility), nigras (by Southern whites), colored people (NAACP is easier to say quickly than the National Association for the Advancement of Colored People, but it was "colored people" who gave the organization that name), blacks, Afro-Americans, and African Americans. There is one word which has been used by both whites and blacks which has become completely unacceptable in white usage, and that is the so-called N-word. A black professor has written a lengthy and provocative book about whether it is ever acceptable for honkeys (my word; certainly not his) to use the N-word. I agree that it is unacceptable in all instances. Nonetheless, many blacks feel they can use the word without shattering a major linguistic boundary. It may be a double standard, but then, blacks have lived with double standards themselves for generations, so perhaps it is only fair play that we whites have a double standard imposed on us.

In the Sixties and Seventies, we went fairly quickly from "black" to "Afro-American," and then as quickly to "African

55

American." Now we seem to be going back to "black" again. In my judgment, that is likely a good thing. Although not all blacks are truly black, and no whites are truly white, "black" and "white" are sufficiently descriptive, and are not at all pejorative, as proper English words.

The word "Oriental" (or oriental) has been replaced by the word "Asian." I suppose this is to prevent too broad a categorization. But in my mind, "Oriental" always connoted eastern Asians: Japanese, Koreans, Chinese, Taiwanese, Indo-Chinese (Vietnamese, Laotians, Cambodians), Burmese, Thais, and Filipinos. Other Asians we defined by where they came from: Siberians, Afghans, Malaysians, Indonesians, Indians, Pakistanis, Uzbeks, Kazakhs, Iranians, Iraqis, etc. "Asian American" is such a broad term that it is almost meaningless, unless it means "Orientals." But "Asian" does not connote "Oriental," at least to me. It connotes the entire continent of Asia, which consists of far more people than just Orientals.

What, you may be wondering, does all this have to do with Jesus and the scribes and Pharisees? Or with the Bible? Or with theology? Hold your horses, for heaven's sake! Such a nudzh you are! Have patience; we'll get there.

The United States of America has always prided itself on being a melting pot. The giant lady standing in New York Harbor says, "Give me your tired, your poor, your huddled masses yearning to breathe free." And so the yearners for freedom started to come. At first it was mainly British (English, Scots, Welsh, Scotch-Irish), but then Germans and Dutch and other Europeans started to arrive. Then immigrants began showing up from Eastern Europe, Russia, the Middle East, China, and elsewhere. Decades ago, we still had Italian-Americans and Irish-Americans in this country. Have you noticed that we don't have any of them anymore? Now we just have Italians or Irish, or more likely just ordinary Americans with names like Corelli and Piraino or O'Connor and Shaughnessy. But when your ancestors in this country got off the boat one or two or three centuries ago, why would you be Scottish-American or Welsh-American or Italian-

American or Irish-American or Asian American - - - or African American? Why aren't you just American, whatever may be your ancestry?

Melting pots are terrific ideas in theory, but they are hard to pull off in fact. And when politically correct language insists on pointing out the **separate** identities of Americans, it undermines the **common** identity of Americans. My parents were born in Canada. They emigrated to the States before I was born, and were naturalized when I was a young boy. I was born here. Am I a Canadian-American? What in the world is that? I am an **American**, for crying out loud! So are you! (If, in fact, you are.) And whether you are Hispanic or Chinese or Russian or Israeli or Vietnamese or whatever, if you are an American, you're an American, and that's good enough!

American seminaries are the epitome of political correctness. Do you realize that half or more of the students in most American seminaries are, by their own unique nomenclature, Euro-Americans? Great Caesar's ghost: Euro-Americans! Give us a linguistic break, will you? Cut us some etymological slack! Euro-Americans indeed!

To use terms like African-American or Asian-American is unintentionally to undermine the very concept of the United States of America. It is more than sufficiently difficult to promote unity in a nation with 50 states stretching from sea to shining sea, and beyond, and with two hundred nationalities represented among its citizens. Why further complicate it by insisting that it is politically correct deliberately to point out differences when we describe ourselves, rather than similarities? We are all Americans, wherever our parents or grandparents or ancestors may have come from!

Harry Truman once sardonically observed, "The United States was created by the boys and girls who could not get along at home." The colonists got honked at what was happening to them in England, so they left to start a new life here. And that story has been played out with every person of every nationality who ever set foot on these sceptered shores to begin a new life.

57

What possible long-term advantage is there in pointing out our other-ness (Hispanic, Oriental, Slavic, Italian, whatever), when it is our us-ness, our American-ness, we want to undergird?

There is one group of citizens with a politically correct moniker whom I have not yet mentioned. They are the Native Americans, formerly known (and obviously incorrectly) as Indians. How long must people's ancestors have lived in central North America (for lack of a better term) for the people themselves to be considered native Americans? Even the Indians were not native to America; they came here from Asia millennia ago. Ultimately, every American is either an immigrant or the descendant of immigrants. Nobody was native from the very beginning.

Sadly, the Indians were first called Indians because Columbus presumably thought he had landed in India. Well, anybody can make a mistake. But the first Americans became known as Indians because a fluke of mistaken geography, and ever since they have been called Indians. Some Indians despise the term, although apparently most others don't, just as some blacks insist on being African-Americans, but with most others it is acceptable to be just black.

Speech that is truly politically correct to all people in all circumstances has become a virtual impossibility. If we think we are correct to describe one person with the proper PC label, we will offend another person with exactly the same background when we refer to him or her in that way. You can't win for losing.

And that's just the point, isn't it? Our **words** are bound to offend certain people, but we have no choice other than to use words, if we are to communicate with one another at all. However, we must be certain that our **actions** do not cause offense. We should treat everyone equally, which is to say, we should **love** everyone. God does not require us to like everybody. In fact, even He probably dislikes a lot of us a lot. But love we must.

I have known people who are absolutely squeaky clean in PC speech. But they are as mean as snakes underneath all their supposedly sensitive wordings. And some of the people who most revile them are those who refuse to follow the PC rules. These proper PC folk talk the talk; oh, do they ever talk the talk! But do they walk the walk? That is what God looks at when He judges us. The walk is far more important than the talk.

Remember *Brave New World*? Or do you remember *1984*? Huxley and Orwell, writing half a century ago, foresaw the dangers of using language for political purposes in very twisted and perverse ways. The double-speak at which they both so furiously railed is reminiscent of much of our PC language today. Many PC words do not clarify; they obfuscate. They do not open up; they cover over. However well intended they may be, they compress meaning into meaninglessness, they create illusions where previously there was reality, and they divert real issues into petty verbal games.

A while back there was a piece in the paper about how the word "squaw" has become offensive to certain Indians around the country. The State of Maine has more "Squaw" place names than any other state. The Maine legislature decreed that everything with Squaw in its name had to be changed to "Moose." So Big Squaw Township became Big Moose Township, and Middle Squaw Brook became Middle Moose Brook, and a mountain called Squaw's Bosom became Moose Bosom.

Does a moose have a bosom? Have you ever wondered about that? Well in Maine there are moose bosoms!

The Minnesota legislature also decreed a name change to be in order. However, some clever Minnesotans fixed the linguistic wagons of those state politicos. Instead of Squaw Creek and Squaw Bay, now they have Politically Correct Creek and Politically Correct Bay. Right on, you Golden Gophers! Minnesota, hats off to thee! And anyway, wasn't it Indians who called squaws squaws? Nobody who hailed from Sussex or Lancashire ever came up with a word like that. If the word was proper at one time among those who coined it, need it be improper now among everyone who has been made familiar with it?

Political correctness sooner or later merges into historical revisionism. If we refuse to use the old terminology, we can create, *de novo*, a new reality, we suppose. So if you don't call

Indians Indians, you can erase the historical context out of which that word originated. Then you can use other words or concoct new words which better suit your revisionist purposes.

I remember when every community had a dump. Nobody has a dump anymore; now we have sanitary landfills. Dumps connote environmental rape. Sanitary landfills connote environmental sensitivity. But a sanitary landfill by any other name is still a dump.

It has become unacceptable in governmental circles to speak of churches, synagogues, or mosques. Those words are too religious-specific. Now we have faith-based organizations. In a *New Yorker* cartoon, a man is speaking to another man at a cocktail party. The other chap is wearing a clerical collar. So the first guy says, "I see that you work for one of those faith-based organizations." Coming from him, it almost sounds like a slur, doesn't it? The smarmy PC nudnik!

Ultimately, political correctness has not evolved because of heightened sensitivities to the thoughts and feelings of others. Instead, it is the result of hypersensitivity, super-sensitivity, sensitivity well above and beyond the call of duty. Liberals have been the primary PC zealots, but some of them are illiberal in their liberalism. They want to force everyone to use their carefully restricted language, supposing it will make the world a better place. What it does is to make the world a much duller place, deliberately attempting to diminish the borders of the most expansive language in the world.

Of course words historically have been employed to damage or to inflict pain upon particular groups of people, and all people of good will must avoid that. In order more effectively to avoid it, however, we need to know the historical context in which these verbal assaults arose. It is unwise to attempt to revise that history out of existence. To refer to a previously cited example, even though we should never again use the N-word, it behooves us to be aware of the racial cauldron in which it bubbled up. Otherwise, not being familiar with the sorry historical context, we might find ourselves repeating it again, not knowing what to avoid, much less how to avoid it.

As a Christian minister, the PC language which has most irritated me is the god-awful God-language which has been created in the last generation to suit the sensitivities of ultra-feminists. In another of these sermons, I fulminate about that at some length. Here let me simply state that I believe it is demeaning to tradition and ultimately it is both silly and fruitless to attempt to refrain from referring to God as being a male deity. Surely God is not fundamentally male or female. But for us to relate to God, most of us must conceive Him as being personal. We are too limited intellectually or philosophically to feel connected to an impersonal deity.

Virtually all traditional names or descriptions of God in Judaism, Christianity, and Islam are male in orientation. The Bible consistently refers to God as "He," although most translations use the lower case "he." Jesus often called God "Father," and always He used male terminology when referring to God. Does that mean that God is male? No. But it does mean that Jesus and the other biblical writers perceived the God Who Is Personal in the terminology of a male divine person.

My teeth are set on edge whenever liberal clergy or seminary or college professors call God "She." I clearly understand what they are trying to do when they say that, but when they do it, it forces me to think about what they are trying to do, rather than to focus on the nature of the God to whom they refer. It is a PC theological affectation to call God She, or to refuse to use any personal pronouns for God. Furthermore, the rationale behind this effort is doomed to failure - - - thank God! Normal people of faith are too wise to be buffaloed into submission by well-intentioned ultra-liberals who have not thought through what would happen to religious faith were they to succeed in their concerted efforts. (I wonder: would buffaloes find it politically incorrect for me to use this particular metaphor? They probably would. But like the boor I am, I shall not give it another thought.)

Fortunately, no biblical translation yet has eliminated personal pronouns altogether when referring to God. The New Revised Standard Version altered some of the most obvious sexist statements in the oldest biblical manuscripts. The New International Version is the translation most frequently used by conservative and evangelical Christians. Astonishingly, a PC NIV has just been published.

Frankly, I have become ambivalent about the NRSV. (Ambivalence about anything is not natural to me, as you may have noticed.) I am unfamiliar with the new NIV. When the NRSV first came out, I bought a copy, and read it. Ordinarily, I used it in conjunction with my preaching during the remaining years of my active ministry. Some changes in it I liked, but eventually, I concluded I preferred the RSV. Beauty of English phraseology was lost from the KJV in the RSV, and the NRSV became even less majestic in its phrasings. Nevertheless, I consciously chose that the biblical citations in this tome would usually be from the RSV.

And that prompts another inevitable facet of this whole PC issue: **personal taste**. Some of us like PC language, and some don't. As has often been stated, there is no accounting for taste. People like what they like and they don't like what they don't like. Often we can offer no rational explanation. That's just the way it is.

I don't like PC. But I try to support my dislike with a rationale. If you like it, you too need to support your position with a rationale. We may never agree on this, but at least we can disagree rationally, rather than irrationally or simply emotionally.

When the Oklahoma City bomber Timothy McVeigh was executed by lethal injection in Terra Haute, Indiana in May of 2001, *The Times* of London carried a story about it. The correspondent, Joanna Coles, referred to T-shirts which enterprising entrepreneurs in Terra Haute were selling prior to the execution. One said, "The Worst Is Yet to Come McVeigh – Hell!" Another declared, "Hoosier Hospitality: Timothy McVeigh, May 16, 2001, Justice at Last." It also includes the image of a hypodermic needle. Another shirt, copying the TV craze, said, "McVeigh: 'You Are the Weakest Link!' Goodbye!" And it had not one, but two, hypodermic needles, suitably touching at their tips. The article said that PETA, People for the Ethical Treatment of Animals, begged Mr. McVeigh to make sure that his last meal was meatless. He wrote them that they might be more successful in trying to convince the Unabomber, Ted Kaczynski, to follow their advice.

Political incorrectness shall continue regardless of the most noble efforts of ethically governed people to prevent it. It is impossible to underestimate the crassness of many members of the human family when major social, political, economic, or philosophical issues are involved. Intentionally inflammatory things shall be said as long as humans have breath to say them. That is a sad fact of life.

Nevertheless, efforts informally to enforce politically correct language are bound to fail. People will say whatever they want to say, unless technically it is illegal according to the laws of whatever nation they say it in. Even then, some might still say it, just to test the validity of the laws.

And that brings us, at last, to Jesus and the Pharisees. (You hoped I had forgotten. Fat chance.)

Most of Matthew 23 is an unrelenting attack on the attitude of the scribes and Pharisees. It is well to remember that these religious leaders were conscientiously devoted to the study and implementation of the Mosaic religious laws. The scribes likely were "strict constructionists" and the Pharisees "loose constructionists," although you would not deduce that from reading the Gospels.

What galled Jesus about these men was that He believed they only wanted to **appear** as though they were following the intent of the law. But in their hearts, they did not follow it at all. "Woe to you, scribes and Pharisees, hypocrites! For you tithe mint and dill and cummin, and have neglected the weightier matters of the law, justice and mercy and faith…. Woe to you, scribes and Pharisees, hypocrites! For you cleanse the outside of the cup and of the plate, but inside they are full of extortion and rapacity…. Woe to you, scribes and Pharisees, hypocrites! For you are like whitewashed tombs, which outwardly appear beautiful, but within they are full of dead men's bones and all uncleanness" (Matt. 23:21,23,25).

Jesus detested the display of religiosity. He constantly attacked people who tried to look as though they were keeping

God's law, but who made no serious attempt to incorporate the law into their very being. "You blind guides," Jesus shouted at His theological enemies, "straining out a gnat and swallowing a camel!" Anyone who fixates on the intellectual study of religious morality without transforming that morality into daily actions may become classic gnat-strainers and camel-swallowers.

Jesus called the scribes and Pharisees hypocrites. This Greek word, *hupokrites*, translates directly into English, and we frequently use it. Almost always we use it of others, of course, and seldom does it become a descriptor for ourselves. However, "hypocrite" literally means "play-actor." A hypocrite is someone who acts the role of righteousness, but is not necessarily righteous at all. Literature is filled with hypocritical characters. Think of Hamlet's step-dad, Tartuffe, or Elmer Gantry, for example.

Is it possible that politically correct language could represent hypocrisy? Do PC people want themselves and everyone else to **appear** righteous, or do they want everyone also to **be** righteous? If we say all the right things, does that make us right? Might it be better to say what might be considered the wrong things, but we still somehow manage to do the right things? If we don't sound acceptably proper, but we act properly, are we —— and the world —— better off? Are words or attitudes the real issue here, as far as God is concerned? Both, surely, but which is more important?

More than most people, it seems to me that ultra-liberals spend far more of their time talking the talk than they spend walking the walk. They are speakers of the word, but not necessarily doers of it. I suspect that were Jesus to live among us again, He would lace into those on the far left of the religious life with as much vehemence as He would those on the far right. For that matter, nobody in between would be very safe either.

Like most trends, political correctness shall soon pass into relative oblivion. I, for one, shall not mourn its passing. It has not corrected what it sought to correct, nor has it sufficiently addressed what it sought to address. It was moralism without solid morality, good intentions without good results. *Sic semper tyrannis*. Good riddance, too.

Scripture – Psalm 89:19-37

Text – The enemy shall not outwit him, the wicked shall not humble him. I will crush his foes before him and strike down those who hate him. – Psalm 89:22-23 (RSV)

THE UNTENABILITY OF BEING THE SOLE SURVIVNG SUPERPOWER

Things seem to go to the head of George W. Bush. The President seems to see himself as a Texas Ranger, or as the Lone Ranger, or as The Divinely Chosen Worldcop.

If W. were to read Psalm 89, it likely would deepen his conviction that he has been called by God to become the arbiter of all things good and true for all nations of the cosmos. Psalm 89, according to the superscription at the beginning of the psalm, is a Maskil of Ethan the Ezrahite. Nobody knows for sure who this Ethan was, or even what an Ezrahite was. If the truth is told, a maskil is a bit of a mystery as well. Scholars can speculate about it till the cows come home (as they are wont to say in bucolic environments), but anybody's guess who wrote this psalm, or why he wrote it, is as good as anybody else's guess.

Whoever wrote Psalm 89, he was a great fan of King David. The first eighteen verses extol God, and all that God had done for Israel in days gone by. Early on, in v. 3, it is stated, presumably by God Himself, that David was chosen as the special servant of God. Then, from v. 19 through v. 37, the psalm extols David, and all that the great king had done for Israel. It is written as though God is praising David, and God exalts the king for his faithfulness to Himself.

In the midst of this royal paean of praise by Yahweh, God explains why David had been so successful as the monarch of the Israelites. God saw to it that no nation could defeat Israel or David. "The enemy shall not outwit him, the wicked will not humble him. I will crush his foes before him and strike down those who hate him" (Ps. 89:22-23). Then the psalmist has

Yahweh say of David, "He shall cry to me, 'Thou art my Father, my God, and the Rock of my salvation.' And I will make him the first-born, the highest of the kings of the earth."

George W. Bush is what he himself would probably call "a Bible-believing Christian." And that's just what makes him so scary. And that's what makes psalms like Psalm 89 so scary. Throughout the Hebrew scriptures there are scores, even hundreds, of passages which suggest that God specially chose Israel for very specific political and military reasons, as well as for religious or spiritual reasons. According to holy writ in numerous passages, God wanted Israel to become the dominant nation of the ancient Middle East.

No doubt there were countless Israelites who proudly shared that notion. It is very comforting, yea, verily, it is exceedingly reassuring, if one can truthfully believe that God has selected one's own particular country to dominate the earth. Ethan the Ezrahite subscribed to the Domination Theory of divine providence. And so, I fear, does George W. Bush. And also Dick Cheney. And also Donald Rumsfeld. And particularly John Ashcroft. Our President and three of his closest confidants clearly are convinced that God wants the United States of America to be the sole surviving superpower. They hope that extremely sobering reality will be the status quo for the foreseeable future. And they want to prevent any other nation of any political stripe from attempting to become a superpower. It was bad enough in the Bad Old Days when the Soviet Union was the Other Superpower. It was very good, W. & Co. conclude, that the Bad Guys fell apart, and the Good Guys won the Cold War. And now, they smugly declare, "No enemy shall outwit us, the wicked shall not humble us. We will crush our foes, and strike down those who hate us."

History is strewn with the wreckage of countries which presumed that God favored them over all other nations. Israel was destroyed by Assyria in 722 BCE. Judah was destroyed by Babylon in 586 BCE. Judea was destroyed by the Romans in 70 CE. The Roman Empire imploded in the 4th and 5th centuries of the Common Era before the advancing barbarian hordes, as did the Byzantine Empire a few centuries later. The Holy Roman Empire went down the historical dumper, the Mogul Empire failed, the Ottoman Empire failed, in 1918 the German Empire, whose soldiers' belt buckles brazenly declared *Gott Mit Uns* (God With Us), failed, the British Empire, upon which, it was claimed, the sun never set, saw its sun set in the 20th century, in 1945 the Japanese Empire failed, and sometime in the 21st century, God willing, the American Empire also shall fail. For the good of the globe, the last of these failures likely cannot come too quickly. The United States of America, at least under the Bush Administration, has gotten dangerously out of hand.

But millions of Americans, many of them Christians, certainly one of them its current President, don't believe that. They believe what the enigmatic Ethan the Ezrahite believed, that God wants certain nations to dominate the world at certain points in human history. These American Christians, many if not most of them from the Religious Right, are convinced that without question, God wants the USA to dominate the world now. Such a view is, and always has been, a dangerous delusion. Far worse, it is horrendous theology. It led to the demise of Israel as a political entity in biblical times (and maybe once again in current times), and if it continues unchecked, it shall lead to the demise of the USA as we now know it.

In the spring of 2001, Vice President Cheney delivered a speech about the US military. It was an unvarnished call to arms of the most belligerent sort. Among other things he said, "Dozens of countries have nuclear weapons that could kill millions of people with the turn of a key." **Dozens**? Unless Dick Cheney knows something the rest of us do not know, he has exaggerated the facts. Maybe a dozen nations have nuclear weapons. Other dozens might develop such weapons if they chose to do so, which wisely they have not done. But, according to our Vice President, there are dozens of nations out there who might decide to detonate us in a happy heartbeat. "Leaders of several countries (e.g., North Korea, Iraq, Iran, Libya, Lebanon and perhaps China and Russia) would love to see the U.S. and its people blown to pieces." Well, perhaps. But **Lebanon**? How did little Lebanon get included in that list? Because Lebanon is not strong enough to keep Hezbollah out, does that mean they want the US blown to smithereens? And do any of those nations seriously want us destroyed any more than we seriously want them destroyed? Mr. Cheney's words play to the basest instincts of his fellow citizens.

Then the Vice President compares classical Athens and Sparta. "In ancient Greece, the people of Athens were unparalleled world leaders in art, philosophy and technology. Their rivals in Sparta were not; instead, the Spartans built massive, well-trained armies. When the two countries fought, who won? Sparta. And guess who lost their entire civilization because they didn't think it was important to build an appropriate army? Athens!"

It takes chutzpah in profusion proudly to express admiration for Sparta over Athens. What colossal militaristic nonsense! Choosing Sparta over Athens is like choosing Germany or Japan in the 1930s over Britain, France, or the USA during the same period! And Richard Cheney is a heartbeat away from the US Presidency!

Since the Soviet Union collapsed in 1989 and the two years immediately following 1989, the USA has achieved a military and political power never before duplicated in human history. Other nations have dominated during other epochs, but nobody else ever had the sheer military and economic supremacy even to come close to matching what our nation now possesses. We think we can do anything we want - - - and with impunity, we do it. Two previous American Presidents presided over the USA when it was the sole superpower, but neither of them, George H.W. Bush nor William Jefferson Clinton, showed a small scintilla of the arrogance illustrated by the presidency and personality of George W. Bush.

Consider some of the major international treaties which Bush II has simply negated by sheer, willful, petulant audacity. Almost every nation on earth signed the Kyoto Treaty on ecological issues and global warming —— but not the USA. Most other nations signed a treaty banning the future use of land mines in warfare —— but not the USA. For three decades one of the key-stones in the balance of power between the USA and the USSR was the Anti-Ballistic Missile Treaty. By means of that agree-ment, both of the superpowers promised not to develop a system for the destruction of incoming ballistic devices hurled by "the other side." An anti-missile shield, it was reasonably deduced, would represent a very de-stabilizing reality. But once George W. Bush became convinced that neither the USSR nor its political successor, Russia, would send missiles against us, but that other "rogue nations" might do just that, he washed his hands of that hard-won treaty. Only Congress can adopt treaties, and only Congress can abrogate treaties, but President Bush has scuttled this treaty all by himself, and Congress has not summoned up the courage to prevent him from doing it. No doubt defense contrac-tors are now working feverishly to concoct the technology necessary to stop missiles in mid-flight, if it can be done, which it probably can't. But that never stopped us before from trying the technologically impossible, did it? The profligate flinging of American dollars at any obstacle is guaranteed to overcome every obstacle —— isn't it?

Some time ago the United Nations approved the establish-ment of an international war crimes court. The treaty, which was first proposed in 1998, was provisionally signed by 139 coun-tries, including the United States. The court is intended to prosecute individuals from any nation who participate in geno-cide, crimes against humanity, or other carefully defined war crimes.

When he became President, George W. Bush, with an arro-gance that is so characteristic of an insecure person of average or below-average intelligence, unilaterally concluded that the US should not be party to such a treaty, and he withdrew the US sig-nature. He and his advisors feared that the court, in future, might prosecute American soldiers for supposedly specious offenses, and that we, the mightiest nation on earth, would be subject to the political whims of rinky-dink countries (my gratuitous guess at his mindset) such as the United Kingdom, France, Germany, or

Upper Volta, should they happen to have justices on the International War Crimes Court. To be fair, W. was not alone in refusing to go along with the concept behind this new court. Russia and China have balked at signing the treaty as well. North Korea, Iran, and Iraq aren't thrilled with it either. Thus we are united with a highly dubious coterie of recalcitrant nations in opposing what those nations want carte blanche to be able to do without anyone telling them they ought not to do it. Swell allies we have here!

Nobody deserves to be thrust into the sole-superpower category. It is an odious status, regardless of how much chest-puffing it seems to encourage. But that is exactly where we Americans now find ourselves. If that were not bad enough, we have a President and a presidential Administration who are obsessive about secrecy. They don't want to tell nobody nuttin' about nuttin'. Dick Cheney came close to apoplexy when the press asked the identity of the people on his energy advisory task force. No one insisted on knowing everything that was discussed by this group; they just wanted to know who was doing the discussing. Mr. Cheney harrumphed, as only he can harrumph, that over his dead body would he divulge the names. And of course millions of Americans assumed, probably correctly, that there must be something to hide, if even the names of the participants must be kept secret.

Bruce Fein is a former Justice Department official who has worked in several Republican administrations. He says that never before has anyone attempted to maintain secrecy over the identity of anyone serving on a government committee or task force. Mr. Fein went so far as to say that the US "has never had a more imperial presidency, at least since Roosevelt during his conduct of World War II." Mr. Bush insists that he will not reveal the names of people who merely consult or confer with him, and Mr. Fein says that is unprecedented. "I've never encountered one individual who told me he's not going to the Oval Office unless he is promised confidentiality. It's the biggest hoax in the world. Why he's making up all this stuff is utterly and completely baffling."

In many places and in many ways the Bible states that David was the greatest of the kings of Israel. Far more frequently than that the Bible implies that David was the unparalleled king of kings. I as quite prepared to believe that assessment as well. If the history of David's reign which is recorded in the Bible is even 50% accurate, he was a magnificent monarch.

Nonetheless, on the basis of what we can all read in I and II Samuel, and perhaps especially what we can read in all the psalms which are ascribed directly to David (not all of which he may actually have written, to be sure), I also believe that David probably suffered from bi-polar illness. Further, he was probably somewhat, if not markedly, paranoid. And if he was paranoid, he may have been a schizophrenic paranoid, besides being a manic-depressive. Despite all that arm-chair headshrinking on my part, however, I am fully convinced David was still a remarkable king. If that mountain of mental baggage accurately describes the historical David, he was all the more remarkable. To do as much as he did with that much stuff weighing him down is little less than astonishing.

Let the reader beware: I am not suggesting that George W. Bush is like King David. Would that it were so! David was brilliant; W. is less than average. David was mentally a complex mess; W. is mentally the essence of simplicity. David was mentally very badly adjusted; W. appears to be quite well adjusted, if in a frightfully unpredictable manner. David understood, appreciated, and utilized complexity; W. seems unable to understand, appreciate, or utilize anything other than the most simplistic of ideologies. **BUT** —— David believed God had specifically ordained him for greatness; W. also believes God has ordained him for greatness, and has so declared to the American people and the world.

Through the course of my lifetime, I have discovered that most people perceive reality either in the stark contrast of black and white or in a plentiful plethora of a huge variety of shades of gray. George W. Bush is a black-and-white person. Being a gray person, black-and-whiters make me very nervous. And gray people make black and white people very nervous. It is a genuine conundrum.

71

In this semi-sermonic essay, as you can clearly observe, I have been gingerly beating around the bush about what I really think of George W. Bush, and I've been doing it for far too long. I shall no longer dodge the issue; I need to come directly to the point. George W. Bush is a dangerous man. He is an exceedingly dangerous man, because he is such a limited man. He has surrounded himself with men who are much more intelligent, if also much more ideologically driven, than he is, and thus they are a **really** dangerous bunch.

Ideologues, even fairly unbalanced ideologues, can still turn out to be excellent rulers. King David is one example of that phenomenon. Richard Nixon, in my opinion, is another. Never did this country have a screwier, more complex, or more devious man in the White House than Richard Nixon. Nevertheless, he was able to overcome some of his deepest suspicions and ideological leanings to achieve some of the most important political and diplomatic successes in American history. Greatness plus mental or political or theological balance do not always go hand in hand. But greatness cannot emerge out of mediocrity, especially when mediocrity appears incapable of growth into something greater. As a President, George W. Bush is mediocre at best. But he is the willing tool of some extremely able, if devious, advisers.

The most able member of the Bush cabinet is Colin Powell, our Secretary of State. Yet he is the person who consistently is undercut by other Administration officials. Early on in the pre-9/11 Bush Administration, Gen. Powell and Condoleeza Rice, our National Security Adviser, frequently locked horns behind the scenes. Relatively speaking, she is a hawk; he is a dove. It is ironic: the preacher's daughter wants war, and the four-star general wants peace.

Nowhere is US foreign policy more tortuously twisted than in its dealings with Israel and Palestine. The Christian Right, and also the Jewish Right, push the President very hard on taking a hard line toward Yasser Arafat and the Palestinians. Moderates in both political parties support the Secretary of State in his efforts to walk the tightrope between the militant Ariel Sharon and the militant Yasser Arafat. An American journalist named Fareed

Zakaria wrote an editorial in *Newsweek* at the time our Middle East policy seemed the most muddled (Apr. 29, 2002). Mr. Zakaria said, "It is for Israel to decide whether Sharon's invasion will bring them security or insecurity in the long run....For America it has been a disaster. Since September 11 we have wanted to push the Arabs on two fronts: first on internal political reform and second on Iraq. But with tensions sky-high, these issues have been drowned out completely. Now the only conversation we will have with the Arabs is the one they always prefer to have – about Israel and Palestine. The big winners from Israel's offensive are Iraq and the political extremists of the Middle East. Reform is on the retreat."

How did the US botch things so badly in the latest Israeli-Palestinian violence? It happened because the Christian Right, who have long had the President's ear, further convinced him of what he already believed, namely, that the US is God's Gift to the Nations, and that the US President is acting on God's behalf to support the Jews in the Jewish land. It is much, much, **much** more reliable to say what God does not want than to specify what He does want. What He does not want is more bloodshed in the Land of Israel/Palestine/Judea/Samaria/WestBank. What God wants, what He always wants, is peace. But how to achieve peace God usually leaves up to the human race, and the human race usually manages to botch up the peace process.

The real danger, however, is the assumption that God is unquestionably directing the actions of any human agent, be it George W. Bush, Richard Cheney, Donald Rumsfeld, Condoleeza Rice, Colin Powell, John McCain, Ted Kennedy, Paul Wellstone, Tom Daschle, or Bill Bradley. God gives us functioning gray matter, not direct divine instructions. It is truly frightening when leaders proudly believe they are directed by God, rather than being gently and unobtrusively led by God's spirit in their lives.

It is painfully clear that President Bush intends to wage war with Iraq in some form or manner. By the time this book goes to press, that war may have already begun —— or have been concluded. Many in Congress oppose such a conflict, and for a variety of reasons which need not to be elucidated here. But it is the *Gott Mit Uns* mentality of the American President and his advisers which impels him in the direction of war. Probably in his mind, most Americans (except those who oppose a war with Iraq) are Good Guys, and most Iraqis (except those who seek the downfall or assassination of Saddam Hussein) are Bad Guys.

Condoleeza Rice has stated that US policy represents "moral clarity." It is that arrogant theology which is so upsetting about this presidency. War ought always to be the last resort of foreign policy for any nation. But war, or the threat of war, seems often to be one of the first factors employed in our current foreign policy. Self-righteously calling three particular nations "the axis of evil" is a statement which is guaranteed to coalesce even many moderate nations against us. When the emperor obviously has no clothes, who among foreign people is going to be so foolish as to ignore the brazen nakedness?

It is much wiser to attempt to **act** with moral clarity, and to refrain from **saying** that is what we are trying to do. Declaring our morality subverts our morality. In this case, it is much better to hide our light under a bushel than brashly to try to shine it into the faces of everyone near and far.

William Bennett, the primary arbiter of conservative morality, recently formed an organization called Americans for Victory Over Terrorism. One of the primary purposes of this new group is to establish an anti-anti-war movement. In other words, anybody on the home front who cautions against going to war with perceived terrorists anywhere in the world is to be thwarted on the home front. The bellicose Mr. Bennett said he will take the fight "to campuses, salons, oratorical societies, editorial pages, and television."

Bill Bennett's virtues may sometimes be vices in virtuous disguise. He is a moralist of the most inflexible sort. And he and his ilk have the ear of this President in an unwholesome, unhealthy, and unpredictable manner. It is the certitude of the Religious Right which is one of the primary factors so off-putting about them. By what authority do they think they possess the exclusive patent on morality?

People who are proudly convinced beyond any humble or humbled doubt that God has big plans for them cause God great alarm. On the one hand, the Bible seems to support such folk. But just as frequently, if not even more frequently, the Bible urges us to beware of such folk. "He who sits in heaven laughs; the Lord has them in derision," as Psalm 2 says, and as Handel said in his *Messiah*. God can use anyone and anything for His purposes. But it is dubious and probably dangerous to go from thinking that God can use us for His ends to thinking that we can use God as a means to our ends. God will be God, whatever we might choose to do.

As edgy and explosive and potentially disastrous as the Cold War was, the USA may actually have been safer during that era than it is today. When any nation is the unchallenged power broker of the world, it is only a matter of time before its power shall not only be challenged, but deliberately shattered. Further, such powerful nations tend to take unilateral actions which would never even be contemplated under the more normal situation of a balance of international power.

Autocracy anywhere and at any time is fraught with great peril. Unhappily, it has fallen upon the USA to become the world's autocrat in the opening years of the 21st century. It behooves us as wisely as possible, but also as quickly as possible, to start sharing power with others once again, either with long-time or newly-discovered allies. The expansion of NATO is probably a very good thing, although the outcome of this expansion is by no means clear. The relationship of President Bush with President Putin of Russia is one of the best things to come out of the Bush presidency. Anything we can do to improve the discourse between the two former super-foes is bound to be beneficial. As many people widely recognize, it is to our benefit and the benefit of the whole world to do whatever we can to help China put its authoritarian past behind it, and to move into the freedom of the world economy as soon as practicable.

For the time being, the most logical political entity to offset the sole-superpower status of the USA is the USE: the United States of Europe. Because we have long seen Europeans essentially as friends rather than foes, the European Union can become the least threatening alternative for Americans to the American hegemony of the world. Of course, that will require the Europeans to work together to a far greater degree than has been their historical tendency.

But truly it is not good for the US either to run the whole show, or to think that it can —— or must —— run the whole show. George W. Bush has stated unequivocally that he wants the US to be the dominating force in the world for decades or centuries to come. To offset that noxious idea, now we need droves of American internationalists in Washington. For far too long we have had far too many American imperialists who took up residence there.

The greatest threat to world peace and stability for the moment appears to be coming from militant Islamic nations. If radical Islam should take control of those countries where Islam is dominant, then radical Christianity shall quickly escalate in those nations where Christianity is thought to be dominant. A more dreary and dreadful prospect is hardly imaginable.

Shall the Al Qaedas and the Usama bin Ladens of the globe become the wave of the future? If too many western leaders sound too "Christian" in their response to Islamic terrorism, that almost certainly shall be the outcome. The only thing worse than having the USA as the sole surviving secular superpower would be for Americans to perceive themselves to be the sole surviving Christian superpower. Politics by itself is sufficiently uncertain; religion, when wedded to politics, produces a fearfully unpredictable combination. Thus Christians, Jews, Muslims and others have always attempted to influence political decision-making, but Christianity, Judaism, Islam, and every other religion must assiduously avoid attempting to forge a united front to control political decision-making.

In 1840, Arthur Cleveland Coxe wrote, "We are living, we are dwelling/ In a grand and awful time." In the USA of his time, he could clearly sense that events were leading toward some sort of cataclysmic denouement. In 1861 the dreadful clash began in earnest. The American Civil War resulted in the death of over 600,000 soldiers. The ill effects of that war continue to this day, not only in the South, but in cities and suburbs and towns and villages throughout the land.

Once again, in the early 21st century, we are living and dwelling in a grand and awful time. Things could get very ugly very quickly.

But that is not a foregone conclusion. In 1916, in the middle of the War to End All Wars, Clifford Bax wrote, "Turn back, O man, foreswear thy foolish ways." Now, even now, we 21st century Americans can foreswear our foolish ways.

For Americans, that means we *must* work toward voluntarily giving up some of the inordinate and destabilizing power which history has thrust upon us, working together with other nations of good will and wise policies for the benefit of the entire earth. Because we **can** do that, we **should** do it. Taking everything into account, the USA has been a relatively decent imperialistic nation. We can become even more decent by casting off some of our unwanted imperial powers.

Thus endeth this highly politicized harangue. Thank God for that, we call all say!

Scripture – Deuteronomy 29:2-16; Joshua 9:1-27

Text – "You stand this day all of you before the Lord your God; the heads of your tribes, your elders, and your officers, all the men of Israel, your little ones, your wives, the sojourner who is in your camp, both he who hews your wood and he who draws your water, that you may enter into the sworn covenant of the Lord your God, which the Lord your God makes with you this day." – Deuteronomy 29:10-12

HEWERS OF WOOD

It is almost the end of the so-called "Wilderness Wandering." For forty years the children of Israel have been schlepping through the Sinai Desert. It has not been a pleasant experience for them. In fact, most of them have groused the whole way, a reality always in the forefront of the mind of Moses, who has had it up to his eyebrows with grousers.

For four books – Exodus, Leviticus, Numbers, and Deuteronomy – Moses has been pontificating almost non-stop. He has recited and interpreted what he believes God's law is intended to be for Israel. Much of what Moses says is what Moses says God says, but it all comes out of Moses' mouth anyway. But to his listeners, and to us, his readers, it is to be assumed that God Himself is the authentic Presenter of the Torah, and God uses Moses as His messenger.

Now, the people are presumably just a few days or weeks or months from crossing the Jordan River into the Promised Land. So God, speaking through Moses, reminds them of what was the essence of the Wilderness Wandering. During that four-decade journey through the desert, what slowly evolved was what Christians call the Old Testament and what Jews describe simply as the Covenant. ("Testament" and "Covenant" are synonyms. The words mean "promise" or "contract" or "agreement.")

God feels it is necessary, via Moses, to give Israel a last-minute reminder of all the people to whom He has made His promise. Obviously it is intended for all the people of Israel, and Moses lists the tribal leaders, the religious officials, and all the men, women, and children of Israel. But Moses goes on to say that the covenant is also meant for "the sojourner who is in your camp, both he who hews your wood and he who draws your water."

"Hewers of wood and drawers of water" is a phrase we hear later, in the book of Joshua, the next book following Deuteronomy. The phrase apparently connotes people who were slaves of the Israelites. They were non-Israelites, but God wanted Israel to know that even their slaves were to be treated as part of the covenant people of God.

Throughout the Hebrew scriptures, there is a clear, compelling, and consistent declaration that there must always be a special concern for "the poor, the widow, the orphan, and the sojourner in your midst." Why? What makes the circumstances of those folks so unique that everyone else needs to be nudged to keep them in mind when social or political or religious decisions are being made?

Israelite society, from the time of Moses to the time of Jesus, was male-dominated. It also was adult-dominated. It also was ethnically dominated. Males got a greater percentage of the economic benefits of the land than females, adults got more than children, and Israelites got more than Gentiles (the sojourners who lived among them). The culture of the people, and the people themselves, accepted all this as a societal given. They were convinced that certain individuals **ought** to get more of the good life than certain others. But God didn't accept that as a social inevitability. Therefore God kept reminding Israel over and over that they were commanded to look out for people whom society tended to overlook.

Among the disadvantaged categories were those the Bible calls "hewers of wood and drawers of water." Because much of the land of Israel was sparsely wooded, slaves would have to go long distances to find firewood for their masters. And because much of the land was desert, slaves often also had to go long distances to find water for their masters. It was never easy to be enslaved anywhere in the world where slavery was common, but it was especially difficult to be a slave in the nomadic culture of ancient Israel. The Israelites might forget that stern reality, but God never did. And so God, by means of His selected spokesman Moses, told the Israelites, just before they entered the Promised Land, to be sure that their hewers of wood and drawers of water were consciously included within the covenant community. To God, even slaves were always to be considered insiders, not outsiders.

Within a few years of entering the Promised Land, God's commandment regarding Israelites slaves was tested, and in a very peculiar way. Under Joshua, the Israelites defeated one Canaanite group after another as they sought to take control of the land. The inhabitants of the Canaanite city of Gibeon, observing their neighboring cities being thrashed one after the other, decided to trick the Israelites. Instead of waiting for Joshua and his troops to come to them, the Gibeonites went out to negotiate with the Israelites. They were dressed in rags, as though they had been on a long journey themselves, just like the children of Israel. Out of compassion for them, Joshua said he would make a covenant with them, and he would not attack them.

Later, Joshua discovered the Gibeonites had fooled him. But because he had promised not to assault them, Joshua kept his covenant with them. However, for their subterfuge Joshua enslaved the Gibeonites, and they became hewers of wood and drawers of water. And, said the writer of the book of Joshua, whoever it was, the Gibeonites "continue to this day" as slaves. There was no question about whether it was legitimate for the Israelites to enslave them; it was, they concluded. Nonetheless, because of the covenant Joshua had made with them, even when they acted with bad faith, the Gibeonites still were to be considered legitimate, if substandard, members of the larger covenant community of Israel. To be treated as slaves of the Israelites was therefore preferable to being categorized as Gentile outsiders by the Israelites. It wasn't much better, but at least some better.

Now, nearly a century and a half after slavery was abolished by Abraham Lincoln in the USA, and almost two centuries after "the peculiar institution" was outlawed nearly everywhere else in the western world, we may logically ask whether God truly approved of slavery in ancient Israel. It is impossible for most of us to imagine that God **ever** sanctioned slavery, and particularly among His people Israel. But that is another issue altogether, and it is not the point of this sermon. For our purposes in the early 21st century, the question is this: **What ought to be our position as a society toward those people who today are the equivalent of hewers of wood and drawers of water? What special provisions should we, seeking to follow God's will in our own unique circumstances, make for the least, the last, and the lost among us?**

Under every economic system which has ever existed, whether capitalist, socialist, communist, mercantilist, feudalistic, or whatever, there always is a class of people at the lowest rung of the social and economic ladder who perform the most menial and lowest-paying kinds of labor. They are the day laborers, the undocumented domestic servants without a "green card," the chronically unemployed or underemployed who take whatever work they can get whenever they can get it on a cash-only, no-deductions basis.

Curiously, in the United States of America, the most successful capitalist country which ever existed, there is a higher percentage of "hewers of wood and drawers of water" among us than among any other essentially capitalist country in the world. Further, as a society we probably make fewer provisions for the welfare of the least, last, and lost among us than is the case for any other wealthy nation.

Innumerable books and doctoral theses have been written to explain why that is so. Stated in an exceedingly brief fashion, here is the main explanation why I think it is so: Americans live under the great self-delusion that everyone can "make it" in this nation, if people will only work hard enough. That simply is not true. Whether in the USA or anywhere else, there are bound to be people who do not possess the necessary mental or physical abilities to succeed in the employment marketplace. Too many are too poorly educated to advance themselves economically. Too many babies are born to too many malnourished, poorly nourished, alcohol-or-drug-laden mothers to have the genetic requisites to succeed in later life. In addition, many people grow up in such impoverished situations that they have absolutely no role models for success to whom they have ever been even marginally related. If "failure" is all a person has ever known, then "failure" is almost certainly all one shall ever know. To put it in biblical terms, it is nearly impossible to escape being a hewer of wood if everyone around you has always been a hewer of wood. Extreme poverty is a form of societal slavery, and relatively few people ever manage to escape from such poverty.

What is accurate on an individual level also seems accurate on a national level. Countries that have a long history of poverty tend to continue in poverty, even in the midst of the most massive expansion of the world economy that has ever occurred. Aid from wealthy countries usually has little effect on permanently poor countries, especially in those countries where dictators siphon off most of the aid for themselves and for the ruling clique. In a book called *The Elusive Quest for Growth: Economists' Adventures and Misadventures in the Tropics*, economist William Easterly described how most aid-receiving nations have frittered away whatever funds or services were provided for them. Mr. Easterly is not an ideological capitalist economist; he simply accurately portrays how ineffective are most foreign aid programs.

That, however, should not surprise anyone. Individuals as well as countries who do not know how to handle money are almost certain to misuse any extra money that is given to them, unless the giver is on hand closely to monitor how the assistance is used. Half the world's population subsists on less than two dollars a day. A billion people – one-sixth of the earth's population – live on less than a dollar a day. And the percentage of the world's people who live in the most debilitating poverty is increasing, not decreasing. Where economies are the grimmest, the most babies are produced. It has ever been thus. And thus the percentage of really poor inhabitants of the planet is constantly rising.

Studies show there is no correlation between the amount of aid given to poor countries and the improvement of the economies of those countries. Therefore many wealthy nations have cut back on foreign aid, assuming that it accomplishes almost nothing at all. In 1990, .02% of the gross domestic product of the USA was designated for foreign aid. By 2000, it had dropped to .01%. The USA devotes the smallest percentage of its GDP to foreign aid of any wealthy nation. Italy and Greece give less than .02%, Germany .027%, Japan .028%, and the UK .032%. The most generous countries for foreign aid as a percentage of GDP are Denmark (1.06%), the Netherlands (0.84%), and Sweden (0.8%). To express these figures in the most glaring and jarring way, the richest nation in the world shows the least concern for those nations whose citizens consist mainly of hewers of wood and drawers of water. Thus by our political decisions we show ourselves to place those people at the greatest distance outside our own covenant community. And thus, as a nation, we almost totally ignore the commandments of God to include the poorest of the poor in our thinking, acting, and planning.

Once again, it should not surprise anyone that the nations most likely to give the highest percentage of their national budget to assist poor countries are those nations where the vestiges of socialism are still the strongest. Northern Europe does not practice pure socialism any more than the USA practices pure capitalism. Nobody is "pure" in any economic system, nor has anyone ever been. But wherever governmental policies very consciously take the poor into particular account, the accounting practices of those governments will provide more for the hewers of wood than will the governments of other nations less committed to the welfare of the people who inevitably inhabit the lowest levels of human society. It is far better to be poor in northern Europe than in the USA or other equally capitalist-minded countries.

"Hewers-of-wood"-type people are much more likely to end up in prison than those of us in the higher strata of human society. A whole host of statistics through the decades will verify that.

Furthermore, poor men, especially poor black men, are much more likely than middle-class men, white or black, to be executed in those states which allow capital punishment. In Florida, if the murder victim is white, the perpetrator is 4.8 times more likely to be executed than if the victim is black. In Oklahoma, the perpetrator is 4.3 times more likely to die under those same circumstances, and in Illinois, he is 4 times more likely to be executed.

There are almost two million people in American prisons and jails; two **million**. That represents two-thirds of one-per-cent of all of us. The Justice Department reported that in 2000, 4.6 million Americans who have been in prison are now out on parole. That number increased 44% since 1990. Of those parolees, 47% are black. In some urban neighborhoods, 10% to 25% of all black males are on parole. Such folks find it almost impossible to find employment. Inevitably their rate of recidivism (ending up in jail again) is very high.

The "lock-'em-up-and-throw-away-the-key" philosophy is not only not working; it is disastrous. Capital punishment is not eliminating the total number or percentage of criminals either. And executing people is far, far more expensive than keeping them in prison for life. Former US Senator Paul Simon says that over the past 25 years it cost the State of Illinois $800 million more to execute people than it would have if they had been locked up permanently.

There are 1.6 million felons in our country who are barred from voting. Nearly a third of them are black. In Florida, roughly half a million people cannot vote because of a state law which prevents felons ever from voting. That is 5% of all eligible Florida voters. Gov. Jeb Bush has initiated a class action suit against a lifetime ban from voting because of felony convictions. Apparently he has concluded it is a crime for criminals to be permanently shut out of the democratic process. May Jeb Bush's tribe increase! (Sort of. And maybe not his **whole** tribe.)

Hewers of wood tend to believe that they are shut out of the system. Many of them eventually believe that they will never escape their status as the lowest folks on the societal totem pole.

In the main, their assessment has proven to be historically correct. Society pays a great deal in fiscal, psychological, emotional, behavioral, and governmental costs to maintain its hewers of wood and drawers of water. And we also pay huge amounts to "keep them in their place," "**their place**" being wherever **we** are not. Financially, we would probably be far better off to guarantee an annual income somewhere above the poverty level to every individual and family who find themselves snared in the virtual slavery which results from being members of the hewers-of-wood class. We spend far, far more remedially than we would ever spend pro-actively.

Undoubtedly some poor people think there is no point in their trying to find employment of any sort. But many would work if they could be guaranteed steady employment somewhere, with the assurance of medical insurance, and possibly the hope of a pension beyond mere Social Security. My wife and I live in the city of Cleveland, Ohio. Our neighborhood is a new housing development of middle class people, two thirds of whom are black. We are surrounded by some of the poorest people in Cleveland, almost all of whom are black. Frequently when I am outside mowing the lawn or shoveling snow, young black men will stop to ask me if I want to hire them to do what I am already doing, and I am usually nearly done with. If I thought I could afford to hire any of them on a regular basis, I would —— especially when my aged vertebrae balk at the contortions through which I put them when removing eight inches of slushy precipitation which comes our way courtesy of Lake Erie.

For the past century, and especially for the past three decades, the pattern of American demographic movement has been one of non-hewers-of-wood moving away from all those who are hewers of wood. By the 21st century, there are far more people in the suburbs of the cities than there are in the central cities themselves. And in most places, the vast majority of those suburbanites are white.

According to the 2000 census, the fastest growing county in the US during the 1990s was Douglas County, Colorado, between

Denver and Colorado Springs. It is 90% white. Elbert and Park Counties, to the east and west of Douglas County, were the third and fifth fastest growing counties in the country. They are even whiter. Forsyth County, Georgia, was the second-fastest growing county; it is 92% white. And only in the Nineties were significant numbers of non-whites even allowed to move into Forsyth County. Historically it was one of the most segregated counties in the land. Of the 20 fastest growing US counties in the Nineties, all but one are more than 80% white.

However, it would be a mistake for everyone to imagine these demographics indicate only "white flight." It is really "hewer-of-wood-flight" that is occurring, because millions of blacks, Hispanics, and other minorities have also moved to the suburbs during the last couple of decades to flee the hewers of wood. When we first came to Ohio, we lived in Cleveland Heights. This first-ring suburb has become blacker and blacker, as blacks from Cleveland proper moved out to avoid the urban decay which increasingly characterized Cleveland, and virtually all other large American cities. Cuyahoga County, in which Cleveland is located, probably does not now have a higher percentage of blacks than it ever had, but it has more blacks living in the suburbs than it ever has had. Everyone else abandons the poorest of the poor, and there emerge ever-larger pockets of either Haves and Have-Nots.

God was right, and Moses was right; you can't cordon off the hewers of wood and have a society that works. The rich, the middle class, and the very poor must live side-by-side if there is to be any social cohesion at all. Societies fall apart when the hewers of wood are left to their own devices, because, as I said earlier, the hewers of wood do not have sufficient devices to make it on their own. They need the constant assistance and encouragement of everybody else. That's what God told Moses just before the children of Israel got to Mt. Nebo, and that's what Moses told the children of Israel. Make the hewers of wood part of the covenant community, or else the covenant community will fall apart by slowly or quickly drifting apart. If the hewers are not **a part**, then they will live **apart**, and it will create an inevitable decay in the entire social order.

When you live close to the hewers of wood, inevitably you become more concerned for their wellbeing. When you move away from them, you tend to forget them. Out of sight, out of mind, you know. For most of its history, but especially for most of its recent history, the USA, like nearly every other nation, has consciously avoided concerted attempts to address the needs of our hewers of wood. It seems so easy to forget the poor if we don't rub elbows with them. But deliberately forgetting the poor carries huge and unavoidable costs. It seems easy to ignore the poor. In reality, however, it always is not only difficult and painful, but also impossible, to ignore them.

D. Stephen Long is a United Methodist minister, and is a professor at Garrett-Evangelical Theological Seminary in Evanston, Illinois. He was baptized by Anabaptists, educated by evangelicals, and now is director of the Center for Ethics and Values. Recently he wrote a book called *Divine Economy: Theology and the Market*. Prof. Long is something of a contrarian, and he attacks the positions of a whole array of theologians, from right to left. His greatest disdain is directed against capitalism, which he says is based on usury. Lending money to anyone at interest is unbiblical, Long points out. And indeed, the Bible speaks out against usury, especially for Jews to lend money to other Jews at interest, but even to require interest payments from Gentiles. If there were no lending of money at interest, the Bible seems to claim, the poor, along with everyone else, could borrow, and thus their problems would be greatly alleviated. And since society at large will never accept an economy without usury, Christians, through their churches, should become lenders, particularly to those least able to repay the loans.

Well, maybe. As wild and wooly a liberal as I am, I doubt that recipe is going to work, because too few Christians will be willing to lend too few dollars to too few people to help them out of the jams they are always in.

Understand this: **there is no permanent solution to the reality of poverty**. There always have been and there always will be hewers of wood. The needs of the poor can be addressed both individually and corporately. You and I, by ourselves, may take very small steps to assist the poor. But together, we can take much bigger steps. But remember, no matter what we do, there will always be poor people. It is an inevitable fact of life for every human society, no matter how it is organized economically, politically, or religiously.

However, government can do more than any other institution, including religious institutions, to alleviate some of the problems of poverty. The government of the children of Israel during the Wilderness Wandering, and for a few generations afterward, was essentially a theocracy. If "the church" runs "the state," then the church can make provisions for helping the poor in their poverty. It can never help all the poor out of poverty, but it can assist in overcoming some of the disadvantages which poor people constantly face.

But we don't live in a theocracy, and we thank our lucky stars we don't. Theocracy is probably the worst form of government imaginable, and is more likely to produce widespread abuses than any other governing option. It is tough enough having politicians running the government; can you imagine how chaotic it would be if the preachers and priests ran the show?

The use of tax dollars, and the programs those dollars fund, is the primary means of aiding the poor. No program is perfect, and the best of programs eventually disintegrate, needing to be replaced by some other program, which also shall eventually fail. One of the troubles of successful people is that they naively suppose everyone can achieve success. If it were possible, it would have happened long ago, and we would all be living in a utopia. But it doesn't happen, because it can't happen. So what happens is what happens. And what happens with, among, and to the poor is largely determined by the political will of the body politic to address the issues of poverty at all times and in all places. Don't look for permanent solutions. Look instead for mere improvements.

And for heaven's sake, don't get discouraged. In the best of all possible worlds, when people set out to try to change the world, it is two steps forward, and one step back. Almost no one can survive an entire career as a social worker. It is simply too exhausting emotionally, physically, and spiritually. Nor can anyone spend an entire lifetime attempting to be a social engineer, whether that person is a politician, preacher, or congenital do-gooder. New recruits are a constant necessity when dealing with hewers of wood. No one knows that better than hewers of wood themselves.

All the difficulties and frustrations notwithstanding, God stands with us at the entrance to the Promised Land. And because it is He who made the promise, the promise shall come to pass — maybe not as we would choose, but as God, working through all of us, provides.

Scripture – Jeremiah 8:22-9:9

Text – Every one deceives his neighbor, and no one speaks the truth; they have taught their tongue to speak lies, they commit iniquity and are too weary to repent. – Jeremiah 9:5

THE DEVASTATIONS OF OUR DECEIT

Jeremiah was not a cheerful guy. In fact, he was a world-class grump. When he was at his best, he was merely pessimistic. Usually he wouldn't see the glass as being half empty; he would usually refuse even to look at the glass, for fear that it was completely empty. If somebody said the sky was a beautiful blue, he would insist it was a dull gray. If they said it looked like rain, he would declare they were going to have a hundred-year flood. A cheerful guy Jeremiah was not.

Jeremiah also was an irrepressible nudzh, at least as far as the royal household was concerned. He was like Rush Limbaugh to Bill Clinton or Molly Ivins to George W. Bush. There were several kings in Judah during the years Jeremiah was a prophet, and Jeremiah constantly laid them all out in lavender. He bugged the gizzard out of them all. He could never discover a kind word to say to any of them. One of them got so steamed at Jeremiah he had the prophet thrown into a deep pit. And the king made the dyspeptic prophet cool his heels there for a long time just to show Jeremiah who was boss. A regular Royal Enemy No. 1 Jeremiah was.

To be fair, in general Jeremiah didn't like the people of Jerusalem or Judah much better. He barely spoke a civil word to them either.

We have a word for the kind of carping criticism which Jeremiah heaped on everybody. We call it a *jeremiad*. A jeremiad is a way of giving somebody what-for in such a way that no one, least of all the person to whom the jeremiad is directed, can mistake what is being said. If any of us really wants to lace into someone, we resolutely fling a jeremiad in that person's direction.

Probably Jeremiah would have gotten along better with people if Prozac or Paxil had then been invented. I suspect he suffered almost constant depression, which is why nearly everything he wrote in his lengthy prophecy is so bleak.

However, just because Jeremiah probably was severely depressed doesn't mean that his criticisms of the society of Judah had no basis in fact. Jeremiah lived at the time leading up to what we call "the Babylonian Captivity." By the time the Babylonians descended on Judah, the whole country had pretty much gone to hell in a handbasket. In 597 BCE, the Babylonians came and laid siege to Jerusalem. They finally captured the city, and they put their own hand-picked puppet on the throne of Judah, a weakling named Zedekiah. Jeremiah considered him a total non-entity, and told him as much. Eleven years after this royal nudnik was given his job by the Babylonians, they got so fed up with him they came back, besieged Jerusalem again, and then burned the city to the ground. They destroyed the temple, and took thousands of people back to Babylon as virtual slaves. It was the end of "the good old days" for the Jews. Never again would they be an independent nation with the political power they had had prior to Zedekiah's reign.

There were numerous beefs Jeremiah had with his fellow Jews, but I will spare you the mind-numbing enumeration of them. Instead, we shall concentrate on one thing in particular to which Jeremiah objected. He was greatly distressed by the pervasive level of **deceit** which characterized the nation of Judah. From the highest stratum of the social swells to the lowest stratum of the social nobodies, he kvetched that lying and deception had become a way of life. And no one else seemed upset about it. Lying had become so common that it was accepted as readily as breathing. In truth, Jeremiah seemed to believe the people lied with far greater ease than they breathed.

What set off Jeremiah the most is that he knew God had already provided the solution to the problem of deceit. It was contained in the words of the Ninth Commandment: "You shall not bear false witness against your neighbor." In other words, don't lie. In still other words, tell the truth. The people had been given the proper medicine by God as an antidote to prevarication, but they refused to take it.

"Is there no balm in Gilead?" Jeremiah asked, speaking on behalf of God, as the prophets so often did. "Is there no physician there? Why has the health of the daughter of my people not been restored?" (Jeremiah 8:22)

Then Jeremiah let loose with the invective of the burr which was perpetually positioned under his prophetic saddle. "Every one deceives his neighbor, and no one speaks the truth; they have taught their tongue to speak lies, they have committed iniquity and are too weary to repent" (Jer. 9:5).

American culture in the first decade of the 21st century is very much like the culture of Judah just before its political collapse. Lying has become endemic among us. Deception is practiced as a finely-tuned art form. In government, education, business, interpersonal relations, and even in religion, deceit has become so common we no longer even perceive it to be deceit.

Look at television sit-coms. Characters lie in practically every episode. Usually they are "little white lies," small peccadilloes which scarcely merit our notice. On the crime or police or lawyer dramas, we see big lies every week. And the deceptions are so ubiquitous that we assume they are part of the fabric of everyday life for everybody. And they may be. And if they are, we are in a far deeper moral morass than we ever imagined.

The Enron-Arthur Andersen debacle is an illustration of systemic deception with disastrous results. Without question, the top officers of the Enron Corporation fudged the truth for years, making their financial picture look far, far rosier than it actually was. Also without question, officials in the Arthur Andersen firm that handled Enron's accounting also hugely fudged the fiscal numbers. The deceit of these people led to the biggest bankruptcy in US history.

Our government and its officials also have engaged in systematic deception from time to time. The biggest example of all in fairly recent memory is Watergate, which ended with the resignation of President Nixon. Iran-Contra was the deceitful legacy of the Reagan administration, Monicagate was the albatross around Bill Clinton's neck, and several major lies have already plagued the administration of George W. Bush.

Happily, the official attempt of our current presidential administration to establish a Bureau of Deceptions ended in failure before it ever came to pass. Somebody (and I suspect it was the malignant brainstorm of Richard Cheney, Donald Rumsfeld, and/or John Ashcroft) decided that what this country needed was an agency which they cynically chose to call the Office of Strategic Influence. This lunatic organization was to be lodged in the Department of Defense. Its purpose ostensibly was deliberately to provide false information - - - **to both friends and foes alike**! In other words, it was reasoned, the business of government has become so compromised by truthful leaks that the government needs an agency which concocts false leaks!

What kind of craziness is this? Whoever came up with such a cockamamie idea?

There is no question that national security necessitates that the federal government must maintain secrets for the ongoing welfare of the people. No serious person would deny that. But by what kind of screwy thinking does the Bush administration (the George W. one, **not** the George H.W. one) come to the conclusion that in order to maintain security, we are obligated to broadcast lies? And what kind of foreign-policy-ignoramuses could ever imagine we should conscientiously lie to our allies as well as to our enemies? What nation in its right mind would ever again trust us if the Office of Strategic Influence had actually come into existence? Whatever were these officially-sanctioned paranoids thinking?

Maureen Dowd, that splendid lady with the powerfully poisonous pen gave this sorry scheme what-for in one of her *New York Times* columns. "Our government shouldn't need to lie to justify its increasingly broad and intricate war of terrorism," she indignantly opined. "Holy Gulf of Tonkin! Besides, there's enough real stuff about the bad guys —— they're Evildoers, after all. We don't need to make up stuff to pin on them. But let's look on the sunny side. At least the Bush administration is trying to disseminate information, even if it's fictional. Usually it's trying to suppress information, even if it's consequential."

John Dean, Nixon's White House counsel and a close observer of political cover-ups, wrote a stinging editorial about Vice President Cheney's refusal to divulge the names of his carefully-picked energy advisory board. Nobody seriously insisted on publicizing the minutes of the meetings of this anonymous group; they just wanted the anonymity to be obliterated. But no, the Vice President, one of the most ruthlessly close-lipped of nationally-elected officials in our country's history, refused even to publicize the names of his energy-policy confidants. A lawsuit by Congress was instituted to adjudicate the impasse.

John Dean wrote, "If the vice president does not believe as a matter of principle that the General Accounting Office should have oversight powers, he should try to sell Congress the statute that empowers it. That he has not done, perhaps because he knows such an effort would be futile." Then Mr. Dean, who thirty years ago told the truth and ended up disgraced, suggested that the Bush administration may believe it can tie this matter up in court for years, never having to provide the names of the Vice President's energy advisors.

But then John Dean wonders if there might be an even more cynical and sinister motive. "Cheney may believe that the five conservative justices (of the US Supreme Court) who put him in his current job will again assist the administration. Such a remarkable political win in the Supreme Court, effectively neutering the oversight authority of the accounting office – and, by extension, that of Congress – would amount to a seismic realignment of power in Washington. Before Bush vs. Gore, I would have considered such a ruling an impossibility. Now I'm not so sure."

The United States of America, politically, socially, and economically, has sunk into a situation where our ready acceptance of lying and deliberate deception is threatening to destroy our viability as a nation and people. Again, we all know it is necessary for government, business, and individuals to keep certain secrets to themselves. But no one has a moral right, let alone a divinely-or-politically-authorized right, to tell lies. We may choose not to tell the whole truth and nothing but the truth for what we consider to be valid reasons, but we must never accept lying as a means to avoid telling the truth. Refusing to answer certain questions, which is what Dick Cheney has done in the energy-advisory issue, may or may not work as a ploy for wending our way through the potential minefields of social and political life. But lying is never acceptable. And if we question that, we need only look to Jeremiah for corroboration.

In an editorial about Mr. Cheney's refusal to make known the names of his energy advisors, Tony Mauro gave some biting observations. Mr. Mauro is the Supreme Court correspondent for *American Lawyer Media* and *Legal Times*, and is a member of *USA Today*'s board of contributors. He said, "So Cheney and Bush want privacy for their conversations, but not for anyone else's. And it may well be that they are entitled to have unchronicled conversations with advisers. But there is no good reason that the names of people who have talked to the vice president about energy policy should be protected. No reason, of course, except the obvious one — that Cheney has something to hide from Congress."

However, it is not only "people in high places" who tell lies or hide the truth. You and I do it on an all-too-frequent basis. When April 15 rolls around each year, we all are required to make an accounting of our income for our very good friends at the Internal Revenue Service. Millions of us use the 1040 Short Form or the 1040A. But millions of others use the 1040 Long form. Are all of us always completely truthful in what we tell the IRS? Or is our 1040 at least partly a work of fiction? We go through the same moral debates every year: "If I tell them this, then I have to tell them that. But if I tell them that, it will prompt questions about this." And so we do what we think is best. But almost always it turns out to be best for us, not for the federal government.

But there are many other personal circumstances where we do not necessarily tell the entire truth. Often we do not want to hurt people's feelings, and so we withhold certain facts from them. But more often than not, we don't tell the whole truth, or we overtly choose to lie, to protect ourselves and our own reputations, rather than to spare or guard the feelings of others. Husbands and wives lie to one another, parents and children lie to each other, friends and business associates lie. And the worst of it is that it doesn't really bother us much, if at all.

In a *New Yorker* cartoon, an attorney says to his client, while another attorney is writing notes on the case, "O.K. —— let's review what you didn't know and when you didn't know it." It is funny - - - but it also is a cutting indictment of our legal system. Lawyers advise their clients on how to avoid telling everything they know without actually lying. "Innocent until proven guilty" is taken to great extremes, so that often the guilty are acquitted, because the prosecution could not prove that some testimony is false, even though the prosecutor, the defense attorney, and the perjuring witness know it is false.

We say to people that we will respect what they tell us, but often we have already pre-judged what they say is not worth hearing. Another *New Yorker* cartoon: a man, perhaps an inventor or salesman, sits in the reception room of a business executive. The executive's secretary says to the visitor, "Mr. Carleson will seriously consider your proposal but ultimately reject it now." A rejection has been the foregone conclusion all along, but Mr. Carleson is willing to go through the motions for the sake of appearances. He is not **telling** a lie; he is **enacting** a lie. And so employers interview people they have no intention of hiring, and editors give a cursory glance at articles or books submitted to them by eager would-be writers, and members of the clergy supposedly listen intently to stories of people that they conclude within two minutes of the opening explanation are fraudulent. Our behavior implies honest appraisal, but our minds have long since been made up.

Not everything that is less than the whole truth is, *ipso facto*, a lie, however. There is the story of the two Irishmen who were hired by Seamus on his farm. One day Pat came running up to

Mike, and shouted, "Pat, come quickly! Seamus just fell into the manure pit up to his ankles!" Mike said, "Well if he's only in the manure up to his ankles, can't he just walk out?" "O no," Pat exclaimed," grab a shovel and come! He fell in head first!"

Pat didn't lie, but he didn't initially tell the whole truth either. He did not mean to mislead Mike, but he didn't clearly tell the whole story from the beginning, and it turned out to be misleading.

Or there was a minister I once knew. We shall say that his given name was General Watson Smythe. That wasn't his actual name, but it was like that, and his first name actually was "General." He told me that he was named after a man who was his next-door-neighbor at the time of his birth, General Watson. "General" was the man's first name, and "Watson" was his last name. So my friend became General Watson Smythe.

Anyway, when he was a very young man General Watson Smythe was drafted into the Army. He was sent to serve in the fire station on his Army post as his first assignment. When he got there the sergeant in charge was bemoaning how short of equipment and supplies they were. General told the sergeant not to despair, that he would get him the supplies he needed immediately. General picked up the phone and dialed the quartermaster. "Hello," he said, "this is General Watson Smythe, and I'm over at the post fire station. We need some supplies and equipment, and I want it delivered right away." The quartermaster agreed, and within hours they had everything the sergeant wanted. When the post commander found out the complete truth of the matter, however, he was greatly displeased, and General experienced the colonel's wrath.

General Watson Smythe had not lied, but he had used the truth in a misleading way. It was the last time he used his name in what he knew would be an unsuccessful attempt to misconstrue the truth. Never again in the military did General use his own name in vain.

That illustration, while quite harmless in itself, points out the delicate tension which always exists between outright falsehood and the truth, or between the truth, the whole truth, and nothing but the truth. Whenever we make any claim for what we assume is truth, we need to be aware of what we are consciously attempting when we make our claim.

We need to ask ourselves four questions whenever we are tempted to tell a lie or to refrain from telling the whole truth. The questions are these:

1. **Why** do we say whatever we say, whether it is true or false?
2. Is there **ever** a valid reason for using deceit?
3. If we don't tell the truth, is not that behavior automatically, by definition, **deceit**?
4. If we try to deceive others, would we want them to deceive us in like manner?

Whenever we tell anyone anything, we need to be clear in our minds about why we tell it to them. For example, if we know some information that we are certain is vital to someone, but we also know someone else **ought** to be the one to tell that person, should we divulge the information? Suppose you know that a friend's spouse is having an affair with someone. Ought you to tell the friend, if the spouse is unwilling to do so? And if the friend asks you if you think the spouse is having an affair, should you say so, or should you urge the spouse to confess? And if the spouse refuses, should you go ahead and tell the truth? **Why** do you decide to do whatever you decide to do? It is not enough merely to tell the truth; we must also know **why** we choose to tell it.

Or suppose you are a physician, and suppose you have a patient who has told you she does not want to hear the truth about her physical condition if it is very bad news. Do you tell her anyway? If you don't tell her, do you tell her spouse or parents or other family members? **Why** do you do whatever you do?

In his *Address to the Unco Guid,* Robert Burns points out the crucial distinction which exists in the "why" of human motivation:

> Then gently scan your brother man,
> Still gentler sister woman;
> Tho' they may gang a kennin wrang,
> To step aside is human:

One point must still be greatly dark,
The moving *why* they do it;
And just as lamely can ye mark
How far perhaps they rue it.

We can never be certain why people do the things they do. Only God is capable of judging that.

Nonetheless, it is never valid to tell a lie to protect ourselves. Life is always a risk, and telling the truth can be very risky. Therefore, telling lies to save ourselves pain or trouble or embarrassment is never acceptable, even though it might be highly preferable to us as a course of action. We need clearly to understand why we do the things we do, and for whose primary benefit we do them. Being deceitful for our own benefit is an example of sin at its lowest common denominator.

Can there **ever** be a situation where using deceit is acceptable? Yes, there might be. For example, if someone shows you his new suit and asks you if you don't agree with him that it is the finest suit ever purchased in the history of haberdashery, and you think the suit looks like it was created by a blind one-armed arthritic sufferer of permanent DTs, are you bound to tell the truth about what you really feel? Nobody should feel forced to say what they know someone else wants to hear. But we aren't forced to be cruel by telling our innermost thoughts, either. We might say, "That is a really interesting suit" or "Your suit has an unusual color" or "Wherever did you find such a unique suit," but God does not require us to say, even if we truly feel it, "That is the ugliest piece of cloth stretched over a lumpy frame I ever laid eyes on." Kindness may necessitate not telling the whole truth, and nothing but the truth. And telling the whole truth in that instance may mean that you are acting falsely with your friend. What is "true" about telling the truth about a suit, when it is your friend to whom you need to be true, rather than to your true thoughts on his new suit?

Or suppose you conclude you need to tell a lie to someone in order to preserve that person's dignity. You are a teacher, and a below-average student who nonetheless always works to capacity asks whether he did the worst in the class on the test. A brilliant student got a higher grade, and should have gotten an A, but got only a C+. In terms of ability, the brilliant student did worse than the below-average student. In order to undergird his self-worth, do you tell the less-bright student that others did worse than he, even though technically that may not be true? In an instance such as this, we might want to ask what Pilate asked when he was trying Jesus, "What is truth?" What **is** truth, when truth turns out to be a multiple-choice reality?

If we choose not to tell the truth in a particular situation for any reason, does that automatically mean that we are **deceitful**? Yes. And no. Some of the above examples show how not telling the whole truth is not necessarily deceitful. Another example. Parents frequently do not tell children the whole truth when the children ask a whole array of questions. When a four-year-old asks, "Are we rich?", it is not helpful to ask in response, "Compared to whom?" Four-year-olds cannot comprehend such comparisons. So the parents mutter something like, "We're not rich, but we're not poor either." It probably still doesn't answer the question, but it's a question that doesn't necessarily need to be honestly addressed, and why on earth did that nosy little tyke ask it anyway, the pesky little gidget? On the other hand, if family finances are really hurting, and the seventeen-year-old asks, "Are we really hurting?", the answer should be "Yes." The teenager needs to ask such a thing, and should be given an honest answer to the question. In fact, it would be deceitful to tell the teenager everything is fine, if it isn't fine, because a child that old is able to assist in improving the situation.

But let us considerably enlarge the issue. Was it right for the Roman Catholic bishops for years to hide the fact that there were widespread allegations of sexual abuse against some of the priests in their dioceses? Was that deceitful? They might answer that they were attempting to protect the Church. But what about the children; don't they deserve protection? What about those who were abused and are now young women or young men? Can deceit "for a good cause" ever really be good? It is easy for those of us who are not bishops clearly to perceive the ethics of this matter, but it was not, and is not, easy for the bishops. People who do not have institutional responsibilities can point the finger much more readily, and safely, than those who must try to balance corporate, as compared to individual, concerns.

Twice I was called to court to testify in divorce proceedings between parishioners. Both times I asked the judge to excuse me on the basis of pastoral confidentiality, and both times, happily, I was excused. But it might not have been so. And had I been required to tell the truth as I perceived it, what would I have said? Is it **always** deceitful if we do not tell the whole truth, and nothing but the truth?

Finally, we need to remember the Golden Rule. If our tendency is not to tell the truth, especially when we think it is for valid reasons, would we want someone else to do the same thing to us? If we want confirmation that the ugly suit we bought is not ugly, then we don't want to hear the truth. If the doctor tells us we are well when we are in fact dying, we may or may not want the truth. For whatever it is worth, I think **everyone in every circumstance** should be told they are dying if that accurately describes their situation. Of course we are all dying, but if our death is coming soon, we need to know about it. Or so says I.

If I lie to protect myself, would I want others to lie to protect themselves? I don't think so. Deception for self-protection is the most dubious deception of all.

Sir Walter Scott said it so well: "O what a tangled web we weave/ When first we practice to deceive!" Probably everyone, including Jeremiah himself, has sought to deceive someone at some time or another. Fortunately, at least for the transmittal of the truth, very few of us are smart enough to weave a sufficiently smooth web when we set out to deceive someone. It is too hard to remember all our lies, so it is always much easier always to tell the truth. Some people, sadly, are pathological liars. In certain kinds of personal matters, a certain recent President may have been such a person. Whether that made him unfit for the presidency was a question hotly debated inside and outside the halls of Congress. But he survived that debate - - - barely.

On the other side of the coin, it may be as equally disastrous ideologically always to tell the truth as ideologically always to lie. Mark Twain's vicious satire, *The Man That Corrupted Hadleyburg,* proved that point. Those who have no regard for how truth can injure people are useless members of society if they refuse never to lie. There must be general discretion in truth, as there also must be general disdain for falsity. Truth and falsehood are not always a matter of black and white; sometimes shades of gray are the only options open to us.

Jeremiah likely was ideologically committed to what he conceived was truth-telling at all times. It is greatly interesting to me, from both a theological and psychological point of view, that Jeremiah once accused God of deceiving him. "O Lord, thou hast deceived me, and I was deceived; thou art stronger than I, and thou hast prevailed" (Jer. 20:7).

But let us look more closely at this particular passage. A few verses later Jeremiah complains to God that people are mocking and denouncing him. When you consider what a nuisance he made of himself, this is not surprising. Jeremiah was a necessary if painful corrective from God Himself for the cesspool that Judah had become, but nobody is ever thrilled to welcome the Roto-Rooter man. What did Jeremiah expect to receive as the result of his four decades of continuous criticisms: the Man of the Year Award?

God did not deceive Jeremiah, nor does He deceive us. God never promised it would be easy if we are always honest and forthright. Sometimes it is not only hard, but it may be incorrect, if not downright painful, when we "tell it like it is," or at least like we think it is.

Still, in the midst of what once was called "situational ethics," it is well to remember that almost always truth is preferable to falsehood, and that honesty ordinarily beats deceit, hands down. And, as Jeremiah declared, it is unwise on a regular basis to insist that falsehood bears more fruit than truth, or to say that all is well if all is not well. Speaking with the voice of God, the prophet cries out, "They have healed the wound of my people lightly, saying, 'Peace, peace,' when there is no peace. Were they ashamed when they committed abomination? No, they were not at all ashamed; they did not know how to blush." And Jeremiah said that not once, but twice, and twice verbatim (6:14-15; 8:11-12).

As a people, we have compromised truth far too much, and have used deceit far too frequently. Jeremiah's jeremiad to Judah is well directed at us also. If we get too much of the truth, we can die from the truth, as Stephen Vincent Benet' once said. But if we get too much falsehood, we shall surely perish from that. May God grant us to live the truth, so that truth may live.

Scripture – Luke 12:13-21

Text – And he said to them, "Take heed, and beware of all covetousness; for a man's life does not consist in the abundance of his possessions." – Luke 12:15 (RSV)

THE INATE WEAKNESS OF CAPITALISM

Capitalism is the most successful economic system yet devised in the history of the human race. It has brought more prosperity to both a greater number and a greater percentage of people who have lived under its influence than any other economic system which has ever been introduced.

Most observers in most nations today would declare that the place where capitalism has achieved its zenith of success is in the United States of America. Since the end of World War II, but especially in the last quarter of a century, American capitalism has made astonishing strides in productivity as well as standard of living. The American gross domestic product is by far the largest in the entire world. Furthermore, a higher percentage of Americans are directly or indirectly invested in the American stock market than is the case for any other nationality. Virtually half of our citizens have personal funds (as compared to employer pension funds) in the market.

This is not to suggest that every day in every way the market is getting better and better. Like a bouncing ball, the stock market goes up and down, up and down. It always has, and always will. But over the long haul, it has been going unsteadily upward. When it goes down, alas, American stockholders' hearts go pitty-pat, pitty-pat pretty rapidly. That also has ever been thus. Nonetheless, when all relevant factors are taken into consideration, capitalism American-style looks remarkably healthy, even given the problems which have afflicted many business enterprises in the down-years of the 2000-2003 bear market.

"The business of America is business," said President Calvin Coolidge, and many a business tycoon has discovered immense internal gratification in that statement. (By the way, have you ever noticed that tycoons seem to be associated only with business? Did you ever hear of a medical tycoon, or an academic tycoon, or a political or philanthropic or military or ecclesiastical tycoon? Not on your philological lexicon, you didn't. The only place for tycoonery is business, and don't you forget it.) "What's good for General Motors is good for America," proclaimed Charles Wilson, an erstwhile CEO of the Detroit company who served in the Eisenhower Administration. We might choose to quibble with that statement - - - but not here. Here we must press on.

The twentieth century witnessed a struggle among three competing economic systems for dominance: socialism, communism, and capitalism. Numerous European nations, along with other nations in Asia, Africa, and Latin America, instituted varying forms of socialism, and some of those nations are still socialistic, though in a decreasing mode. In the former Soviet Union, China, Eastern Europe, North Korea, Cuba, and Southeast Asia, communism was the primary economic system. Communism is still practiced to some extent in China and Viet Nam, and to a large extent in North Korea and Cuba. But when the Soviet Union collapsed in 1989, communism ceased to be a serious alternative as a viable economic system. There are perhaps a handful of true Marxists still alive in the world — but they are just barely alive. They are ancient codgers who continue to be true believers even when there is nothing serious left to believe in.

Probably there are still at least six or seven American socialists who hold out hope that what Sweden or Denmark or post-war Laborite Britain or Tanzania once were is what the USA shall one day become. Those lonely socialist holdouts would be well advised not to hold their breath, because the probability of the triumph of socialism in the US is as likely as the Jamaican bobsled team winning at the next Winter Olympics. For the past century and a half, at least, capitalism has been synonymous with The American Way, and it is almost certain to continue that way until long after everyone now living has shuffled off this mortal coil.

105

In fact, the past fifteen years or so have seen the growth of a new capitalistic phenomenon which never could have been foreseen by Adam Smith, Andrew Carnegie, John D. Rockefeller, or any of the captains of industry of previous generations. (Why is it that they are always "captains"? Did you ever wonder that? They are at least colonels, or brigadier or major or lieutenant generals. Some are even general generals, with four stars, and a few are generals of the Army, with five stars. But no, in common parlance, they are merely "**captains** of industry." Strange.) Anyway, what no previous capitalistic bigwig could have forecast was the rise of what we now call "globalization." Capitalistic globalization knows no national boundaries. It seeks to do business everywhere it can any way it can with whomever it can (or must).

Globalization has American and European capitalists salivating like hungry hounds at an outdoor barbecue. They see a world unified by international corporations and laws which promote the free flow of good and services to every remote corner of the globe. Globalization is believed to be an inevitable result of the complete victory of capitalistic progress.

Allow me now to make a pastor's observation. Most of my ministry was spent in congregations which had a heavy preponderance of people who worked in various kinds of businesses. The only denomination more likely to have more capitalists than the Presbyterians are the Episcopalians. But hey, theirs is really old money, and ours is only moderately old. Many of the parishioners I served were middle-management types, but a substantial number were high-level executives. I discovered that, in general, the higher the level of income, the greater the faith in the capitalist system. And I do mean "faith," in the religious sense. Millions of people believe in capitalism in exactly the same way that other people believe in God. Nobody can **prove** that capitalism is the best economic concept, but countless numbers **believe** that it is. Thus capitalism can become a secular religion. God may or may not be worshipped by the capitalist faithful, but free enterprise is definitely worshipped.

And therein lies the first weakness of capitalism. It can become a religion for some of its most ardent proponents. By no means am I suggesting that everyone who prefers or supports capitalism sees it as a religion, but without question, some do. Thus an economic system become an idol, which, by definition, means a false god. It is biblically unacceptable for anyone to put ultimate trust in any economic system, even capitalism, which almost certainly is the best economy for the greatest number of human beings.

The second weakness of capitalism is that, in theory at least, it presupposes that everyone is essentially good. "How so?" you may wonder. For capitalism to achieve maximum success, everyone must work as hard and effectively as possible, and none should take advantage of anyone else. Thus the corporations whose employees from top to bottom are the happiest are those companies in which all "share and share alike." This isn't to say they are all paid the same amount, for that would be corporate socialism. But all get a **fair** share of whatever they put into the corporate enterprise by sweat, cerebral, financial, or executive equity.

The problem is this: everyone is not essentially good. If John Calvin and his ilk are correct, we are all essentially corrupt, corrupting, and corruptible. When it operates as it should, according to the theory, capitalism should have as few rules and regulations as possible, because all workers will blissfully do what they ought to do. But nearly everyone, if not virtually everyone, bends the rules to his or her own profit from time to time, and lots of people end up getting — as they say in the hardware-manufacturing business — screwed.

Do you need some corporate names to authenticate that observation? Here are a few: Enron, Arthur Andersen, WorldCom, ImClone, Merrill Lynch, AOL Time Warner, Adelphia, Martha Stewart Living Omnimedia Inc., Ernst & Young, Qwest, Harken Energy, Warnaco, Microsoft, Citibank, Halliburton, and Morgan Stanley. Some individual names? Kenneth Lay, Andrew Fastow, Scott Sullivan, David Myers, Al Dunlap, Dennis Kozlowski, Mark Swartz, Mark Belnick, Samuel

Waksal, Bernard Ebbers, George W. Bush, John, Timothy, and Michael Rigas, James R. Brown, Michael Mulcahey, Martha Stewart, and Richard Cheney, to name a few. All took advantage of "the system" when "the system" had insufficient controls to prevent them from doing what they did. The most egregious offenses were the cooking of books and insider trading. A few of these people have been arrested, and some shall presumably spend time behind bars. But the ultimate result has been that hundreds of thousands of people, who were dutifully following the rules, have lost their jobs.

It is a major mistake for any social organization or system to be based on a belief in the essential goodness of human nature without providing careful scrutiny to make sure that goodness is being pursued. The Church cannot function well unless the clergy are closely watched, as we recently have learned to our chagrin, and business certainly cannot operate effectively if nobody is looking over anybody's shoulder. It simply is a bad idea to trust that people who believe in capitalism will always do the right thing, because they won't. Nobody who believes in anything, including believing in Almighty God, will always do the right thing.

In a lengthy *Harper's* article (December, 2001), John Gray addressed the notion of globalization and capitalist philosophy. He wrote, "What is striking is how closely the market liberal philosophy that underpins globalization resembles Marxism. Both are essentially secular religions, in which the eschatological hopes and fantasies of Christianity are given an Enlightenment twist. In both, history is understood as the progress of the species, powered by growing knowledge and wealth, and culminating in a universal civilization." Characterizing the foundations of both Marxism and globalized capitalism, John Gray goes on to say, "History's crimes and tragedies are not thought to have their roots in human nature: They are errors, mistakes which can be corrected by more education, better political institutions, higher living standards. Marxists and market liberals may differ on what is the best economic system, but, for both, vested interests and human irrationality alone stand between humankind and a radiant future. In holding to this primitive Enlightenment creed, they are at one."

How true that is! The idealism of the true-believer Marxist and the true-believer capitalist is essentially the same. But the ideal has **never** been actualized in any reality anywhere, nor shall it ever become actualized. **Sin** is the problem; **greed** is the problem; **selfishness** is the problem.

How soon we forget our history! Some of the greatest and most philanthropic of capitalists have also been some of the most ruthless of businessmen. It is estimated that John D. Rockefeller gave away more dollars in actual-dollar-value than anyone who ever lived, although Bill Gates is currently giving him a run for his money. But for all his goodness, Rockefeller also had huge faults. He could be absolutely heartless in his quest for whatever he wanted. He tried to get complete control of the world oil market. By the 1890s, he did manage to control 80% of the US market. Finally, under Republican President Theodore Roosevelt in 1911, Standard Oil was broken up into several companies, much as AT&T was broken up nearly seventy years later. Whether either of those "de-constructions" was a good thing shall always be fiercely debated, especially by the most enthusiastic of capitalists.

In the early 20th century, and continuing through the presidency of Harry Truman, numerous regulations were set in place to attempt to prevent the capitalist abuses which occurred under people like John D. Rockefeller and Andrew Carnegie. But from Ronald Reagan on, there was a strong movement toward de-regulation. Now we are starting to see some of the same patterns which bedeviled our country in the early part of the last century coming home to roost as the first years of the new century are unfolding. In 1904, Ida Tarbell published her pivotal book, *History of the Standard Oil Company*. Sounding as though she were describing the thousands of workers who have lost their employment in the spate of current business implosions, Ida Tarbell wrote, "It was that man after man, from hopelessness, from disgust, from ambition, from love of money, gave up the fight for principle." With a reformer's revulsion, she decried "the open disregard of decent ethical business practices by capitalists."

Harry Truman powerfully addressed this issue when he said, "Material things are ashes, if there is no spiritual background for the support of those material things." **And that leads to the third weakness of capitalism, which is that it encourages people to pursue wealth for its own sake**. In the words of the reptilian Gordon Gekko, one of the two main characters in the movie *Wall Street*, "Greed is good." But greed isn't good. Greed is never good. It **always** is evil. Even though greed in the short run may produce more or better mouse traps, ultimately it will destroy whomever falls victim to its avaricious clutches.

Despite all the pious capitalistic trappings described by Max Weber in *The Protestant Ethic and the Spirit of Capitalism*, nobody truly glorifies God by making money. We glorify God by glorifying God, which may or may not occur in the making of our money. As it says in the Westminster Catechism, "Man's chief end is to glorify God and to enjoy Him forever." Nobody ever glorified God simply by acquiring more and more income.

Furthermore, there is a genuine sense in which "money making money" is not really the same as making money. That is, when we invest in someone else's efforts, **they** are the ones doing the work, and **we** are the ones deriving income from their labors. I realize that owning stock helps to create jobs and so on and so on and so on, as high business executives keep reminding us, and that is all well and good. But by no means is it the whole story.

Republicans, who should be Calvinists and believe in the total depravity of the race, according to Max Weber, believe in the goodness of human beings, particularly those who are Republicans, and they strongly support governmental de-regulation of business. Democrats, who should be Wesleyans and believe in the potential perfection of each person, particularly those who are Democrats, strongly support the government looking over the shoulder of every business in every city and hamlet in the country. In other words, conservative capitalists cheer for human goodness when it suits their economic philosophy, and liberal strong-government advocates cheer for heavy regulation of business when it suits their economic philosophy. To generalize, Republicans want the greatest profit possible, while Democrats want what is best for all the people, and especially for the lower-paid workers.

And that leads to the fourth major weakness of capitalism, which is that its major focus is always to provide a dividend to the stockholders. If that doesn't happen, capitalism doesn't work. Well, the fact is, sometimes that ought not to happen. Sometimes, boards of directors should decide that the stockholders should get no dividends for this quarter, and maybe the next quarter, and maybe the next quarter after that. But of course, if that happens, they fear that people won't invest in the XYZ Corporation.

But what about the XYZ **employees**? Does not the board of directors have even a prior obligation to them? Must "the bottom line" always be the bottom line? However, with their enormous stock options, the highest-paid executives are also directors and shareholders, and, as we have seen, some of them have shown themselves to be far more concerned for the income of the stockholders (of whom they possess some of the greatest blocs of stock) than they are for the employees. The callous disregard for employees in some of the shakiest corporations has shown the directors to be exactly what they are: zealots for profits at the expense of all other considerations.

In capitalism, the pursuit of profit should always be perceived as a means to an end, and never as an end in itself. Unfortunately, that has never been a factor in capitalist philosophy. Profit has always been the primary, and perhaps the only, purpose of capitalistic economics. But in the bull market of the 1990s, even profit took a back seat for investors. They didn't care very much about earnings from the stock they owned; the rising price of the stock is what motivated them to keep pouring money into the market. And for many stocks, the price kept rising, almost astronomically.

Even now, when a bear market has devoured seven trillion dollars of stock-market wealth since April of 2000, stocks are still probably greatly overvalued because of excessive — and unsubstantiated —— faith in capitalism. Since 1870, on average stocks have traded at about fourteen times their annual earnings. Nonetheless, in August of 2002 they were trading, on average, at twenty-two times their annual earnings.

What this means is that the profits from owning stock, whether in the earnings produced or combined with the profit made in buying and selling stock, is still about 50% higher than traditionally has been the pattern. And what that means is that Americans have placed too much faith in their economic system. There is little historical justification for supposing that the boom years of the Nineties were normal. They were abnormal, and a precipitous bear market has borne out that truth. The economic ebbs and flows of the past dozen years have illustrated the folly of putting too much faith in profits as the be-all, end-all of economics. Too many people made too much money on what was, essentially, misplaced faith. Furthermore, millions of people have lost their employment as the capitalistic bubble burst. If investors had not been so greedy, and managers so duplicitous in their accounting practices, the adjustment might not have been nearly so painful or disastrous.

And what does the Bible have to say about all this? Many, many things, actually, but we will look only at one of the parables of Jesus. It is a story found solely in the Gospel of Luke, and it is an unusually short parable at that. It is often called the Parable of the Rich Fool (Luke 12:13-21).

As is true of most of the parables of Jesus, the story is prompted by a particular incident. Someone in a crowd to whom Jesus was speaking said to Jesus, "Teacher, bid my brother divide the inheritance with me." From the very nature of that statement, we may deduce that the man who spoke to Jesus was a younger brother in their family, and not the oldest brother. In medieval England, and even into the time of the Industrial Revolution, primogeniture was the primary English law of inheritance. By it, everything in a father's estate went to the oldest son, and nothing went to any other sons or daughters. If there were no sons, then a daughter or daughters could inherit from their father, but the estate might also go to nephews or other male relatives.

In Judea in the first century of the Common Era, the law of inheritance is what we might call "double-geniture." That is, at the death of the father, the estate would be divided into equal shares, there being one more share than the total number of heirs. The oldest son would get two shares, and the younger sons would each get one share. In the so-called Parable of the Prodigal Son, for example, the estate would be divided into three equal shares, since there were just two sons. The older son would get two shares, or two-thirds of the estate, and the younger son one share, or one-third of the estate. If there were five brothers, there would be six shares; the oldest would get two shares, or one-third of the total, and the four younger brothers would each get one share, or one-sixth of the total.

Therefore, it is a logical deduction that the man asking Jesus to convince his brother to divide the inheritance with him had to be a younger brother. Their father obviously had died, and the oldest son had not yet properly divided the estate. The younger son wanted Jesus to convince the older son to do what he should already have done.

Jesus did not do what the younger son asked, however. Instead, He said, "Man, who made me a judge or divider over you?" Then, as He so often did when responding to such matters, Jesus told a parable. But before doing that, and unlike with many other parables, Jesus preceded the story by saying what was the point of the story. **"Take heed, and beware of all covetousness; for a man's life does not consist in the abundance of his possessions."** Then came the parable.

There was a rich farmer whose land produced so prodigiously that he could not fit all the harvested crops into the barns he already owned. So he decided, with understandable justification, to tear down his barns and build bigger ones. He said to his soul, "Soul, you have ample goods laid up for many years; take your ease, eat, drink, and be merry." We sometimes use the phrase, "Eat, drink, and be merry." In the Greek language in which Luke wrote his Gospel, the word for "be merry" is *euphrone*. *Euphrone* is not so much a word as a deep expression of fleshly satisfaction. It is the sound one makes at the end of the

113

Thanksgiving dinner: "Aaaaaaaaahhhhhhh!" So the farmer was saying to himself, "I have made a lot of money, and now I can sit around eating, drinking, and saying 'Aaaaaaaahhhhh' over all the good fortune which I, myself, have created!"

"But," said Jesus, "that very night God said to the wealthy farmer, 'Tonight your soul is required of you. This is your moment for dying, guy! And all this wealth you have acquired, to whom will it now belong?'"

Capitalists, take heart: neither Jesus nor God are opposed to riches per se! What good news that is, huh! But both God and Jesus are greatly opposed to anyone who makes wealth the center of his or her existence. Anybody who places more importance in investment portfolios or bank accounts or pieces of real estate than in God has created an idol, and the sin which most upsets the Almighty is idolatry. The first two of the Ten Commandments specifically are directed to idolatry, and it was idolatry which most drove the biblical prophets into a frothy frenzy of prophetic dudgeon. The sober truth is that wealth is more likely to become our god than any other single thing we might encounter in the Department of Idolatry.

When you think about it, it makes so much sense! If **anything** is more important to us than God, then by definition whatever that might be is a false god. Wealth by itself is neither good nor evil, but it can become evil if we allow it to become our god. And, as I have tried earlier to suggest, millions of capitalists make the product of capitalism, namely profit, their god. The pursuit of profit consumes countless numbers of otherwise sensible people with otherwise genuinely sensitive and carefully considered values.

God has no problem whatever with anyone making money through honest labor, or through honest investments, for that matter. Our problem arises when we start to believe that, rather than our making our money, **our money makes US.** But money doesn't make us! Our money says absolutely nothing about our worth as a person! God **alone** makes and sustains and redeems us, and that has **nothing whatever** to do with any efforts of our own, in **anything** we might choose to do or not do.

The notion of "the self-made man" is one of the most mistaken and dangerous ideas ever to emerge from American capitalism. **Nobody** is self-made, not even in terms of what any of us "makes" in the American capitalistic system. Our assets are not our own; everything we have belongs to God. It is the height of human hubris to suppose that "we" **make** whatever "we" have. Whatever we have is not ours! All of it is a gift from God, who gave us the intelligence, drive, and perseverance to acquire it. God gets really ticked at anybody who thinks his or her stuff belongs to him or her alone. It steams Him to His divine core. Remember it.

And remember this: in the Parable of the Rich Fool, God is not angry with the farmer for having done well on his farm. Instead, God is angry because the man is more concerned to conserve his wealth than he is to glorify God.

Political and economic conservatives strongly believe in conserving something or other; that is perhaps the main reason they are called conservatives. Economic conservatives particularly believe in conserving wealth. That's okay — so long as it does not become the deepest basis of one's faith. If people devote more time and energy to the conservation of wealth than they do to supporting and undergirding the kingdom of God, then God and Jesus Christ shall certainly take them to task for their foolhardy and thoughtless idolatry.

Once again, the curious thing is that in general, theological as well as political and economic conservatives should be convinced of the sinfulness of human nature, and theological as well as political and economic liberals should believe in the goodness of human nature. But when it comes to making and protecting money and on taking a stand on human nature, conservatives are liberals, and liberals are conservatives. Or, to describe it in terms of American political leanings, Republicans are liberals and Democrats are conservatives. Amazing. And profoundly discombobulating.

Capitalism, as it has been exhibited in the USA or anywhere else, has its priorities in exactly the wrong order. The capitalist's sense of obligation is always **first**, to the stockholders, **second**, to the government, in order to stay within the rules and stay out of trouble, and **third**, to the employees of the corporation, who always come in last in the capitalistic pecking order.

But the proper order should be as follows: **first, the public wellbeing** (which far too few capitalists [corporate officers or investors] ever consider)**; second, the employees; third, the government** (don't spend so much time worrying about following the rules; just follow them, for crying out loud, and then you won't have to worry!), and **fourth, the stockholders**. If a company is well managed and promotes a strong internal work ethic, it will succeed as a corporation, unless time passes its products by. Unless buggy manufacturers got into the automobile business or some other line of production, or telephone companies diversified into other communications products, they went out of business. Even if they did change with the times, some of them still went out of business. But that is not the end of the world, however terminal, and even eschatological, it might have seemed at the time.

The greatest innate weakness of capitalism, as is true for any other economic alternative, is that people may end up putting more faith into their particular system than they put into God. And that God won't abide. You can bank on it.

Scripture – Genesis 11:1-9

Text – And the Lord said, "Behold, they are one people, and they have all one language; and this is only the beginning of what they will do; and nothing that they propose to do will now be impossible for them." – Gen. 11:6 (RSV)

A RIGHT-BRAINED SKEPTIC'S TAKE
ON SCIENCE AND TECHNOLOGY

In seminary we were taught that everything from Genesis 1 to Genesis 11 was what was called "myth." To most people, the word myth probably connotes a made-up story, a fiction, a fairy tale. Thus for modern people, myths by definition cannot "be true." "Being true" to us means being factual, being historical, that whatever is claimed to have happened actually did happen, and pretty much as portrayed by whoever tells the account.

To the ancients, myths represented that which was **really** true, whether or not it happened, or was historical, or factual. Probably most ancient Hebrews did not suppose that Adam and Eve actually existed in time, but, as Mircea Eliade, the Rumanian expert on mythology, explained, Adam and Eve certainly existed *in illud tempore*: in **those times**. "Those times" were not like **these** times. **These** times are quite pedestrian. They are measured in minutes, hours, and years, but *in illud tempore* there were giants, and dragons, and angels, and sneaky serpents, and trees of the knowledge of good and evil and trees of knowledge and all kinds of other wonderful stuff. Time was different *in illud tempore*.

The point of ancient myths was to explain what God was doing before there were any people there to know or understand or interpret what God was doing. What was God doing when the world was created? Read Genesis 1 and 2, and you'll find out. What was God doing when people started to sin and rebel against God? Read Genesis 3, and you'll find out. What was God doing when the human race seemed totally to go to hell in a handbasket? Read Genesis 6 through 9, and you'll find out.

117

Did the Hebrews consider the early part of Genesis to be historical? No doubt many did, but many others didn't. The **historicity** of the Genesis 1-11 myths didn't matter all that much to them; the **truth** of the myths mattered immensely. And what was true about the myths is that God was always there, guiding, directing, reproving, scolding, flattering, and flattening humanity, in order once again to guide, direct, reprove, scold, flatter, and flatten. God does that with all of us too in these times, just as He did in those times.

The myth of the Tower of Babel is one of the most problematic passages in the whole Bible, it seems to me. What it intends to explain it doesn't explain, and what it doesn't mean to suggest at all, it clearly states.

The myth begins by telling us that Way Back When (which is another way of saying *in illud tempore*), all the people in the world had just one language, and that language had only few words. **Do Not** get hung up on whether that was ever historically true; it is mythological truths we are looking at here.

So, these were these ancient people living on the Plain of Shinar, which was in Mesopotamia (the Land Between the Rivers: the Tigris and Euphrates), which is now modern Iraq (does God have a sense of humor, or what?). And the Shinarites (the Bible doesn't use that word; I did) said, "Hey, let's make bricks, and then let's build a city, and then, in the city, let's build a tower that reaches up to heaven. Pretty slick, huh?" the Shinarites said to one another.

A few tidbits: for nearly all of their history, the Hebrews used stone whenever they built anything. Stone they had by the beaucoups of metric tons, so why should they bother to make bricks? But they were intrigued that the Mesopotamians made bricks, because the Mesopotamians didn't have much stone in their between-the-rivers flatlands.

For reasons unexplained, but merely stated, the Shinarites built a high tower. By means of it, the story says, "We will make a name for ourselves, lest we be scattered abroad upon the face of the whole earth." Why they would be scattered all over creation if they did **not** build the tower is beyond me, and maybe you too, but these Mesopotamian towers certainly did manage to make a name for their builders. The towers are called ziggurats, and there are still many decrepit examples of them throughout Iraq.

The Tower of Babel myth is what Old Testament scholars call an *etiology*. Etiology is the study of the causes of things. It is especially important in the science of medicine, and for obvious reasons. If a disease is diagnosed, it is much more quickly overcome if its cause can be pinpointed, because then particular medicines may be developed to eradicate it.

The Book of Genesis was finally put together from many sources when the Jews were captives in Babylon (in Mesopotamia) in the sixth century BCE. They has noticed the brick ziggurats here and there in the fertile countryside, and they wondered why they had been built way back when. The myth of the Tower of Babel is the etiological explanation. People got too big for their britches, and they decided to "make a name for themselves." If that doesn't sound too plausible to you, you're not alone. But that's the tower etiology.

Anyway, God didn't like what the people of Shinar did, and God said, "Behold, they are one people and they have all one language; and this is only the beginning of what they will do; and nothing they propose to do will now be impossible for them. Come," said God, presumably to Himself, "let us go down, and there confuse their language, that they may not understand one another's speech." And God, yea, verily, the **plural** God of Genesis, "Let **us** go down," *Elohim* rather than merely *El*, scattered them everywhere, which is exactly what they didn't want to happen, and why they built their tower in the first place. And the tower, we are informed, was called *Babel*. Babel means either "confusion" or "Gate of Bel." Bel was one of the primary gods of the Babylonians.

In Genesis, as elsewhere in the Bible, Babylon is an evil place, and the Babylonians (or Akkadians or Chaldeans or Sumerians) were never thought to be nice folks. Furthermore, they were **confusing**. Their language was confusing (what other

119

nationality's language isn't?), their culture was confusing (everyone else seems odd to us, except us), and their religion certainly was confusing (why did they concoct all those gods and spirits and demons?).

At the deepest level, Genesis highly disapproved of what the Babylonians did in constructing their Tower of Babel (Confusion), their Tower of Babylon (Gate of Bel). To describe their actions in contemporary terms, they used **technology** for the wrong purposes. And because they did, God confounded them by confusing their language, scattering them to the four corners of the earth.

To the captive Jews in Babylon, bricks could be utilized to build houses or shops or even palaces, but they were convinced nobody should ever construct towers reaching up to heaven. (Might September 11, 2001 have illustrated a similar kind of primitive religious antipathy to such human hubris? I wonder.) The Tower of Babel was a colossal affront to God, the biblical writers thought, a technological marvel which mightily irritated the Almighty One of Israel. But instead of casting down the tower, God cast out the tower builders.

The technology of the ancient world was amazing, even by the standards of the modern world. The Seven Wonders of the World were truly wonderful. The Lighthouse at Alexandria, the Colossus of Rhodes, and the Hanging Gardens of Babylon have long since disappeared from our view, but the Great Pyramids of Giza stand to this day. The Great Wall of China (not one of the Seven Wonders, which, alas, were reckoned to exist only in the Western World)) is the only man-made structure which can be seen from the space shuttle, they say. Astonishing.

But what if the human race uses science and technology in the wrong ways? What if we increase life expectancy to one-hundred-and-twenty (Moses' age when he died: Deut. 34:7), and God want us to live for only three-score-years-and ten, or even by reason of strength, four-score (Ps. 90:10)? What if, intentionally unleashing the power of the atom, we also unleash a Three-Mile Island or a Chernobyl? Or what if, through scientific research we develop anesthesia, but we also develop chemical weapons? Will God confuse or confound or dispel us as He did the builders of the Tower of Babel? And if He doesn't, what then?

John Lukacs wrote a book called *At the End of an Age*. In it he said, "A great division among the American people has begun – gradually, slowly – to take shape: not between Republicans and Democrats, and not between 'conservatives' and 'liberals,' but between people who are still unthinking believers in technology and in economic determinism and people who are not. Compared with that division, the present 'debates' about taxes and rates and political campaigns are nothing but ephemeral froth blowing here and there on little waves, atop the great oceanic tides of history." Prof. Lukacs says of the thesis of his book, "Its theme is simple. It has to do with conscious thinking. We have arrived at a stage of history when we must begin thinking about thinking itself.... At the end of an age, we must engage in a radical rethinking of 'progress,' of 'history,' of 'science,' of the limitations of our knowledge, of our place in the universe."

John Lukacs is right on target. There are too many people today who are too uncritical in their blind belief in science and technology. Not all scientific or technology research and development is morally and ethically neutral. Some avenues of knowledge ought not to be explored, just as some kinds of behavior should always be avoided. Dostoevsky wrote *Crime and Punishment* to suggest that even though a man might attempt to get away with murder, considering it not to be murder, his action was found to be socially, ethically, and religiously unacceptable. In like manner, the results of certain kinds of research are so likely to result in evil usage that the research should never be pursued. And if it is pursued, then wisdom will require the destruction of the evil results of the research.

Jim Sollisch is a commentator for NPR's *Morning Edition*. He wrote a somewhat tongue-in-cheek piece in which he suggested that many technoklutzes, such as himself, marvel at technology without ever wondering about how techno-marvels work. And he upbraids the techno-whizzes when they get so steamed at the snail's pace of their newest gadgets. "I've heard you in Starbucks, cursing the speed of your brand-new laptop's processor, whining about your puny modem. There is no joy in you early adopters. Never a pat on the back for technology, never a kind word. You are miserable in your superiority, while I, in my inferior state, am filled with joy. You think of technology as your religion, and yet it brings no comfort. I stand in awe of every bit and beep and byte.... I am happy for my ignorance. I'm glad I wasn't required to take math and science all four years of high school like kids today have to do. As a result, I don't understand technology. I revere it. I'm not waiting for the next new thing; I'm still enjoying the last new thing."

And that suggests a modern truth. **The world is divided into two kinds of people: those whose lives are devoted to technology, and those whose lives are affected by, but not driven by, technology.** As an example, I am sure you have encountered many people who insist you need to get connected to the Internet, if that great leap forward has not yet happened in your life, and they badger you to become proficient in the use of e-mail. You may be such a badgerer yourself. But as one who is **on** but not **of** the Net, and who would much rather talk to people on Mr. A.G. Bell's horn than send e-mail missives to them, I say this: nobody is ever going to convince me that I am an incomplete human being unless I use the Internet and e-mail more than I already do. Get off it, Internetophiles! Get over it! Some of us, millions of us, do not see this the way you do, nor shall we ever! I am serious! Stop bugging us!

Fortunately, I use the Internet so little that nobody (and I suppose it would be the company I pay $96 a year to beam me up) has sold my name to spammers. "Spam," which used to be bits of crushed meat of dubious origin shoved unceremoniously into a can, is now defined as unsolicited ads which come unbidden daily via e-mail. Ellen Goodman had a column about it a while back. "My spam, your spam, everyone's spam is nothing if not a growth industry. On average, 11 per cent of all e-mails now are spam.... As Internet guru Esther Dryson says, 'The magic of e-mail is that you can e-mail almost anyone. The tragedy is that almost anyone can e-mail you.'"

I have never been hooked by the Internet, nor shall I ever be. But when I first got hooked up, I felt morally bound to read every blasted word that appeared on my morally-neutral screen. No more. Some stuff I don't even open because of who sent it, and some I scan sufficiently quickly to delete into eternal oblivion without a nano-second of ethical qualm. You probably do the same.

Even so, I am subjected to more and more incoming words that I don't want to read that I have less and less time for reading words that I do want to read. In the pre-tech days of the US Postal Service, it took too much time and postage money for everybody to write everybody about everything, but now, courtesy of Microsoft or somebody (I neither know nor care who), all of us who got connected get bombarded. Who gave anybody the right to do that? I am serious; who did? I realize we can disconnect entirely, but most of us probably don't find this so offputting that we want to do that. Are we therefore consigned to endure these cybernetic insults to the last syllable of recorded cyberspace?

The Internet is not satisfactorily regulated by any government anywhere. And if the US government outlawed certain features of its usage, e-mail pushers would just move offshore to continue doing their dastardly deeds.

Furthermore, all kinds of nuts put all kinds of nutty stuff on Internet web sites which all kinds of other nuts think isn't nutty. There is a plethora of misinformation, disinformation, and just plain lies out there in cyberspace, and droves of gullible people believe it is the Gospel truth. If it is **there**, these unreasonable folk "reason," it **must** be true. But much of it isn't true! It is a pack of packaged prevarications!

And then there is the world-wide host of e-mail and Internet addicts, people who spend dozens of hours every week senselessly surfing. Dr. David Greenfield is the founder of the Center for Internet Studies. He estimates that 6% of Americans are compulsive e-mail checkers. I don't know if that means 6% of everybody, or just 6% of those who are hooked up to e-mail. Either way, it represents millions of addicts. And I am not being facetious when I say that all the people who helped develop the Internet (and it was not just Al Gore all by himself) must bear at least some measure of culpability for this colossal human waste of precious time.

Now somebody has come up with yet another new technological widget to appear unbidden on computer screens. It is called Instant Messaging. While you are innocently writing a report or letter (or sermon), or when you are having a civilized conversation with another humanoid in your office, somebody can instantly message you, and a cute little block appears on your screen, telling you a cute little statement. Businesses are starting to buy IM like it's going out of style. Many executives love it, but others are not so convinced. IMs bother people when they are writing, these nay-sayers say, and employees frivolously send messages to one another on company time. This is yet another illustration of technological advancement which may result in a sociological retreat.

Computers and the Internet and e-mails and instant messages are here to stay; don't get me wrong. The genie is out of the bottle. And the genie can perform wondrously well. But it is, at best, a mixed blessing. Anyone who does not perceive the pitfalls and dangers of cybernetics, as well as the immeasurable advancements represented by computers, is missing one of the great ethical conundrums of our time. Certain features of our lives are out of control because there are no controls yet conceived to prevent a good thing from turning into an all-too-frequent nightmare.

Phillip Bobbitt wrote an unusually thought-provoking essay in *Time* Magazine called "Get Ready for the Next Long War." He said that a group like Al Qaeda can become a "virtual" nation because of computers. "The virtual state has many of the same characteristics of other states.... But it is borderless; it declares wars, makes alliances with other states and is global in scope but lacks a definable location on a map.... We are entering a period in which a small number of people, operating without overt state sponsorship but using the enormous power of modern computers, bio-genetic pathogens, air transport and even small nuclear weapons, will be able to exploit the tremendous vulnerabilities of contemporary open societies."

Without question, Al Qaeda could not accomplish what it has accomplished, it could not even exist, without computers. Modern industry and business could not exist without computers either. But it is especially sobering to think that modern terrorists also could not succeed without the benefits of cybernetics.

However, the issues are much greater than merely computerization. Consider cloning or cryogenics or genetically engineered foods or the safe treatment of nuclear waste or fetal tissue research or test tube babies or voluntary or involuntary sterilization or a thousand other such ethical concerns. Because we **can** do many things does not mean we **should** do everything we can. Maybe Ted Williams' body can be frozen, and maybe in the future wealthy parents can purchase a few cells of the cryogenized Boston Bomber to have inserted into the genetic program of their own soon-to-be dear little Teddy. But is it **right**? Is it **moral**? Is it ethically acceptable? And what about other parents, who can't afford the genetic boost, and whose sons – or daughters – will thus never bat .400?

Libby Purves is a writer for *The Times* of London. She always packs a piquant punch in her pungent prose. Ms. Purves wrote about a four-line verse which she was told by two sources was pasted to the walls above the urinals in the men's rooms of some of Britain's motorway rest stops. Certain men might be relieved to read, "Was it me or was it him?/ The truth is hard to find/ What you need is Dadcheck/ To give you piece of mind." There is now a company in the UK which sells a product that will determine if the DNA in any given child is or is not connected to the man who pays the money to take the test to determine the paternity of Child X or Y.

But what happens if it is determined the putative father of a certain child biologically could not possibly be the actual father? And what if the child – or mother – believes the supposed father is truly not the father: then what? Is it always good to have incontrovertible proof of such matters, Libby Purves asks.

Class action tobacco suits have rocked the tobacco industry. But what if, three or five or ten years from now, millions of people start showing up with malignant tumors above their telephone ear as a result of frequent usage of cellular telephones? Or what if genetically engineered foods turn out undeniably to produce cancer or other diseases, as many techno-skeptics are claiming will happen?

"Cute nukes" are one of the latest concerns prompted by technological and scientific advancements, or so says the irrepressible Molly Ivins. President Bush has ordered the Defense Department to conduct research on small nuclear weapons which can be used against terrorists or other enemies, such as Saddam Hussein, who build bunkers deep underground. In the jargon of Mil-Speak, these miniature nukes are called "offensive strike systems." Molly discovered that the Defense Department declared that these new weapons are to be "employed against targets able to withstand non-nuclear attack (for example deep underground bunkers or bio-weapons facilities)." In other words, it's okay to use tiny nukes, even if we have forsworn the offensive first-strike use of big nukes. Ms. Ivins quotes the ending of the play *Rosencrantz and Guildenstern Are Dead*, where the one tragic character says to the other, "There must have been a time, somewhere near the beginning, when we could have said, 'no.'" Lisbeth Gronlund of the Union of Concerned Scientists stated it so powerfully in a different way: "If the world's greatest military power with all its conventional weapons needs to use nuclear weapons, doesn't everyone else?" Think about it, dear heart; for God's sake, **think** about that. It appears that too many people in Washington DC are not thinking about it at all.

There is **always** a time, though unfortunately it is usually well toward the beginning of the process of scientific and technological inquiry, when we could say, "No." As a right-brained chap, who admittedly was behind the door when they were passing out the scientific smarts, it seems to me, as an outside observer, that too many pure researchers are too oblivious about where their findings might lead them. Either that, or they are too impure in their morality about those potential findings. As Robert Frost said, though in a very different context, "Before I built a wall I'd ask to know/ What I was walling in or walling out/ And to whom I was like to give offense." There is no moral high ground in any kind of research or inquiry where there is a strong possibility that the knowledge gained will much more likely become a detriment than a boon to the human race or to the world which God alone has created.

Even if that is true, however, and I firmly believe it **is** true, saying it will not prevent every conceivable kind of scientific research from going forward anyway, **unless** there are strong and enforceable international agreements to prevent it. And even then, of course, subterfuge could and would be used for scientists, mad or otherwise, to continue to do their thing. And they can and will do it either independently for personal profit or with funding from rogue governments or international groups of various sorts. Such is human nature, which always has been somewhat red in tooth and claw.

Nevertheless, there are certain actions which can and should be taken by thoughtful, altruistic citizens of the world community.

No one should engage in any form of scientific or technological research on anything that is more likely to be used for evil purposes than for good purposes. And because ethicists are almost never consulted before such research begins, it is the scientists themselves who must do the primary policing of their own endeavors. But this may suggest that everyone who aspires to any kind of scientific research should be given several rigorous courses in ethics as part of their academic training, just as most medical schools require their students to receive training in medical ethics.

All of us should purchase only those products which are thought to be the least harmful to the earth's environment. Up until the past few centuries, humanity was incapable of disturbing the ecology of the world. Now we have numerous means of destroying the global environment altogether. Therefore it behooves us, especially those of us who are well educated, to refrain from products which rapidly deplete rather than enhance the delicate balance of ecology. So, for example, we should probably outlaw SUVs and mandate wind-driven power generators, regardless of the expense. To spend too little now is to guarantee spending too much later.

We should support **wise**, as compared to merely **smart**, political candidates. And we should avoid nominating and especially electing any candidate who seems to possess only average intelligence. Further, we need politicians who have moral, as compared to simple political, courage. The world has become too complex for average leaders adequately to lead. But we need people who are not only smart, but also who are wise and courageous.

Every resident of our planet needs constantly to think about whether the innovations which confront us at an ever-increasing rate are more likely to result in the benefit or the degradation of the world. Everything from hula hoops, frisbees, and Velcro to in-vitro fertilization, Methadone, and silicon chips are basically good. And everything from DDT, Thalidomide, and polyunsaturated fat to nuclear weapons, chemical weapons, or biological weapons are likely to turn out for the bad. Even when used with the best of intentions, bad stuff almost always results in bad stuff.

William Rees-Mogg is another writer for the London *Times*. In an editorial about Rowan Williams, the then-newly named Archbishop of Canterbury, Mr. Rees-Mogg said, although not directly about the new archbishop at all, "The contradiction of scientific materialism – and incidentally of global capitalism – is that it totally depends on human relationships, but does not generate love by its own logic. Science plus religion, or globalism plus religion, works for the benefit of mankind. Science without religion, or globalism without religion, must be destroyed by a lack of social coherence."

Truer words were never written. The days when it could be claimed that science and technology are morally neutral are long over. Nobody can hide under the shield of technological amorality any longer. That goes for those of us who purchase the fruits of technology as well as those who produce its fruits. We need to be far, far, **far** more careful about what we have done, are doing, and shall continue to do. Our individual choices affect the corporate nature of the cosmos more now than ever before.

In the myth of the Tower of Babel, the tower technocrats did not think through the consequences of their actions nearly well enough. That, despite the inconsistencies of the story to modern readers, was their downfall. And so, because they did not anticipate the end results of their choice to build what to them was a modern marvel, they were thrown by God into a maelstrom of confusion and division.

Do you remember Neville Shute's novel *On the Beach*? Or did you see the movie? It takes place in Australia, which in the story was the last place on the earth to survive a worldwide nuclear war. As the tension between the West and the USSR rose, it became evident to most people in the drama that a nuclear exchange was almost inevitable. But a Christian group – and I think it was the Salvation Army – had placed a banner in a prominent place in – I think – downtown Sydney. It declared, **"THERE IS STILL TIME, BROTHER."** At the end of the movie, when the American submarine submerges with its pitifully small contingent of relatively healthy men and women, the camera moves back to the now-deserted city streets. All the people have died. The last scene shows the tattered banner, fluttering in the wind of a nuclear winter. And we are left wondering: Is there still time? Is there?

Back in the Fifties, when the novel was written and the movie was made, the political and military situation was very different from our present circumstances. Nonetheless, the godly reminder is as valid now as it was then: There Is Still Time, Brother.

Science and technology have been much more of a blessing than a bane to the world. But unless they are to become the Ultimate Bane, we need more **conscientiously** (did the etymological connection between "science" and "conscience" ever really strike you before?) to seek the best from our technical endeavors, and assiduously to avoid the worst.

The Plain of Shinar lies glistening before our eyes. What shall we construct - - - and **why**?

A Thicket of
Theology

Scripture – Luke 15:1-32

Texts – "Even so, I tell you, there will be more joy in heaven over one sinner who repents than over ninety-nine righteous persons who need no repentance." – Luke 15:7; "And when she has found it, she calls together her friends and neighbors, saying, 'Rejoice with me, for I have found the coin which I had lost.'" – Luke 15:9; "And he arose and came to his father. But while he was yet at a distance, his father saw him and had compassion, and ran and embraced him and kissed him." – Luke 15:20; "And he said to him, 'Son, you are always with me, and all that is mine is yours. It was fitting to make merry and be glad, for this your brother was dead, and is alive; he was lost, and is found.'" – Luke 15:32 (RSV)

GRACE: THE GREATEST OBSTACLE TO FAITH

No preacher would ever read all of Luke 15 in the context of a service of worship. It is just too long, and it would take up too much time. By the time the preacher or lector had finished reading the entire chapter, a third of the congregation would have left in a hurried huff. For those who remained, half of them would leave if the preacher announced that there were four verses, comprised of six separate sentences, which were the texts for the sermon. Then, most of the remaining parishioners would put the preacher against the chancel wall, and hymn him with their hymnbooks. Death by stoning would not last as long as death by hymning. However, hymning him would be more fitting, in light of his egregious behavior.

But since this is a book, and not a service of worship, and since however long it takes you to read all of Luke 15 and then all of this sermon is however long it takes, take the time right now to read all of Luke 15 - - - again. I know you've read it before, but read it again. It deserves to be read again, in any case, but it is essential to grasping the content of this sermon. So, please read it. Really. Seriously. Read it.

…. There. Now we can begin this, the first theological sermon that is too hot to preach. Or at least it would be too long to preach on a Sunday morning, because this will be the longest of all of these sermons. There is much biblical background to be covered before the actual sermonizing can begin.

Note how Luke 15 starts. "Now the tax collectors and sinners were all drawing near to hear (Jesus). And the Pharisees and the scribes murmured, saying, 'This man receives sinners and eats with them'" (Luke 15:1).

Most Christians seem never to have tumbled to the glaring fact that Jesus appealed most to the kind of people most Christians like the least. Jesus hung out with the "wrong crowd" continually. Perpetually. Brazenly. As my mother would say, He had more nerve than a canal horse. He knew He was provoking the religious powers-that-be, but He went right on, provoking the living hell out of them. Literally. He was ruthless about whom He hung out with; relentless; regard-less. Obviously He didn't give a rat's backside about what the religious mucky-mucks thought, or else He would have been more careful in choosing those with whom He associated Himself.

But you see, what Jesus said and did, what He *was*, was the best thing that crooked tax collectors and sordid sinners had ever encountered. Jesus said time and again that even though their sins were numerous and in-your-face kinds of sins, nonetheless God loved them, and He (God) would never let them get away from Him. Jesus suggested that they couldn't escape His (Jesus') love, either. God's love for sinners, any kind of sinners, **all** kinds of sinners, is unconditional. That's also the way Jesus loved. The rest of us don't love like that; none of us does. We all love with strings attached. But with God and Jesus, there are no strings attached.

Luke 15 is maybe the most important single chapter in the whole Bible. Certainly it is the most important chapter in the Gospels, and indeed, in the whole New Testament (or the Greek Bible, as some Christians say, remembering that the Hebrew Bible comprises most of the Bible. It is a useful distinction, and also a thoughtful one.)

Luke 15 consists of an opening observation, the one about the "wrong kind" of people hanging around Jesus, and the "right kind" of people being put off by that. That persistent reality gave Luke the opportunity to string together three of the parables of Jesus. The third, which is known as the Parable of the Prodigal Son, is the greatest of all the parables, says I. In fact, if there were nothing else in holy writ except Luke 15:11-32, it would suffice. If I am ever sent to a deserted island in the south seas, and I am told I can bring along only part of one chapter of the Bible, any part of any chapter of my own choosing, that's what I'll take. I'd first try to negotiate for the whole Bible plus a lot of other books, but if that didn't work, then just the whole Bible, and if that failed, then Isaiah and Luke, and if that didn't work, then just Luke. But if I couldn't talk my way into that, I'd settle for Luke 15, or merely Luke 15:11-32. However, it is probably rare to end up on a deserted island after lengthy negotiations for all or just part of the Bible, so maybe neither you nor I need to worry about that eventuality. Still, it's the kind of thing I think about, when I am thinking about such things.

In the first parable, the one about the lost sheep, a shepherd has a hundred sheep, and he loses one of them. Apparently sheep were behind the door when the brains were being passed out in the cosmic or celestial creature-creation department. They get lost easily, I have read. In the parable, when the shepherd finally finds his lost sheep, he drapes it around his shoulders and brings it home. Again, I have read that a lost sheep is so traumatized by being lost that it can't – or won't – walk. I don't know this from experience, but I assume it is true. Even if it isn't true, it's a pastoral falsehood which helps us understand the parable better. And when the shepherd gets home, he calls to everyone in the village, and asks them to rejoice with him, because he has found his lost sheep. And they, who also presumably are shepherds, and thus live by an equally tight margin of profit and loss, are only too glad to rejoice. They know how they'd feel if they lost one of their own sheep. "Even so," says Jesus at the conclusion of His first parable, "there will be more joy in heaven over one sinner who repents than over ninety-nine righteous persons who need no repentance."

And who, parabolically, are the ninety-nine righteous folk? The scribes and Pharisees who are put off by the creepy cast of characters Jesus hangs around with, that's who! Whodjuhthink?

But listen: *the Pharisees get a bad rap in the Gospels.* They really do. Most of the Pharisees were good guys. They honestly sought to do what they thought was right. But the Gospels were written by zealous Christians who did their writing from thirty to seventy years after the death and resurrection of Jesus. By then, they figured **all** the Jews were bad guys. Three of the four Gospel writers themselves were born Jews, but apparently they decided you couldn't be both a Jew and a Christian. So they forsook their Jewishness (a mistake) and bellowed their Christianity (also a mistake?), and they said the Pharisees were bad guys.

The above paragraph is a gratuitous theory about some first-century AD (CE) history. Whether or not it is correct, it seems undeniable to me that Jesus was telling His detractors, whoever they actually were, that righteous people should rejoice in the salvation of unrighteous people. In other words, good guys should be glad when bad guys are brought on board, because it is good not only for the bad guys but also for the good guys. Having everybody on board is a good thing, Jesus by inference is telling everybody.

And right there is why all the good folks who are likely to read a book like this encounter the painful truth that grace is the greatest obstacle there is to the discovery of genuine faith. Most believers in God consider themselves to be at least moderately good. They may not see themselves through the rose-tinted spectacles of outright narcissism, and they may not be duplicates of Little Jack Horner (who stuck in his thumb/ and pulled out a plum/ and said...), but they figure they're at least OK. I'm OK, you're OK, and all that. Well, actually, you may not be OK, but I'm OK; of that I am almost certain.

That attitude is the greatest threat to the Christian Gospel. Calvin had it basically right, even if he grossly overstated it. We are not totally depraved, but none of us is AOK, or even merely OK, either. We are all somewhere between "depraved" and "barely-acceptable-as-is." The best of us is not fully acceptable, and the worst of us is not fully unacceptable, in the eyes of God. To God, we are all lost souls, to one degree or another. We are lost sheep, or lost coins, or lost sons and daughters, but He (God) is going to find us, and it is He (Jesus) who came to tell us that, in God, we shall be found. **All** of us.

That assertion mystifies many believers, whether Christian or otherwise, and it irritates others, it angers others, and it absolutely enrages still others. The most conservative followers of any religion, whether Jewish, Christian, Muslim, Hindu, or whatever, are the most likely to deny that God has the freedom to exercise His grace on behalf of all His children. Bleeding-heart liberals might approve of grace, even if many of them haven't a clue as to its cost. But most of us, and maybe all of us, in our deepest heart of hearts, are as peeved as we can be by the very idea of grace.

Grace is, as has often been stated and has earlier been implied, unconditional love. God loves all of us like that. If pressed far enough, however, we are all burned up by such a notion. Who does God think He is, loving people like the Roman Emperors Caligula or Nero, or Ghenghis Khan, or Tamerlane, or Napoleon or Hitler or Stalin or Muammar Khadafi or Saddam Hussein or Usama bin Laden? Or what about the mothers who drowned their children, or the husbands who slay their wives, or the serial killers, or, or, or? Does God love them as much as He loves you or me? Yes, the Bible says so. Some, though not all, of the prophets say so. Jesus certainly says so. It is illustrative of grace abounding. And to the world, to most people, to all of us at some point, grace is the pits. It is clearly so unfair.

Grace *is* unfair. Truly it is. And that is precisely why it is grace. If God loved us with a conditional love (you do this for me, and then I'll love you), it would be a kind of love, but it wouldn't be grace. To be grace, grace ***must*** represent unconditional love. And that bugs the living bejeebers out of us.

So Jesus comes to the second of His "lost" parables, the one about the lost coin. It is short, only three verses. A woman lost a coin somewhere inside her house, and she swept every inch of

136

every floor until she found it. As with the shepherd, she calls everyone together to celebrate with her. And once again, Jesus says, "Even so, I tell you, there is joy before the angels of God over one sinner who repents" (Luke 15:10).

Jesus wasn't saying that only to scribes and Pharisees, or, more likely, to scribes, and priests, and Sadducees. He is saying it to **us**. Be glad when bad guys get on board, He tells us. But we aren't glad, because we still think bad guys are bad, and good guys are good, and **they're** bad, whoever they are, and **we're** good, whoever we are. Terrorists are bad (which is true), but we are good (which is not nearly as true as we think).

So then comes the third parable, which is the greatest of all the parables, which is called by a misnomer, the Parable of the Prodigal Son. It should be called instead the Parable of the Loving Father, or maybe the Parable of the Loving Father and His Two Unloving Sons, or maybe the Parable of the Loving Father and His Two Highly Unlovely Sons. But "Father" should be in the name of this parable, because it is really about a father and his love, not about the two sons of a father who both acted like sons of Lucifer Satanicus.

Fully to understand this parable, we need to understand something about the culture of first century Judea. In that society, property passed in a proscribed way from one generation to the next. If a man had three sons, his estate would be divided into four equal parts at his death. The oldest son would get two parts of the estate (or in that particular instance, half), and the younger sons would each get one part, which would be a fourth of the estate, using that example. If there were six sons, the estate would be divided into seven equal parts, and the oldest would get two-sevenths, while the others would each get one-seventh.

In Jesus' parable, there are only two sons. Therefore, at the father's death, the older son would get two-thirds of the estate, and the younger one, the so-called prodigal, would get one-third.

There is a major problem in this story, however. It is so odd as to be skin-crawling strange. Upon hearing it, the people to whom Jesus told the parable would be in shock.

The problem was this: the younger son asked his father for his share of the inheritance *while the father was still living*! He wanted his third *before his father had died*! In other words, by making this request of his father, the younger son was saying, in effect, "Dad, I want you dead, and I want you dead **now**! Show me the money! Show it to me now! Give it to me now, Dad, because I'm gonna be outahere!"

Can you imagine the chutzpah in such a request? No, it's a demand, not a request! I want **mine**, and I want it **right now**!

Jesus very deliberately told His listeners a story that He knew would shock them. But, as we shall see, the true shock is not the behavior of the younger son, or even of the older son. In the end, the most shocking behavior is that of the father. What kind of love does this father have for his two sons? How can justice or righteousness or fairness or equity allow him to love the way he does?

It is astonishingly jarring that the father in the parable agrees to give the younger son his share of the inheritance. What we modern readers do not immediately perceive is that it also means the father, in order to be fair to the older son, was required to give him his two-thirds of the estate. If the father did it for the one, he was obligated to do it for the other. And this compounded the cultural astonishment of this story, because it meant that, *while he was still alive*, the father willingly gave up everything he owned to his two sons. No Middle Eastern father in the first century, nor in the twenty-first century, would ever do that.

But carefully pay attention to this: **on the basis of subsequent behavior, NEITHER SON DESERVED WHAT THE FATHER GAVE THEM!** They both were ungrateful twits!! They both were horrible to their father!!! They both deserved to be utterly disowned by the father, to be cast into the other darkness, where men weep and g-nash their teeth!!!! In life, people who weep and g-nash their teeth **always** deserve to weep and g-nash their teeth! We get what we deserve - - - don't we? If we mess up our lives, our lives of necessity must become messy — correct? Not so, says Jesus of Nazareth by means of this unparalleled parable, through Almighty God, we don't get what we deserve! Thank God, we don't! We get what we don't deserve (the unconditional love of our Creator), and we don't get what we do deserve (the unceasing punishment of a permanently peeved Creator)!

After the younger son had spent all his money in what the King James Version so colorfully calls "riotous living," Jesus tells us the young man "came to himself." What a magnificent little detail! He "came to himself"! He remembered! He remembered his father! He recalled the kind of father he was, not an ordinary father, but a kind father, a fair father, a father who would love him no matter what the young man might do! So the younger son started home, and all along the way he rehearsed the speech he would give to his dad; "Father, I have sinned against heaven and before you; treat me as one of your hired servants.... Father, I have sinned against heaven and before you; I'm not worthy to be called your son; treat me as one of your hired servants."

And of course he's right! He **has** sinned; he has sinned greatly! He has treated his father as though he wanted him totally out of his life, as though he wanted him dead, he has blown his entire inheritance, and now he can do nothing except go back home and work on the farm like a hired servant. The Greek word, *doulos*, can mean either "servant" or "slave." Either way, the younger son is willing to take his medicine; he is ready to get what, sorrowfully, he knows he deserves.

But there is yet another of these little cultural details which we in the 21st century cannot fully appreciate about life in 1st-century Judea. Jesus so deftly inserts this snippet into the story. "And he" (the younger son) "arose and came to his father. **But while he was yet at a distance**, his father saw him and had compassion." While he was yet at a distance! And what does that small phrase tell us? It tells us that the father had constantly been looking for his son to return! It says that the father was **watching** for his son, he was **watching out** for him, he was earnestly **waiting** for him to come home! And in that culture, fathers were *primus inter pares*! They were *il capo de tutti capi*! They were the first among equals, they were the head of all the heads. It was a highly male-dominated society, and a father who had been shunned as this father was had every reason to ignore his younger son completely. But not only did the father not ignore his son, he had actively been looking and yearning for his return since that day long ago when the young man had trudged off to the far country in search of fame and fortune, or good times, or whatever it was he thought he was needing, or at least seeking.

The Father awaits us! When we get lost, He looks for us! He searches for us! He is the Love that will not let us go, ever! He is the Father who cannot **not** love us, the one who loves us no matter what, the one who will not give up on us regardless of whether we do or do not do what He demands of us! He gives us His laws, and tells us we must follow them! But He also gives us the ability and the will to follow them, when that may not be our inclination! And if we don't follow them, if we throw His laws back into His face, He will still be our Father anyway! There is nothing we can do to escape from His love, because it is offered to us without condition!

Then there is the next sociological snippet, the kind which so easily evades 21st century notice. The father saw him and had compassion, "and **ran** and embraced him and kissed him." It is the three-letter word "ran" which makes this an even more disjointed story. Because it was such a glaringly male-dominated society, and because the father of the family, the *paterfamilias*, was the biggest cheese in the entire social structure, it was incumbent on the father always to act with dignity. Big cheeses don't run to welcome returning prodigals. Big cheeses wait for prodigals obsequiously to return, they insist on giving prodigals the required amount of time to grovel before them, they remain impassive for inordinate lengths of time so that miscreants may have sufficient opportunity for everyone to know just how miscreant-y they are. Little shots may run, but big shots walk; they stroll, at best they amble.

But that isn't what this father does. He **runs** to throw his arms around his son, he picks up his long robe and races down the village street, with all its filth and grime, shamelessly showing his ankles and lower legs, which Middle Eastern men would never do. A true father, a genuine father, a father who understood his elevated status and the much lower status of his younger son who had so abased himself, would never run to welcome home the sinner who had the fling in the far country, which means Gentile-land, which means Them, as opposed to Us. No, this is a self-effacing father such as none of the people to whom Jesus told the story had ever seen. Nor could they believe such a father could exist. Nor can we believe it. Grace is just too good to be true. It is the greatest obstacle there is to faith.

As we all remember, instead of allowing the son to finish his well-rehearsed speech, the father embraces the son, and kisses him, and tells his servants/slaves to bring a robe, and a ring, and shoes, and to clothe his son as he should always have been clothed had he not chosen to take his inheritance and flee the family homestead. The astonishment on hearing this continues. It is as though this worthless cur of a son had never left home, nor demeaned his father so much, nor brought so much shame on the father, and the older brother, and the extended family, and the village. This is Al Capone, coming back from prison to Chicago, and everybody treats him like a prince! "What wondrous love is this/ O my soul/ O my soul/ What wondrous love is this/ O my soul?"

But then there comes the second part of the parable, the part about the older son. Before you get too impressed with him, you need to know this: he gladly took his two-thirds of the estate when his brother demanded his one-third. He didn't nobly object; no, not he. He didn't say, "Dad, Dad, Dad, you mustn't do this! It is wrong for you to give your second-born son his share of the inheritance while you're still alive. But I'm not going to compound the insult by accepting my two-thirds share" —— oh, no, the older son never said that. He took over the farm right then and there, and the father instantly became a kind of social supernumerary, a familial fifth wheel, an unnecessary appendix in this whole sorry saga.

In lots of ways, the older son is an even worse skunk than the younger one. By taking over the farm, by staying there instead of selling everything and taking off for the bright lights of Jerusalem or wherever, his very existence diminishes the status of the father on a daily basis. All the neighbors can see for themselves what rotters these two sons turned out to be, but the older one is even more rotten than the younger, hard as that may be to believe, because he now controls the farm, and everyone can see what is happening. The father is like an old bull who has been put out to pasture. Obviously he is too old to cut the mustard anymore, and everybody can see it, just because there is he is, out in the familial pasture!

When the older son hears what his father has done for his brother upon the brother's return, he is incensed. He has given the dirty flatarap a robe, and ring, and shoes! He has ordered the slaves to prepare a party! But it was not within the father's rights to do this! Only the older son could do this, because he alone, the older son, runs the total show now! Who the hell does the father think he is, showing compassion and unconditional love to the confounded prodigal! The father's behavior is just that — hellish! He acts with misguided love, and he thwarts true justice! If anything, the younger son **should** be treated like a slave, because that is all he deserves! But no, the father treats him like a **son** again, and a beloved son at that!

"But he" (the older son) "was angry, and refused to go in," said Jesus, toward the end of this parable without peer. His father begged him to come inside the house for the celebration. Defiantly, the older son shot out his jaw, and snarled, "All these years I have served you" (which wasn't true; he had been serving his own self-interest; after all, he now owned everything) "and I never disobeyed you" (which may or may not have been true, but I'll give him the benefit of the doubt, the self-righteous son-of-a-sea-cook), "and you never gave me so much as a baby goat upon which to feast with my friends. But when **this son of yours**" (not "my brother," but "this son of **yours**") "came, **who has devoured your living with harlots**" (who said anything about whores? Did Jesus say anything about whores? I don't think so!), "you killed for him the fatted calf!"

In my family there were four boys, of which I was the fourth. The oldest was probably the hardest for my parents to raise. Over time he became, in many ways, the most exemplary of all four of us. He left home sooner, had less education, had to work harder to get where he got, but he got there. However, when he was a teenager, he was, if not hell-on-wheels, at least a trial-on-shanks-ponies. I remember one time when he had done something or other about which my parents were considerably less than pleased. Dad was ready to put a tin ear on him, as Mom would have said. Dad took off his belt, and took Bob down into the basement, and we on the upper floor heard the snap of the belt against a cowering backside. But there was nary a whimper to be heard. Then, when at last the whipping ceased, Dad and Bob emerged from the menacing dungeon of the cellar. It was such an ordeal for both father and son that the father told the son and the rest of the family that we were going out to a restaurant for dinner. In those days (it was the mid-40s), we did not go out to restaurants, and certainly not out for "dinner." Supper, maybe, but not dinner. But it was a Sunday afternoon, if memory serves me correctly, and out to the restaurant we all went, including the sadder but presumably wiser Bob.

The father in the parable was like our father in Dixon, Illinois, on that long-ago Sunday, except that the father in the parable didn't whip the tar out of the younger (who in our case was actually the oldest) son. But our dad did kill the fatted calf. We who never went to the restaurant because we couldn't afford to go to the restaurant went to the restaurant. We made merry to a fine fare-thee-well, and it got us all over a rough patch, most of all Bob, for whom it was the roughest, except for Mom, for whom undoubtedly it **was** the roughest. Oh, how she suffered when any of us suffered!

And so, at the end of the parable, the father says to the older sibling, "Son, you are always with me, and all that is mine is yours [literally true]. It was fitting to make merry and be glad, for this **your brother** *was dead*, and is **alive** again; he *was lost*, and *is found*."

143

Do you recall how Jesus ended the first two of three "lost" parables? "There is more joy in heaven over one sinner who repents than over ninety-nine righteous persons who need no repentance," and "There is joy before the angels of God over one sinner who repents."

There's something very peculiar in this third parable, however. **We aren't told whether either son repented!** We do know that the younger son came home, and we know that the older son stayed home, but we don't know whether either of them decided that they way they were living was wrong, and that they'd better get their act together!

Did they repent? Did they "change their mind," which is what the Greek word *metanoia* really means? Jesus doesn't tell us! In fact, He doesn't tell us what was the response of the older son at all, other than that he was angry at what their father had done. But when the father told the older son that it was proper to be joyful at the return of the younger son, whether or not he had had a genuine change of heart, did the older son accept the father's assessment? Or did he continue to hold a grudge? And if he did, what should the father do then?

I can't tell you what all human fathers would do in such circumstances, and I'm sure they would vary in what they did. But I am certain of what the father in this parable would do, because I am sure of who Jesus metaphorically meant that father to be. The parabolic father is meant to be our heavenly Father. And God would accept the older son regardless of what his response might be. Of that I have not the slightest doubt.

* * * * * * *

Now we have finished the biblical part of this lengthy sermon. And it is only fair to tell you that I am already 33% beyond where I would have gone in a normal-length Sunday sermon, and we haven't even started the primary sermonizing yet. That's one of the few beauties of reading, as opposed to listening to, a sermon: it can be any blasted length the blasted sermon-writer wants it to be. But I've already told you this is going to be the longest of all the sermons in this book of sermons that are too hot to preach, so you haven't been suckered into anything.

However, what's so hot about this sermon? *Grace*, that's what. Those three parables, as I earlier averred, are all about grace, and grace is the greatest obstacle to faith. None of us truly loves grace, particularly if it is offered to anybody else. But we aren't thrilled about it when it is offered to us, either. We have a natural aversion to grace, because it violates much if not most of what we hold sacred.

The Bible tells us, in book and chapter and verse after book and chapter and verse, that to be proper followers of God, we must do what God tells us to do. That's what the whole *Torah*, the Law, is about, isn't it? If we follow the Ten Commandments, if we do all that other stuff, all will go well. Well, maybe not **all** of it. If we stoned to death everyone who has ever committed adultery, there wouldn't be very many people left to be stonechuckers. If we cut off the hands of all thieves, especially all who have ever stolen anything, no matter how inconsequential, there would be few of us with any digits or paws left. Some parts of the Torah are absolutely blood-curdling in the punishments they prescribe. But in the main, we are correct in assuming that God wants us to keep the laws of ethical and acceptable moral behavior.

The one thing we forget, though, is that keeping God's law has nothing whatever to do with earning or meriting or being rewarded by God's love. We must follow God's law to show our love for God, but God will love us regardless of what we do or do not do. The offer of His love has no conditions attached to it, nor does the acceptance of that love. We are free to reject it, and all of us do reject it, and all too often. But it shall be offered to all of us anyway.

We naively assume that we must repent, and therefore we will believe in God. Quite the contrary. We must believe, and therefore we will repent. Faith precedes repentance; repentance never precedes faith. If we repent, ever, it means that we have already believed.

And from whence cometh our faith? From God, and God alone. Nobody chooses to believe. Belief or faith are not acts of volition. Whoever believes does so because that person has accepted the free gift of God's grace. Grace results in faith; faith does not result in grace. Grace produces faith; faith does not produce grace.

Grace is pre-venient, as St. Augustine and others have insisted through the centuries. That is to say, God gives us His grace before we have done anything to merit it. God's love for us is guaranteed to us even before we are born, and it shall continue forever after we are dead in eternity. Grace was extended to us long before we have even thought of doing God's will.

To put it in judicial terms, we are **justified** by grace through faith. We aren't really justified by faith, but rather by grace **through** faith, despite what Habakkuk and then Paul said. To be justified means to be declared not guilty of sin.

But we **are** guilty of sin; we are **all** guilty! "There is none who is righteous, no, not one," said the tentmaker of Tarsus, and he's right. Nobody is — in the terminology of the courtroom — - "not guilty;" everyone is "guilty."

But the Judge (God) through His grace (unconditional love) decrees that by His love we are made innocent, and thus we are justified. And if we are **justified**, we should become **sanctified**. To become sanctified means literally to become saintly, or perhaps better, holy. It means at a minimum to want to do the right stuff all the time, and actually to do the right stuff most of the time.

But again, we do not become justified because we are first sanctified; we are sanctified because we are first justified. We don't do the right and therefore we become righteous; we are given God's grace, and therefore we naturally seek to do the right. Nonetheless, righteousness and 95 cents will get you a cup of coffee on the way to salvation. Only grace will get you salvation, and salvation has nothing whatever to do with our attempts at goodness.

How do we know we are the recipients of God's grace? We can know that only by faith. But how do we get faith, if we don't have it? God gives it to us. No man comes to faith on his own. No woman can will her faith into being. Faith is a gift of God, freely offered to all.

Not everybody accepts the gift, however. You have surely noticed that sobering fact among family members, friends, classmates, or business associates. Some people do not believe in God, or in His grace, or in anything that transcends the bounds of this planet.

Truly to accept grace means we must change the way we live. We can no longer live for ourselves; now we must live for God. And to do that means to do what God's law tells us to do.

But even if some of us don't accept God's grace, His grace is still offered to all, and in the end, everyone will be saved by it. God desires ultimate salvation for everyone. Temporally, many of us shall live in hell, usually of our making. But eternally, we shall all live in heaven. Universal salvation is God's choice for His children. And if that's what He wants, that's what He will get.

Nearly four decades as a professional preacher has taught me that idea rankles more Christians than anything else I have preached. And I have intentionally made it my business to preach lots of rankling things. But grace, which finally issues in salvation for all, is the hardest thing for many Christians to believe, and thus grace proves to be the greatest obstacle to their faith. We all want to be worthy of salvation. It's an uplifting and edifying thought. But it will never happen. Only those who are not worthy of salvation can be saved.

In the past several years, increasing numbers of parishioners became connected to the Internet. Until I myself finally joined the 20th century at the end of the first year in the 21st century, I used to receive increasing numbers of old-fashioned hardcopy pages through the mail of wisdom which seem to traverse the Internet like cosmic dust passing through space. Now that I too am connected, I receive more and more soft pages of e-mail wisdom. If I live another twenty or thirty years, I will probably have been sent everything ever known by everyone that needs to be known by anyone.

One of the aphorisms of out of cyberspace I was given before I was properly hooked up myself says this: A clear conscience is usually the sign of a bad memory. Because a person (unknown) put this wisdom-snippet in my mailbox at church, without identifying the person who originally said the wise-snip, I can't properly credit the sagacious originator. But she/he is correct; a clear conscience usually is the sign of a bad memory. We tend to remember everyone else's sins, slights, and mistakes like elephants, but we are sand fleas when it comes to recollecting our own sins, slights, and mistakes.

Why is that? I believe it happens because, as the Book of Common Prayer so eloquently declares, we think of ourselves more highly than we ought to think. To us, we are as bright and shiny as stars in the sky. We delight in deluding ourselves about ourselves.

The Wizard of Id by Brant Parker and Johnny Hart is one of my favorite comic strips. Frequently its evangelical creators insert their theology into the land of Id, with its motley cast of delightfully flawed characters. One day the watchman on his tower looks down on a passerby, and he shouts, "Who goes there?" The answer wafts up from below, "A man of the cloth seeking lost souls." "Congratulations, Padre," says the watchful guard, "you've hit the mother lode."

Indeed. We are all lost souls. But the good news is that all lost souls have been found, not because we have made ourselves available to be found, and not because we have done anything to deserve our being found, or because we have engaged in any serious finding on our own, but simply because The Finder has found us. The Hound of Heaven is on the search, and He will not desist until He has found us in such a way that we will know beyond any doubt that we have been found.

Ronald Goetz, the emeritus Professor of Theology and Ethics at Elmhurst College in Elmhurst, Illinois, was asked to preach at the funeral of an atheist. He wrote about the experience in *The Christian Century* (Oct. 18, 2000). He said, "I would hope that grace, which God intends for the salvation of all humanity, is not so fragile that it cannot stand up to human unbelief. Surely the God who dwelt among us in the person of Jesus Christ is both too powerful and too gracious to take our rebellious rejections for final answers. Surely the one true Holy God, who out of love has made all things visible and invisible, is not so intimidated by human rebellion as to despair of the power of God's gracious love to win us over. Surely such a God could never conclude that there is no other choice, given the trouble we make for God, but to damn all but a chosen few to eternal rejection. No, the free and sovereign God is in no sense bound or intimidated by the enormity of our sin. God, in God's freedom, has left open countless avenues to God's grace."

Another Internet story sent to me: After the christening of his baby brother in church, little Tommy sobbed all the way home in the back seat of the car. His father asked him three times what was wrong. Finally, the boy replied, "That preacher said he wanted the baby and me to be brought up in a Christian home, but I want to stay with you guys!"

We think of ourselves more highly than we ought to think. We imagine we are something we are not. Out of the mouths of babes… Others are often much better than we think they are, and we are often much worse than we think we are. In a *New Yorker* cartoon, a young man is ascending through a swirl of clouds toward the celestial regions. A sour-looking elderly couple are watching this surprising ascent, and the old geezer says to the geezerette, "Damn, looks like that snotty kid of Ben and Edna's is coming up the tunnel of light!" That's exactly the way it happens, folks. People come swooping up that tunnel who will astound the gizzard right out of you. Why, your ascent itself will astound lots of people who are already at the top of the tunnel! Grace is the only solution for the problem of who gets into the swirl. But because it is the grace of God, everybody gets in.

Still, we can never perceive grace to be grace until we affirm the call of God in our lives. Grace abounds, but unless we respond to it, we cannot move on to our earthly sanctification.

Over a century ago, telegraph was the fastest form of communication. A certain telegraph office needed a Morse code operator, and a number of men showed up to apply for the job.

The office was noisy, and part of the clatter was the constant click of the Morse letters coming out from the telegraph wire. A sign on the secretary's desk instructed applicants to fill out a form, and then they were to wait until summoned to an inner office. There were seven applicants. After a time, one of the men got up, walked over to the door to the inner office, and went in, unsought and unannounced. The others were upset that he had been so forward, and they assumed he had made a mistake.

In a few minutes the office manager came out, along with the brash young man who had just walked in. He told the other applicants the job had been filled. They began to grumble, and they said to the manager, "He was the last of us to come in to apply, and yet you have given him the position. It isn't fair!"

The telegraph manager said in response, "I'm sorry you feel that way. But all the while you were sitting here, a message in Morse code was going out over the telegraph: 'If you understand this message, then come right in. The job is yours.' None of you heard it. This man did. The job is his."

Grace is always there. It is always being offered. It will always be offered to all of us. But in this life not all of us will accept the gift. Those who do not will not be cast out; they just won't know they are in until after they have left this world.

And that's a tragedy. Why should anyone reject grace, when it is always available to everyone?

William Stringfellow was an attorney-theologian whose writings touched many Christians for over a generation. He once said, "The most obstinate misconception of the gospel of Jesus Christ is that the gospel is welcome to this world. This conviction – endemic among church folk – persists that, if problems of misapprehension or misperception are overcome, and the gospel is heard on its own integrity, the gospel will be found attractive to people, become popular, and a success of some sort. The idea is curious and ironic because it is bluntly contradicted in scripture and in the experience of the continuing biblical witness in history."

How true that is! The Gospel is good news only to those who understand themselves to be bad news. Good people don't need unconditional love; only sinful people need it. And because most people consider themselves good, they choose not to respond to God's gracious invitation to live a new life in harmony with Him. They assume they are already in harmony with God.

"There is more joy in heaven over one sinner who repents than over ninety-nine righteous persons who need no repentance." But what if someone doesn't repent? Or what if they do repent, but still do not accept the Good News of the Gospel? To God, that does not ultimately matter. In the Parable of the Father and the Two Lost Sons, neither son overtly repented. That did not prevent the father from continuing to love each of his sons with an unconditional love. Only when the children recognize the costly nature of the Father's love can they wear the rich robe of kinship which God has prepared for them from before the foundation of the world. The Gospel can do its work for us solely when we realize that whatever we are doing for ourselves is not working. Thus, to say Yes to God requires saying No to ourselves. And that's hard.

Scripture – Romans 5:1-11

Text – But God demonstrates his love for us in that, while we were yet sinners, Christ died for us. – Romans 5:8 (NIV)

THE MISAPPROPRIATION OF THE CROSS

The cross of Jesus Christ is the central symbol of the Christian faith. In nearly every church everywhere in the world, there is either a cross outside, on the steeple or in some other prominent place, or inside, on the wall in back of the chancel, or above the altar, or on the communion table, or in another very visible location.

The most common form of religious jewelry for Christians is the cross. Not a dove, or a fish, or a flame: the cross. Crosses hang from chains around the necks of both males and females. They are used in earrings, and in these days, for both males and females. As tattoos have become more popular for both women and men, crosses have become a common choice in a tattoo. It may seem a bit barbaric to some, or even bizarre, but then, there's no accounting for taste, is there? Many Christian Bibles have a cross emblazoned on the cover or the spine of the book. Large crosses may be seen on hillsides along highways or roads, sometimes small crosses are placed along the roadside where there was a fatal accident. And of course there are literally millions of crosses in Christian cemeteries all around the world. Have you ever wondered how many soldiers would turn over in their graves were they to know that a cross had been placed above their decaying bodies? Or what about the family members of those soldiers: how do they feel in seeing a cross over their loved one's grave, especially if that person was an agnostic or atheist?

Each of the four Gospels devotes from 20 to 30% of its entire narrative about the life of Jesus to the events of Holy Week, and the reporting of the actual crucifixion takes up a considerable percentage of the Holy Week narrative.

For the apostle Paul, the crucifixion was by far the most important event in the life and ministry of Jesus of Nazareth. It became the very heart of his theological understanding of God's purposes in the world. It was the *summum bonum*, the highest good, in the great scheme of God for the salvation of the *cosmos*, the *mundus*. Paul perceived the resurrection of Jesus to be of utmost importance as well, but to Paul, the resurrection was the flip side of the crucifixion coin. In Paul's mind, it was pivotal that Jesus died on the cross, but He died in part so that He might be raised from the dead. Each event has meaning only in conjunction with the other. There could be no crucifixion in the fullest sense without the resurrection; there could be no resurrection in the fullest sense without a crucifixion.

In other words, Paul would argue that had Jesus simply died from a ruptured appendix or an aortal aneurism or a staphylococcus infection, His resurrection would have had far less meaning. Or had Jesus merely died on the cross, but had not been raised from death, Paul would insist the cross would never have carried the meaning it has had for Christians during the past twenty centuries. Both the crucifixion and the resurrection were central to Paul's interpretation of the life of Jesus, but it was first and foremost the cross which became the foundation of that interpretation.

In his first letter to the Corinthians, after some opening greetings, Paul launched headlong into his theology of the crucifixion. Apparently there were conflicting notions of what the cross actually meant among the Corinthians, and Paul was intent that they get it straight, which meant getting straight as he would interpret it for them. Further, they needed to get it straight from the horse's mouth, and he, Paul, was the only proper horse to deliver the message.

Paul was one of the most intelligent, wise, observant, and shrewd human beings who ever drew breath. He knew the stakes were exceedingly high in the arguments going on among the Corinthians, and he wanted to stake a claim to what he was convinced was the only correct way of understanding the crucifixion of Jesus. Paul clearly saw that things might get out of hand if he didn't give them what he was believed was the scoop, the whole scoop, and nothing but the scoop.

So, in the very the first chapter of the first letter Paul sent to the Corinthians (New Testament scholars deduce that he wrote not two but as many as four letters to the obstreperous Christians of Corinth), Paul wrote these words: "For Jews demand signs and Greeks seek wisdom, but we preach Christ crucified, a stumbling block to the Jews and folly to Gentiles, but to those who are called, both Jews and Greeks, Christ the power of God and the wisdom of God" (I Cor. 1:22-24).

There are pages and books of hidden scholarly meanings between the lines in those words, and all of it is important. Unfortunately, we don't have time to give it enough attention. Suffice it to say that Jews looked for direct signs from God, and Greeks looked for the wisdom of God. Both "signs" and "wisdom" were code words to describe two quite different cultures and approaches to religious truth. The *semeion* of God were observable historical happenings which were signs of what God was doing in the world. The parting of the waters of the Red Sea would be a really big sign (*semeion*), as would be God's presentation of the Ten Commandments on Mt. Sinai. The wisdom (*sophia*) of God, on the other hand, was more of a mental or intellectual exercise, and was not something people could readily see. By His wisdom God imparted truth to people through a direct spiritual means, but only those who received this wisdom could fully benefit from it. Wisdom did not come from **seeing** things happen; it came from **feeling** things happen within. Signs were external; wisdom was internal. Signs were historical; wisdom was supra-historical, or perhaps extra-historical.

All that having been said, let us return to what Paul said to the Corinthians. And what he said was, "Jews demand signs and Greeks seek wisdom, but **we**" (which really means **I**; preachers do that all the time; you have to keep your eye on them) "preach Christ crucified, a stumbling block" (*skandalon*) "to Jews and folly to Greeks." Most Jews don't get it, said Paul, and most

Greeks don't get it, but those who **do** get it, either Jews or Greeks, are people who know what *I* know, said Paul, namely, that the cross is the central event in an understanding of God's plan of salvation for the world.

The crucifixion as a "stumbling block" is truly a *skandalon* (scandal) to many people, both inside and outside the Christian religion. It is the undoing of Christianity for millions upon millions of people. If the cross as it has been widely proclaimed has to be accepted for anyone to be a proper Christian, these folks say, then I want no part of it.

So, in what ways has traditional or orthodox or mainstream Christianity understood the cross? From the earliest days of Christianity, many Christians have associated the crucifixion with the concept of **atonement**. The word atonement connotes a proper reparation which is made to take away an offense or injury. The concept arose in the religion of the early Hebrews, although it did not originate with them. On *Yom Kippur,* the Day of Atonement, a scapegoat was driven out into the wilderness. Symbolically the scapegoat took the sin of the people with it, and their offenses were covered over or carried away or taken care of. Atonement cannot eradicate or obliterate sins, because they happened. But atonement can pay the price of the sins; it can assume the punishment; it can, to use American slang, "take the rap."

On the cross, Christian tradition says, Jesus **atoned** for the sins of the world. But in what way did He atone, the Church through the ages has asked itself. Was it an *expiationary* **atonement**, or a *substitutionary* **atonement**? "Expiation" means "to make appeasement." Thus, this idea proposes that Jesus appeased God's anger toward our sins by dying on the cross. His death was sufficient appeasement in itself to take away God's wrath over the sins of everyone who ever lived. No, no, said (and say) other Christians, Jesus' atonement on the cross was a **substitute** for our own atonement. He died **in our place**. His death was therefore a **vicarious** (i.e., an "in the place of") death. We should have been crucified ourselves for our own sins, each of us, but Jesus was crucified in our place.

Now look, unless you had the distinct pleasure of being subjected to all these dandy theological nuances in a seminary somewhere, and you somehow managed to live to tell it, you probably are not doing intellectual back flips because of your excitement to cogitate upon all this wonderful stuff. But these questions are foundational to how we should or could or might or may understand the meaning of the cross. So, dear heart, carefully read on. Together, we're headed somewhere, I hope.

Let me brutally candid. I don't believe Jesus atoned for anything on the cross. He did not appease God's anger by dying there, and He certainly did not take our place by dying there. God doesn't need to be appeased! What a primitive notion that is! Besides, what good would it do us if you or I died on a cross? Would God want it? I hope not! Would He demand it? Most assuredly not! Even if our sins are sufficiently horrendous as to warrant our being nailed to two cross beams of wood, God is not the kind of despotic deity who would demand such a punishment! And if He is, then we should want no part of Him! We should demit from God, if that's the sort of God He is!

But then, what **does** the crucifixion represent? For what reasons **was** Jesus crucified?

Here, I think the Jesus Seminar scholars are right on target. Probably it is instructive, if also unproductive, to debate, and much less to vote, on what sayings and events in the four Gospels are historically accurate. Only the most rigid would insist that everything happened exactly as it is written, because there are numerous inconsistencies and contradictions. No doubt most of what Jesus said or did failed to make it into any of the Gospels, and much that did make it didn't happen and wasn't said. However, a majority vote cannot authenticate what Jesus said or did, either. It is a fascinating scholarly exercise, but there's something flawed in the very democratic process of it all.

Nonetheless, the Jesus scholars are surely correct when they insist that Jesus died on the cross primarily for historical reasons, and not for theological or Christological or fundamentally suprahistorical reasons. Jesus died because He attacked too many sacred cows and fought too many philosophical, theological, and religious battles, and He deliberately acquired far too many political and religious enemies.

The purpose of this sermon is not to address whether it was the Romans or the Jews who killed Jesus. Historically, it was neither, at least not collectively. Nor did **we** crucify Jesus, you and I ("'Twas I, Lord Jesus, I it was denied Thee; I crucified Thee"). **A few** Jews and **a few** Romans, Pilate in particular, conspired to crucify the Nazarene, but that is history, and into that particular history we shall not here go.

Then does the cross have meaning at all? Without question it is the central symbol of Christianity, as I said in the introduction, but **should** it be? **Ought** the cross be at the heart of our concept of who Jesus was and is, and what Christianity has been and is?

For seventeen years I was the pastor of the First Presbyterian Church of Hilton Head Island, South Carolina. It was the last of four permanent pastorates in which I served. A year before I left the Hilton Head pastorate, I preached a sermon called *The Cross: The Demonstration of GOD'S Salvation*. I said at the time that I thought it was the most important sermon I ever preached. I also preached it in three out of the four interim pastorates in which I was engaged. I didn't preach it in the first of those congregations, because I knew too many of those truly fine folks were too conservative even to listen to it. Discretion is the better of valor, and all that.

This sermon is a longer and, I hope, more reasoned copy of **that** sermon. I don't mean the other one wasn't "reasoned;" I mean it was just less "thoughty." than this one.

The morning after I preached *The Cross: The Demonstration of GOD'S Salvation*, the three associate ministers stormed into my office. Well, one stormed; two just stepped. The one, who had just accepted a call to another congregation as their pastor, said that were he not leaving, he would have brought me up on heresy charges before the presbytery (the key governing body in the Presbyterian Church), and intimated he would like to see me defrocked. The other associates took different approaches. One wondered why on earth I ever preached such a sermon (a good question), and the other simply wondered whether it had been a good idea to do it, even though she was neither surprised nor upset by it.

After considerable spirited, committed, and heated discussion, one of the associate parsons opined that fortunately, probably only 10% of the congregation really understood the sermon, but loved it, another 10% understood it, and hated it, and 80% didn't really understand it. No, said another associate (not the one who wanted me chucked out), 5% understood it and loved it, 5% understood it and hated it, and 90% didn't really understand it. In retrospect, those guesstimates may well have been accurate reflections of reality.

What I said there, and what I am saying here, is very clearly unorthodox. Whether it is truly heretical is something which presumably can officially be decided only by a presbytery of the Presbyterian Church (USA). If anybody wants to challenge a retired geezer, this retired geezer is willing to be so challenged. I am not sure I would welcome the opportunity, but I certainly would not shrink from it either. Retired clergy are sometimes pretty pathetic, but when I was still officially in harness, I would not have avoided the theological confrontation which that sermon, as well as this, illustrated.

What I said then included statements such as these: Jesus does not save us; God saves us. The cross does not save us; God alone can save us. But the cross is the quintessential demonstration of God's salvation. Because Jesus ended up on a cross, we can see that we have **already** been saved. Further, our being saved does not require us to believe in God or Jesus or the cross; we are all saved by God regardless of what we do or do not believe or do or think.

But let us come back to the apostle Paul. Paul got it right in Romans, but he got it wrong in I Corinthians. Christian preachers should never preach the cross as the central feature of the Gospel of Jesus Christ, because the cross simply is not the core of the Gospel. "Preaching Christ crucified" may have led many people to believe that they were saved, but they were saved long before they heard the cross preached. And it wasn't – and isn't – the cross which saves them; it is **God** who saves them. Once again, in this matter the Jesus Seminar folks are right. Jesus never taught that He (Jesus) was the Savior. Instead, the genuine Jesus, the historical Jesus, the Jesus sadly lost in the mists of antiquity, taught that **God** is our Savior. He proclaimed the kingdom of **God**, not the kingdom of **Jesus**. **God** was the message; Jesus saw Himself as being merely the **messenger**.

In that regard, Christians are absolutely correct is claiming that Jesus is the Messiah, the Christ, the Anointed One of God. Jesus is not God; He is not the Second Person of the Trinity; He is not Yahweh Incarnate. There is no Trinity, really. There is only God. The idea of the Trinity was a third, fourth and fifth century attempt of the early Christians to put distance between themselves and the Jews, and to come up with a novel concept for Gentiles to buy into. Historically, it worked, but theologically, it's a mess. What does it **mean**, to say that God is One-in-Three and Three-in-One? People believe in the Trinity because they know they are supposed to believe in the Trinity. For sixteen centuries the Church has insisted on it. But the Arians and the Unitarians are right. The doctrine of the Trinity is an idea without substance, a concept without merit, and an equation without genuine theological, biblical, or mathematical usefulness.

S. Mark Heim teaches at Andover Newton Theological School. He wrote two very carefully constructed essays about the crucifixion for *Christian Century* a couple of years ago (March 7 and 14, 2001). The first was called "Christ crucified," which had the subtitle "Why does Jesus' death matter?", and the second was "Visible victim: Christ's death to end sacrifice."

Dr. Heim refers to the Trinitarian doctrine which is implicit in the traditional Christian understanding of the cross, but he reminds us of a central problem in it that was clearly seen by the German theologian Jurgen Moltmann. "Trinitarian theology which attempts to explicate the Christian conviction that it is God who suffers and is punished can only further the confusion at times – now it is the Father who insists on the blood and the Son

159

who sheds it." Then Prof. Heim further describes the dilemma so thoroughly described by Moltmann in *The Crucified God*: "The sacrifice is not directed to God: it takes place within God. There is no difference in will between the Father and the Son; both act out of passion for human redemption. And there is no difference in suffering. Both suffer, only they do so in different dimensions of the same event...."

Early Christians, and indeed millions of Christians today, believe that Jesus of Nazareth was the Incarnation of God. And if that is so, they reason, then Jesus is the Second Person of the Trinity, because Jesus is God, or perhaps more precisely, God is Jesus. Therefore, in dying on the cross, God died, at least in some sense. So, it is not only **Jesus** (the Son) who dies on the cross; it is also **God** (the Father).

But hold on here! What do these words *mean*? Does God Himself become the substitute for our atonement? Is it necessary that either God or Jesus die in order for us to be saved?

Mark Heim describes the notion of the substitutionary atonement as follows: "That doctrine, substitutionary atonement, can be summarized this way: We are guilty of sin against God and our neighbors. The continuing sins themselves, the root desires that prompt them, and the guilt we bear for making such brutal response to God's good gifts – all these together separate us from God and are far beyond my human power to mend.... Thus a gap, a price, remains to be reckoned with. Christ stands in this gap, pays the price, bearing the punishment we deserve and he does not. In so doing, Christ offers something on our behalf that could never be expected or required. Christ offers the 'over and above' gift that clears the slate and brings sinners into reconciled relation with God."

Do you find all that difficult intellectually to follow? I do! In my formative years, and in my first years in the ministry, I accepted all of it, because I knew that is what was expected of me. But I never understood it. Later, when I tried to understand it, I couldn't, because it didn't make sense. And it still doesn't make sense. In his article "Visible victim," Mark Heim claims that by means of the cross, Jesus shows that never again shall

160

there be a need for a substitutionary atonement. Never again shall anyone require a scapegoat in order to be granted atonement. In fact, says Heim, scapegoating itself is a sin.

Each of these theological terms, individually examined, is comprehensible. It is when they are all strung together, with the intention of proclaiming or defending enormous life-altering theological claims, that they become cerebral mush, at least for me. I confess that I just don't get it.

I am convinced that neither God nor Jesus conceived the crucifixion from before the foundation of the world, despite what Paul, the early Church, and the creeds proclaim. The crucifixion happened; of that I have no doubt. But, as I stated earlier, it happened for **historical**, not for **theological** or **Christological**, reasons. Jesus could have avoided the cross, as He Himself indicated, both in Gethsemane and at Golgotha. And surely God did not insist that Jesus had to be crucified in order for His life to achieve its deepest meaning.

Nonetheless, by means of the cross we are shown that God has *already* saved us! Because Jesus understood the divine nature more fully than anyone else who ever lived, He knew that God did not require any kind of sacrifice in order for anyone ever to be saved. All of us are saved, simply because we are children of God, and God wills that all should be saved and come to a knowledge of the truth. But Jesus also knew that many of us are permanently convinced that sacrifice is a necessity, and therefore He reluctantly accepted what appeared to be a sacrificial death. By it He illustrated the reality of His very name, *Yeshua*, which means, **God Saves**. But it is **God** who saves us, not **Jesus**. The death of Jesus shows that we are saved, but in itself it does not save us.

Normally I prefer the Revised Standard Version of the Bible, or, if my arm is sufficiently twisted, the New Revised Standard Version. The New International Version is not my biblical cup of tea. However, in the text for this sermon, I think the NIV has it exactly right: "But God demonstrates his love for us in that, while we were yet sinners, Christ died for us." God didn't just **show** His love for us, as it says in the RSV, and He certainly didn't **prove** His love for us, as the NRSV says, because not even God can **prove** that. But God does **demonstrate** His love for us through the crucifixion of Jesus. In Christ, as in no one else, God was reconciling the world to Himself. Paul was so wonderfully and powerfully correct in that declaration, and the cross of Christ is the most compelling demonstration of that inexpressible truth. When we see a cross, anywhere and under any circumstances, we are reminded of **THE Cross**, the cross of Jesus.

It was God who was doing the demonstrating via the cross, not Jesus, although it certainly seems as though Jesus was illustrating whatever was being illustrated. And whether we do or do not believe in "the atonement," or in any particular theory of the atonement, and whether we do or do not believe that it is the death of Jesus which saves us, the cross demonstrates that we all were saved, and are saved, and shall be saved, because that is God's will for all of us. God loves us like **that,** to the death, as it were. And that means God's death, if such a thing were possible, or Christ's death, or our own death.

James Denney was one of the greatest preachers of yesteryear in the Church of Scotland. In his time the Scottish Church was regrettably quite anti-Catholic. But as he journeyed about the Lowlands and the Highlands, he frequently employed the most common symbol of Roman Catholicism to make his point about the nature and depth of God's love for all of His children. Steadily building up toward the climax of his sermon, James Denney would finally arrive at his most dramatic moment. Reaching down onto the shelf of the pulpit, which the congregation could not see, the Scots pulpiteer without peer would pick up a crucifix, lift it high above his head, and proclaim, "God loves us - - - like **that!**"

What a tremendous way to demonstrate that truth! And what a tremendous truth that is! The cross illustrates God's salvation, it shows God's salvation, it demonstrates God's salvation, but it is the cross **of Jesus** which provides the demonstration! Jesus knew fully what we can only know in part, that God loves us to

162

the greatest degree possible, and that because that is true, God has already provided for our salvation! Since God Himself could not die on a cross, He used the willingness of Jesus to be crucified to demonstrate God's intentions!

All of that notwithstanding, it seems to me the cross is misappropriated when anyone insists that it must absolutely become the central and primary symbol of Christianity. As good as Good Friday ultimately was and is, and as tragic as the cross was and is, surely it is the teachings of Jesus about God, more than the death of Jesus, which convince and convict us of God's love for us. We know who God **is** because we know who Jesus **was**. To hear the echoes of the historical Jesus is to perceive the voice of the eternal God. It isn't that Jesus was God or is God, but rather that He knew God as none of us can know God. In seeing what Jesus saw, we see God as completely as is humanly possible.

I fully realize that what I have attempted to say here is not traditional, and that its thesis would be rejected by most Christians. My primary purpose in saying it, however, is to give encouragement to those Christians who are unable to understand or accept the orthodox position of Christianity with respect to the cross. The cross ended the life of Jesus, but it is not required of us that we believe it gives birth to new life — or to eternal life — for us. God wants for us to have new birth with or without the cross, and He will grant us eternal life, again with or without the cross.

God Himself cannot die for us, because God cannot die and continue to be God. But God allowed Jesus to die on the cross, just as He allows all of us to die in whatever manner it is by which we shall die. If the cross is more effective than anything else in demonstrating God's love to us, then long live the proclamation of the cross. But even more important than **that** proclamation is **The** Proclamation, which is the love of God and the kingdom of God. Long, long live Jesus. Even more so, long, long, **long** live God.

Scripture – John 10:22-30

Text – "I and the Father are one."

DO WE DEMAND TOO MUCH OF JESUS?

Jesus of Nazareth is the centerpiece of the Christian religion. He is the *summum bonum*, the highest good. It is He who gives us our faith. He is our Savior and our Lord. Without Him, we would dwell in a land of deep darkness. He is the light of the world, the bread of life, the good shepherd, the Alpha and the Omega. As the Gospel hymn says, "Jesus is all the world to me."

But is He? Is He? Is **Jesus** the centerpiece of Christianity, and the highest good, and the Savior and Lord, or are those more accurately descriptions of **God**? Or, are God and Jesus one and the same? When we think about Jesus, do we expect Him to do everything we expect God to do? Normally we would never ask such questions, but let us ask them now, because in formulating our answers, we may discover whether we demand too much of Jesus.

What do we want Jesus to be? Who do we think He was in His own time? Who is He in our time? Did Jesus call us primarily into a relationship with Jesus, or did He come primarily to call us into a relationship with God?

For twenty centuries, the Christian Church has answered those questions in a wide variety of ways. We might suppose this issue is clear, but it is far from being clearly explained or clearly understood. Whatever you want Jesus to be, you can find support for that in the Gospels and in the rest of the New Testament. Whatever you don't want Him to be, you also can find in the Gospels and New Testament.

We **suppose** that the Church has spoken with one voice on these matters, we **imagine** it has done so, we **deliberately believe** the Church is unequivocal in establishing one "party line" about Jesus, but that is simply not the case. There are Christians who have perceived Jesus as the be-all, end-all of faith and the single

164

indispensable feature of orthodox religion. There are other Christians who see Jesus as a great moral teacher and guide, but they do not believe that He is divine, and they seriously doubt that He was raised from the dead. There are other Christians who hold positions on Jesus somewhere between those two extremes.

If we are to be genuine Christians, what **ought** we to demand of Jesus? Are there specific criteria which authenticate Him as Messiah, Savior, and Lord?

The Gospels themselves do not speak with one voice about that. If personally we have a clear understanding of who Jesus is, we can pick and choose certain passages to authenticate our choice. But there are other passages which may paint a picture quite different from the portrait of **our** Jesus.

The common tradition is that Jesus was without sin. The letter to the Hebrews expresses it this way: "For we have not a high priest who is unable to sympathize with our weaknesses, but one who in every respect has been tempted as we are, **yet without sinning**" (Hebrews 4:15). Through the centuries the Church has insisted that Jesus never sinned, not even once. But Jesus Himself did not seem to support that notion. According to Mark and Luke, a would-be disciple said to Jesus, "Good teacher, what must I do to inherit eternal life?" In response, Jesus said to him, "Why do you call me good? No one is good but God alone" (Mark 10:17ff., Luke 18:18ff.). Should we demand perfection of Jesus? In this episode Jesus appears not to demand it of Himself.

An ancient tradition declares that Jesus is to be our judge at the end of our lives. The Apostles Creed states of Jesus that "He ascended into heaven, and sitteth on the right hand of God. From thence He shall come to judge the quick and the dead." There is widespread support for that idea in the Gospels and elsewhere in the New Testament. However, there are other biblical passages which seem to undercut that notion. The Fourth Gospel in general has the highest Christology for Jesus, but even it has Jesus say the following: "If anyone hears my sayings and does not keep them, I do not judge him; for I did not come to judge the world, but to save the world" (John 12:47).

The real question is this: shall it be **God** or **Jesus** who will judge us in the end? In the Hebrew scriptures (the Old Testament), always it is God who is the judge. In the Greek scriptures (the New Testament), sometimes it is claimed that God shall be our judge, and sometimes Jesus. In Matthew's account of the Last Judgment, clearly it is Jesus who shall be the judge (see Mt. 25:31ff.). So which is it? How do we want it to be? Does it matter?

The disciples James and John, who were brothers, came to Jesus and tried to twist His arm to allow them to sit at His right and left hand when Jesus came in His glory. Jesus told them, "The cup that I drink you will drink; and with the baptism with which I am baptized you will be baptized; but to sit at my right hand or at my left is not mine to grant, but it is for those for whom it has been prepared" (Mark 10:35ff.). I infer from those words that Jesus did not feel He would be the judge of this matter, that instead, God would be the judge.

Do you want Jesus to decide your eternal destiny? If so, how would you feel if He refused, and turned that task over to God? Would you accept God as your judge?

Christian tradition teaches that Jesus is both fully human and fully divine. That concept is fraught with enormous intellectual difficulties. If Jesus was human, He could not know everything, but if He was divine, He **had** to know everything, because God knows everything. Our word for "all-knowing" is "omniscient." A couple of days before Good Friday, four of the disciples asked Jesus when the end of the world was coming. Jesus answered, "Of that day or that hour no one knows, not even the angels in heaven, nor the Son, but only the Father" (Mark 13:32). Thus on at least one question, the precise time when the world would end, Jesus pleaded ignorance. Does that diminish the claim about Jesus' divinity? Or, if Jesus is to be the Messiah, do you demand that He also be divine?

There is some ambivalence in the Gospels over whether Jesus even perceived Himself to be the Messiah. In some passages He definitely states He is, but in others He sidesteps the issue. When Jesus instructs the disciples to procure a particular upper room for Him and the disciples in which to celebrate the Passover seder, He says they should say to the owner of the building that "the Teacher" has need of it (Mk. 14:14). Here Jesus sees Himself as a rabbi, and not even as the Messiah, even though during the Last Supper there were unmistakable messianic overtones. So another question is asked of us: are we willing to accept Jesus as a mere rabbi, or do we insist that He must be more than that?

In the Garden of Gethsemane, just before His arrest, Jesus prayed the famous prayer, "Father, if it be possible, let this cup pass from me; nevertheless, not as I will, but as thou wilt" (Mt. 26ff., Mk. 14:32ff., Lk. 22:40ff.). Here Jesus very clearly distinguishes between Himself and God. Do we want both a human and divine Jesus? If so, did —— or does —— such a Jesus exist?

In the synoptic Gospels, the "cleansing of the temple" occurs either on Palm Sunday or the day afterward. In John, however, it occurs very early in the ministry of Jesus (Jn. 2:13ff.). In the synoptics, Jesus quotes Isaiah (56:7), where it says, "My house shall be a house of prayer." In John, however, Jesus says to the moneychangers with their tables, "Take these things away; you shall not make my Father's house a house of trade." It is very curious: the Gospels with the lower Christology (the synoptics) have Jesus saying, "**My** house shall be a house of prayer" (although it is a quote from Isaiah), and the Gospel with the higher Christology, John, has Jesus say, "You shall not make my **Father's** house a house of trade." What did the Gospel writers demand of Jesus? Did they want Him to be God Incarnate, God in-the-flesh, or did they want Him to be God's unique servant, but not God Himself? Is it surprising that we can't be consistent in what we demand of Jesus if the Gospel writers themselves lacked consistency?

The traditional Christian doctrine of the Trinity is perhaps the most problematic of all Christian beliefs. The third of the three "Persons" of the Trinity is the Holy Spirit. The Old Testament on fairly rare occasions refers to "the spirit of God," and three times it uses the actual term "holy spirit." Twice it is "holy **Spirit**"

167

(Psalm 51:11 and Isaiah 63:11), and once it is "holy spirit" (Isa. 63:10). However, there are many references to the Holy Spirit (both words capitalized) in the New Testament, including quite a number by Jesus Himself. But it is evident from one of those references that Jesus does not equate Himself with the holy spirit (or Holy Spirit), and thus, presumably, He does not equate Himself with God ("the Father") either. Jesus says, "Whoever says a word against the Son of man will be forgiven; but whoever speaks a word against the Holy Spirit will not be forgiven, either in this age or the age to come" (Mt. 12:32).

In fairness to the traditional understanding of the Trinity, it was always insisted that "the Father is not the Son, the Son is not the Holy Spirit, and the Holy Spirit is not the Father." But each "Person" is nonetheless "God," according to orthodox Trinitarian teaching. My point in using this particular passage is to suggest that Jesus apparently considered Himself "lower" than the Holy Spirit, when He said that any sin against Jesus could be forgiven, but no sin against the Holy Spirit would be forgiven. Once again, do we demand that Jesus be God, or not? In some Gospel episodes, Jesus equated Himself with God, and in others He did not. For us, which shall it be?

Another ancient belief in the Church is that Jesus is the Son of God. Indeed, in the Fourth Gospel Jesus occasionally refers to Himself as such. But **never** in the synoptics does He call Himself that. **Others**, including the devil, call Jesus God's Son, but **Jesus** never makes that claim. Should we make it on His behalf? Does our faith demand that Jesus be the Son of God? Scripture gives warrant for such a belief. It also gives warrant for questioning such a belief.

Is Jesus "the Lord?" The disciples and others often called Him "Lord." There also are a number of instances where Jesus called Himself "Lord." But others gave Jesus that honorific title far more frequently than Jesus applied it to Himself. When Jesus called Himself "Lord," or when He allowed others to call Him "Lord," what did He mean by the use of that term? Did He mean "God?" Is Jesus "the Lord" in exactly the same way that God is "the Lord?"

I find it curious, and bordering on bizarre, that many Christians now seem to use the word Lord **only** in conjunction with Jesus. **God** is not the Lord to them; Jesus **alone** is the Lord. How could that happen? By what linguistic detour did God stop being "the Lord" and Jesus became "the Lord"?

When you go to church, or when you hear someone on the radio or television referring to "the Lord," does the context in which the word is used clarify whether the speaker is talking about Jesus or about God? In my opinion, we should use the word **Lord** to refer **only** to God, unless we use the two-word expression "**Lord Jesus**." To say "Lord" when we mean Jesus unintentionally diminishes God, because **God** was "*the* Lord" or "Lord" long before Jesus was Lord. Perhaps we can now see how our very use of words may demand more of Jesus and less of God than the use of words should allow.

What do **you** usually mean when you say "Lord?" Do you mean God, or do you mean Jesus? If you mean both, does the context in your use of the word clearly suggest which you mean? If you are not sure whether you mean God or Jesus, then are you certain in your own mind who God is and who Jesus is? In the very language you choose to use, what do you demand of Jesus?

Think about the meaning of the following passage from Matthew. It is set during the original Holy Week, and Jesus is grieving because Jerusalem has not recognized Him or the purpose for which He was sent into the world. Jesus says, "O Jerusalem, Jerusalem, killing the prophets and stoning those who are sent to you! How often would I have gathered your children together as a hen gathers her brood under her wings, and you would not! Behold, your house is forsaken and desolate. For I tell you, you will not see me again until you say, 'Blessed is he who comes in the name of the Lord'" (Mt. 23:37-39).

It should be obvious to everyone that here, Jesus sees Himself as being the one who "comes in the name of the Lord," but He is **not** Himself "the Lord." It appears proper to call Jesus "the Lord Jesus" if it means "the Master, Jesus," but not if it means "the God Jesus" or "the God, Jesus." Jesus **IS NOT** God;

He isn't; and it is Christian excess, it is **un-Christian**, to insist that Jesus **is** God! And yet for two millennia the Church has insisted exactly that, and even with increasing frequency!

The so-called "cry of dereliction" indicates beyond dispute that Jesus neither was God nor perceived Himself to be God. As Jesus was dying on the cross, impaled there by cruel spikes driven through His wrists and feet, Jesus said, "My God, my God, why hast Thou forsaken me?" It is true that, as has been oft-noted, that verse originated as the opening verse of Psalm 22, and it was probably accurate, as many New Testament scholars have suggested, that Jesus was reciting scriptural passages as He hung upon the cross. But regardless of the actual historical circumstances in which these words were uttered, they transparently imply that Jesus the man was crying out to the God whom He called Father, genuinely feeling that God had abandoned Him. Never was the distinction between Jesus and God more painfully obvious than it was at Golgotha.

Jesus prayed to **God**; He did not pray to **Himself**! On the cross, He cried out to **God**; He did not cry out to **Himself**! As He desperately gasped for His last labored breaths, He quite understandably felt forsaken by God, as would any of us in those same terrible circumstances!

And yet we often require of Jesus that He be God, because we fear that if He isn't, He can't be the Messiah, nor can He be the Lord. But He **is** the Messiah! He **is** Jesus **Christ**! He **is** the **Lord** Jesus; He **is** Jesus the **Lord**! He's just not God. He never was, and never will be. Some of the biblical writers claimed He was, and the Church has almost always insisted He was, and is, but He wasn't. And isn't.

"O magnify the Lord with me, and let us exalt his name together!" Who is "the Lord" whom we are invited to magnify, and who is the one whose "name" we are asked to exalt together? Millions of Christians, on hearing this, think automatically of Jesus. But the verse comes from a Psalm, Psalm 34 (v.3), and the Psalm was composed perhaps a thousand years before the time of Jesus. **The Lord** is **God**, and God's **name** is **Yahweh**; it is not **Jesus**.

Why, you may ask, do I keep going on like this? Why do I make such a huge fuss about this? I do it because I am certain the Church has made huge fuss of this in the wrong direction! I do it because Christianity as it has evolved has done a great disservice, both to God and to Jesus! The Church does not sufficiently magnify or exalt God, and it magnifies and exalts Jesus too much! It nudges God out of the picture too often, and it thrusts Jesus into the picture too much!

Jesus Himself did not do that. To Jesus, God was the *summum bonum*, the highest and the only Truly Good One. To many of the followers of Jesus, Jesus became the *summum bonum*. In effect, God became an also-ran. Without question, no one intended that. Nonetheless, that has been the result.

Please understand: if you insist on the divinity of Jesus, or if you perceive Him to be "the Lord" —- period, end of story —-, you are in good company. Countless Christians through twenty centuries of Church history agree with you. It's just that I am convinced the historical Jesus would not agree with you, nor do I, (although nobody needs to be concerned about the latter!).

However, I do want you to ruminate on what your position, whatever it is, ultimately means. And I want to try to provide a context for your ruminations by highlighting another Holy Week episode.

One Easter several years ago, I said in a sermon that Jesus did not **rise** from the dead, that instead He **was raised** from the dead. Very few people picked up on that distinction, but of those who did, they were about equally divided in being strongly opposed or strongly favorable to the idea. Scripturally, one is on far safer ground to say that Jesus rose from the dead than to say He was raised from the dead. Matthew, for example, has the angel say about Jesus to the women at the empty tomb that "he has risen" (28:6). Mark uses exactly the same words (16:6). Luke carries through the same idea, when he has the angels (two, not one, but no matter) remind the women that Jesus had said he would be crucified, "and on the third day **rise**" (Lk. 24:7). In John, the incredulous disciples couldn't imagine what had happened to Jesus' body when they arrived at the empty tomb, because, says John, "as yet they not know the scripture, that he **must rise** from the dead" (Jn. 20:9).

The Apostles Creed further solidifies this particular way of understanding the resurrection. "He descended into hell. The third day **He rose** again from the dead, He ascended into heaven" etc., etc.

So if all four Gospels say that Jesus **rose** from the dead (active verb), and the early Church said it as well, then why do I insist that Jesus **was raised** from the dead (passive verb)? I insist on it, I **demand** it (to the degree I can, which I really can't), because **that is what Jesus Himself demanded** we should understand. Remember the Caesarea Philippi incident? Jesus very clearly told the disciples that "he must go to Jerusalem and suffer many things from the elders and chief priests and scribes, and be killed, and on the third day **BE RAISED**" (obviously my bold-faced tampering with the text —- Mt. 16:21). Jesus did not say He would rise from the tomb; He said he would be raised! It is a critical difference, a major distinction, a **crucial** (i.e., literally "at the cross") issue.

Jesus did not raise Himself from death; God raised Him! The crucified Jesus could not produce a resurrected Jesus; only God could do that! People who die cannot raise themselves, and that includes Jesus of Nazareth! Only God can raise the dead, and Jesus is not God, not really! (Or might I already have said that?)

Look, although I realize three pages back I began to sound like a broken record, and my insistence on this matter may long since have become what appears to be no more than an infuriating quibble, I consider it to be anything but a quibble. And wherever you stand on this matter, you should not see it as a quibble either. From my perspective, and I hope yours as well, it is at the heart of what is, and what ought to be, believed. Fundamentally, this issue is not really a question of either/or, that either the one side is correct or the other side is correct. It is rather that the Church is careless in the use of critical terminology, including the very books of scripture to which the Church gave its early blessing. Both sides can demand anything they want of

Jesus, and they can find plenty of support for their position. Further, the side which demands a great deal of Jesus has a great deal more support for its stance than does the side which wants much less demanded of Jesus.

Nevertheless, I somehow have engendered sufficient chutzpah to say that the majority side became far too sloppy in its terminology about Jesus. It is too Christocentric, too Christ-centered. It is not sufficiently theocentric; it is not nearly enough God-centered.

Currently there is a major debate going on in the Presbyterian Church (USA), the denomination with which I have been affiliated my whole life. The issue is complex and multi-faceted, but boiled down, it comes to this: some of the liberals in the denomination have implied or courageously stated that untold millions of people have been and are being saved outside "a saving knowledge of Jesus Christ." Nobody needs my vote on this issue, but I vote with the liberals. Some of the conservatives, on the other hand, are insisting, as has the Church insisted for the most part through most of its history, that salvation is possible through Jesus Christ alone.

In the typical waffling way our historic American denomination has adopted in the Christological wars of the past few decades, the 213th General Assembly of the Presbyterian Church (USA) made a statement it hoped would placate both sides in this ongoing brouhaha. I shall quote from the statement, asking pertinent questions as we go along.

"We confess the unique authority of Jesus Christ as Lord." I can accept that, provided more clarity is given to the words "confess," "unique," "authority," and "Lord." As it is, I can only guess the nature of the exceedingly fine line the drafters of this statement were trying to dance along. But if those words are clearly explicated, and I agree with the explication, then I can agree with that whole statement. I shall not hold my breath for that eventuality, however.

"Every other authority is finally subject to Christ." That statement is borderline heresy, if not over the border. Does it mean that **the authority of God** is also subject to the authority of

173

Christ? If that's what it means, then I could not disagree more strongly, and I hope you will join me in my strong disagreement. If it means that God and Christ are one and the same, then I would say such fuzzy wording is utterly unhelpful, and ultimately hopelessly confusing.

"Jesus Christ is also uniquely Savior." If Jesus is uniquely Savior, meaning Savior **alone**, then is God **not** our Savior? And if it is demanded of us that we accept that orthographic construct, I for one demur; I recant; I object. Only **God** can save us. Over the centuries God has chosen to save many millions of us **through** Jesus Christ, but it was **God** who saved us, not **Jesus**. Furthermore, God saves far more of His children **apart from** Jesus than **by means of** Jesus. Throughout history, far more people have not heard of Jesus than have heard of Him, and therefore anyone who hasn't heard of Jesus and yet has been saved (and that's everybody, says I, but say relatively few other Christians), has been saved specifically by God apart from Jesus. Even those who have been saved through Jesus have been saved **by God through Jesus**, and not through Jesus apart from God. Apart from God, who is Jesus, anyway, for heaven's sake? I realize what I am saying here will drive Christian conservatives into a frenzy. But hey, what they say drives me into a frenzy too. Must Christian frenzies go only one direction?

"Although we do not know the limits of God's grace and pray for the salvation of those who may never come to know Christ, for us the assurance of salvation is found in confessing Christ and trusting in Him alone. We are humbled in our witness to Christ by our realization that our understanding of Him and His way is limited and distorted by sin. Still the transforming power of Christ in our lives compels us to make Christ known to others." I have reservations about saying that that exact way, and I vociferously object to the word "alone," but in essence, I agree with what I perceive to be the meaning of those words.

Christianity would be better served, and would be better received, if Christians always tried to say what they mean, and mean what they say. We are far too careless in our proclamations

174

of what we believe to be truth. I realize that everything we say is subject to misinterpretation or reinterpretation or deliberate mis-representation. Nonetheless, we must try to exercise more care when we attempt to present what we believe is the essence of the Christian faith.

Let me conclude this particular sermonic harangue with what I hope shall be some helpful suggestions.

1. Beware of making any categorical statements about Jesus, such as that He alone is the Savior or that He and the Father are one or that He is, *ipso facto*, God Incarnate.
2. If you feel you must make any categorical statements about anything (which probably is not too wise, even though we all do it), make them about God, not Jesus.
3. When you attempt to elevate Jesus by means of any statement you make about Him, might that statement unintentionally diminish the role or reality of God in your life, or the life of anyone else? If so, I suggest you avoid making the statement. Both God and Jesus will be greatly pleased.
4. Elevate Jesus in your mind and heart, if He is not already elevated in either sector of your being. Jesus of Nazareth is the clearest describer of the nature of God and the kingdom of God who has ever lived, and no one ever got into trouble by studying Jesus too closely or for too long a time.
5. That having been said, we nonetheless are more likely to be disappointed if we demand too much of Jesus than if we demand too little of Him. Those who demand too much tend to focus too much on Jesus and too little on God. Such a focus lowers the ability of their minds to expand beyond themselves and human history to that realm where God alone dwells. To use terminology which J.B. Phillips most certainly did not use but which may nonetheless apply, if their God is solely Jesus, their God is too small.

Because I am such a congenital contrarian, I look to the most Christocentric of all biblical writers to end this plaintive plea.

175

That, of course, is the apostle Paul. In his second letter to the Corinthians (which the scholars would say is actually his third or maybe fourth letter, but no matter), Paul said, "All this is from God, who through Christ reconciled us to himself, and gave us the message of reconciliation" (II Cor. 5:18). (The "himself" in that statement obviously refers to God, not Jesus; "Through Christ God reconciled us to himself" i.e., to God).

Then Paul leads into what for me is perhaps the finest Christological proclamation ever inscribed in holy writ. "That is, God was in Christ reconciling the world to himself, not counting their trespasses against them, and entrusting to us the message of reconciliation" (II Cor. 5:19). **There it is**. It could not be stated better. In the man Jesus of Nazareth, God was reconciling the world to Himself, to God. And God did it on behalf of Himself, not on behalf of Jesus. God always wanted to be at one with the world He created and all the people who ever lived in it. And Jesus was one of the means, we Christians believe the primary means, of effecting that reconciliation. Ultimately, it is more accurate to say this entire scenario is specifically the activity of God, and not the activity of Christ. God used Jesus, and Jesus was more willing to be used by God than anyone else who ever lived. But it was **God** who did the reconciling, **not Jesus**.

Oh, one last question, lest I forget to ask it. What do **you** demand of Jesus?

Scripture – Job 1:1-12

Text – And the Lord said to Satan, "Behold, all that he has is in your power; only upon himself do not put forth your hand." So Satan went forth from the presence of the Lord. – Job 1:12 (RSV)

THE HELL *YOU* SAY!

Hell is a bad idea. It also, unfortunately, is a biblical idea.

But it was not always a biblical idea. Historically, there was no concept of hell among the Israelites until they were taken as captives to Babylon in 586 BCE. It was there, when they began rubbing shoulders with Zoroastrians and Zoroastrianism that the Jews first encountered the notion of a place of eternal punishment.

There is widespread uncertainty about when Zarathustra, the founder of Zoroastrianism, lived. Very little historical background is available on him. The religion he founded is starkly dualistic. That is to say, there is good and evil, and a good god and an evil god, and the good god commands the earth for a thousand years, and then the evil god commands it for another thousand years. And the two warring deities go back and forth and back and forth through the unfolding millennia until the end of time. Then the good god shall win, the evil god will ultimately be defeated, and all the good people will be saved, and the evil people will be forever damned.

There is a lot more to Zoroastrianism than just that, and that is not even a fair or accurate summary. But it's all I'm going to say anyway.

Presumably from the time of Abraham, about 1800 BCE, or maybe from the time of Moses, about 1250 BCE, until the time of the Babylonian Captivity in the 6th century BCE, the Israelites had no concept of either heaven or hell, in the sense in which Christians understand those terms. But there was no idea of heaven either. There was virtually no notion of either a place of eternal reward or punishment for anybody. Rather it was believed

177

that after death, everybody went to a shadowy existence in a place (or maybe a state of being?) called *Sheol*. The Hebrew word Sheol simply means "the pit."

Is Sheol nothing more – or less – than the grave (i.e., **the** pit)? Is it a physical reality at all? Or is it purely spiritual? And if spiritual, then why is Sheol so ill-defined?

While the Hebrews were wrestling with the meaning of Sheol, the Greeks during that same period of time came up with a similar concept: Hades. Hades is not hell. Hell is supposed to be a place of punishment. Hades is more like Sheol. Everybody goes there when they die: the good, the bad, the indifferent — everybody. However, the geography of Hades eventually became much more certain in the popular mind than the geography of Sheol. To get to Hades, you went across the River Styx on a ferryboat, owned and operated by a chap named Charron. People didn't like to go to Hades, I guess, because they didn't much like to die. It has ever been thus. But to the Greeks, there was no choice in the matter. You died; you went to Hades; end of story.

If you deduce from this that Sheol and Hades do not seem like adequate synonyms for hell, you have correctly deducted. It took many centuries for hell to get as real as it is in the minds of many people today. My mother, for example, almost never said the word "hell," unless she was talking about what everyone else means by hell. And she would **never, ever** say "Go to hell." I suspect she mildly feared that she might end up there if she said it. "Go to Hades" was as far as Mom would go, when she wanted to point an obstreperous son or anyone else in an extra-earthly direction. But because she figured Hades couldn't be nearly as bad as hell, she reluctantly concluded that in moments of extreme exasperation she might opine that someone would have her permission, or even encouragement, to go there.

There is one central character thus far missing from thus whole hellish exploration, and that of course is Old Scratch himself, the devil, *el diablo*, the prince of demons (or daemons, in the English of King James). After all, what would hell be without Satan?

Satan is another of those cockamamie ideas the Jews encountered when they were hanging around Babylon as political prisoners. People who languish in prison often get wild ideas from other prisoners. You could ask some of the people who have become the most zealous of Al Qaeda operatives. The word Satan literally means "Adversary." In Zoroastrianism he was not *Satan*; he was *Ha-Shatan*: **The** Adversary.

To comprehend what hell is, or isn't, we need to follow the religious evolution of the notion of Satan. It is one thing to have **an** adversary. Sooner or later we all have adversaries, and we have them due to many matters and issues. But it is quite another thing to be confronted by **The** Adversary, **The** Satan, the fallen angel Lucifer. (By the way, the Jews also acquired angels in Babylon. They never had them before.) Now I know that these days many people are really into angels. But they're also into crystals, magnets, and bean sprouts. What can I say: most of the most far-out ideas in the Bible came from non-biblical, (i.e., non-Yahweh-inspired) sources. The Bible writers were fascinated by these non-Hebraic notions, so they shoved them willy-nilly into scripture. Our lives would have been ever so much less complicated without them, but, as they might say in Spanish, but don't, *Que estaba, estaba*: Whatever was, was. We are stuck with what we're stuck with.

Thus we are stuck with Satan. According to some very obscure passages in the Book of Revelation (see esp. ch. 12), which itself is the most obscure book in the Bible and in my opinion should have been left out but nobody asked me, some time in the dim and distant past Satan tried to launch a revolt against God in heaven. He enlisted a phalanx of easily duped angels with whom he used to spend time on the celestial street corners, smoking cannabis, and they attempted to overthrow Yahweh. According to every source (of which there are few) in which this angelic battle is cited, Satan & Co. lost.

If the truth is told, Satan doesn't get much coverage in the Bible. Nor does hell, for that matter. Satan is mentioned eleven times in the Old Testament, but seven of those citations come from the Book of Job, to which soon we shall turn. In the New Testament, Satan is noted by name 26 times, but a few of those are variations of repeated episodes in the synoptic Gospels. The Book of Revelation itself accounts for seven of the "Satan citations."

How, then, did Satan and hell come to command such a central place in contemporary Christianity and Islam, if it was so peripheral in both the Bible and the Quran? Judaism doesn't get too wound up with Old Harry, but Christians and Muslims devote an amazing amount of thought, speculation, and anxiety to the Prince of Demons. *Que pasa*?

Well, the medieval period contributed greatly to the advancement of Satanic thinking. Medieval art has numerous depictions of a fiery underworld. All by himself, John Milton expertly, if unintentionally, promoted hell through his epic *Paradise Lost*.

It is a curious phenomenon that many if not most people seem more intrigued by their imaginings of hell than they are by heaven. Many spend more time pondering the devil than the Creator of the ends of the earth. For droves of folks, hell seems to be fun, but heaven seems to be a drag.

Why is that? Why do so many people concentrate on evil or the negative or the devil, and meditate so little on the good, and the positive, and God?

The following hypothesis is only that: an hypothesis. I can't validate it by any kind of statistical proof, and I doubt that anyone could ever validate it. But here goes anyway: **People want a readily grasped EXTERNAL explanation for the existence of evil.** We are rationally unwilling and psychologically unlikely to admit that we ourselves cook up our own evil behavior. Somebody **out there** has to be responsible for it, since we have convinced ourselves that none of us could possibly be guilty of engendering our own evil actions. As Flip Wilson used to declare on television in the old days, "The devil made me do it!"

It is my firm opinion that a belief in Satan and hell is theologically irresponsible. Nobody who wants to be truly serious about attempting to live a proper life in service to God can conscientiously go along with the terribly skewed idea that there is a devil, or that evil people will end up eternally in hell. Such thinking is nothing less than a theological cop-out.

"But Satan and hell are in the Bible!" it will be argued. Yes, they are. And as I said in the beginning, it was all a mistake. It was a very bad idea, and they should immediately have perceived it as such. If Jesus actually talked about Satan and hell, which I sadly suspect He did, then with all the theological courage I can muster I insist that He made a big mistake. He never shoulda dunnit.

I am very serious about all this — **deadly** serious. It is not only a deficiency to believe in Satan and hell; it is deleterious to a proper understanding of who God is and what He is all about. Eternal punishment is utter nonsense. It is total nonsense. It is dangerous nonsense, because it leads so many people astray. It is not **Satan** who leads people away from God; it is the **teachings** about Satan which delude the spiritually weak and vulnerable into supposing that the prince of darkness has tempted them into rejecting God and His laws.

Here is the very hell of the entire notion of hell: the concepts of Satan and hell are meant to scare the hell out of people! But no one can be scared out of damnation into salvation! The only way toward salvation is to accept salvation as a gift. That's what the Bible at its best always says! That's what Jesus at His best always says. There is no Prince of Demons, nor are there any real, physical, or metaphysical demons, nor is there a place of eternal punishment called hell. There is and always has been only the kingdom of heaven, so magnificently elucidated by Jesus, and everybody, always, has always been part of it. Salvation is finally understood when that truth is finally grasped. But until it is grasped, people continue to be seduced by the Imaginary Seducer, and they continue to fear the Imaginary Pit of Perdition, and it is all such a terrible waste of time and psychic energy.

Postulating hell is easy. Living as God has taught us to live is hard. It is exceedingly demanding. And often it is so complicated that we can scarcely decide what we ought to do. But it is still a sorry cop-out if we give a fleeting moment of thought to the slightest possibility that there might be a devil and hell, because there isn't, and there isn't.

It would obviously be foolish to attempt to deny all the biblical and extra-biblical references there are to hell. Hell is **there**, for heaven's sake. But it **isn't**; it isn't **there**; it doesn't **exist**. Heaven exists. None of us can know where, or how, though we do know why. But I am absolutely positive that hell doesn't exist. And if you want not to believe in hell, but you want somebody to blame it on if you decide not to believe in it, so that you won't go to hell for not believing in hell, blame it on me; it's okay with me.

A while back I said we would come to the Book of Job, and so, now, we shall. Job is one of the most fascinating books in the Bible. It also is one of the longest. Its focus on really tough theological issues is absolutely marvelous. If you have never read Job, I encourage you to do so. It will be one of the most enlightening, as well as perplexing, mental exercises in which you shall ever engage.

Biblical scholars are all over the map about who wrote Job, or when, or for whom it was written. Its Hebrew language is technically very ancient, much like Chaucerian English is to Modern English. But did somebody in the 5th or 4th century BCE write it to make it look old? Nobody knows for certain.

Job starts out with a prose prologue, which lasts for two chapters. The rest of the book is in poetry. The story itself is vaguely familiar to many people, but few actual verses are well known. The most famous lines are also some of the most difficult properly to translate, according to the experts who study such things. George Frederick Handel gave them immortal currency in his oratorio *Messiah*; "I know that my redeemer liveth, and that he shall stand at the latter day upon the earth. And though worms destroy this body, yet in my flesh shall I see God" (19:25-26).

The first few verses of the first chapter declare that Job was a blameless and righteous man from the land of Uz who followed God in everything he did. He was very rich, he had a large and happy family, and he was always listed in *Fortune* Magazine as being in the Top Ten in the land for accumulated wealth. (Actually I made up the last part. *Fortune* had not then been invented, even though Job possessed one —- a fortune, that is.)

Verse 6 of Chapter 1 is loaded with captivating ideas. "Now there was a day when the sons of God came to present themselves before the Lord, and Satan also came among them." Who are these "sons of God" —- lower-case *s*ons? Are they angels? Are they another category among the heavenly host? And if Satan **also** came among them, did he sneak in, or was he too a "son of God?" It doesn't explain any of this; it just states it. The scholars have a field day over it, but I guess we are free to believe anything we choose, because by no means is the true meaning evident in this enigmatic passage. I assume that the story of Job is intended to be understood as fiction, not historical fact. But nobody will ever know that beyond dispute.

Anyway, God instantly notices Satan among the others, and He asks, "Whence have you come?" Smug, smarmy, son-of-a-gun Satan says, "From going to and fro on the earth, and from walking up and down on it." What chutzpah! To answer **Yahweh** like that! "I've been around, God; I've been around. But I'm not going to tell you where." Ignoring the insolence, God says, more or less, "Have you considered my man Job, and what a straight arrow he is?" And Satan says, "Straight arrow, my cloven foot! You protect old Job as though he's a hothouse plant, God! But take away his main mansion and his five vacation homes, his fleet of Rolls Royces and his flock of Harley-Davidsons, his lofty stack of stock and his membership on the boards of the five biggest banks in Uz, and you'll see just how much of an Eagle Scout he is."

Now note: God Himself does not lay a finger on Job. Instead, He says to Satan, in so many words, "Have at 'im, yuh creep." God treats Satan like the pond scum he is, if he *is* at all, which he isn't. So, a series of instant and terrible tragedies befall Job. He loses all his livestock and servants, and his whole family, with the exception of his wife, is killed when the house in which they were gathered collapses. Every company in which Job had ever invested instantly went belly up, with both CEOs and CFOs ending up in the Uzian hoosegow. All in a manner of speaking.

Then, in Chapter 2, Smarmy Satan appeared again before God, and God noted to the Prime Seducer that Job was still a straight arrow, despite all the calamities which Satan had thrust upon him. "Yeah, yeah, yeah," said Satan, "but let me personally have a whack at Job's own person, and then see how much he blesses you, Yahweh." "Okay," said God, "but on one condition; you cannot take his life." So Job was afflicted with a terrible case of carbuncles, presumably. His skin was a crimson mass of crusty sores. His wife, that marvelous matron who survived the collapsed house, said to her agonized spouse, "Do you still hold fast your integrity? Curse God, and die."

Nice touch, Mrs. Job! A regular angel of mercy you are! On top of everything else, poor old Job must have a marital comforter such as you? Oy, veh!

But still Job refuses to curse God. "Shall we receive good at the hand of God, and shall we not receive evil?" he plaintively asks. What a Mensch is Job! Who is more admirable than he? Truly, who is?

I'm not going to summarize the rest of the story; you can read it for yourself. And then you can ponder its deep probings, and ruminate on its unanswered questions, and cogitate upon its circuitous and confusing answers.

But here's what we're looking at in this particular sermon: **Satan**. Satan is such a slippery character. He is so mean, so spiteful, that our instant inclination is to despise him. If there were a Satan, we should probably despise him. But, as I have attempted to convince you, there isn't, so we needn't.

Does the devil, as Luther said in *A Mighty Fortress Is Our God*, and as the book of Job implies, "work us woe?" Is Satan's "craft and power great?" Is he "armed with cruel hate?"

I guess if people insist on ascribing evil to someone or something outside themselves, maybe it is inevitable that Satan evolves into become that devious being in the popular mind. Certainly we "give the devil his due" far more than he is due it. From the medieval morality plays to *Rosemary's Baby*, from the dark art of Albrecht Durer to *The Omen*, Satan has taken on a much-larger-than-life life, especially since he had no life in the first place. But many people **need** Satan; they **want** Satan; they **demand** the existence of a Satan and a hell, because otherwise, God and life demand too much of them, and they feel they cannot supply the demand.

Pay close attention: hell is really a very silly idea cooked up by people who don't want to get sufficiently serious about God and faith and valid religion. Hell is a convenient escape from thoughtful reflection on the way things truly are. Lazy or shallow or childish thinking gravitates toward Satan and hell. Disciplined and deep and mature thinking gravitates toward God and the kingdom of heaven and the King who best explains and describes the kingdom of heaven.

No one, least of all I, can deny that millions of very serious Christians and others down through the ages have believed in and preached about Satan and hell, and they were intelligent and committed people. None of these people concocted hell or Satan out of a vacuum. There is a long litany of demonology to support the notion of the prince of darkness and the place in which the prince resides with all the damned souls of all time. Nonetheless, in my judgment it all leads to – you should pardon the expression – a **dead** end. If there were a hell, it would be death - - - unending death, the perpetual cessation of all awareness of life.

By the time of Jesus, the Jews called hell *Gehenna*. Gehenna has an interesting etymology. To the south of the Old City of Jerusalem there is a narrow, steep valley called the Valley of Hinnom, or sometimes, the Valley of the Sons of Hinnom. The valley provided an excellent natural defense for Jerusalem, because its walls are so steep that they served as a kind of castle wall without a wall having to be built.

Over the passage of centuries, the Valley of Hinnom gradually became the unofficial Jerusalem city dump. People would carry their garbage into the valley, and burn it there. City dumps always seem to take on a life of their own. They get bigger or smaller, depending on how much trash is thrown into them, and if the stuff tossed there is deep enough, and combustible enough, the dump seems never to stop burning. Those of us who are sufficiently long of tooth remember that in the old days, before ecology was discovered, dumps were always sputtering and fuming.

Thus the Valley of Hinnom became like — you guessed it! — - **Hell** in the popular mind of the Jerusalemites. The Valley (*Ge*) of Hinnom (*Henna*) was what hell was like. Flames would suddenly erupt from the smoldering refuse, sparks would ascend into the night sky, and the place felt alien and creepy and foreboding.

If hell exists, at all, surely it is like every city dump which ever existed. Sooner or later the fire goes out. Fire cannot continue in perpetuity. No fire can, including the purported fire of hell. If anybody ever went to hell, that person died, and was truly dead. *Kaput. Finie.*

An obscure passage in the Apocalypse of John (the Book of Revelation) and also the Apostles Creed declare that Jesus descended into hell. That is absolutely true. Further, it is true that Jesus is the only person ever to descend into hell. Everyone else who ever died went immediately from temporal to eternal life. It happens, as Paul declared, and as Handel musically proclaimed (although Paul was referring to the resurrection), "in a moment, in the twinkling of an eye, at the last trumpet." Jesus tasted death on behalf of all humanity, so that humanity need never taste actual, perpetual, unending death.

B.C., by Johnny Hart, is one of my favorite comic strips. I don't always agree with everything Johnny Hart says, but he always says it very well, and he is a man of profound convictions. One day the blonde chick was looking at a stone tablet. (In *B.C.* there are no pages in books; there are only flat stones with chiseled inscriptions.) The blonde chick exclaims, "Oh, my goodness...says here... Jesus descended into hell." The fat broad (these are Hart's terms, not mine!) is lying there on a little hillside. And she says, "You're kidding!" "Oh, no... not to **stay!**" says the blonde chick. "He just dropped in to cancel our reservations!"

Exactly so, blonde chick! If ever all of us had reservations for hell, which I don't think any of us ever did, Jesus — or more precisely, **God** — cancelled the reservations! The life, death,

186

and resurrection of Jesus of Nazareth illustrate that truth for everyone to see! Not everyone sees it, not everyone shall ever see it, but nonetheless, the reservations have been forever nullified! We shall not die, not forever, not perpetually! Temporally, some day at some hour and minute and second, we all shall pass from this world to the next, but it will be instantaneous! God wills it! And whatever God wants, He gets!

Hell is useful for fanciful writers and imaginative painters and *New Yorker* cartoonists, but it is useless for everyone else. It apparently has helped millions of people deftly attempt to move the guilt of their own sinful actions onto the sloping shoulders of the crimson-skinned chap with the cloven hooves and forked tail. But that guilt is **their** guilt, not Satan's, and their hellish behavior emanates from them, not from hell.

The degree to which believers want to ascribe excruciating reality and vivid detail to hell is determined by the degree to which they want to absolve themselves or others of any responsibility for their own bad actions. Those who strongly believe in hell tend to fall into two categories. First, there are those who feel terribly sinful, whether or not they actually **are** terribly sinful, and they fear they are headed for hell. Second, there are those who are exceedingly judgmental of the behavior of others besides themselves, and they think everyone else is, and ought to be, headed for hell.

On the basis of continuously trying to please God in all we do, absolutely none of us deserves to experience the salvation of the Holy One of Israel. But, thank God, God does not ultimately decide on our eternal destiny based on our goodness, but rather, on His unconditional mercy and love.

What I now shall say might seem as though I am putting myself way, way, **way** out on a very thin and precarious limb, and I am furiously sawing away at the tree-ward section of my quavering branch. If I truly thought that was what I was doing, I would not say what I am now going to say. So I'll go ahead and say it.

If there really is a hell as hell is popularly understood, then you may be certain there is no God as God should be

popularly understood. Any God who would allow a place of eternal punishment is not a God worth having. "Forever" is forever, and no sins committed during the lifetime of anyone on this planet are sufficient to warrant everlasting torment because of them. Should there be a hell, and should I end up there (as perhaps you devoutly wish), I would join the legions of His Satanic Majesty to help wage war against the Creator of the Universe. No God who would countenance everlasting torture for temporal sins is worthy of remaining God for even another celestial second. On this subject the science fiction author Arthur C. Clarke once made a sagacious observation. "Sometimes I think we're alone in the universe, and sometimes I think we're not. In either case, the idea is quite staggering." To say the least, dear hearts; to say the least.

On the other hand, should I end up in heaven, and somehow I should discover that in fact there is a hell, I will do everything in my power to help organize my fellow celestial subjects for the overthrow of the Almighty One of Heaven. I am very serious when I fulminate that no God who would allow the existence of hell deserves to be God.

"The hell!" you say. No, the hell *you* say.

Scripture – I Corinthians 15:12-19

Text – If for this life only we have hoped in Christ, we are of all men most to be pitied. – I Corinthians 15:19 (RSV)

THE GOSPEL OF DEATH

Carl Jung was one of the greatest psychologists of the 20th century. He inspired numerous students, who helped numerous people, and his legacy lives on in the hearts and especially in the minds of those who have been aided by his insights, even when they do not know it was he who gave them strength for the lifting of their mental burdens.

However, Dr. Jung was pointedly rueful about the realities of aging. He wrote, "When an aging person secretly shudders and is even mortally afraid at the thought that his reasonable expectation of life now amounts to only so many years, then we are painfully reminded of certain feelings within our own breast; we look away and turn the conversation to some other topic.... Naturally we have on hand...one or two suitable banalities...such as 'everyone must die sometime'...but when one is alone and it is night and so dark and still that one hears and sees nothing but the thoughts which add and subtract the years, and the long row of disagreeable facts which remorselessly indicate how far the hand of the clock has moved forward, and the slow, irresistible approach of the wall of darkness which will eventually engulf everything you love, possess, wish, strive, and hope for —- then all our profundities about life slink off to some undiscoverable hiding place, and fear envelops the sleepless one like a smothering blanket."

Well, that's cheerful, isn't it? A regular bundle of chuckles was old Carl, eh?

But the eminent student of the mind aptly described in incandescent if lengthy prose the way millions of people feel as they come to the rude awakening that now they are older, and soon they will be old, and then they will die. And then what? Then what?

Death is one of the pre-eminent subjects of life. It has fascinated playwrights and poets, philosophers and screenwriters, novelists, ethicists, and actuaries. Our personal financial plans necessarily include our awareness of the inevitability of death. When we are young, most of us purchase life insurance, which is actually death insurance. When we are older, we set up living trusts, which may or may not benefit us when we are living, but will certainly benefit someone else when we are dead. Even Social Security provides us with a death benefit, although by this juncture, it barely scratches the surface of what it truly costs to die. If we had nothing other than that paltry sum to care for our carcass after we have shuffled off this mortal coil, nobody could ever afford to die.

George Bernard Shaw had an outstanding philosophy about both living and dying. He said, "I am of the opinion that my life belongs to the whole community, and as long as I live it is my privilege to do for it what I can. I want to be thoroughly used up when I die, for the harder I work, the more I live. I rejoice in life for its own sake. Life is no brief candle for me. It is sort of a splendid torch which I have got hold of for a moment, and I want to make it burn as brightly as possible before handing it on to future generations."

Would that everyone lived as the immortal GBS lived, crafty, gifted, giving curmudgeon that he was. But we don't. Many of us cling so tightly to our days and years that we seem never to live at all. We are so obsessed with longevity that we never learn how, really, to live each day as it comes. We are like the person who brashly declared, "I intend to live forever. So far, so good." Yeah, right. We become adroitly adept as perpetual whistlers in the dark.

I have discovered that one of the most helpful means for managing to survive "this world of woe" (as the old spiritual describes it) is assiduously to read *The New Yorker* cartoons. Reading other stuff in *The New Yorker* is instructive and interesting as well, but the cartoons are an essential element for coping with a highly eventful and unpredictable existence.

There is the one where two older men in dark suits standing on clouds appear before St. Peter at the Pearly Gates. (People in cartoons like that always are standing on clouds like that. It is an excellent skill, to be able to stand on clouds. It leads one to wonder, are there actually fleecy puffs of glistening vapor supporting the Pearly Gates, and the celestial kingdom enclosed beyond? The cloud-capped towers, the gorgeous palaces, the solemn temples, and all that?) The first man, a squat, stout, large-proboscissed fellow, has a briefcase in one hand. He reaches out the other hand with a proffered business card toward the preoccupied celestial gatekeeper, and he says to the Big Fisherman, referring to his silent client beside him, "Archibald Monroe —— I'll be heading Mr. Billing's transition team."

Thank heaven someone is willing to assist Billing as he adjusts to his new life! Thank God for anyone who helps anyone cross over from this life to the next! Life doesn't end when life ends - - - does it? Death is not our finale - - - is it?

The apostle Paul was the prime biblical proponent of the Gospel of Death. He was so totally convinced that the resurrection of Jesus from the dead assured our own future resurrection that he kept coming back to this theme, again and again and again. When the Nazarene carpenter was raised by God from death, it was far more than an unprecedented historical happening to Paul; it was a cosmic occurrence with universal and perpetual consequences. When God conquered death for Jesus, He conquered death for everyone, Paul resolutely decreed.

Initially, it is clear that Paul believed Jesus would return to earth sometime very soon, certainly during Paul's lifetime. When that happened, Paul implied, the world would cease to exist, and all proper believers would be swept into heaven as a glorious cloud of witnesses. Nonetheless, Paul never claimed that actual physical death would be avoided for all who were Christians. (He probably believed that non-Christians would die for sure, but that's another thought for another sermon, one of which is carefully tucked away elsewhere in this sermonic tome.) As time went on, and Jesus did not return, Paul changed his tune. He figured all the Christian faithful had better plan on cashing in their terrestrial chips at some point, because nobody could know when The End was coming. Therefore, Paul came to accept the inevitability of death for all people, believers as well as unbelievers. I suggest that it would be good for the rest of us to accept that as well. Death is coming to each of us, to all of us. Count on it. Be ready for it. And even if you never get ready for death, death will always be ready for you.

The entire 15th chapter of I Corinthians is Paul's summary of what I am calling the Gospel of Death. The old Anglo-Saxon word *Godspel* means "Good News." There is good news in our dying, says Paul, because it is a prelude to our living eternally with God. And we know that shall happen, says the relentless Tarsus tentmaker, because of the resurrection of Jesus of Nazareth. "Now if Christ is preached as raised from the dead, how can some of you say there is no resurrection of the dead?" What is wrong with you schlemiels anyway, Paul wanted to know. How can you possibly think that death might be **The End**? "The end is the beginning!" said Paul. "We preach Christ as raised from the dead," said Paul, "and so also do we preach that **you** shall be raised," said Paul. "If for this life only we have hoped, we are of all people most to be pitied," said Paul.

Yeah, right, Paul. It's easy for you to say. You hadn't died yet when you said that. Did you say it when you died? Huh? Did you?

It is easy to be blithely philosophical about death when you don't think you're dying, but when you know you're looking the Grim Reaper in the eye, and that the one who is blinking is you, not him, death becomes a fearful existential reality. Death is theologically and spiritually captivating to the living, but to the dying, death is deadly.

Lance Morrow is an editorial writer for *Time*. Not long after Vice President Cheney took office, Mr. Morrow was comparing his bad heart to Mr. Cheney's bad heart. Heart people, said Lance Morrow, look at life differently from those who have no heart history. (Tricky language, this. Doesn't your heart have a history? I thought so. Mine too. Mine has been pumping for 63 years. So far, so good, as they say. But there **is** a history, even if my particular cardiac muscle has never needed any cardiological scrutiny.) Anyway, Lance Morrow wrote, "My approach to life for many years has been ascetic, robust and provisional. Every mortal lives with the fact of his own death. Most people are not disabled by the thought; they are able to forget about it on most days. We pretend we are immortal. And of course, we are —- for the moment. People with a history of heart attacks, like me and Cheney, do, however, listen to the engine more carefully than most other drivers. We cock an ear inward" (*Time*, March 19, 2001).

Those of us who have been blessed with remarkably good heath do not and cannot see life in precisely the same way as someone who constantly knows she is "on borrowed time." We **all** are on borrowed time, of course. But from whom do we borrow it? From God? From fate? From death? From our unavoidable physicality? And why does Smith, who has exactly the same health problems as Jones, outlive Jones by 27 years? Or why does Brown, whose health has always been as outstanding as Green's, live to be 103, whereas Green checks out at a mere 94?

Lance Morrow further explicates the insights of a heart person. "After a heart attack, you feel as if someone has broken into the house in the middle of the night. You know there is a killer waiting in the dark basement…. A heart attack leaves you feeling that your most intimate friend has breached a fundamental trust. The body – bright youth, now tarnished and corrupted – loses its mind and violently assaults you, a monster within. You live thereafter with a strange sense of alienation."

Look, the **body** is not going to make it out of this world. The body is done for, doomed, *kaput*. Paul talks about this at the end of I Corinthians 15. "Lo, I tell you a mystery. We shall not all sleep, but we shall be changed, in a moment, in the twinkling of an eye, at the last trumpet" (15:5152). Then, said he, the perishable would put on the imperishable, and the mortal would put on immortality. And **then** death would be swallowed up in victory.

But the **body**, the *sarx*, the *corpus*, shall not make it. *We* shall make it out of this world intact, but our bodies won't. They shall revert to the ground from which they came (*Adam*: Humanity; *adamah*: ground.) "Earth to earth, ashes to ashes, dust to dust," as it says in the committal service at the graveside.

William Rees-Mogg is a columnist for *The Times* of London. "William Rees-Mogg": what better handle could there be than that for a man who writes for what declares itself to be, and is, simply **The Times**, and of course it has to be always and only of London, don't you know? Mr. Rees-Mogg was arguing for a belief in the existence of God on the basis of much evidence in the world, both substantial and circumstantial. At the end of his editorial, he wrote, "Early in the summer I met the late Archbishop Runcie in the House of Lords. I asked him how he was. He replied, 'Dying, but in the best of spirits.'" Then Mr. Rees-Mogg completed his piece with these words: "The existence of God is no mere debating point. It gives purpose to life, and it gives purpose to death."

Would that we all were aware in our heart of hearts that we are dying! But that being so, may we all also be in the best of spirits! There is good news in death! Because of it, and **only** because of it, we are going to live again — forever! You can rely on it with absolute confidence! As Paul stated, since by a man (Adam) came death, by a man (Jesus) came also the resurrection of the dead!

The new Archbishop of Canterbury is Rowan Williams. He is a Welshman. The fact that a Welshman has become the highest official in the Church of England illustrates that God has a marvelous sense of humor. But that's not why I refer to Rowan Williams.

It happened that Archbishop Williams was next door at the Trinity Church in Lower Manhattan on the very day the World Trade Center was attacked. The experience of being so clearly and closely in harm's way so moved him that he quickly wrote a little book called *Writing in the Dust: After September 11*. In it he noted that "it was Plato who said that philosophy was about learning how to die." Seeing the Twin Towers come crashing down all around him gave him new appreciation for that truth, an appreciation made possible only by the destruction he witnessed through his own incredulous eyes. Archbishop Williams decided to "reflect on theology as learning about death, and also death as a teacher of theology. It seems to me that when we are faced with a real, concrete possibility that death is going to happen to us, we immediately have one of the deepest possible challenges posed to the way in which we think about ourselves. We're brought up against a plan in which we have no part at all to change the future. So often we as humans construct our sense of freedom and worth around our capacity to change the future. What happens when we cannot?"

There is one very sobering reality about the future of each of us which none of us can change. We are going to die. There is no way around it. We might be able to stave off death a little, to waylay it, temporarily to stem its inexorable tide. But come it will. And are we properly prepared for it?

Nearly all of us would do nearly everything we could to avoid dying sooner rather than later. Only the gravely depressed or the gravely ill want death to come as quickly as possible, or to hasten what we call its "natural" course. (By the way, in this context, what does "sooner" or "later" mean? Or what is "natural" about **when** we die? Whom are we trying to kid with the use of such language?)

Because we don't want to die "too soon," as a society we spend billions of dollars in our futile attempt to thwart the early onset of death. In 1988, Americans spent 10.9% of the gross domestic product on health care. By 1993, that figure rose to 13.4%. "Managed care" was supposed to halt the increase, and to some extent it has done so. But now we are spending over 15% of our GDP on health care, which is virtually twice the level of any other industrialized country. And still it is true that whatever is spent on the health of the average American over her or his lifetime until the last six months of life, that amount doubles during those final six months. Dying is hugely expensive. And everybody dies anyway, regardless of how much is expended. So why don't we decide to die sooner, and save the wasted expense?

Further, conservative politicians are doing everything they can to prevent people from choosing to end their lives "sooner" rather than "later," with those words – and concepts – in quotation marks. Usually these conservative politicians act on the basis of a conservative, evangelical, or fundamentalist theological position. But ought not such people, of all people, understand the **Gospel** of Death? Why can we not all see that sometimes it is far better to die in peace than to live in misery? Where is the Good News for anyone who is forced to continue breathing in a body which is doing its best to end the suffering quickly? Why are the "death with dignity" laws fought so strongly by the "right to life" folks? Should the right to life also guarantee the necessity to suffer?

In 1997, the State of Oregon passed a law which said that a patient may choose to be given a legal dosage of lethal drugs, but only under very closely supervised conditions. The hue and cry went up that there would literally be murder and mayhem as a result of this law. Nevertheless, since its inception, only 75 people or so have taken the opportunity given them to end their lives. John Ashcroft, our Attorney General, and George Bush, our President, are threatening to use federal officials to investigate the amount of pain medication doctors prescribe for their patients, seeking thereby to prevent active or passive euthanasia.

Is death **bad**? Is it **evil**? Ought we to take every possible measure to avoid death for every possible person? Why should government, or anyone else, for that matter, attempt to lengthen the time it takes people to die, especially people who want to die as soon as possible? Living is **bad news**, when death is cruelly thwarted, when all continued living can guarantee is physical, psychological, and spiritual suffering of the most unimaginable kind. Death is **good news**, it is **gospel**, when the time to die has come. It is inhuman to bypass death when the natural process is providing every opportunity to allow the patient to escape a body which life has transformed into a prison. Save us from the savers of life, when life is doing everything it can to cease living!

Dr. Jerome Groopman is a professor of medicine at Harvard. When John Ashcroft announced the plan to take punitive action against physicians who prescribe lethal drugs for terminally ill patients, Dr. Groopman wrote an editorial for the *New York Times*, which was circulated in other newspapers. He told of a woman who was in the final stages of leukemia. With her husband and physician, she had talked over what she wanted done when nothing more could be accomplished by attempting to make her better. Her lungs began to fill up with blood, and the doctor ordered a strong dosage of morphine. A respiratory therapist vehemently objected, saying that the morphine would impair her breathing, which was true. The therapist righteously declared that the doctor was in effect a murderer, and the husband an accomplice to murder.

The hospital review board said the charge against the doctor was unfounded, as did the district attorney's office. But under the rules written by John Ashcroft, the doctor and husband conceivably could be charged and convicted. Dr. Groopman states that "it is medically impossible to dissociate intentionally ameliorating a dying patient's agony from intentionally shortening the time left to live." He then says, "If the Justice Department's action is a political bone thrown to religious conservatives, it shamefully miscasts health professionals as agents of the devil rather than angels of mercy. If it represents an earnest attempt to protect the dying, it in fact makes them more vulnerable."

When I began the Christian ministry nearly forty years ago, people died much more quickly then than now. That was especially true of cancer patients. Then, the actual onset of death might take mere hours or days; now it might take weeks, or months, or years. And for what? For what?

Atheists and agnostics legitimately might choose to fight death with every means at their disposal. Since they believe this life is the only one they shall ever have, it probably behooves them to live as long as they can. But believers should have the courage to die with confidence, because for us, death is not death.

Johnny Hart is the cartoonist for *B.C.* While he is sometimes a bit too obviously evangelical for one so unorthodox as I, he nevertheless gets in some dandy comedic zingers from time to time. One of the lightly bearded guys in his comic strip comes up to another lightly-bearded guy, who stands beside a rock into which is chiseled the word "ANSWERS." The first man asks the second one, "What could a dead atheist, a dead agnostic and a dead saint possibly have in common?" And the Answer Man answers, "They all *know* there is a God."

You have that right, Johnny Hart! In death we shall discover that there is no death! In death we shall see God, and God shall see to it that we shall never again see death! Ultimately, there is Gospel, and only Gospel, in death, for all of God's children!

But let us be honest, with one another, and with ourselves. Most of us have at least some degree of fear about death, because it is the only unknown that is certain to affect everyone. God might not exist, but we know death does exist. And no one can ever avert whatever it has in store for us.

And yet, **and yet** the authentic Christian faith tells us that beyond the unavoidable is the unimaginable. And even though we cannot adequately imagine or understand it, we can find an invulnerable hope which assures us that not only will all be well, it will be wonderful beyond description. Skeptics will call it a pipedream, and cynics will insist it is without foundation. But for us, it is the conviction which enables us to live optimistically and to die victoriously.

A friend sent me something which had come to her via e-mail. A woman who knew she would die very soon asked her pastor to come to see her for one last visit. Calmly and objectively she talked over everything she wanted included in her funeral service. Then she made what she considered her most important request. She wanted an open casket during the service, and she wanted a fork placed in her right hand. Not surprisingly, the minister was nonplussed by this, and he asked her why she would make such an extraordinary request. "Well," said the dying lady, "whenever there is a church dinner, and they take away the plates after the main course has been served, they always say, 'Save your fork!' Whenever that happens, I know that something even better than what I have had is coming. On the day of my funeral, I want everyone to think that something better is coming for all of us."

During the funeral, the minister recalled meeting with the parishioner just before she died. In the period of visitation prior to the service, he said he had noticed many people asking one another why in the world the deceased lady had a fork in her hand. It seemed absolutely bizarre. So he gave her explanation to the congregation. "She understood far better than I the essence of the Christian Gospel, and it is this: After death, something much better is coming. Remember it always, and you will never again live as you did before."

Sometimes the syrupy evangelical hymns present the Good News of God more winsomely than the older, more theologically accurate, historic hymns. *Shall We Gather at the River* tells the Christian truth about death in its own unique way. No one who ever heard the tune can forget it. But the saccharine words convey the sweet story in their ever-memorable manner: "Shall we gather at the river/ Where bright angel's feet have trod/ With its crystal tide forever/ Flowing by the throne of God?" Then there comes the chorus: "Yes, we'll gather at the river/ The beautiful, the beautiful river/ Gather with the saints at the river/ That leads by the throne of God."

The next to last stanza says, "Ere we reach the shining river/ Lay we every burden down/ Grace our spirits will deliver/ And provide a robe and a crown." Then comes the final stanza: "Soon we'll reach the shining river/ Soon our pilgrimage will cease/ Soon our happy hearts will quiver/ With the melody of peace."

Is it great music? No. Is it even a very good text? No. But nonetheless it powerfully captures the Gospel of Death. Yes, we'll gather at the river/ The beautiful, the beautiful river/ Gather with the saints at the river/ That leads by the throne of God.

Always be as prepared to die as you have tried to be prepared fully to live every day of your life. And above all, remember this: Keep your fork.

Scripture: Isaiah 66:6-14

Text: "Shall I bring to the birth and not cause to bring forth? Says the Lord; shall I, who cause to bring forth, shut the womb? says your God." – Isa. 66:9 For thus says the Lord (Isa. 66:12); "As one whom his mother comforts, so I will comfort you; you shall be comforted in Jerusalem." – Isa. 66:13

THE GENDER OF GOD, AND RELATED IMPONDER-ABLE PONDERINGS

It was about 1959 or so, and I was in the University of Wisconsin A Cappella Choir. The choir had combined with three other University choral organizations, and this huge ensemble sang the Brahms *Requiem* under the direction of Robert Shaw.

I had never sung in the German *Requiem* before (we did it in English; what can I say?), but I will never forget the magnificence of that enormous throng of singers, doing their best with some of the most beautiful musical sequences ever inscribed onto printed choral staffs. The baritone soloist, Ara Berberian, sounded like he had been sent directly from heaven, and Robert Shaw was inspiring beyond description, as he led us through the gorgeous harmonies.

When Johannes Brahms composed his *Requiem*, his mother had recently died. He was disconsolate. In large measure, he wrote the music to ease the pain and loss he so sharply felt. And in the middle of this wondrous work of sharps and flats, he inserted a soprano solo. It was as if his mother were speaking to him from the sounds of his own music, bringing him solace and hope.

Adele Addison sang the soprano solo. She was electrifying, and she brought a flood of tears to my eyes as the glorious text unfolded.

> Ye now are sorrowful, howbeit, howbeit,
> Ye shall again behold me, and your heart shall be joyful,
> And your joy, your joy, no man taketh from you.

Look upon me; ye know that for a little time
Labor and sorrow were mine,
But at the last, I have found comfort.

As she sang these lines, we in the chorus sang part of the words of our sermon text. We were, in Brahms' choral conception, the voice of God. "Yea, I will comfort you, as one whom his own mother comforteth; I will comfort you; I will comfort you."

That Sunday afternoon, long ago, I heard the voice of God in the voices of four hundred other singers. And His voice was a feminine voice. God sounded like Adele Addison. But Adele Addison was Johannes Brahms' mother, telling him that his *joie de vivre* would return, and that she had at last found comfort for herself, after going through the labor and sorrow of dying. But to me, she sang the song of God, and God was a **She**.

* * * * * *

What is the gender of God? It is a serious question. What is the gender of God?

For most Christians through most of Christian history, indeed, for most Jews and Muslims as well, the question was never a question. God is masculine. The Bible says so; the Quran says so; end of story: masculine.

There is no theological rationale whatever for the masculinity of God; none. It is tradition which has insisted that God is masculine, western tradition in all three western religions.

In other religions, both historical and contemporaneous, there are goddesses. The Canaanites had them, the Greeks and Romans had them, the Babylonians and Egyptians and Assyrians had them. Certainly the Hindus also had (and have) goddesses.

But **goddesses** are different from **God**, aren't they? Monotheists don't believe in goddesses, do they? We believe in only one God, who alone is God, we believe.

The Hebrews called God *El*, and sometimes *Elohim*. The first word means "God," and the second literally means "Gods" (plural.) The Muslims call God *Allah*, and curiously, that word literally means "**The** God." Go figure.

It is complicated by the fact that to the Hebrews, God's *name* was not **God**; His name was *Yahweh*. But because the biblical Hebrews thought God's name was so sacred, they never pronounced it. Whenever they came to His name in their reading of the Hebrew Bible, they substituted the word *Adonoy*, which means, "Lord."

Linguistically, both **God** and **Lord** are, by definition, **male** nouns. A female god is a goddess, as earlier noted, and a female lord is a lady, a' la' **Lady** Diana, **Lady** Jane Grey, etc.

So again, we ask, what is the gender of God? In the language of the Bible, as well as the Quran, God is male. Of this there can be no doubt.

But because the biblical writers and Muhammad conceptualized God as male, and Jesus referred to God as being male, does that automatically mean that God **is** male? Likely not. They were merely reflecting the male-dominated thinking of their society in their time. And most people who continue to use the traditionally male terminology for God, including the very use of the word "God," probably have no serious problems with male-dominated thinking. But that **IS** a problem, says I. However, it is a different problem.

The sort of people who would choose to read sermons from a book with a title such as that imprinted on the cover of this book are people for whom the gender of God is a genuine issue. But such folk need to understand that it is not an issue for the vast majority of the human race. That anyone would even raise the question would prompt this huge number of human beings to react with a) incredulity; b) anger, c) guffaws, or d) yawns. There is enormous indifference out there over this question. For nonbelievers the issue is a non-issue, but even for most believers, it is also a non-issue. To try to make it into something for discussion is likely to provoke either indignation or accusations of silliness. Why would anyone even wonder about this?

Then what sorts of people do get exercised about God's gender? **People who are unusually concerned about women's liberation; that's who**. People who feel a deep need to debate human gender roles; that's who. People who think the females of our species have been discriminated against for most of human history; that's who.

Liberals, in other words, are the ones who want to discuss the gender of God. Most conservatives have no interest in the subject, nor do moderates. Most "conservative" revisions of the Bible do not use "inclusive language," to cite an example. Years ago, when the conservative Zondervan Press published the original New International Version of the Bible, they wanted to use inclusive language for human beings ("humanity" rather than "man," etc.). Traditionalists insisted they would not buy a politically correct NIV, and Zondervan relented. But not they are coming out with a PC NIV called Today's New International Version. Still, not even the New Revised Standard Version of the Bible, the version of choice for most liberal Christians, de-sexes God. He is still **He** in the NRSV.

Those who have ears to hear, let them hear: the **gender** of the deity is a sensitive subject, but the **debate** about the deity's gender is equally, if not more, sensitive. To multitudes of believers from at least the three western religions, God is male, and there is no debate. For those people it is non-productive, and even inflammatory, to seek to address the matter. But if anyone insists on debating it, that person needs to be prepared for some exceedingly heated and emotional responses. Because liberals tend to join only liberal churches, however, they are ignorant about how strongly most people feel about this. Many liberals have no qualms about using what is called "inclusive God-language" (which turns out to mean that one must never use a personal pronoun for God), and those liberals may blithely assume everyone else goes along with them on this. But they don't. Not even most of the people in most liberal churches go along with it. They do, however, put up with it; they acquiesce in it; they silently defer to it.

Most liberal clergy never use a personal pronoun when referring to God. They just clumsily keep on saying "God" all the time, without referring to Him as either "Him" or "Her." A few of them constantly alternate between calling God both Him and Her.

For every "Him" there must be an equal and equally weighted "Her."

I know I shall offend some readers by what I am now going to say it, but I believe it needs to be boldly stated nonetheless: **such sensitivities are simply superciliously silly.** As well intended as both these practices are, they create a dreadful language of liturgy. It sounds mildly peculiar or possibly daft or probably inexplicable or definitely awful or utterly mystifying when the liberal clergy either refuse the use of personal pronouns with respect to God, which is alarmingly common, or they slavishly alternate between the male and female personal pronouns, which is happily quite uncommon.

There are essentially three major points I want to make in this sermon. They are:

1) The ongoing liberal debate about proper God-language is neither truly about God nor language, but rather is a most unfortunate extension of another very important debate about women's liberation, or the equality of men and women, or male/female issues, or the battle of the sexes.

2) It is imperative that we perceive God to be **personal**, however we may choose to perceive His/Her gender.

3) The current liberal concern about the gender of God shall mercifully be a passing one, I am convinced. (This could, however, merely be wishful thinking on my part.)

Let me therefore address each point in its turn.

ONE. The question of God's gender in the recent past first arose in the 1960s and 1970s. To my knowledge, it arose first in the USA, and if it became a question in other countries at all, it was a later phenomenon which resulted in little serious debate.

But the gender of God became a large question in liberal American society because in liberal American society, gender roles became a large question. Such movies as *Some Like It Hot, Tootsie,* and *Mr. Mom* explored the issue. Feminists such as Bella Abzug,

Gloria Steinem, and Betty Friedan rightly proclaimed the need for equality between the two sexes, an equality which sadly is still very far from being achieved. For that matter, feminists need not be feminine in gender. Most of the male liberal clergy, including yours truly, I hope, can legitimately be considered feminists.

However, regardless of how anyone might respond to the matter of the gender of God, everyone should understand that it is in no way truly a feminist issue. God is who He/She is, but the nature of God is a totally different question from matters of human female/male behavior or status or rights. It is wrong to usurp the debate over the nature of God by attempting to force it under the umbrella of the injustices which males have visited upon females for lo these many generations.

There probably have been infrequent other instances where the gender of God became a genuine question for debate among people of good will, but I suspect they have occurred during times such as our own when human gender roles were being hotly contested. In the medieval period, for example, such stellar females as Hildegard of Bingen, Julian of Norwich, and Theresa of Avila were advocates for the greater recognition of women. For the most part, however, humans of both sexes have either actively accepted or passively acquiesced into believing that God is male. In any case, they believed that God is personal. Within Christianity, the doctrine of the Trinity speaks of the three **persons** of the Godhead. Forget Sophia (Wisdom) as the feminine third-person of the Trinity; this was **never** a widely-held theological formula, despite what many late-20th century feminist theologians have claimed.

Among liberal Christians, there has been a movement toward altering the traditional Trinitarian terminology. Instead of referring to the Father, Son, and Holy Spirit (two out of three of those words are unquestionably male), many liberals now say Creator, Redeemer, and Sustainer. Nice try. The intention may be above reproach in political correctness, but it is a gross violation of nineteen centuries of Christian thought to placate a few language zealots in the last quarter of the 20th century and the opening years of the 21ˢᵗ century. And in any case, Jesus was a male, whether or not God the Creator and God the Holy Spirit are male. Who is trying to kid whom here?

TWO. This leads into my second point, which is that it is a necessity for biblically- or Quran-based Jews, Christians, or Muslims to conceptualize God as being personal. We do not and must not perceive God as a force, a power, an impersonal something "out there." "May the force be with you" may cut it in *Star Wars*, but it won't work in Jewish, Christian, or Muslim theology. We cannot relate to forces. We may be affected by them (gravity manages to bring us back down to earth every time we jump up in the air), but we cannot personally relate to — or be related to — forces or powers. Philosophers may be happy with concepts of an impersonal creator, but theology requires that our Creator must be personal.

But is the Creator male or female? The only persons we know are either male or female. Surely God consists of the best qualities of both human females and males, but He is ever so much more than that. And thus **He** is not fundamentally **Him** at all.

Still, in order for limited minds to conceptualize God in personal terms, we need to see God (see there, I didn't use a personal pronoun, now did I?) as being personal. If everyone agreed to use the female personal pronoun, it would be fine. Truly it would. But because the traditional language refers to God in the masculine form, it is the most helpful to the greatest number to continue using that language. It is both wrong-headed and wrong for liberals to attempt to de-sex God at this late date in the history of theology. And this leads to - - -

THREE. Happily, the concern about the gender of God is a passing one. I think so, anyway. More than that, I hope so, anyway. Most sensible people choose to ignore what all the fuss is about, and they go on in their benighted old ways, thinking that God is male. Technically they are wrong, to be sure, but at least they see Him to be a personal, rather than an impersonal, deity. The deliberate insistence never to use personal pronouns for God would, if followed for three generations, almost completely undermine the four-thousand-year-old scriptural concept of our God as being personally related to us. That would do incalculable damage in the future to viable faith. Fortunately, the common folk are too clever to allow the quibbles of the liberal clergy to stand in the way of a palpable understanding of the nature of the Almighty. Whatever else God might be, She is essentially personal in His being. People in general are too bright to let a discussion of the divine gender waylay them in their attempts to be faithful witnesses to God and His love as they perceive Him and His love.

It may well be the height of hubris for liberal Christians to insist on politically correct God-language, especially when someone has carefully thought through the issue, and chooses to use the traditional language. Hundreds or thousands of pulpit committees from mainline churches assiduously listen for slips of the tongue in potential candidates, slips which betray a dreaded theological political incorrectness. Many a member of the clergy, especially older ones, have lost out in being called to these churches, never realizing that their God-language was the unaddressed offense which torpedoed their candidacy.

I once got fired from an interim pastorate. Besides the fact that my style of leadership was at odds with several key people on that church's staff, my God-language was unacceptably offensive to the three associate ministers. I, who had been frequently shot at for over thirty years in the pastorate for being too liberal, was too conservative for them, and for others on that church's governing board. When I have told long-time friends about this episode, many of them have absolutely hooted with laughter. A fine kettle of fish that is, when people who have been railed at by me for being too conservative take immense pleasure when the railer is getting his just deserts from folks who are even more liberal than he. Well, I suppose it does indicate that God has a sense of humor. At the time, though, it didn't seem too hilarious to me.

It would be to the great advantage of the Christian religion if my fellow liberal clergy would revert to the use of the traditional language about God. The arcane debate about the gender of God has little or no relevance to most other Christians, whether clergy or laity. We should go back to the biblical language, not because it is more accurate in describing God, but because the new language only confuses or befuddles the great majority of Christians. The vitally important questions behind the God-language debate appear picayune to most of the laity, as well as to many of the clergy. The Body Ecclesiastic is being damaged by the tension, but the proponents of the new language are unaware of how badly viable theology is being eroded by their celestial sensitivities.

Is God or our concept of God enhanced by this highly nuanced discussion? Almost certainly not. Is the Church edified by it? Again, it is not.

If it is widely agreed upon that God's gender is neither male nor female, but that God unquestionably is personal, then it behooves Christendom to come up with some new personal pronouns which refer only to God. Perhaps *Heshe* or *Shehe* would do, although both sound oppressively awful. But following along this non-euphonious line of thinking, the divine personal possessive pronoun could be *Herhis* or *Hisher*. (Merely to write these horrendous suggestions on paper makes my skin crawl! And all this just to give liberal Christians their linguistic victory!) Such an outcome is highly unlikely, however. Words like this will never play in Peoria.

The God who is God is infinitely greater than the ability of anyone, regardless of how bright or gifted, properly to conceptualize Him. Nonetheless, it is incumbent on all of us to do our best to understand God as best we can, thus the better to relate to Him. Heaven knows God has always done His best to understand us and relate to us. And it always has been a severe test of His divine nature to do so.

We need to appreciate why so many liberal Christian clergy have raised the issue of the gender of God. They mean well. Truly they do.

But as one who shares many of their concerns, and who relishes many of their positions and also prejudices, on the God-language gambit I say this: Get off it. Get over it. Get on with it.

What **is** the gender of God? I don't know. And neither, I suspect, do you.

Jesus the
Radical

Text – "For whoever would save his life will lose it, and whoever loses his life for my sake will find it. – Matthew 16:25

DOES JESUS DEMAND TOO MUCH OF US?

The text for this sermon is found in all three of the synoptic Gospels (Mt. 16:25, Mk. 8:35, Lk. 9:24). In fact, it is found twice in Luke (also Lk. 17:33).

In Matthew and Mark, the setting for this statement by Jesus is one of the most beautiful in the entire biblical land of Israel. Jesus was with His disciples at what the New Testament calls Caesarea Philippi, the Greeks called the Panias, and the Arabs call the Banias. It is the place where the Jordan River begins it winding course to the south. Water from Mt. Hermon far above the Banias comes gushing out of the sedimentary rock of a sheer cliff, and several small streams come together there to give birth to the Jordan.

The Greeks carved a statue of Pan, the god of nature, into the side of the cliff. Hence the name "Panias." But because Arabic has no letter "P," it must substitute the letter "B." Thus it became known as the Banias to the Palestinian Arabs who have lived in the region for many centuries. A more beautiful setting than the Banias could not be found anywhere. And it was there where the first person in all of history recognized Jesus to be the Messiah, the Anointed One of God.

As they sat by the frigid water, Jesus asked the disciples what identities they had heard anyone give Him. "Who do people say that I am?" He asked. They provided some of the suggestions they had been told: John the Baptist, Elijah, Jeremiah, or others of the prophets, who had been brought back from death via the person of Jesus. "But who do you say that I am?" It was then that Peter blurted out his own answer. Maybe Peter had thought about it before; maybe not; we don't know. But, in typical fashion, Peter exclaimed, "You are the Christ, the Son of the living God!"

Speak now; think later; that was Peter's motto. But this time Peter hit the nail squarely on the head. "Blessed are you, Simon, son of Jonah!" Jesus said to Peter. "For flesh and blood has not revealed this you, but my Father who is in heaven!"

In the Fourth Gospel, other people recognized Jesus as the Messiah and as God's Son long before Peter did in Matthew, Mark, or Luke. But in the synoptic tradition, which is almost certainly more accurate from an historical viewpoint, Peter was the first person to perceive Jesus as the Christ. And if the synoptic chronology is correct (and we have no reason to suppose it is not), this incident at Caesarea Philippi happened only a few weeks before Holy Week. So it was nearly three years into the ministry of Jesus before anyone ventured the opinion that Jesus was the long-awaited Messiah whom God had sent into the world.

"From that time," Matthew tells us, as do Mark and Luke, "Jesus began to show his disciples that he must go to Jerusalem and suffer many things, and be killed, and on the third day be raised." We all remember that Peter rebuked Jesus, declaring, "God forbid, Lord! This shall never happen to you!" Instantly Jesus retorted to Peter, "Get behind me, Satan! For you are not on the side of God, but of men."

I suspect Peter hoped the Jordan River would rise out of its banks, swallow him up, and carry his mortified body swiftly down to the Dead Sea. What a bummer! Peter meant well! He always meant well! But such a nudnik he could be!

Then Jesus got down to what for Him was the brass-tacks moment in this whole episode. As Jesus had done on many previous occasions, He used this incident further to explicate what Dietrich Bonhoeffer called the cost of discipleship. "Those who would come after me must deny themselves and take up their cross and follow me. Those who would save their lives will lose them, and those who lose their lives for my sake will find them."

In Matthew and Mark, this episode is recorded almost exactly identically, word for word. And when Luke repeats our text later on, it too is the same, although it is used in a different context. We may therefore deduce that the early Church obviously remembered this statement of Jesus, first, because it is so easy to memorize, but more importantly, because it states with no ambiguity whatever that becoming a disciple of Jesus is a very hard thing to do.

On one occasion Jesus said, "My yoke is easy, and my burden is light" (Mt. 11:30). But only once did He say it, or anything like it. Most of the time Jesus laid out an extremely challenging course of action for any who would become His disciples. He placed huge demands upon the Twelve, and upon all the rest of us who want to be His followers.

Take the Beatitudes, for example. According to Matthew, these words, which serve as the opening of what the Church has come to call the Sermon on the Mount, promise great blessing, but they also assume great sacrifice. "Blessed are the poor in spirit, for theirs is the kingdom of heaven. Blessed are those who mourn, for they shall be comforted. Blessed are the meek, for they shall inherit the earth." Then comes that final zinger: "Blessed are you when men revile you and persecute you and utter all kinds of evil against you falsely on my account. Rejoice and be glad, for your reward is great in heaven" (Mt. 5:1ff.). And with all this stuff happening to us when we follow Jesus, we are going to feel **blessed**? Yeah, right!

Cheer up; it could be worse. In only a few more verses, it **does** get worse. "Think not that I have come to abolish the law and the prophets; I have come not to abolish them but to fulfil them…. Not an iota, not a dot will pass from the law until all is accomplished…. For I tell you, unless your righteousness exceeds that of the scribes and Pharisees, you will never enter the kingdom of heaven" (Mt. 5:17-20).

Is Jesus telling us that we must keep every Old Testament law to the letter, to the "jot and tittle," as the King James Version had it? But who can do that? If the scribes and Pharisees couldn't do it, who were much more devoted to keeping every single law than we are, then how can we ever hope to enact the law in our lives, every waking moment of every day?

In this particular instance, I don't think Jesus was telling the whole story of what He believed about the religious law. He was deliberately withholding some of His thoughts on the matter. Later on, He Himself intentionally broke some of the sabbatarian laws. So how could He say here that not a jot or tittle would pass from the law until He had accomplished all of it? No, this part of the Sermon on the Mount was stated the way it was for political reasons. Jesus did not want to raise the hackles of His enemies too early in His ministry, so He said what they wanted to hear, just to placate them. Certainly Jesus was not the first person in biblical history to do that, nor would He be the last. For carefully considered reasons, we all keep some of our cards close to our vests at certain times. If we always revealed everything that was on our minds all the time, we would be in terrible trouble all the time. Nobody, not even Jesus, could operate like that.

"You have heard that it was said, 'You shall not kill.' But I say to you, whoever is angry with anyone shall be liable to judgment, whoever insults anyone will be liable to the council, and whoever says 'You fool!' to anyone shall be liable to the fires of hell" (Mt. 5:21ff.). Holy Moses! Who can never become angry? Who has managed never to insult anyone? Who hasn't thought certain people were the epitome of foolishness, whether or not we ever actually called them fools? Jesus, don't you think you're asking too much of us?

"You have heard it was said, 'You shall not commit adultery.' But I say to you that everyone who even looks at a woman lustfully has already committed adultery with her in his heart. If your right eye causes you to sin, pluck it out and throw it away…. If your right hand causes you to sin, cut it off and throw it away" (Mt. 5:27ff.). If you're really serious about this, Jesus, almost nobody, at least almost no males of the species, would live past puberty with eyes or hands still functioning! Is this hyperbole, Jesus, or are you serious?

"You have heard that it was said, 'An eye for an eye and a tooth for a tooth.' But I say to you, do not resist one who is evil. But if anyone strikes you on the right cheek, turn to him the other also, and if anyone would sue you and take your coat, give him your cloak as well" (Mt. 5:38ff.). **Maybe** we could do this, Jesus, as **individuals**, but do you expect nations to follow this advice?

215

Do you want only your individual followers to be pacifists, or do you want all the nations of the world to be pacifists as well? Again, are you asking too much? Is this a reasonable expectation for anyone under any circumstances?

"Do not be anxious, saying, 'What shall we eat?' or 'What shall we drink?' or 'What shall we wear?' For the Gentiles seek all these things, and your heavenly Father knows you need them all. But seek first his kingdom and his righteousness, and all these things shall be yours as well" (Mt. 6:31ff.). No disrespect, Jesus, but you didn't have a family, you didn't have anyone depending on you. Some of us have or have had dependents, and some of those dependents have required a great deal of us. Could we just turn our backs on them and go off to become homeless disciples for you? Is it **right** to walk away from responsibilities, especially when many if not most of those responsibilities are worthy endeavors, ethical choices, moral decisions which we have carefully, and not frivolously, made?

One time Peter asked Jesus how often he was required to forgive someone who had wronged him. "As many as seven times?" said the wary prince of apostles, who had on many previous occasions firmly inserted his flapping foot into his gaping mouth. "Not seven times," said Jesus in answer to Peter, "but seventy times seven" (Mt. 18:21-22). Surely Jesus was not literally telling Peter that the statute of limitations on forgiveness runs to 490 offers of forgiveness. Then on the 491st offense, Pow! you can let him have it. No, Jesus was telling us that we must **always** forgive **everyone** for **everything**. But is that reasonable? Is it possible? And even if it is possible, which it probably isn't, is it wise? Does permanent forgiveness of everybody for everything create a better world, or does it merely create a climate in which the bad guys will always take advantage of the good guys, because they know the good guys will never retaliate for anything? Do you demand the proper kinds of things of us, Jesus? Did you thoroughly think through the long-term effects of your demands?

When Jesus first sent out the twelve disciples on their mission, He gave them some very stringent instructions. "Take nothing for your journey, no staff, no bag, no bread, no money, and do not have two tunics. And whatever house you enter, stay there, and from there depart. And wherever they do not receive you, when you leave that town shake off the dust from your feet as a testimony against them" (Lk. 9:1-3). The first part of that sounds almost like the behavior of Buddhist monks. They deliberately choose to have nothing, and depend entirely on the generosity of others to sustain themselves. To state it baldly, they live by begging. Did Jesus intend those instructions to be followed by the twelve only on their first mission, which presumably was a very short one? Or did He mean it for all of His followers through all of their lives? If the latter, no one, save for those who live in monasteries and convents, follows this advice. Actually, they don't either. Cloistered monks and nuns do not go out into the world on missions; they remain in the secluded safety of their monastic communities. Or is there more to Jesus' instructions to the twelve than meets the eye, something the Gospel writer left out? Could **anybody** ever live like that, particularly people in the opening years of the 21ˢᵗ century?

Mark's Gospel has the account of Jesus passing the withered fig tree that He had cursed (11:20 ff.), which has echoes in Matthew (21:20-22). In response to this highly peculiar incident, Jesus told Peter and the other disciples, "Have faith in God. Truly, I say to you, those who say to this mountain, 'Be taken up and cast into the sea,' and do not doubt in their hearts, but believe that what they say will come to pass, it will be done for them." Only the most wooden of literalists would imagine Jesus intended us to follow these observations literally. But it seems impossible to have faith like that even in a figurative sense. Maybe this statement of Jesus isn't technically a demand, but it still seems as though He is asking too much of us!

Or there is that unfortunate chap Jesus asked to follow Him. "Lord, let me first go and bury my father," he said to Jesus. Then Jesus said to him, "Leave the dead to bury their own dead; but as for you, go and proclaim the kingdom of God." Then, to another would-be disciple who wanted first to go say goodbye to his family, Jesus icily responded, "Those who put their hand to the plow and look back are not fit for the kingdom of God" (Lk. 9:57ff.).

Pay close attention: **Jesus of Nazareth was an extremist; He really was.** We can try to talk our way out of this truth, or try to wend our way around it, but in the glistening light of reality, we are bound to agree that Jesus was an extremist.

Had most of us lived when Jesus lived, most of us would have avoided Him like the plague. We may try to kid ourselves into believing that we would have been every bit as devoted to Jesus as were the Twelve. The problem with that optimistic assessment is that we overlook the fact that the devotion of the disciples wasn't all that much to write home about either. The one we hear the most about, Peter, seemed often to act like a dunce. And his fidelity in the face of danger wasn't anything to extol either. In the moment of Jesus' greatest need, in the Garden of Gethsemane, "they all forsook him and fled," it says in two of the Gospels (Mt. 26:56, Mk. 14:50). None of the apostles came through in the clutch; not one.

What I am suggesting is that the original disciples were not much better at following Jesus with utter abandon than we are. **We are incapable of doing everything He demands of us!** It is imperative that we realize that, or else we shall catapult ourselves into the muddy wallow of self-pity, crying, "Woe is me, woe is me! I am a totally worthless disciple!" None of us is worthless, but none of us is perfect either. We all are somewhere between the deepest hole in the garbage dump and the highest peak of the mountain. Wherever we are on that continuum, it is imperative for us to understand that we are simply not capable of doing everything Jesus demanded of us.

But also remember this: **Jesus did not always follow His own advice.** He did not always practice what He preached. It may seem scandalous to say that, even heretical. But if you read the Gospels, if you read every word of every Gospel, and you cogitate carefully on all of it, you will have to admit that even Jesus didn't always do what Jesus told us we must always do. He got angry, as we do, although He insisted we must never get angry. He called some of the scribes and Pharisees blind fools, although He insisted we must never call anyone a fool. He resisted evildoers, not with the lashes of a whip, but with terrible tongue-lashings. He was **not** "gentle Jesus, meek and mild;" He really wasn't.

Earlier I mentioned Dietrich Bonhoeffer. Bonhoeffer had an outstanding phrase. He declared that Jesus was edged out of the world and onto the cross. From early in His public ministry, Jesus knew that somehow, through one subterfuge or another, He would be executed. And since the cross was the universal means of execution in the first century Roman Empire, that was probably the method by which He knew He would be killed. I don't think Jesus possessed that certainty by divine foreknowledge; I think He knew it because He was very shrewd observer of individual and corporate human behavior. He knew that nobody could be as radical as He was without paying the ultimate price for His radicality. Jesus intentionally put Himself on a slippery slope which He was sure would terminate upon on a cross.

I can't personally imagine what it would be like to become increasingly convinced that I would be executed. To the very limited degree I can put myself into that mindset, it seems likely that anyone who felt that way would feel a greatly heightened sense of the importance of "getting on with it." Jesus knew that He had to get on with it, and He strongly, maybe even impetuously, urged His followers to get on with it too. "The cup that I drink you will drink," Jesus told the disciples (Mk. 10:39), and that came to pass. Most of the twelve, the tradition declares, also died violent deaths, as did Jesus. When you think you don't have much time, you don't always measure carefully everything you say. And so, yes, Jesus did demand too much of us, as He demanded too much of Himself. But it could not be any other way, given the circumstances under which He lived, and the shortened time constraints He felt closing in on Him.

"If you would come after me, then deny yourself, and take up your cross, and follow me" (Mt. 16:24). When Jesus said that to the disciples, He knew that His days on earth were swiftly coming to an end. Did Jesus actually say to them, "**Take up your cross** and follow me?" If He did say it, could He possibly expect them to know what it meant? Prior to Good Friday, it would have been a statement with no context, a saying without meaning. Or perhaps He did say it, and since He said it so close to Good Friday, later its meaning struck them like a thunderbolt, even if it mystified them when they first heard Him say it.

In any event, all who seek to follow Jesus must do exactly what He said. We must **deny ourselves**, and we must **take up our cross**. We have talked ourselves into a Christianity that is too easy, a discipleship that demands little. "When Jesus calls a man," said Bonhoeffer in the opening statement of *The Cost of Discipleship,* "He bids him come and die." The German theologian literally died as a Christian martyr. We are called figuratively to die.

The Bible says we should be tithers. Most of us are so well off financially that we can give much more than a tithe, and everyone, regardless of how poor, is capable of giving away 10% of their income. Yet we choose to live "better" than we might, in order not to die.

The Bible suggests, in many places and in many nuances, that we should live within our means, that we should not be extravagant in our lifestyle. Extravagance comes easily to us; simplicity seems almost impossible, especially in an age that is economically so complex. So we choose to live "better" than we might, in order not to die.

Jesus tells us to go the extra mile for people, but usually we don't go out of our way at all for anyone. He tells us not to retaliate, but when we are in a store, buying something with our hard-earned money (just ask us how hard; we'll tell you), and the clerk acts like the nincompoop he is, we petulantly dress him down for his incompetence, never thinking for a moment that anybody who accepts his low level of pay is not likely to be the rocket scientist we consider ourselves to be. But we go ahead and buy whatever it is we wanted, and thus we choose to live "better" than we might, in order not to die.

The Bible tells us to do, do, do, to give, give, give, to believe, believe, believe, and we don't, don't, don't, and we keep, keep, keep, and guard, guard, guard. And we don't trust, and instead we distrust and mistrust. Does Jesus demand too much of us? Heavens, yes! What did we expect? Denying self doesn't come naturally to any of us; protecting self is as natural as falling off a log!

Three days before the crucifixion, Jesus told what would happen when He, the Son of man, came in His glory. It is the famous illustration of feeding the hungry and giving drink to the thirsty, of clothing the naked and visiting people in prison, of "doing unto the least of these." At the end, said Jesus, when the history of each of us has played itself out, we will be divided like sheep and goats. The sheep will go on God's right hand to eternal life, but the goats will go on God's left hand into eternal punishment (Mt. 25:31-46).

Most of us, maybe all of us, are goats. We do what we shouldn't do, and we don't do what we should do. Our catastrophic capricornian actions make us sinister and gauche, and we deserve to be herded to the left side, where men weep and gnash their teeth.

Does Jesus demand too much of us? I hope to tell the world. If He doesn't, we wouldn't do nearly as much as we somehow manage to do. But however much we do, it is never enough. As Elizabeth Barrett's husband, Mr. Browning, declared, "A man's reach should exceed his grasp, or what's a heaven for?" Jesus demanded more than He knew we could accomplish, so that we might accomplish more than we are wont to do.

James O'Toole is an associate professor of history at Boston College, a Roman Catholic institution in one of the most Catholic of American cities. In the *Boston College Magazine* (Fall 2001), he wrote about trends in the Roman Catholic sacrament of confession. Since Vatican II, he said, the very name of the sacrament has changed. Previously it was known as penance; for the past few decades it has been the sacrament of reconciliation. In the Fifties, there were long queues in Catholic churches beside the confessional boxes; from the Sixties on, the lines disappeared. What once was considered a necessity on a weekly basis has become an option, even on an annual basis, although canon law requires confession at least once a year.

Prof. O'Toole asked, "Does confession have a future? As a historian, I am more comfortable describing and analyzing the past than predicting the future, but I find it difficult to believe that the long lines at the confessionals of earlier times will return.... We stand today in the same position as the Christians in the early Middle Ages: The older form of confession and absolution is dying out, and what the newer form will be is not clear."

In Marge Piercy's novel *Summer People*, the author says this, describing one of her characters: "The Church was a dark place she had escaped. Oh, the Protestants thought they had religion but what they had was something comfortable, tidy. Something that was kept in its place and bothered them little. A place to expose their new clothes and feel pious. There was an odor of sin and sanctity, no great weight of the centuries pressing down. The polite Protestant sects weren't real religions, which is why she liked them. They offered as much religion as a truly civilized person needed."

Today, only the most rigidly fundamentalist of churches or Christians feel terribly uneasy with the knowledge of how greatly they have failed in their Christian discipleship. The rest of us, mainline Protestants, Pentecostals, evangelicals, Roman Catholics, or Eastern Orthodox go through the motions of admitting our shortcomings, but those failings don't really weigh us down. We have learned how gracefully to avoid the awareness of our need for grace. We acceptably accept our unacceptability. Our knowledge of our sin is skimpy, and our determination to improve our lives is wimpy.

Jesus was sometimes relentless in His insistence that we become transformed beings. "Do you think that I have come to give peace on earth?" He asked. "No, I tell you, but rather division; for henceforth in one house there will be five divided, three against two and two against three; they will be divided, father against son and son against father, mother against daughter and daughter against her mother, mother-in-law against her daughter-in-law and daughter-in-law against her mother-in-law" (Lk. 12:51-53). Where people take the teachings of Jesus extremely seriously, clashes are inevitable. They don't happen much among most of us, because we don't really take Jesus' teachings all that seriously.

Shortly after saying the things quoted in the above paragraph, Jesus said, "If anyone comes to me and does not hate his own father and mother and wife and children and brothers and sisters, yes, and even his own life, he cannot be my disciple. Whoever does not bear his own cross and come after me, cannot be my disciple" (Lk. 14:26-27). There is no way that statement could be taken literally, but there also is no way it can be dismissed out of hand, either. Jesus clearly implied that being His disciples is going to create some tension between us and those we love the most. If it does not happen, then we have not conscientiously attempted to put into practice the demands He makes on us. All of us will never agree on everything we think should be incorporated into the Christian life, but none of us shall have the luxury of avoiding Christ's demands altogether. If being a Christian is ever going to pay, it must start to cost. We delude ourselves if we think otherwise.

A convenient Christianity is likely no Christianity at all. Only in terms of the power of God's love is Christ's yoke easy, or is His burden light. God's grace saves us; His grace alone saves us. Were it not for God's unconditional love, our sins would turn our lives into an horrendous hell. But in the meantime, Jesus has placed a test before us, and we all need to pass it. Don't plan on dotting every "i" and crossing every "t," or satisfactorily finishing every question; it won't happen. But don't think it will be acceptable to turn in a blank blue book either.

Attempting to live a Christian life without self-denial is like attempting to win an Olympic gold medal without any kind of training. Victory in Jesus necessitates the defeat of self. So get with the program and start denying yourself - - - for heaven's sake!

Scripture – Mark 10:17-22

Text – And Jesus looking upon him loved him, and said to him, "You lack one thing; go, sell, what you have, and give to the poor; and you will have treasure in heaven; and come, follow me." At that saying his countenance fell, and he went away sorrowful; for he had great possessions. – Mark 10:21-22 (RSV)

JESUS AND RICHES: A CASE STUDY

This scripture passage from the tenth chapter of Mark's Gospel is often called the Story of the Rich Young Ruler. It is found, almost verbatim, in each of the three synoptic Gospels. In all three versions, the man who sought out Jesus was rich. In Matthew (19:20) it is noted that he was young, and in Luke (18:18) he identified as a "ruler," which means an authority in a synagogue, as opposed to a political authority. Thus, by the accretion of interpretation through the centuries of Christian history, he becomes "the rich young ruler."

Because the rich young ruler was wealthy, we may deduce that he had all the creature comforts he needed. But that isn't why he wanted to talk to Jesus. A particular question had been bothering this sensitive, admirable man, and he correctly decided that Jesus was the best person to propose an answer for him. "Good Teacher," he said to Jesus, "what must I do to inherit eternal life?" Because Mark later informs us that Jesus instantly was attracted to the goodness in the young man's heart, we may infer that his greeting was genuine when he called Jesus "Good Teacher" or "Good Rabbi." Unlike many of the people who approached Jesus, who intended to trip up Jesus, this man was very honest and without guile when he spoke to Jesus.

Jesus might have said to the man that nobody can do anything to **inherit** eternal life, because nobody can do anything to inherit anything. An inheritance comes to us from the generosity of another. Perhaps this young man had already inherited a great deal from his deceased father, which is what made him rich, as all three of the Evangelists tell us, and such an inheritance had guaranteed him a cushy temporal life. Eternal life is a gift from God, and solely from God; no one else can give it. Jesus might have reminded the eager young synagogue leader of these things - - - but He didn't. No, instead Jesus answered the man's question with another question. (Was Jesus a Jew, or what? Was the rich young ruler a Jew, or what? Do Jews answer questions of Jews with questions, or what?)

"Why do you call me good?" said Jesus. "No one is good but God alone." Some readers might assume Jesus was being deliberately ironic here, as if to say, "If you call me good, you must think I am God incarnate, because only God is good." I don't accept that interpretation. I think Jesus didn't want to start off on the wrong foot with the young man. From the very outset, Jesus reminded the man that God alone is good. Maybe Jesus told the young man He was grateful for the compliment, but none of the three synoptic writers bothers to tell us that.

Then, knowing that the opening repartee didn't really get to the root of what was germinating in this outstanding would-be disciple, Jesus continued on. Jesus recited a few of the Ten Commandments as a way of probing further to help the rich young ruler find his own answer to his own question. "Oh," said the rich young ruler, probably with relief in his voice, "I have faithfully observed all these divine laws from my youth." By looking in the man's eyes, and by peering into his heart, as only Jesus could do, Mark tells us that Jesus immediately loved him. Jesus perceived the man to be what Yiddish calls a *Mensch*, a genuine, upright, noble human being. The man's *Menschlichkeit* shone with a pure radiance which brought joy to Jesus' heart.

So, **because** Jesus was so taken by the purity of the rich young ruler, He said, "There is one thing you still lack in your devotion to the law. Now you must sell everything you have and give the money to the poor. When you do that, your true treasure will be in the kingdom of heaven, rather than in the finest things of the earth. And having taken that bold and courageous step, then you will be able to come, and follow me, and be one of my disciples."

It is imperative for us to understand that Jesus wasn't trying to set up a huge impediment in the path of this man. That's the last thing Jesus wanted to do. Jesus would have been thrilled to have such a magnificent specimen of true devotion as one of His followers. Standing there, resplendent in his hand-tailored Brooks Brothers suit and his fitted Egyptian cotton button-down shirt and his $150 Saks Fifth Avenue designer silk tie and his $325 Gucci loafers, the Man from Nazareth immediately recognized a high-quality human being, a first-class sort of person, a committed, caring, earnest seeker-after-truth. Jesus was not put off by the man's wealth, and He may even have been attracted to it. After all, the young man represented a huge contrast to the rest of the motley crew who were The Twelve. Jesus had no intention of trying to trick the rich young ruler; He just wanted him to know the nature of the cost of our discipleship when we become subjects in the kingdom of God rather than citizens of this world.

Further, it is imperative that we understand this: **Jesus had no implicit problems with wealth, nor does God.** No, *Jesus* has no problems with wealth per se; *we* are the ones who have the problems! Every penny of the world's wealth is ultimately a gift from God, so obviously God has no quibbles with wealth either. But for human beings, here is the issue with respect to wealth: **What do we do with our money?** Do we use money, or does money use us? Do we own our wealth, or does our wealth own us? Who is in charge of our wealth: us, or God? For whose primary benefit do we have or save or spend our wealth, for us, or for God?

None of the Gospel writers provided us with a credit rating for any of the twelve disciples, or for anyone else who followed Jesus. My guess is that only a few of them possessed even the proverbial receptacle in which to relieve themselves. It would have been far easier to follow Jesus as a poor fisherman, which is maybe what Peter, Andrew, James, and John were, or a penniless revolutionary, which is maybe what Simon the Zealot and Judas Iscariot were. Matthew the tax collector may have been rich, especially if he had dipped into his IRS cash proceeds. But then, would Jesus want somebody like that as a disciple? Maybe. Who knows? In any case, Matthew **was** one of The Twelve, however much money he did or didn't have.

Anyway, when Jesus said the rich young ruler must get rid of all his riches, He was telling him, as He tells all of us, that there is a price to be paid in becoming associated with the Messiah. You must give up whatever is nearest and dearest to you. You must be totally unencumbered of everyone and everything else in order to become totally encumbered by your newly-designated discipleship. To have everything, you must have nothing. Or, as Jesus put it, "Whoever would save his life must lose it," or "Whoever loves parents or spouse or children more than me is not worthy of me," or "Having set your hand to my plow, you must never look back," or "To get with my program, you have to give up your program." (Actually Jesus never said that last thing; I made it up. But He **might** have said it.)

Mark expresses the reaction of the rich young ruler in such an imaginative, colorful manner. "At that saying, his countenance fell, and he went away sorrowful, for he had many possessions." The eager, engaged, energetic young would-be follower was instantaneously deflated. With inexpressible sorrow, all the air went out of him with a great whooshing sound. "His countenance fell." In a flash he looked like death warmed over, like he had been kicked by a mule, like he had just heard the worst news ever to assault a human aural cavity. In a mere moment, he knew that his future had vanished, and his world had collapsed, because Jesus required him to do the one thing he could not do.

If you figure the problem with the rich young ruler is that he was rich, you have missed the point altogether. Whether or not any of us is rich is a tertiary concern to God; what we do with our wealth is of primary importance to Him. Again, do we own our wealth, or does it own us? Or, to look at it from another perspective, if we are unusually healthy, do we own our health, or does it own us? If we were born brilliant, do we own our intelligence, or does it own us? If we can tear the cover off a baseball when we hit it, or throw a football like a bullet seventy yards down the field, or serve a tennis ball at 139 MPH, are **we** the ones who do that, or is it **God in us** and **God through us** who does it? To whom do we and our talents and abilities and possessions belong: to ourselves, or to God?

Money isn't the issue; ownership is the issue! Are **we** ours, is **it** ours, or are we and it **God's**? That's what Jesus wants to know! That's what God wants to know! And it is a mistake to start out, supposing that we are our own person, when there is no other option than to be God's person! There is a hell of a price to be paid in order to get into the kingdom of heaven!

And so, money isn't the problem ... unless it **is** the problem. And sadly, for most of us, money is a problem, and for some of us, money is **the** problem, the primary problem of our existence.

Probably more than any other economist, John Maynard Keynes has been the primary philosophical forefather of contemporary American capitalism. Keynes believed in money. But he also believed that money is meant to be spent, not saved. If people make money, and spend it, then the economy grows, and everyone benefits. There are two or three more features of Keynesian economics than that, or maybe even fifty or a hundred, but that is a key to Keynes.

There are three things anyone who has money can do with it: we can save it, we can spend it, or we can give it away. Obviously we can do all three at the same time, but those are the only choices open to anyone who has money.

We don't know why the countenance of the rich young ruler fell. Maybe he was a saver, or even a miser, somebody who loved to invest money and see it grow. Or maybe he was a spender; someone who loved all the material pleasures which money can buy. (That business about the Brooks Brothers suit I also made up; there is nothing in any of the three synoptic accounts which even hints at that. But hey, when you're working on a sermonic essay like this, or an essayic sermon, you have to amuse yourself somehow.) However, we may infer that the young man was not delighted with the prospect of giving away all his money to the poor or anyone else. By the rapid plunge of his countenance, it seems evident that giving away his wealth was not high on his list of To-Do things prior to becoming a disciple of Jesus.

Are we to assume Jesus insists everyone must give up whatever wealth we have to become His disciple? No, no, no! That is not the point! The point is not that we must give up **anything in particular**; it is rather that we must give up **everything in general** that stands between us and genuine discipleship.

However, money or wealth can be a major impediment in our pursuit of discipleship, which is why Jesus talked so much about money. It has been stated that Jesus talked more about the stewardship of wealth more than any other single subject. That seems difficult to support in a close study of scripture, but it may well be true.

But **why** is it so hard for us to feel comfortable about our money — or lack of it? Why are we so defensive and closed-mouthed and guarded about our lucre, whether filthy or otherwise?

One of John Grisham's most recent novels is called *The Summons*. It is about two sons who are summoned by their elderly father to return to the home in which they grew up in Mississippi, because the paterfamilias is about to die. They are to arrive there at such-and-such a time on such-and-such a day. The older son, Ray, is a professor of law at the University of Virginia, and the younger one, Forrest, is a ne'er-do-well drug addict. Ray gets to the house first, and he finds that their father has died only an hour or so before his arrival. In the process of waiting for Forrest to come, Ray discovers three million dollars in cash in some boxes stashed away in the house. This, to say the least, was a non-plussing discovery. Their father was a judge, who never could have managed to save three million dollars, especially in cash. The plot becomes instantaneously thick. What to do with that much cash? And should Forrest get his half of the money outright, or should Ray set up a trust fund so that Forrest cannot spend it all in a plethora of profligate purchasing, particularly on drugs and alcohol?

Toward the end of the novel, Ray explains the situation to Harry Rex Vonner, the closest friend of their father, who also was the judge's attorney. When Ray divulged the existence of the huge stash of cash, Harry Rex said, "You should've told me." But Ray retorted, "I wanted to keep the money, okay? I had three million bucks in cash in my sticky little hands, and it felt wonderful. It was better than sex, better than anything I'd ever felt was. Three million bucks, Harry Rex, all mine. I was rich. I was greedy. I was corrupt. I didn't want you or Forrest or the government or anyone in the world to know I had the money" *(The Summons*, pps. 308-9).

Right there, Christian or otherwise reader, is how money can take possession of us! It can corrode our ideals! It can eviscerate our resolve! It can transform generosity into greed, sanctity into selfishness! The possession of wealth does not automatically do any of those things, but it **can** do it, and often it **does** do it.

According to *The New York Times,* 87,000 American taxpayers made $1 million or more in 1995. By 1999, that number had risen to 205,000. In 1995, the 87,000 had 5.4% of the total American income. By 1999, the 205,000 had 11.2% of the total income. The 205,000 garnered more than 25% of the nation's total personal income growth. The capital gains tax cut of 1997 favored the 400 taxpayers with the most income in the USA. They took in 7% of all the capital gains in 1998, but they paid only 22% of their income in taxes in that year, which was down from the 30% they paid in 1994.

It is very difficult for people with incomes like that not to expend enormous mental and spiritual energy to continue making incomes like that. Everyone at every income level wants, minimally, to stay at her or his level, or better, to move up the ladder. But the more income we make, the harder it is to cast aside everything to follow Jesus. Riches are not sinful by their nature, but they can be a major distraction to discipleship. And so can power or position or sex or status distract us. Being a disciple is a terrible and demanding enterprise. Jesus never led anyone to believe anything other than that.

Nonetheless, wealth poses a particular problem for discipleship, because by its very essence, it is so **tangible**. Power, position, sex, or status are also tangible, but not nearly as much as wealth. Money or other assets are more readily quantifiable than other impediments to our faithfulness to God and Jesus. Who can objectively measure such things as power or status? But we can quickly add up how much we have in the bank or in investments or in the value of our material possessions. For that reason, most people discover the accumulation of wealth is more likely to deter us from total commitment to God than any other single factor.

Let us consider some specific examples. One of the best-paid players in the National Basketball Association was given a three-game suspension for a flagrant infraction of the rules. In his case that three-game dismissal amounted to $800,000 in salary. That comes to $267,000 per game. You probably agree that it's a fairly sizeable chunk of cash for flinging a round ball through a round hoop. For whom would be it be easier to drop everything and go off to follow Jesus: a skinny kid on a crumbling asphalt court in a city playground, or a superstar center who pulls in $267,000 per game?

A certain football coach went from being the highest-paid coach in college football to being the highest-paid coach in the NFL. He gets $5 million a year. Assuming he coaches his team in 20 games throughout the season, excluding exhibition games but including post-season playoff games, he gets roughly $250,000 per contest. Of course he does other things for the team, but on a per-game basis, it comes down to a cool quarter of a million dollars for each 60 minutes of official game time. Were Jesus to appear before that coach and an unpaid volunteer coach with a pee-wee team, and He urged both of them to drop everything to follow Him (as He did with Peter, Andrew, James, and John), who would be more likely to respond instantly in the affirmative?

Suppose an excellent home-run hitter in baseball decided that God wanted him to volunteer as the hitting coach for a struggling parochial school baseball team. One hitter has been retired from professional ball for ten years, and another is in his prime, having hit 70 home runs a year for the last two years. His salary is $18 million a year, which equates to $250,000 per home run. Of course he too does other things for the team: he catches fly balls, he throws the ball a few times each game, he gets other hits, or he walks, or he strikes out. But any way you slice it, he makes about $250,000 for each of his home runs. Of the two hitters, who is probably going to help out the parochial school team, if either of them does?

Since founding a major technology company in 1997, a CEO sold $700 million of stock options which the board of directors, which he controlled, awarded to him. The company went into a multi-billion dollar bankruptcy five years after he started it. The CEO of another company used millions of dollars of corporate funds to purchase and furnish several homes for himself, and sold over $100 million in stock shortly before the stock lost over 95% of its value. The founder and CEO of another corporation was arrested for mismanagement of company funds, along with other family members, but not until the family had taken $3.1 billion from the company prior to its bankruptcy.

When wealth like that is being amassed that fast, it is hard to concentrate on much else. Who is going to stop to smell the roses when the fleeting moment required for a good whiff costs the sniffer the equivalent of $15,000 per sniff?

After the collapse of the World Trade Center, contributions flooded into the Red Cross and other charitable agencies. In the Tribeca section of Lower Manhattan, the Red Cross offered to pay up to three months of mortgage and maintenance payments or rent, along with money for groceries, utilities, transportation, and medical expenses, if such expenses were applicable. Some people in some buildings were devastated by the terrorist attack, and others were virtually unaffected. Nonetheless, many people in undamaged buildings were offered — and accepted — up to $15,000 of this "free money." "WWJD?", the bumper sticker asks; What Would Jesus Do? I don't think He'd take the money. And I don't think He'd take any disciples who took the money. Money, especially that kind of money, corrupts the kind of commitment Jesus wants from us.

There are instances throughout religious history where individuals gave up a life of wealth and privilege for a much larger, if also much less plush, good. Siddhartha Gautama was the son of a noble landowner in northern India, but he cast aside his background to become the Enlightened One, the Buddha. St. Francis of Assisi was the son of a wealthy merchant. His father disowned him when he gave away everything he owned, including the very shirt off his back. Francis' younger contemporary, St. Clare, did much the same thing. Ever since, Buddhist monks and Franciscan brothers and the Poor Clares have chosen a life of poverty, not because it better serves God, but because they have felt it frees them to be better disciples for God's causes. And a young man from Nazareth had a father who was a carpenter, although some scholars say the Greek word actually connotes "homebuilder." Joseph was middle class, to the degree that first century Judea had a middle class. But Jesus turned aside from relative wealth and better-than-average privilege and became an itinerant preacher, depending solely on the generosity of those who affirmatively listened to Him.

We all lack at least one thing in our discipleship, but the rich young ruler lacked one thing only. "Go, sell what you have, and give to the poor, and come, follow me." Was it harder for him to give up the single thing lacking in his commitment than it is for us to surrender whatever impedes us? Each of us must answer that question. And until it is answered, we will never be free to move forward.

Curiously, most American Christians do not consider themselves to be wealthy. Affluent, maybe, but not really wealthy. Compared to the vast majority of the world's population, however, we are rich, regardless of our position on the scale of income of our fellow citizens. Eighty to ninety per cent of the people sharing the world with us do not have sufficient spare cash to purchase a book such as this one, even if they wanted to read it, which most would not, but most of us can buy far more things than we need.

We take our wealth and income for granted. "We're just like everyone else," we tell ourselves. We may be like most of our peers, like most of the people with whom we are closely acquainted, but we are far above nearly everyone else on earth in the possession of assets.

In the industrialized West, or, more appropriately, the post-industrial West, it is the middle and upper classes who are the people who go to church or synagogue. The underprivileged and the underclass do not have time to bother with church. They are too busy trying to exist to give much thought to the quality of their existence. In the Third World, however, it is the poorest of the poor who are attracted to religion, religion of any sort. And it is in the Third World where both Christianity and Islam are currently making their greatest numerical headway. The percentage of people living in poverty in the poor nations is so large that they are powerfully unified in their hope for something or someone, anything or anyone, to lead them out of their physical impoverishment into a more plentiful and hopeful spiritual dimension. In Jesus' own time, it was likely the poor and dispossessed who were most drawn to His teachings, not the kind of people who would read books of dyspeptic sort-of-sermons by unreconstructed liberal retired preachers.

The life to which Jesus calls us is clearly not a life of ease or pleasure. From time to time we may encounter both ease and pleasure, but they are by-products of Christian existence, not the purpose or measure of it.

We have made Christianity too comfortable. "Comfortable Christianity" is an oxymoron. If our discipleship is not hard and demanding, it is neither real nor realistic. "People who have everything," which describes most of us, have convenience etched into our existence. Convenient Christianity is also an oxymoron. And yet we try to co-exist with this contradiction in terms, even when we know in our heart of hearts that it is not possible.

We are too hard on others, and too easy on ourselves. We see their faults as though on a large-screen television, and we see our own failings on a battery-operated three-inch portable-in-a-pocket screen. And the batteries are almost completely out of oomph.

Half-hearted discipleship is, by definition, also half-baked. We want discipleship on the cheap, while at the same time we demand a life of comfort and ease. We have grown flabby in our commitment. Physically many of us are fitness fanatics, but spiritually we are candidates for a twelve-step inner spa of the soul. We talk much, but do little. In our own quiet way, we give the world our testimony, but it is so timid, so soft, so unobtrusive, that almost no one ever hears it. Because we lack the courage or conviction to shout it from the mountaintop, the world never realizes that we want to pass it on. As subdued as it is, the world doesn't even know what "it" is.

"And Jesus looking upon him loved him." When Jesus looks on us, He also loves us. Jesus loves me, this I know, for the Bible tells me so.

But if we love Jesus, or, more important, if we love God, we need to do something to reciprocate their love for us. We cannot truly receive the divine or the messianic acceptance unless it results in a total transformation of our lives. In our time it has become far too easy to adopt a Christianity that is far too easy. We must die in order to live. Our self must suffer if we are ever to discover our true selves.

"At that saying his countenance fell, and he went away sorrowful." Shall we accept the lively death which Jesus offers, or shall we choose the deathly life which the world offers? And are we ready to count the cost?

Scripture – John 20:1-18

Text – Soon afterward he went on through cities and villages, preaching and bringing the good news of the kingdom of God. And the twelve were with him, and also some of the women who had been healed of evil spirits and infirmities: Mary, called Magdalene, from whom seven demons had gone out, and Joanna, the wife of Chuza, Herod's steward, and Susanna, and many others, who provided for them out of their means. – Luke 8:1-3

THE LADY WHOM JESUS LOVED

It is an unfortunate truth that there are too many women named Mary in the Gospel narratives. It is hard to keep them all straight.

Most of the time, the context tells us which Mary is being written about. The most-frequently cited Mary is the mother of Jesus. She, of course, was the wife of Joseph, the carpenter. She is very big in the two birth narratives (Matthew 1&2 and Luke 1&2). She also appears several other times in various places in each of the four Gospels. When she does, we know it is she, because she is identified clearly.

Then there is that other Mary, who is the sister of Martha and Lazarus. She lived in Bethany, just outside Jerusalem. At least that's where the two sisters and brother lived in John (see ch. 11). In Luke, they may have lived somewhere in the Galilee, rather than in a Jerusalem suburb, as identified by John. Further, in Luke there is no mention of Lazarus; only Mary and Martha reported on (see Luke 10:38-42). Earlier in Luke, as is true of all the other synoptic Gospels, Jesus had been spending all His time in the northern part of the country, that region called "the Galilee" by Israeli Jews today, and just "Galilee" by Christians for the past nineteen centuries.

Anyway, Luke says, "Now as they went on their way, he entered a village; and a woman named Martha received him into her house. And she had a sister named Mary, who sat at the Lord's feet and listened to his teaching" (Lk. 10:38ff.). That leads into the

236

famous incident of Martha fretting about feeding Jesus and Mary wanting to be fed spiritually by Jesus. When I was a boy, my parents used to have periodic go-rounds about who really chose the better part: Mary or Martha. Jesus said Mary did, and so did my father, but my mother sided with Martha. Somebody had to fix dinner, said Mom. So we four boys would cheer for Dad, and then for Mom, just to egg them on in their biblical dispute. (We had a disputatious household. Having read a sufficient number of these hot homilies, you will not be surprised to hear that, no doubt. It was true; in our house we reveled in arguments and debates.) However, all this is by-the-by, because Mary of Bethany or wherever is not the Mary this sermon is about.

Nor is it about "Mary the wife of Clopas" (John 19:25), who stood at the foot of the cross with Mary the mother of Jesus, and Mary Magdalene. That Mary, the wife of Clopas, is identified as Jesus' mother's sister in John 19:25, which would make her Jesus' Aunt Mary. But how could there be two Marys in the same family, the one who ended up married to Joseph, and the other who ended up married to Clopas? Why would any parents give two daughters the same name? Wouldn't it be confusing? Now of course maybe this Mary the wife of Clopas was actually Mary the sister-in-law of Jesus' mother, and not Mary (the mother's) sister.

Are you following all this? Are you keeping all these Marys straight? What did I tell you about there being too many Marys?

There are three other Marys mentioned later in the New Testament, outside the Gospels. We know for certain who the first one is. "All these devoted themselves to prayer, together with the women and Mary the mother of Jesus, and with his brothers" (Acts 1:14). So that Mary is, again, Jesus' mother. Then we learn that the mother of John (or John Mark, or, better known to us, as just Mark, the Gospel writer) is also Mary. "When he realized this, he went to the house of Mary, the mother of John whose other name was Mark" (Acts 12:12). Finally, at the end of Romans, Paul says, "Greet Mary, who has worked hard among you" (Rom. 16:6). There is no further specific identification, but we may deduce this lady was none of the other previously mentioned Marys.

So that it is clear whom I am talking about in this sermon called *The Lady Whom Jesus Loved*, I am talking about **Mary Magdalene**. That Mary was the Mary for whom Jesus had a unique love and affection, as I hope this sermon shall indicate.

So who was Mary Magdalene? What do we know about her? Unfortunately, not much. Presumably Mary Magdalene came from the village of **Magdala**. Thus Mary *Magdalene* actually connotes Mary of Magdala. Magdala was located on the northwest corner of the Sea of Galilee. It was the first village to the north of the city of Tiberias. Tiberias still exists, and it existed in the time of Jesus, but Magdala has long since disappeared. Today there is almost nothing there other than a small abandoned archaeological dig. But in Jesus' time, apparently Magdala was a wealthy community.

Curiously, one of the most important details about Mary Magdalene comes to us in two of the Gospels almost as an afterthought, or as a throw-away fact which maybe all the early Christians then living knew, but which certainly none of us would ever have known had not Mark and Luke told us. Our text from Luke gives the first citation of this critical fact. In a list of women, Luke includes a note about "Mary, called Magdalene, from whom seven demons had gone out" (8:7). Luke gives no specifics other than to say Mary was called Magdalene, and "from whom seven demons had gone out." He does not say **how** these demons were driven out of her; he only tells us that **somehow** they went out.

Mark gives us more — and far more pivotal — information. The last chapter of Mark is fraught with some problems, because it contains not one but three possible endings. In all biblical versions Mark 16:1-8 is the same. That is, it tells that Mary Magdalene and two other women went to the tomb where Jesus had been buried, and that they did not find the body. Instead, they encountered a man dressed in a white robe, who told them that Jesus was now risen from the dead. The man told the three women to tell Peter and the other disciples that Jesus would meet them back in Galilee. But, says Mark, "they said nothing to anyone, for they were afraid" (16:8): end of sentence, end of chapter, end of Gospel.

The footnote says there is alternate ending, which has two sentences. The first says they women did tell Peter and the others, and the second sentence says that Jesus sent the disciples out with "the sacred and imperishable proclamation of eternal salvation."

But there is yet another, longer suggested ending. Its first verse, which would be Mark 16:9, says, "Now when he rose early on the first day of the week, he appeared first to Mary Magdalene, *from whom he had cast out seven demons*" [my italics]. In other words, Luke simply says that seven demons went out of Mary Magdalene, but Mark says that it was Jesus who cast out the seven demons. I believe that Mark provides us with an immensely important fact in the story of Mary Magdalene.

In order to proceed further in a plausible sequence, I hope you will now grant an assumption, which is this: Jesus, in historical point of fact, did cast seven demons out of Mary Magdalene. Maybe it didn't happen as Mark says, but please, for the sake of proceeding further, at least grant the possibility that this exorcism happened. Whether or not there actually were —— or are —— demons is another matter altogether. The Gospel writers thought there were demons, Mary Magdalene thought there were demons, and Jesus probably also thought there were demons.

To people in the 21st century, "demons" equate to mental or psychological illnesses of a particular sort. Where we likely would say someone suffers from bi-polar illness or schizophrenia or paranoia or a personality disorder, 1st century people would say they were possessed by demons. Mental illness was then and is now a terribly distressing and befuddling form of illness, because we still know relatively little about its origins or successful treatment. When 1st century people could not determine the origin of a sickness, they called it demon-possession. When 21st century people cannot determine how particular forms of sickness occur, we call it "mental illness." Either way, it is a huge problem, and it is very difficult entirely to eradicate.

So, let us agree that before Mary Magdalene met Jesus, she suffered from mental illness (or demon-possession, in their terminology). At some point in her life, she encountered Jesus, or

Jesus encountered Mary. We don't know when or how, because none of the Gospel writers tells us anything about it. But somehow it happened. Did Mary ask to have her demons cast out, or did Jesus volunteer to cast them out without being asked? Again, we don't know. But somehow it happened.

Have you known anyone for whom a modern medication has virtually eliminated a mental condition? Some of the new pharmaceuticals have remarkable results for certain people under certain conditions. When they are cured, it seems both marvelous and miraculous.

That is what happened for Mary Magdalene. For years she had been plagued by the demons of depression or lethal delusions or hallucinations or psychotic illusions or who knows what. Then she met Jesus - - - and her demons were gone! She was cured! Jesus merely spoke the words, He spoke The Word, and Mary was made well! For the first time in her life, she felt like a normal person! She saw reality through clear lenses, instead of hallucinations through her theretofore terribly clouded vision! *Miriam ha-Magdalit*, Mary the Magdalene, was made well by *Yeshua ha-Notzri*, Jesus the Nazarene!

I suspect this particular miracle occurred fairly early in the life of Jesus. In Luke, where we first hear about Mary (8:1ff.), the miracle must have happened only a few months after Jesus started His public ministry. As Luke describes it, Jesus began going about the region of the Galilee, preaching and bringing the good news of the Kingdom of God. Luke further tells us that twelve were with Him, "and also some women who had been healed of evil spirits and infirmities," of whom one was Mary Magdalene.

And here is where the plot unfortunately thickens in the imagination of historic Christendom. It is the improper conclusion which results from the notion of the "evil spirits." Both Mark and Luke say that seven demons went out of Mary. As previously stated, Mark merely says that seven demons had gone out of her. But Luke insists that it was Jesus Himself who cast out the seven demons.

240

Demons, by definition, must be evil spirits. Whoever heard of a good demon? After all, isn't the word "demon" a synonym for "devil"? People might have **good** spirits within them (the spirit of truth, the spirit of kindness, the spirit of healing or prophecy or whatever), but an **evil** spirit is, well, quite obviously, **evil.**

So what evil might Mary Magdalene have done? To many Christians through the ages, she had a very tarnished reputation before she met Jesus, a reputation which rendered her to be "that kind" of woman. But upon what behavior was that bad reputation based?

There is an ancient tradition which declares that Mary Magdalene had been a prostitute before she met Jesus. Nothing scriptural warrants that conclusion, not one word. So how did that idea ever come about?

It came evolved through a deliberate tampering with circumstances. There is **nothing** factual to suggest that Mary was a prostitute: **nothing!** Nonetheless, to millions of Christians through twenty centuries, Miriam of Magdala was a practitioner of the world's oldest profession.

Here, I think, is how that misinformed notion became a widely held tradition. In John's Gospel, chapter 12, it says that Jesus went to the home of Mary, Martha, and Lazarus six days before Passover. In other words, the incident recorded by John in chapter 12, verses 1-8, occurred the day before what Christians have come to call Palm Sunday. On that occasion, John says, Mary (the sister of Martha and Lazarus, *not* Mary Magdalene) took some very expensive ointment and anointed Jesus' feet. Judas was angry that she spent so much money on such expensive ointment, says John, but Jesus upbraided Judas by saying that Mary had anointed Him for His burial, **before** He had died. Jesus praised Mary for Her kindness and devotion. But remember, **it was Mary, the sister of Martha and Lazarus**, who did this anointing.

Now go back to Luke's Gospel. **Immediately before Luke first tells us about Mary Magdalene,** he tells us the story of Jesus in the home of Simon the Pharisee (Lk. 7:36:50). In that

241

particular episode, Jesus had been invited to the home of a Pharisee whose name was Simon. While Simon, Jesus, and other guests were eating dinner together, "a woman of the city, who was a sinner" (7:37) came and sat down at Jesus' feet. Weeping uncontrollably, she began pouring ointment on Jesus' feet, and she wiped His feet with her hair.

A couple of parenthetical cultural points. In the first century, when a rabbi was invited into someone's home, anybody off the street could come in and stand or sit at the edge of the room or the courtyard to listen to the rabbi. To us that may seem a very peculiar idea, but it was an acceptable custom nevertheless. Secondly, for this "woman who was a sinner" (i.e., a prostitute), the wiping of Jesus' feet with her hair was a skin-crawling and shocking thing for her to do. In that culture, women never uncovered their hair, just as in ultra-Orthodox Jewish or very traditional Muslim cultures today women never "let their hair down." (That is the origin of that expression, by the way.) It is a social taboo of the most obvious and widely accepted sort; women in the most rigidly traditional cultures must never expose their hair in public. It would almost be as bad as exposing their naked bodies.

But here was this village prostitute, pouring ointment on Jesus' feet, and wiping His feet with her hair! To her, her action was a symbol of the deepest devotion, because in Jesus she sensed someone who had both the power and the willingness to forgive her for her life of sin. Simon had acted very badly by not offering to have Jesus' feet bathed, which social custom demanded Simon should do, but Jesus praised the woman for washing His feet with the ointment and wiping His feet with her hair. She had lived very badly, and by uncovering her hair she was acting very badly again, but Jesus saw in her unprecedented act a sign of great love toward Him, and He declared that her sins, which had been many, were all forgiven.

Now pay especially close attention. In John's Gospel, it was a woman named Mary, albeit it Mary the sister of Martha and Lazarus, who anointed Jesus with ointment. In Luke's Gospel it was an unnamed prostitute who anointed Jesus with ointment.

And immediately afterward, Luke introduces us to Mary Magdalene. Therefore, **by a complete fluke of inaccurate recollection**, many people in the Church through the centuries have deduced that the woman who anointed Jesus was Mary Magdalene. **But there is nothing WHATEVER to support that hypothesis! It is a TOTAL fabrication!! Mary Magdalene was NOT a prostitute, and it was not she who anointed Jesus!!!**

However, if we are to believe what Mark — and especially Luke — tell us, Jesus **did** cast seven demons out of Mary Magdalene, whatever you choose to make of that episode. I have never thought Mary was a prostitute, nor shall I ever believe that. I think she was a woman who suffered from some form of mental illness, and Jesus cured her of that illness through His miraculous powers. Whether her "seven demons" were truly evil spirits, I am agnostic; I just don't know. But I have no biblical basis for supposing Mary was a prostitute, nor should you suppose she was. She was simply a very troubled woman who was cured of her troubles by the miracle-worker from Nazareth.

That singular miracle changed Mary's life. From that moment on, she became a disciple of Jesus. And I mean exactly that: Mary became a **disciple**. She, along with several other women, became disciples of the Master as surely as were the Twelve also disciples. But put this is historical and cultural context. First-century Judea was a highly male-dominated society. None of the Gospel writers would ever dare openly state that Jesus had female disciples, because it would instantly undermine anything else they might say about Him. Can you imagine orthodox Jews paying any attention at all to a would-be Messiah who had close *women* followers? Perish the very thought!

Nonetheless, when Luke tells us that Mary Magdalene, Joanna, Susanna, and many other women were followers of Jesus, along with the Twelve, he is telling us something radical and revolutionary, without actually explaining it to us. However many weeks or months or years the Twelve followed Jesus as disciples, the women also followed Him that long. To Jesus, the women were as fully His disciples as any of the men. And, if my hypothesis is correct, Jesus saw Mary as His Number One Disciple.

Jesus treated women as being equal to men. He treated both men and women as equals! In those days nobody thought women were equal to men. But Jesus thought so, and that was a dangerous position. Anyone who messes with so strong a social convention as the **obvious** superiority of men to women is going to get into trouble, **big** trouble! You might not get killed for it, but if anybody needed added evidence to secure a death penalty, the radical nature of that position would certainly help pound the nails into the coffin — or the cross! Jesus freed women from the slavery of being women, and thus chattel, **things**!

But Luke also gives one other crucial, even potentially scandalous, detail. He says that the women "provided for them out of their means" (Luke 8:3). Who is the "them" for whom the women provided? **It is the disciples, but especially it is Jesus!** Jesus and the twelve were **"kept men!"** How else do you think that financially they were able to wander around the Galilee for three years? Jesus had nobody at home to support, but presumably all the other men did. Somebody had to pay their expenses! So who was it? **It was the women!** It may especially have been Mary Magdalene who bankrolled most of the whole Jesus Movement!

There is a tradition which holds that Mary was a wealthy widow. The tradition comes from one of the Gnostic Gospels. The Gnostics were a group of first-and-second century heretical Christians who had their own stories of Jesus, stories which frequently were at odds with the four canonical (or officially authorized) Gospels. One of the Gnostic Gospels tells that Mary Magdalene was a wealthy widow. Another goes so far as to claim that she was the wife of Jesus. Yes, you read correctly: a Gospel which was rejected by the early Church states that Mary Magdalene was married to Jesus.

I don't buy it. I think the four canonical Gospels are correct in suggesting that there was a unique relationship between Jesus and Mary, but there is nothing to support the notion that Jesus ever married her. In fact, were it accurate, that concept would cre-

244

ate immense problems for both the establishment and the continuation of the Christian religion. A married Abraham or Moses or Hosea or Peter or James or John in okay, or even a married Muhammad, but a married Jesus is a notion that would send Christianity into a spiral of historical oblivion. Given the nature of how Jesus has come to be perceived through the intervening centuries since He lived on this planet, it is impossible to accept the notion of a married Jesus without a total revision of Christian Christology.

Nevertheless, years of pondering this relationship have convinced me that Jesus had a bond with Mary Magdalene which was unlike that of any of His other relationships with anyone else. There was a unique love between them, though they were not "lovers." Jesus felt more deeply fulfilled by Mary than by any other person, and she felt the same way toward Him, but I am certain it was not a sexual fulfillment *per se*. The uniqueness of the relationship came about **because** Jesus was a man and Mary was a woman, but it was not **based** on that fact.

You are probably wondering: "Just what is this biblical meddler trying to say?" Perhaps I can best explain it through my own experience as a pastor. Through nearly four decades of being a preacher, I found that in general, men either found my preaching to be helpful and edifying, or they didn't find it that way. But males in general did not and do not see me to be anything especially unique as a parson. Women, on the other hand, have tended either to be unusually complimentary and supportive to me, or very cool and even hostile; in general, I mean.

Obviously I can be all wrong in this assessment. I may have missed the boat entirely on this matter, and I may have made some cockamamie conclusions for cockamamie psychological reasons which no one, least of all I, could ever fully understand. Other people are in a far more objective position to assess these statements than I am. Nonetheless, I still maintain that my ministry seemed to be more effective with women than with men.

Whether or not that is true, it seems true to me that Jesus profoundly affected women in His ministry more than men. We insist there were twelve disciples, because four males told us there were twelve disciples. But I believe beyond doubt that there also were many women whom Jesus considered to be among His closest friends and associates.

There is an indefinable something that sometimes occurs between certain males and certain females. It definitely is not the result of "consummated sexuality," to coin a term. Rather it happens precisely because it is "unconsummated sexuality," or because it is sexuality without sex.

Let me give an analogy. I realize this analogy is fraught with peril, but it may help you understand the deeper level of the relationship between Jesus and Mary. Throughout the decades of the growth of popular music as a social phenomenon, and particularly with the rise of numerous rock stars, there have been many examples of young women, teenage girls, and even pre-pubescent girls going nearly bonkers over their male-singer heroes. Think of the Beatles or Elvis or some of the current superstars, and you will at least acknowledge the phenomenon of which I am speaking, even if you strongly deny where the analogy seems to lead.

Male rock stars also have innumerable male fans. But the nature of the "fan-dom" is different between male and female fans. The same is true in reverse; female singers are more likely to have strongly devoted male fans than female fans.

Now, please put the notion of being a "fan" on the back burner, or, better yet, completely out of your mind. And come with me back to Jesus and Mary Magdalene. There was a powerful "indefinable something" between the two of them. Whatever "it" was, it was a latent "it," and not an active "it." But it was real, nonetheless. Both of them felt it, and each of them drew great strength from it. Although none of the Gospels even hints at it, I speculate that Jesus was able to summon up the courage to go to the cross far more because of His love for Mary and her love for Him than for the love of all the Twelve put together.

And that brings us to the crucifixion, the next-to-last chapter in the earthly story of Jesus. In three of the Gospels (Mt. 27:56ff., Mk. 15:40ff., and Jn. 19:25ff.), Mary Magdalene is specifically

246

identified as one of the people standing at the foot of the cross. **Further** (and please note the importance of this), **in no Gospel does it say that ANY of the Twelve, except John, even stood close to the cross!** In other words, only "the beloved disciple" (as John presumably describes himself) was in the immediate vicinity of the cross. **However, several women were there, and in three of the Gospels, Mary Magdalene is specifically identified as one of the women!**

Now are you starting to get the picture? Now do you see why I call Mary "The Woman Whom Jesus Loved"?

But that is not all! There is yet another factor, or more accurately, four more factors, which authenticate the unique relationship of Mary Magdalene and Jesus. **In every Gospel**, Mary is reported to have been there at the empty tomb on Easter morning. In fact, **ONLY** Mary is there in all four Gospels (Mt. 28:1ff., Mk. 16:1ff., Lk. 24:10ff., Jn. 20:1ff.). No two Gospels agree on exactly who went to the tomb, but they all agree that Mary Magdalene was one of the tomb visitors. Furthermore, John states that **ONLY** Mary went to the tomb, that no one else came, at least initially.

And what are we to make of these assertions? From my perspective, at least this: no one loved Jesus as much as Mary Magdalene, and Jesus loved no one as much as Mary! Mary could not pull herself away from the tomb! She could not believe that Jesus truly could be dead! And when He was raised from the dead, and appeared to her, paradoxically she could not initially believe that He was alive again!

Although I am convinced the Fourth Gospel is by far the least historically accurate, I still am most drawn to its account of the first resurrection appearance. Let us look at some of the details (Jn. 20:1ff.). "Now on the first day of the week, Mary Magdalene came to the tomb early, while it was still dark, and saw that the stone had been taken away from the tomb. So she ran, and went to Simon Peter and the other disciple, the one whom Jesus loved, and said to them, 'They have taken the Lord out of the tomb, and we do not know where they have laid him.'"

Peter and John ran back to the tomb with Mary, and they saw that indeed, Jesus' body was gone. In English it says simply that Peter stooped and looked in the empty tomb, and he "saw the linen cloths lying." The Greek text is ever so much more magnificently powerful. It says that he "saw the linen cloths lying *in their folds*." This implies that the linen bandages which had been wrapped around Jesus' body were lying there as though Jesus' resurrected body had risen straight up from them, and they were lying in place, as though wrapped around a body, but there was no body there! They were not pulled off or unwound; they were still in place, but the body was gone! What a spine-tingling detail that is!

Anyway, after Peter and John saw for themselves that the body was not there, they left. What nudniks they were! How like males they were! They saw, but they did not **see**! They absorbed a crucial fact, but the fact did not **register**!

Not so with Mary. She could not pull herself away. Though she did not yet understand that Jesus had been raised from the dead (NOTE: **Jesus did not rise from the dead; He was raised from the dead. It is an all-important distinction**), Mary's love for Jesus also prevented her from fully accepting the fact of His death.

It was at that moment, according to the Fourth Gospel, when the two angels, who were inside the tomb, appeared to Mary. They asked her why she was weeping. (I know that angels are not supposed to be sexual beings, but this pair had to be males; only males would ask such an obviously stupid question!) She told them why she was crying. Then, she turned around and saw Jesus standing behind her. John has Jesus ask Mary the same question, "Woman, why are you weeping? Whom do you seek?" Somehow I can't imagine Jesus ever asking that, but for the sake of moving along, let us go along with John's historically mistaken report.

Then come some of the most mystifying words of the entire Bible: "Supposing him to be the gardener, she said to him, 'Sir, if you have carried him away, tell me where you have laid him, and I will take him away.'" It was Jesus speaking to Mary, but Mary did not know it was Jesus! Then the single most electrifying word in the entire Bible: "Mary." And then, at last, Mary understands! Her heart, which had been totally shattered by grief, was suddenly completely revived by joy: "*Rabboni!*" Mary shouts. Rabbi! Teacher! One word from His mouth, her **name**, *Miriam*, and she knows the truth that transforms this world: He is risen! He is risen indeed! He calls us by name! He knows us! He knows all of us!

But Jesus knew and knows and shall always know the heart of Mary Magdalene better and more thoroughly than anyone else who ever lived, because in her He found his deepest and most profound soul mate. Jesus was attuned to Mary as to no one else among His closest friends and disciples. And therefore it was to Mary that He first appeared in His risen form.

The Greek novelist Nikos Kazantzakis wrote a book called *The Last Temptation of Christ*. It is the story of the public ministry of Jesus, but the primary character in the story, other than Jesus Himself, is Mary. The writer proposes that the last temptation of Jesus was to use His miraculous power to come down from the cross for the sake of Mary, thus to extend further His deep love for her. When the novel was made into a movie by Martin Scorsese, it caused both a scandal and a sensation. Never was a movie more thoroughly praised and panned.

It is quite conceivable that Jesus may have been tempted to remove Himself from the cross for the sake of His relationship with Mary. Had He done so, however, He would not have been Jesus, for He would not have been a human being, inextricably caught up in a cruel death engineered by men He could not defeat. He would have been the incarnate God, using divine powers for human purposes. That Jesus could not and did not do. Whatever powers He had, He used for God, and not for Himself. That is what makes Him unique among all the human beings who have ever lived.

Andrew Lloyd Webber and Tim Rice collaborated on the religious rock opera *Jesus Christ Superstar*. In it Mary Magdalene has a haunting song called *I Don't Know How to Love Him*. I'm sure that lyric perfectly captures the ambivalent love relationship which existed between Jesus and His most devoted disciple. Mary really didn't know how to love Him, and He didn't know how to love her. But love each other, deeply, if ambiguously, they did.

On Easter Sunday, April 3, 1994, at the First Presbyterian Church in Hilton Head Island, South Carolina, I preached a sermon called *Mary Magdalene: Love, Wounded and Restored.* In it I said some of things I have tried to say in this much longer version of that particular sermon. The delivery of that sermon was the next to last in a series of sermons called *Voices Near the Cross.*

In retrospect, it was probably a mistake to preach such a sermon on Easter. It is too untraditional, too thought-provoking for a typical Easter congregation. Afterward, one of the associate ministers spoke to a parishioner in the parking lot. The minister, who is female, said to the parishioner, who also is female, "As he was preaching that sermon, I was asking myself, 'Where the hell is he going with this?'"

Everything you have read above is where I was trying to go, except that here I devoted more background study to the topic. In several respects, this sermon is both hotter and less hot than all the other sermons in this collection. It is hotter, because it can truly get under some people's skin like nothing else said here. But it is less hot, because it contains far, far more biblical background. People who will most dislike the content of this sermon might appreciate the methodology behind it the most, even if they strongly oppose my conclusions.

Why would I ever write such a sermon as this? Or why would I ever preach such a sermon as that one? For this reason: **Jesus of Nazareth was a man like all other men**. He was human like all other humans. He experienced the same hopes, the same desires, the same feelings and yearnings that we all experience. And it is my growing conviction that His deepest humanity was made manifest in His relationship with Miriam of Magdala. He had a radically unique love for her, and she for Him.

It was not a sexual relationship. Jesus' devotion to God and to the commandments of God would not allow Jesus ever to enter into such a relationship outside marriage. And, as I have tried to indicate, Jesus did not marry Mary Magdalene. So their relationship could not have been essentially sexual.

250

Nonetheless, the love between Mary and Jesus was probably the single factor which enabled Him to go confidently to the cross. If she could love Him to Golgotha, He could trust God to lead Him beyond Golgotha. And more than any other relationship which Jesus had with anyone, it was Jesus' unique love for Mary which God used to lift Him from the tomb.

Christos anesthe! Alethos anesthe! Christ is risen! Indeed He is risen!

Letters

Text – But whatever anyone dares to boast of – I am speaking as a fool – I also dare to boast of that. Are they Hebrews? So am I. Are they Israelites? So am I. Are they descendants of Abraham? So am I. Are they servants of Christ? I am a better one – I am talking like a madman – with far greater labors, far more imprisonments [etc., etc. etc. (*my etceteras*)] – II Corinthians 11:21-23 (RSV).

AN OLDER MAN'S LETTER TO
THE OLDER MAN PAUL

Dear Paul,

Let me begin by pointing out the obvious, Paul. Without you, there would be no Christianity and no Church. Period. Jesus didn't initiate Christianity. You did. A religion separate from Judaism was the last thing in His mind. Eventually it was an idea which could never be dislodged from your mind.

For that matter, you may have been surprised, perhaps even amazed, to know that Christianity and Judaism went their separate ways in the manner in which it happened. It didn't occur immediately after your death, and there was no single incident which resulted in the divorce. But the two religions split up anyway. By the third or fourth centuries *Anno Domini*, as we Christians are wont to say, nobody either inside or outside Judaism or Christianity could possibly mistake the one for the other.

I suspect you have not been pleased with how things turned out. You wanted Judaism to focus on Jesus, and Jesus wanted a universalized Judaism to focus on God. Neither of you got anything close to what you wanted. History is often like that. Most revolutions produce something quite different from what the revolutionaries had in mind. You and Jesus must be shocked, yea verily, aghast, at what the Church has done with and to your teachings. But don't feel bad, Paul. It has twisted Jesus' thoughts far more than yours. Since you appear not to have known much at all about Jesus' teachings, I hope you'll trust me on this.

Nonetheless (to come back to my opening paragraph in this epistle), you, much more than Jesus, are responsible for the establishment of the Christian religion. When you proclaimed your understanding of the crucifixion and resurrection of Jesus, you transformed whatever Jesus said about those events before He died (if He actually said all those things, which He probably didn't) into the mighty foundation of a faith constructed primarily on the Risen Christ. You said almost nothing about the teachings of Jesus, or about other events in His life. But, holy Toledo, about the crucifixion and resurrection you said a huge bunch! Incidentally, had nobody told you *anything* of what Jesus said or did, other than that He died and was raised? If not, why not? And if so, why did you ignore it so blatantly? I have often wondered about that, Paul. Too bad you – or somebody – didn't explain this mystery to us.

But I'm getting ahead of myself. I will come back to that theme again. Whatever happened back there on the Damascus road, it has had incalculable influence on everything that followed. When you were converted, Paul, you were **really CONVERTED!** As you told the Philippians (3:4 ff.), you were a Jew among Jews, "circumcised on the eighth day, of the people of Israel, of the tribe of Benjamin, a Hebrew born of Hebrews; as to the law a Pharisee, as to zeal a persecutor of the church, as to righteousness under the law blameless." And, as to humility, we might add, a regular paragon as well.

Had you not made such a huge swing from one form of zealous religion to a different, but not totally opposite, zealous form, we might never have heard of you. If you had just been Saul Q. Jew, you never would have become Paul T. (for THE) Christian. For reasons we shall never fully understand or know, you had a "thing" for the religious law that was far above and beyond the call of Jewish duty. Like many other people, Paul, you were a legalist. Prior to that profound conversion, "Do's and Don'ts" were what motivated you in your religious life. Jesus was not like that, as you came to realize, but boy, you were! And when you threw over all that stuff, you certainly chucked it out altogether. But of that, also, more later.

Paul, probably your most important contribution to subsequent history is not something you wrote, as influential as your letters have been. It was something you did, or something you said when you did it. We read about it in what we call Acts 15, although you of course knew nothing about the finished Book of Acts, since it was finished after you had been executed.

There is no way you could forget the incident. You had been schlepping all over the Mediterranean world, preaching about Jesus to both Jews and Gentiles, but more and more to Gentiles. So the early Church decided to have a Grand Ecclesiastical Clambake in Jerusalem to decide whether, in order to become Christians, Gentiles first had to become Jews.

Now, to us that is a no-brainer. Of course not, we Gentile Christians say. But we say it only because, virtually single-handedly, you carried the day in the Acts 15 Theological Brouhaha. We are Gentiles, and Gentiles wouldn't recognize a sabbatarian requirement or a kosher commandment if we fell over it. There never would have been an Acts 15 Theological Brouhaha, Paul, had you not been such an inestimable and insufferable *nudzh.*

The whole debate started with the question of whether or not Gentiles had to be circumcised. That, to see the least, would be a matter of vital interest to 50% of the Gentile coverts you were somehow able to corral. A bris may be okay for boy Jewish babies, but for grown Gentile men, it is another tissue altogether.

However, circumcision was only the opening salvo in that particular churchly confrontation. Did Gentiles have to follow all the other religious laws which were required by the Torah and codified and explained by the rabbis and scribes? You and Barnabas had been preaching to Gentiles, and some Jewish Christians from Jerusalem came and insisted the Gentiles had to accept the whole nine yards of Old Testament law, including circumcision, before they could sign on as Christians.

Paul, nobody but you could have done what you did! You demanded that the meeting of all the high muckety-mucks had to be held. And although to read Acts 15 it was Peter who convinced the crowd, I have no doubt it was you who did it. Peter is a terrific chap; don't get me wrong. If you want to know the truth, which you probably don't, he is a whole lot more likeable than

256

you are. But when they were passing out the brains, you were the first in line, and Peter — shall we just put it delicately — wasn't. Furthermore, when push comes to shove, I would far rather have you than Peter there either to push or shove. Nobody was ever more pushy than you, Paulie. And, as you said in your letter to the Galatians (2:1-10), you were the one who demanded the Jerusalem meeting, not Peter. Peter has a fetching personality, and you a forceful one. Fetch wouldn't have worked; force alone would suffice.

I'm sure of this: *I* wouldn't be a Christian today, were it not for what you said and did at that early-church council in Jerusalem. It is almost impossible for **Jews** assiduously to observe everything in the Torah, which is why there are, relatively speaking, so few Orthodox Jews. And those Judaizers way back there wanted us Goyim to become **that**? I can imagine your Tarsusian voice sounding through the cavernous hall even now; "Whaddayou, crazy? *Meshugge*, you are! This'll never woik!" you said in your own diffident, uniquely-unassuming demeanor. And you were right. Those Jerusalem ersatz Christians would have killed Christianity before it even got started, if they had won. Thank God you were there, Paul; you did it for us, guy. You.

Your whole beef about following everything in the religious law to the letter was essential, were there to be a Christianity at all. By the time of Jesus, which is to say, by your time, too many Jews had become too committed to the religious law as the be-all, end-all of religion. In Romans, you forcefully said that you were not capable of doing what the law required you to do. Holy cats, is that ever the truth for all of us. Many times we know what we ought to do and we don't do it, but other times we don't even know what we ought to do. No set of laws speaks clearly to all situations for all people through all time. If keeping the religious law is our requirement for salvation, we are all goners, Paul, just as you said.

In the early years of my ministry, I preached frequently from your epistles. Then, as time went on, I went more often to the Gospels, though in that process I also avoided the Fourth Gospel with even more frequency than I avoided what you wrote.

I guess I came to see you and John (or whoever wrote "John") as the two most prominent Super-Christians of the New Testament Church, and I think your emphasis was misplaced. Jesus talked mostly about God, and you and John talked mostly about Jesus. You see almost everything through "Jesus lenses," meaning that all vital theological points can be understood only through Jesus. I try to see everything through "Jesus eyes," meaning that I attempt to understand God as Jesus understood God. There's a major difference in approaches there, as you are well aware.

Maybe I'm like you in personality, Paul, except that for me there was no Damascus road. I too accepted the essence of the religious teachings I was taught in my childhood and youth. As a young man, I too believed the "right things," thought the "right things," preached the "right things." But the more I cogitated on it, the more I decided that Christianity in general and you in particular put too much emphasis on Jesus, and that you short-change God. Perhaps that was not your intention, but sadly that is its result.

Nowhere is that more evident that in what you said about the crucifixion. It seems as though, for you, the crucifixion of Jesus is the sole event through which all beliefs are to be filtered, if I read you correctly. Unless the cross is the foundation of our faith, valid faith is utterly impossible. I agree that the crucifixion was pivotal, but I don't perceive it as you do. I did, because that is what all of us were taught, but I no longer do.

Here is how I see it, for whatever it is worth. Jesus died on the cross, not because God willed it (although obviously He allowed it), and not because Jesus took our place there, but because Jesus got caught up in an historical set of circumstances from which He could not extricate Himself with integrity. Oh, He could have run away, except that then He couldn't be true to Himself. He so thoroughly riled the religious authorities of His time they demanded that the Romans execute Him. And the Romans, not wanting matters to get out of hand (governments in the Middle East are still like that, Paul, believe me), reluctantly complied with the demand.

So what is the significance of the crucifixion? There are several factors which come instantly to mind. It shows that sin can triumph over righteousness, if righteous people are unwilling to stand up for what is right. It shows that institutional religion can get really nasty if it feels severely threatened, even when it has much to commend it. It shows that political authority can choose expediency over ethics. Historically, it shows that even the most devoted of disciples can fail their Master in His time of greatest need, which suggests that we too can — and do — fail.

Paul, you see the crucifixion as a theological necessity. I see it as an historical inevitability. By it you believe God saved the world, or at least the world of those who believe the right things. I believe that by the crucifixion, God used Jesus to show that the world has already been saved: all of it, everyone who lives in it, everyone who has or ever shall live in it.

You yourself said it with the most wonderfully astonishing clarity, Paul. "But God demonstrates his love for us in that while we were yet sinners Christ died for us" (Romans 5:8 NIV). On the cross Jesus demonstrated *His* love for us, but even more, **God** showed us *His* love. Nobody ever embodied the nature of God more than Jesus, nor shall anyone, ever. God could have miraculously saved Jesus. But He chose not to do so, because He wanted us to perceive that as Jesus demonstrated His (Jesus') love for us to the fullest by going to the cross, God also demonstrates His own love, simply by not stepping in to prevent it. We killed the Brightest and the Best; we really did, ... and do, ... and shall do yet again ... all of us. In that you were right once more, Paul. Each of us crucifies the Messiah by being unwilling always to follow what He teaches us about God.

When you told the Corinthians that "God was in Christ reconciling the world to himself" (II Cor. 5:19), I'm sure you didn't mean that in Jesus, God was reconciling the world *to Jesus*; you meant that in Jesus God was reconciling the world *to Himself*, that is, to *God*. Jesus thus is the primary means to God's primary earthly end, namely, the salvation of the human race, and indeed, of the entire created order.

So then, why did you insist that Jesus was "sacrificed," or that He was sacrificed on our behalf, or that He died in our place? "Then as one man's trespass led to condemnation for all men, so one man's act of righteousness led to acquittal for all men" (Romans 5:18). Apparently you implied the first man was Adam, and the second man was Jesus. The doctrine of original sin presents more than enough problems, but the doctrine of substitutionary atonement: is that supposed to be a dogma of Christian faith, Paul? Are we required to believe it? I admit it: I don't. And I'm not alone in that. Does that mean I'm out? Really, truly, honestly out?

And that leads me to another quarrel I have with you, Paul. In numerous ways, you said that faith is needed for our salvation, and specifically, faith in Jesus Christ. "Therefore, since we are justified by faith, we have peace with God through our Lord Jesus Christ""(Romans 5:1). But that prompts some questions. Is faith an act of will? Are we capable of either choosing or rejecting faith? If faith is an act of will, then isn't it a kind of "work" of sorts, something we decide to do? And if it isn't an act of will, then how do we acquire it?

Here's what I think, Paul; I think you never fully answered these questions to your own satisfaction, let alone to the satisfaction of the rest of us. You vacillated on them. In that you are just like me, and probably like everyone else as well. We all try to fit all this stuff into nice, neat pigeonholes, but in the process, we create some weird-looking pigeons which somehow don't fit into any of our carefully-crafted apertures.

I have come to believe that faith is a gift which God alone can give us. We cannot will ourselves into belief. Faith is a gift, and either we accept it, or we don't. If we believe anything, if we believe everything we are supposed to believe, it is because God led us to do it. We can botch it up, and we do, but still, only God can grant faith. Nobody can will to have faith.

Therefore I would express it like this: we are not justified by faith *per se*; we are justified by God's grace alone, which we understand through God's gift to us of faith. In other words, the faith God gives us by grace convinces us we are justified by God. Ultimately, it isn't **our** faith in **God** that counts; it is **God's** faith in **us**.

Am I finished disputing with you, you, who are the smartest and sharpest of the New Testament writers, who are far smarter and sharper than I could ever hope to be? What chutzpah I have, Paul! But then, I'm only acting as you often did, am I not? Finished I'm not, friend; finished I'm not!

There is this little matter about your believing that the world was going to end soon. But you can't be solely blamed for that. Other Christians in your time believed the same thing. If we can accept the authenticity of every word in the Gospel accounts (which by now you may deduced I don't), Jesus also claimed The End was nigh.

But *oy*, such a *tsimmes* it has caused ever since, such a colossal fuss, this conviction that any moment The End shall come! "For the Lord himself will descend from heaven with a cry of command, with the archangel's call, and with the sound of the trumpet of God. And the dead in Christ will rise first; then we who are alive, who are left, shall be caught up together with them in the clouds to meet the Lord in the air" (I Thessalonians 4:17). Do you remember writing that in your first letter to the Christians in Thessalonika? Then, some years later when you wrote your second letter to them, you changed your tune. "Now concerning the coming of our Lord Jesus Christ and our assembling to meet him, we beg you, brethren, not to be quickly shaken in mind or excited, either by spirit or by word, or by letter purporting to be from us, to the effect that the day of the Lord has come" (II Thes. 2:1-2).

Nice touch, Paulie! You got them uncontrollably stirred up in the first place, and years later you desperately tried to get them un-stirred! You can't have it both ways! Either Jesus was coming soon and the world would end, or He wasn't, and it wouldn't. He didn't. It didn't.

But this going "in the clouds to meet Jesus in the air": do you have idea how many well-intentioned Christians have gone off the deep end because of that statement? If the world had ended every time some cockamamie Christian said it was going to end, we would have had millions of The Ends by now. The world couldn't contain the finales which had been predicted for it. Yet, like Old Man River, the world just keeps rolling along.

Good marks for writing II Thessalonians, tentmaker. Bad marks for writing I Thessalonians, at least that part about meeting Jesus in the air. But hey, we all make mistakes. For this and everything else you said that I disagree with, I certainly forgive you. I just want you to know I disagree, that's all.

Next, you attitude toward women. Paul, never was there a more phobic feminophobe than you. What happened back there before the Damascus road, huh? What feckless female "done you wrong"? Was it your mom? Your sister? Your wife? Your mother-in-law? Who?

Oh, I know there are scholars who claim you were one of the first century's prime liberators of women, that you were a feminist long, long, long before anyone ever thought to coin the word. With all due respect to them and you, such a notion seems totally ridiculous to me. **Jesus** was a genuine libber, but **you**, you were a male whose notions about females sprang directly from the bleakest recesses of cultural darkness.

"As in all the churches of the saints, the women should keep silence in the churches. For they are not permitted to speak, but should be subordinate, as even the law says. If there is anything they desire to know, let them ask their husbands at home""(I Cor. 14:33-35). Let me tell yuh, chum, if you said that in any ecclesiastical gathering of any denomination anywhere west of Iran, you would get hooted, or maybe booted, off the stage! Those words are a red flag before a charging bull! Well, maybe not a **bull**, but one very honked heifer. "If they want to know something, let them ask their husbands" indeed! Even the most fervent of MCP fundies would never try to pull that stuff in the 21st century. I realize there are oodles of differences between your century and ours, but honestly, Paul, you'd be taking your life in your hands with most women and many men if you tried to convince anyone of those sentiments today.

"It is well for a man not to touch a woman. But because of the temptation to immorality, each man should have his own wife and each woman her own husband" (I Corinthians 7:1-2). Now there's a lofty commendation, first, for women, and then, for marriage! A swell fellow you are, Paul! "It is well for a man not to touch a woman" indeed!!! In what theological landfill did you ever find that piece of advice? Or did you truly think The End was near, and nobody should touch anybody "in that way," that all should look beatifically toward heaven, waiting for the instantaneous return of Jesus?

"To the unmarried and the widows, I say that it is well for them to remain single as I do" (I Cor. 7:8). Now, really! "But if they cannot exercise self-control, they should marry. For it is better to marry than to be aflame with passion" (I Cor. 7:9). For crying out loud! Were you serious? Do you realize how much this makes you look like you have a pressing need to have your head shrunk? Are you a woman-hater, or merely a man who happens to be a-sexual, and thus you think everyone should be as you are? What's the deal?

"I mean, brethren, the appointed time has grown very short; from now on, let those who have wives live as though they had none, and those who mourn as though they were not mourning" (I Cor. 7:29-30). Then, trying to make matters better, you made them worse: "So that he who marries his betrothed does well; and he who refrains from marriage will do better" (7:38). Writing about those who currently are widows, "but in my judgment she is happier if she remains as she is." And "I think I have the Spirit of God" (7:40). Yeah, right!

Again, who did it to you, Paul? Did you and Portnoy have the same complaint? Was it your mother whom you thought did you wrong? Or maybe your wife? You lead us to believe you never married, but what Jewish man, especially a Pharisee, never married (Jesus being another possible exception)? I have read that your "thorn in the flesh" (II Cor. 12:7) might have been a nagging wife; is that possible? Why are you such a woman-basher, and yet you refuse to provide any of the psychological baggage which would explain your twisted thinking? We'd all like to take you off the hook on this one, Paul, but you make the off-taking so difficult!

"I want you to understand that the head of every man is Christ, the head of every woman is her husband, and the head of Christ is God" (I Cor. 10:3). With the first and third statements I agree, especially with the third. But the **second**? C'mon! "For a man ought not to cover his head, since he is the image and glory of God; but woman is the glory of man. (For man was not made from woman, but woman from man. Neither was man created for woman, but woman for man)" (I Cor. 10:7-8). Paul, if you said that stuff in most mainline churches today, you would be hooted into silent submission, driven from the room with your tail between your legs, if not beaten to a squishy pulp. If you had just allowed more females into your sacred presence, you never would have made such foolish pronouncements! Even the most subservient of first-century females would have attacked you with undisguised glee!

But your attitude toward women in particular illustrates your most peculiar attitude toward sex in general. I hesitate to be the one to tell you, Paul, but sometimes you sound like a eunuch. Or if not a eunuch, a man whose libido was somehow lost in life's unpredictable shuffle.

And such a homophobe you are! You opened the letter to the Romans with a magnificent greeting, and then commended them for their faith, which was itself commendable. But then, why did you launch immediately into a Litany of Stuff Done By Bad Guys? "Therefore God gave them up in the lust of their hearts to impurity" etc., etc (Romans 1:24). "For this reason God gave them to dishonorable passions. Their women exchanged natural relations for unnatural" (what, precisely, does that mean?), "and the men likewise gave up natural relations with women and were consumed with passion for one another, men committing shameless acts with men and receiving in their own persons the due penalty of their error" (Rom. 1:26-27). Again, exactly what does that mean? We can all guess what we think you meant, but what did you actually mean?

Many people are homophobic, Paul, possibly even a majority of people. And you were simply reflecting particular social mores of your own time (though surely well above and beyond the call of duty.) But still: you sound so hopelessly judgmental and puritanical! Then, just a few lines after writing those spiteful words, you had the audacity to say, "Therefore you have no excuse, O man, whoever you are, when you judge another; for in passing judgment upon him you condemn yourself, because you, the judge, are doing the very same things" (Rom. 2:1). Paul, didn't you hear yourself? Didn't you see yourself in what you said? **You** were doing some quite severe judging, so who are you to tell **us** not to judge?

Do you happen to know the story of the mother-in-law who went to see her daughter-in-law, a newly-wed, late one afternoon? Without knocking, the mother-in-law opened the door, and there was her new daughter-in-law, standing without a shred of clothing on her beautiful body. "What are you doing?" asked the aghast mother-in-law. "I'm waiting for your son in my love dress," she explained. "He is always delighted for me to greet him in my love dress when he comes home from the office." The mother-in-law decided discretion demanded her not to pursue this conversation further, so she quickly retreated, and left for home.

On the way, she got to thinking about her daughter's love dress. "Maybe I need to put on my love dress when Sherwin comes home," she decided. When her husband Sherwin came through the door, there she was, resplendent in her birthday suit. "What are you doing?" asked the singularly surprised Sherwin. "I'm wearing my love dress for you." Without skipping a beat as he hung up his coat in the closet, Sherwin muttered, "It needs ironing; what's for dinner?"

Paul, if you ever married, and if your wife had ever greeted you like that when you came home, I bet you wouldn't even notice she was wearing her love dress. All you would do is ask what was for dinner. Since you wouldn't want her to be good at the one activity, all the more would you demand she be good at the other.

You may well be the World's Record-Holder of Hang-ups. You didn't write volumes about yourself, but what you did write speaks volumes about you anyway. A psychoanalyst would wear out his friend Freud trying to figure you out.

It must be that you were very short or very homely or very chubby, or your hair stood straight up in the air and the other kids made fun of you, or you got the first 4.5 average in the honors track in the history of Tarsus High School, and it made everybody else jealous, or something else or something else or something else. You were simply too defensive not to have had some factors which made you want constantly to defend yourself. In several of your letters, you go out of your way to establish your credentials with the people to whom you were writing. Heavens to Murgatroyd, Paul! All we need do is read three or four paragraphs of anything you wrote to realize that you are one uniquely brilliant and gifted guy!

But no, if you ever felt the slightest bit under attack, you lashed out with all the fury of a cornered cobra. "But whatever anyone dares to boast of — I am speaking as fool — I also dare to boast of that. Are they Hebrews? So am I. Are they Israelites? So am I. Are they descendants of Abraham? So am I. Are they servants of Christ? I am a better one — I am talking like a madman" (II Corinthians 11:21-23). Truth to tell, Paul, you **did** sound just a tad bit out of control. Maybe not completely *meshugge,* but like a *schlemiel* all the same. So did you let it go? No, not you! "Five times I have received at the hands of the Jews the forty lashes less one. Three times I have been beaten with rods; once I was stoned. Three times I have been shipwrecked; a night and a day I have been adrift at sea" II Cor. 11:24-25), etc., etc., etc., almost as though you might go on to the last syllable of recorded time.

You never knew when to let well-enough alone. If people acted as though you were a pain in the tuckus, it was because you *were* a pain in the tuckus. Telling them what a great guy you are didn't help win over anybody, and it probably just confirmed the mistaken impressions some of them already had about you.

Nevertheless, as often as you have driven me half-crazy with your irrepressible Paulishness, and as often as I have disagreed with you on major points of theology and especially Christology, in conclusion I salute you with genuine affection and respect. You did what nobody else in the New Testament cast of characters, including Jesus of Nazareth, ever could have done: you founded the Church of Jesus Christ. You, and you alone.

Your imprint is in the minds of all Christians everywhere. Your ferocious commitment to the one you initially persecuted, solely by itself, has rendered Christianity a reality, whereas before you came on the scene it was only an unlikely possibility. You destroyed the viability of Christian legalism, even though it has reared its petrified head countless times throughout Christian history, only to be slain once again. You firmly established the notion that only God can save anyone, that we are incapable of saving ourselves by our own good deeds, no matter how plentiful or exemplary they may be.

From my subjective standpoint, I wish you had heard the voice of God on the road to Damascus, rather than the voice of Jesus. Your zeal then might have been better directed. However, you heard what you heard and saw what you saw, which is the way it is for all of us, I guess. We cannot determine the litany of events in our theological formation; we can only do our best to use them to the fullest for the Good News of God.

You did that, Paul; boy o boy, did you ever do that!

One last un-requested piece of advice, Paul. Lighten up. Calm down. Chill out. You provided a service to subsequent generations like that of no one else, an inestimable, invaluable gift, the gift of your deep and abiding insights and convictions. Most certainly you did fight the good fight, and finish the race, and keep the faith. Blessings on you forever and forever, Tentmaker of Tarsus! The world would be infinitely poorer without you. But because of you, we Gentiles know Jesus as the Messiah, and through Him, we know God as Creator and Savior.

As some these days might put it in idiomatic English, "Paulie, youduhman!"

Your (I hope!) friend,
John

Scripture – Luke 3:15-23

Text – Jesus, when he began his ministry, was about thirty years
of age.... – Luke 3:23 (RSV)

AN OLDER MAN'S LETTER
TO THE YOUNG MAN JESUS

Dear Jesus,

For all of my life I have tried to be one of your disciples. My
parents were always Christians, as much as anybody can be
"always" a Christian. My three brothers, all of whom were older
than I, also were Christians. Ours was a Christian family, and we
lived in a Christian home.

When I was in fifth grade, I decided I wanted to become a
Presbyterian minister. (We were Presbyterians, so I never
thought about becoming any other kind of parson. Knowing
what I know now, I guess I would still join the ranks of
Presbyterian clergy, although God knows being any kind of parson, especially a Presbyterian one, isn't an always-joyous
vocation. But then, that's not your fault, and that isn't why I am
writing you this letter.)

When I made my decision for the ministry, there was no bolt-
from-the-blue, no voice from either you or God. In my youthful
exuberance, I probably admired the three ministers I had had up to
that time, and I figured I would like to follow in their footsteps.
However, this was a subconscious process, not a conscious one, I'm
sure. Anyway, I was just a boy who really liked church. What can I
say; the world has always had its share of peculiar kids, and I was one.

The result is that mentally I was preparing myself to become
a minister for fifteen years before I finally became ordained. Not
many classmates in seminary had lived for that long in that
tightly-wound little mindset of mine. But I was, and am, an
unusually hardheaded chap, and I never wavered from my decision to enter the ministry.

I was ordained on December 19, 1964, and I officially started as a paid parson on January 15, 1965. I then was a couple of weeks short of 26 years old. So, if Luke is right in saying you were about thirty years of age when you began your public ministry, I was four years younger than you were when I began mine. Your ministry lasted three years; mine has lasted almost forty. And Jesus, that makes a difference. At least so it seems to me.

I am not meaning to suggest that you were what we used to call "a clergyman" in the old politically incorrect days, Jesus, because you weren't. Many people, particularly your followers, considered you to be a rabbi. I also have always thought of you as a rabbi, a brilliant one, the most brilliant ever. But then, Jews don't exactly perceive rabbis to be clergy, do they? I wonder if the fairly recent practice of ordaining rabbis is an imitation of a Christian way of setting apart the clergy. But you were a Jew, Jesus, a first-century Jew, and Jews then did not have clergy or ordination; they just had rabbis. And for some of the Jews who knew you, you were *Rabbi Yeshua ha-Notzri*, Jesus, the Teacher of Nazareth.

Your three years of serving God has had more influence in the world than all the clergy of all time put together. What a magnificent proponent of the kingdom of God you were, Jesus! You made God so real, so close, so personal! Because you knew Him so well, we came to know Him ever so much better. For those of us who are Christians, we see God through your eyes. Thank God for that priceless gift, Jesus!

And you were absolutely fearless in your ministry. What you said and did enormously rankled all kinds of people, many of them very powerful and influential. Clearly you intended to do that, or otherwise you would have gone about everything much more cautiously. We who are "professional ministers," as you were, Jesus, are not nearly so bold. Usually we have chosen assiduously and with great effort to make friends and influence people, using tried-and-true techniques of salesmanship and diplomacy. But not you. You were a tiger of truth, a polemical proponent of reality, an in-your-face proclaimer of what you believed was the Gospel, the Good News of God. Had more of us round-collar types (whether or not we ever wear round collars) acted like you, more of us probably would have ended up prematurely dead, as you ended up. But that's another story, and that isn't why I'm writing this letter either.

So why am I writing it, you wonder? Well, I guess I want to get some things off my chest. I have lived twice as long as you, Jesus, and my ministry has lasted at least twelve times longer than yours, and I just want you know I now see things far differently from the vantage point of a relatively young old codger than I did when I was, like you, a young Turk for truth.

It isn't that I am any less feisty than I was when I was your age. If anything, I am more ornery than ever. But I just can't get worked up so much anymore about the foibles of the human race, or my own foibles, for that matter. To you, everything seemed black and white. To me, most of the world looks grimly or greatly gray. There are multitudes of shades of gray, mind you, from very light to very dark. But hardly anything seems either completely white or completely black to me.

Take individual human beings, for example. There are oodles of folks with heads it appears to me are filled with coarsely-ground sawdust, and I would sometimes gladly rip those heads from their quivering shoulders. I think you felt that way sometimes too. But still, I can't continue to be as perennially peeved with them as you seemed to be. Once you got really steamed, Jesus, you appeared to stay steamed. Or am I wrong about this? Have the four Gospel writers made you out to be too much of an Angry Young Man?

Like you, I know that lots of people have the most atrocious, cockamamie ideas about this and that and the other thing, especially about God and religion, and like you, that riles me. But I have lived long enough to understand that is not likely ever to change, that droves of folks will have droves of daffy beliefs, no matter how hard you or I might try to straighten them out. (This, of course, pre-supposes I myself understand the difference between straight and crooked. Heaven knows that is highly debatable, and heaven also knows lots of people have suggested to me that I am full of cerebral cowpies. They may be correct. But

I'm not penning this epistle to address that issue.) Had you lived another thirty or forty years, Jesus, you too might have concluded that all of us inevitably have some faulty notions banging around in our crania, but you didn't, and you didn't. So should I, a young geezer, still see things the way you saw them? Is that a requirement for proper discipleship?

You put up with a lot, Jesus, but it lasted for only three years. I've put up with a lot too, and it went on for four decades. You never had to deal with a few individual church officers on church boards whose brains seemed to have become thoroughly disengaged somewhere along the line, but I did that - - - a bunch, if you want to know the truth. Some of them thought *I* had a broken brain as well, but of course I didn't, and you know that; don't you. Eh? A regular paragon of smarts I am, Jesus.

I have officiated at over five hundred funerals, and have had to proclaim good news to the thousands who mourned their dead. Of everything I did in the ministry, I liked that challenge almost the best. Because God raised you from the dead, I could honestly promise that those hundreds of dead people also would be raised, along with all those living people who gathered to pay tribute to the dead.

But you didn't have to do that, Jesus. You started the Church, sort of, but you never had to serve in the Church. You initiated the institution, in a manner of speaking (although it was the apostle Paul who really got the ball rolling, although that too is another story), but you never had to serve institutionalized Christianity, any more than you were a servant of institutionalized Judaism. You worked outside The System. I worked in it, and for it.

I realize you never intended that there would be an institutional Church. But it happened anyway. People turned your teachings about God into an organization fostering teachings about you. I am certain you have never been pleased that The Messenger became The Message, but once God raised you from the dead, the matter was out of your hands.

In order to be perpetuated, your teachings had to become institutionalized. That's the way it is for anything that truly mat-

271

ters. So, "The Church of Jesus Christ" came into being, whether you approved of it or not. And that was the outfit to which I devoted my entire adult life. I'd do it all again, I'm certain. But that doesn't mean I don't have a churchly complaint . . . or five.

But here's my kvetch, Jesus; you spent three years battling institutional religion, and I spent thirty-seven years working for it. You being you, and I being I, I suspect battling is better, or at least personally more fulfilling. If a guy is pugnacious by nature, he is happier fighting for truth, justice, and what he thinks is the divine way. And you are a theological pugilist, Jesus, which is what I have no problem admitting I am, also. But one can't do too much battle with Mother Church, or she will cut one off at the fiscal knees, she will. And so I made my prostituted peace with my necessarily-compromised profession.

Not you. You went at it hammer and tongs for as long as you could, which is as long as they would allow you to do it, which wasn't very long. And then they killed you. I never had the satisfaction, or at least the finality, of getting killed. You were shredded to a quick death by sharks. Sometimes I felt like I was nibbled into a long professional life by guppies.

I readily admit I could have acted differently, and there would have been far different results. But I felt *called* to the ministry of the Church, I always believed —— and still do believe —— that it was my *vocation*. And so my life turned out as it turned out.

Well, enough of that, Jesus. On to other things.

I confess I have a major beef with you about some of the things you said. You were so - - so - - - *immoderate*. Take the Sermon on the Mount, for instance. Did you **really** mean all that stuff? "Blessed are those who are persecuted for righteousness' sake, for theirs is the kingdom of heaven": that's easy for **you** to say! Well, come to think of it, it wasn't easy for you to say, not easy at all. No one was ever more persecuted than you were. Still, those who feel pervasively put upon don't normally feel as though they are dwelling in the luxuriant safety of the kingdom of heaven.

You said we shouldn't murder anyone, but then you said that "everyone who is angry shall be liable to judgment, whoever insults anyone shall be liable to the council" (what did that mean?), and "whoever says 'You fool!' shall be liable to the hell of fire." But *you* said "You fools!" to the scribes; you called them blind fools. Was it okay for you to get angry with people and call them names, but not okay for us?

"Everyone who divorces his wife, except on the grounds of unchastity, makes her an adulteress, and whoever marries a divorced woman commits adultery." Were you serious about that? Are you really that doctrinaire? Divorce is surely a huge failure, but can it legitimately be utterly forbidden?

You quoted the *lex talionis*, the law of limited retaliation, which says that you may take no more than one eye of your enemy when he takes one eye from you, or only one of his teeth for each of your teeth which he knocks out. But then you said, "Do not resist one who is evil." In theory you are absolutely right about that, Jesus, but in practice it doesn't seem to work. Who can be so self-possessed as never to resist someone who constantly does evil? Is not evil encouraged when good people do nothing to stop bad people from being bad? To stop bullies from being bullies, doesn't somebody need to give them a good wallop?

"Do not be anxious," you said, and I agree. I have tried to live by that advice. But what about those who, by dint of very deep-seated human psychology, are bulging bundles of awful anxieties? What about those who are congenital worriers, genetic fretters? Surely some people can train themselves to become much less anxious, but just as surely, others will never overcome their anxieties - - - will they?

"You must be perfect, as your heavenly Father is perfect": now **that** I just can't buy, Jesus! Nobody can be perfect! Even you weren't perfect! Oh, I know we have been taught that you were perfect, and that we should believe in your perfection without question. Those Christians way back there figured that the divinity they claimed for you demanded your proclaimed perfection. But in you, Jesus, I see at least minuscule traces of me, and my undeniable imperfections. If the Gospel writers have portrayed you correctly (and in the main I think they have), I see you doing a few of the same things you told us not to do. You didn't always practice what you preached. None of us does either. But we all expect more of you. Perfection is not an option for us; it was supposed to be a necessity for you. You passed the test better than any of us, but unless I am totally mistaken, you didn't score a 100.

So here's what I have concluded, after having cogitated on this matter for many years. You never told us that we must be perfect, as Matthew said you said (Matt. 5:48). Instead, I think Luke was the one who got it right; "Be merciful, as your Father is merciful" (Luke 6:36). Being merciful is definitely possible for all of us; being perfect is simply not in the genetic hand of cards any of us has been dealt.

It is comforting to me that you seemed to feel some of the same frustrations I have felt. "O faithless and perverse generation, how long am I to be with you? How long am I to bear with you?" I like that, Jesus. It convinces me that you, as I and everyone else, had, and have, bad-hair days. It goes with the human territory. "If your hand causes you to sin, cut it off": great hyperbole, Jesus! I have told you a thousand times not to exaggerate, but I love it! I say the same kind of stuff. Doesn't everyone?

"I say to you, do not forgive (only) seven times, but seventy-times-seven." That must mean we must **always** forgive, that we must forgive everything. With that I also agree, Jesus. That we are capable of doing. We all have the human potential for accomplishing that lofty ideal. As Thomas a' Kempis wrote, "Know all and you will pardon all": right, Jesus? Right.

It isn't only in the Sermon on the Mount, though, where you said some pretty outlandish things. There are so many other instances as well. "It is easier for a camel to go through the eye of a needle than for a rich man to enter the kingdom of God." I realize that "the needle's eye" was a small gate within the large gate of a Judean city, so that your hyperbole is not as great as it sounds to western ears. But still…. If you had lived another decade or two, and encountered many more rich folks whom you came to love and admire, would you still say that? Or would you state it with such vehemence? Was it merely youthful brashness which resulted in such a statement, or would you always have said such a thing, regardless of how long you had lived?

When you were told that your mother and brothers were waiting at the edge of the crowd to speak to you, you said, pointing toward the adulating throng — almost with deliberate and spiteful coldness — "Here are my mother and my brothers!" Did you have to state it like that, Jesus? How do you think your mother felt when you said that, or your brothers, or sisters? **We** can deduce what you were attempting to convey, but how about **them**? They had to feel awful! "Woman, what have you to do with me?": what kind of way is that for a son to speak to his mom? Or did you speak to the family afterward to explain, and the Gospel writers either didn't know it, or didn't bother to tell us? Sometimes you sounded so **cold**, Jesus! If you had lived longer, would those rough edges have been honed away?

"Get behind me, Satan!" you said to Peter. No one knew better than you that the prince of apostles could be a pain in the tuckus, but did you have to lace into the poor guy so hard? He meant well, Jesus; he always meant well! For crying out loud, he had just become the first person ever to perceive you to be the Messiah! Sure, he could be a schlemiel, but then, can't we all? Satan? **Satan!** I realize you were having your own internal struggle with your own motives and intentions at that exact moment, Jesus, but did that necessitate your laying out Simon in lavender? You were so **young**, Jesus, and you were so filled with youthful zeal! Might you have been a tad easier on people if you had been a tad older?

"Woe to you, scribes and Pharisees, hypocrites!" Holy Moses!!! There seems to be no slack in that statement! And you said it not once, but many times! Without question by them you had had more than your fill of their venomous resistance to everything you stood for, but even so, did you think God required you to chastise them so severely? I'm not suggesting you shouldn't have told them off. It's just that it sounded like you nearly tore their heads off in the process. And didn't that violate some of the things which you yourself said in far less heated, more dispassionate, moments?

And all these references to hell: did you truly say all that, Jesus? I can't believe it! It seems so unlike you! Even if you did say it, I wish you hadn't! And if you said it, respectfully I think you were wrong. I truly mean it. I will always respect you, but if the "hell sayings" are accurate historically, I firmly believed you stepped across the line which God placed around you, as He places a line around all of us. How can the multitude of things you said about God's grace square with the far fewer things you are purported to have said about hell? If God's grace counts for everything, which you said in ever so many ways, then hell counts for nothing, Jesus; for *nothing*!

Or did you say that stuff just to try to scare the hell out of people? If so, do you really think that works? I choose to believe you didn't say any of it, that the Gospel writers put those words in your mouth, because those thoughts were in their heads, and they wanted to write the story as *they* wanted to write the story. If you did say all that hellish business, I forgive you for it - - - but if you will forgive me, I don't buy it. Never. Ever. I never did. There; I've gotten that off my chest too.

Look, I'm not trying to tell you that in some things you were wrong and that I am right. Well, maybe I am doing that, and if so, I am wrong once again. Please forgive me. I really mean that. I know I will never get everything right in either my head or my heart. But my main purpose, as I have tried to make clear, is that I think you would have been less confrontational if you had not been so — as we might say in these days of exceptional political correctness — age-challenged. I find that most people become more tolerant as they get older, Jesus. Not everyone, to be sure, but most. And sometimes you didn't seem to have the sufficient accretion of years to be able to tolerate the sin which inevitably pervades every human spirit. Certainly we don't always do the best we can, but **sometimes** we do! Give us a break, Jesus! We're only human! You of all people should understand that - - - shouldn't you? Remember all those hymn titles? O master workman of the race... O Son of man, our hero strong and tender... Strong Son of God, immortal love....Immortal love, forever full, forever flowing free....What a friend we have in Jesus....

As you know (or as God knows if you don't), I long ago jettisoned many of the sayings ascribed to you by the writer of the Fourth Gospel. *Oy vey*, what a collection of poisonous proclamations!

> "Indeed, just as the Father raises the dead and gives them life, so also the Son gives life to whomever he wishes."
> "The Father judges no one, but has given all judgment to the Son."
> "Truly, truly, unless you eat the flesh of the Son of Man and drink his blood, you have no life in you."
> "Truly, truly, I tell you, before Abraham was, I am."
> "The Father and I are one."
> "No one comes to the Father, but by me."

The writer John believed those things (if that was indeed the writer's name), but you didn't believe them. How could you? God is God, Jesus, and you are you! Your followers declared you to be God Incarnate, but you never declared that. You were deliberately humble, but they greatly exalted you. You made almost all of your claims about **God**, but they made almost all of their claims about **you**. You pointed constantly toward God, but they pointed constantly toward you. You certainly can't be blamed for that. The master cannot ultimately direct what the disciples choose to make of him, can he, especially after he is gone?

Nor can the master control the arguments the disciples have with one another about the master. Nor can he determine what they think about one another. Thus is this unorthodox letter being written by an unorthodox disciple to one whom he considers to be the wondrous epitome of the purest unorthodoxy.

Jesus, my life would be infinitely poorer, were it not for the influence you have had in it. More than anyone else who lived on this earth, you have been the light to overcome my darkness, the hope to overcome my despair, the calm to overcome my fear, the love to overcome my disdain. I have thought about you more than any other person, with the sorry exception of myself. I have tried to imagine who you really were in your own time, apart from the things others said about you. I have tried to sort through everything the four writers and the other non-approved writers said about you, separating as best I could what I considered to be the wheat from the chaff. I have often pondered what you had to endure, how you persevered, how you managed to maintain your magnificent integrity in the midst of so much adversity.

My knowledge of God would be so much more diminished were it not for that incandescent knowledge of God which you passed on to us. I know God most fully because I have known you, if only in the smallest measure.

I have no doubt that I often misunderstand you, and sell you short, and also dwell too much on you and not enough on God. But I want you to know that I was and am and always will be one of your disciples. I have tried to preach your Gospel as winsomely and well as I could. I am pleased beyond the ability of words to describe to have been called by God into what came to be your Church. It occurred from the moment I was born to my particular parents in my particular life setting. Regardless of the dispute others would make about this, by being born to whom I was born and where I was born, I was always a Christian, however unorthodox.

Nevertheless, I still have these quibbles with you, Jesus. You're a younger man, and I'm an older man, and I continue to wonder: Would you have lived your life differently if you had lived longer? And would that make a difference in how we have come to understand you?

I love you, Jesus.
John

Scripture – All 22 Chapters of the Book of Revelation —— I am **serious** about this!

Text – This calls for wisdom: let him who has understanding reckon the number of the beast, for it is a human number; its number is six hundred and sixty-six. – Revelation 13:18 (RSV)

AN OLDER MAN'S LETTER TO THE REALLY OLD MAN, JOHN OF PATMOS

Dear John,

John, I hardly even know where to begin. What a fine mess you have caused! And what a fine mess for such a long, long time!! For twenty centuries Christians have gone over the edge, with predictable regularity, and all because of your apocryphal, elliptical, illogical, numerological, phantasmagoric, hallucinogenic, dreamlike, nightmarish, clandestine, subversive, revolutionary, and sometimes revolting Apocalypse!!!

Now I admit, you weren't the first to come up with the style of writing you used. It existed centuries before your time. Ezekiel used it in the 6th century BCE, and Daniel employed it to the nth degree in maybe the third or second century BCE. So nobody can blame you for inventing the apocryphal or apocalyptic writing method. In times of persecution, earlier Jews had written in the same enigmatic way.

But oy veh, Ioanni, you ratcheted up the whole genre about 7 notches! Or should it be 4 notches, or 3, or 24, or 666, or 144,000 notches? You didn't choose to boil *The Revelation to John* as a huge cauldron of alphabet soup, oh no; it is instead a huge kettle of numerological soup. And God alone knows what the numbers mean - - - if even He knows.

I'm not going to spew out to you some of the many theories New Testament scholars have posited to explain what you were doing. Only you knew what you were trying to do. But I can assure you of this: whatever you intended to happen as a result of

279

writing your "revelation," it didn't happen. Nobody has ever gotten what you wrote "right." Nineteen centuries after you wrote it, and when we are light years outside the context in which and for which you wrote it, nobody is ever going to get it right. You may as well have written the Apocalypse in a language nobody before or since ever knew, because it is that confusing to everybody who seriously attempts to interpret what in the name of heaven you were trying to say.

Having said that, I have no doubt that you wrote what you wrote *in the name of heaven.* You weren't munching mushrooms, you didn't clumsily pitch into the poppy patch, and you didn't stumble into the smoke of a hemp field on fire. I am positive that you never intended to create so many problems for Christianity in the centuries which followed your scribal gambit. You meant well, John; I'm certain you did. And maybe somebody in your own time figured out what you were really talking about. But if so, they never bothered to tell the rest of us. And believe me, that is a major drawback, because what people in our time make of the Revelation reveals a limitless reservoir of untrammeled religious imagination.

You wrote under the threat of persecution to people who also were being persecuted, and you wrote in such a way that *they* (the persecuted) would understand what you were so cryptically saying, and that *they* (the persecutors, the Romans) wouldn't be able to figure it out. It's just that it is all so (please pardon the expression, but I hope you know what I mean): it's all so ***damned*** cryptic! Who in hell, or anywhere else, can genuinely decipher it? Your Revelation is written in early-second-century code, but the code book, if it ever existed, has long since disappeared. Nobody in Langley, Virginia, or Moscow, Russia, or in Scotland Yard in London can find the cryptological key to unlock the philological and numeric mysteries of your many cryptic words, numbers, and images. Even the clever chaps of Al Qaeda, who are excellent at devising codes, would be lost in the plethora of numbers and vivid pictures which you so plentifully splashed across your panting parchment.

When I was a boy, a group of my friends and I joined DeMolay. DeMolay was an organization for male youths, sponsored by the Masons. DeMolay had noble purposes, I guess, but we joined because there was a pool table in the Masonic Lodge, and we liked to go downtown and shoot a few games, acting like we were Paul Newman or Jackie Gleason. We had a secret handshake, a secret ritual, and all kinds of other secret stuff, all of which was so secret I have forgotten every single part of it.

But this much I remember: if you were a tried and true DeMolay, you were in the know. And being in the know was good, because it gave you a leg up on everybody else who wasn't a DeMolay and therefore wasn't in the know. Besides, we had these dances with the Rainbow Girls, and everyone got all dressed up and acted like we were very hot items. Its juvenile exclusivity appealed to our juvenile ignorance.

The Masons have secret stuff too, I hear. I don't know what it is, because I never joined. It has to be secret, though, because Masons never ask anyone to join them; they just wait till somebody expresses an interest, and if he passes muster with them, they let him in. And then he too learns the secret stuff.

Beta Theta Pi also had secret stuff, but I never got far enough into it to find out what it was. In my freshman year in college, I pledged that fraternity, but I got steamed at a particular brother, a football player he was, who seemed to delight in making life miserable for us lowly pledges. So I de-pledged. Who needs fraternity behemothic bullies beating you about the head and ears when graduate assistants were doing the same thing and getting paid for it? But had I hung in there, I would have learned the Beta secret stuff. Like maybe what the Greek letters beta, theta, and pi stand for. Now I'll never know. Rats.

John, your Revelation has oodles of secret stuff, scads of it. But you hid its meaning so thoroughly that nobody now can even come close to accurately declaring what it means. Oh, all kinds of people all the time say what they think it means, but it is all just hyperventilated guesswork. Furthermore, all the time they make predictions about things that will soon happen, especially that the world will end in a spectacular explosive war in almost no time at all. But they have been doing that for centuries, and it hasn't ended yet. And the short times have gotten longer and longer. I'm not suggesting that it won't end; sometime it is bound to expire, if not with a bang, then with a whimper. But neither you, John, nor anyone else knows when, and it is much, much, **much** ado about nothing when anyone claims to know when When will be.

Of course this isn't directly your fault. You wrote your secret script, and they think they have figured it out. They haven't; obviously they haven't, or all the things they said would come true **would** come true. But the fact that nobody ever gets it entirely right or even mainly right doesn't stop others from trying to unlock the secrets. There is never a shortage of Avid Apocalypse Unlockers.

They taught us in seminary that "apocryphal" means "hidden." It's like a murder mystery. When we read the mystery novel, we are constantly trying to figure out whodunit. Until the end, the mystery lies hidden in a plethora of possibilities: the butler, the chauffeur, Col. Mustard, Hannibal Lector, or somebody else who is equally stunning and cunning and very smart.

"Apocalypse," on the other hand, they told us, means "uncovered," or perhaps more literally, "the lifting of a veil." Both words have the same root as their beginning, but supposedly they end up very differently. Except that in your case, John, they don't. **Nothing** in your Apocalypse is uncovered; **everything** is still hidden. Well, almost nothing, and almost everything. Whatever was not veiled, you veiled, and whatever was veiled you didn't unveil.

The opening three chapters are rather straightforward. Particularly the Letters to the Seven Churches in chapters 2 and 3. (Boy, did you love the number 7!) But there is nothing that is especially cryptic or hidden in what you said to those people in those particular congregations. You had encouraging words for most of them. But not for the Laodiceans. *Uff da*, for those poor schlemiels you had no sympathy at all! But then, maybe they deserved what you said about them, and more.

It's when you started chapter 4 that things start to get hopelessly fuzzy for us. For three chapters it is Twain or Hemingway or Bellow, and then suddenly we are in Faulkner or James Joyce or e.e. cummings. There is no prelude or interlude; we are just yanked from normal prose into a host of hidden messages, into a completely covered uncovering. There are no footnotes to help us, no revelatory Cliff Notes, no notes at all. We are thrust into a bottomless sea of numbing numbers, ignominious images, and meaningless metaphors. **That** you **are** accountable for, John.

But let's step back and try to decide just who you are, O Ancient One of Patmos. One hoary tradition in the Church declares that you are the same person who wrote the Gospel of John, the Epistles of John, and the Revelation to John, and that you were also "the beloved disciple," the brother of James, the fisherman and apostle John. People can believe whatever they want, of course, but that seems patently absurd. How would a commercial fisherman, who didn't even have a union card for crying out loud, learn to write like that, "that" being either the style in the Fourth Gospel or the Epistles **or** the style in the Apocalypse? Whoever wrote the Gospel surely also wrote the Epistles, because the writing style is so similar. Nobody needs a Ph.d. in linguistics to deduce that. But the writer of the Revelation was surely somebody else. **You** wrote the Revelation, John, you, the elder, the very old man who lived on the Aegean island of Patmos. You weren't the disciple John; you were the really old man John, the Patmos John, John the Elder. (By the way, isn't it sometimes a caution to be named John? There are so blasted many of us, it's hard to tell us apart!)

And when did you write? Our professors said you wrote about 120 CE, or AD as we used to say. That is, you wrote in the early second century, almost a century after Jesus had been crucified. The professors can't prove that, and I certainly can't prove it, but I have no reason to deny it. Besides, your book didn't get put last in the New Testament for no reason. Supposedly there is a generalized historical progression to the books, although (so we are told) the Gospels were written **after** the letters of Paul were written. They say the Gospel of Mark was written about 60 CE, Matthew 70 CE, Luke 80 CE, and John 100 CE. Setting aside the inconsistency of Paul's writings actually preceding the Gospels, presumably the other New Testament material was written more or less in the order it ends up in the New Testament. And since your Revelation is in last place, I guess we are to assume that it was the last book of the New Testament to be written. Nobody knows any of this beyond dispute, John, and only you know when you wrote what you wrote, or even, for that matter, **that** you wrote it. But most of us think you did, "you" being the very old man who lived on Patmos.

I've been there, by the way. I've seen your cave. I've climbed up to the church on top of the hill too. We didn't have a lot of time, because we were told the ship would leave without us if we didn't get back for the departure hour. As beautiful as it is, Patmos is not a place I'd like to be permanently left on. Until I went there, I always pictured the island differently in my mind, and now I'm not sure whether the pre-visit Patmos of my mind was better than my post-visit Patmos. Both are fine, if the truth is told. But like so many other biblical sites, the mental and the geographical realities are almost always very different from one another, and often at extreme odds with one another.

But let's get back to what you actually wrote. There are all those numbers which are so numerous they numb us. Twenty-four thrones, twenty-four elders, seven torches, seven spirits, four living creatures, seven seals, four angels, four corners of the earth (does the earth have **corners**?), a hundred forty-four thousand sealed (what does **sealed** mean?), twelve thousand of this tribe and twelve thousand of that tribe (in 120 CE, did **anybody** in Israel still think about tribes? And if they didn't, then why did **you** think of them, John?), seven angels, one thousand two hundred and fifty days, etc., etc. etc. Without the code book, how do you expect us to understand what any of those numbers mean?

And then there are the images: the Lamb standing as though slain, harps, golden bowls, a white horse, a red horse, a black horse, a pale horse, stars falling to the earth (did you know how big stars actually are, compared to the earth?), a golden altar, fire, earthquakes, trumpets, an eagle, scorpions, Babylon, a measuring rod, a woman clothed with the sun, a red diadem, the Beast, the sea of glass, Armageddon, etc., etc. etc. We can **guess** what these images might mean, but it is only a guess! Did you ever think we would **know** what you meant? Lots of folks think they know, but they only **think** it; they don't **know** it! People who think they know are much more worrisome – and wearisome – than those who know they don't know!

But when you came up with 666, John, and the Beast, John, you really threw us a curve ball! (That's an American expression; it has to do with a game we call baseball. But never mind.) Years ago, fundamentalists gave Procter and Gamble fits because somebody thought they saw a 666 in the company's logo, and they were ready to forego their Crest toothpaste or anything else P&G sold. **You** did it, John; **you**. The Masons or DeMolays or Betas might have an idea what you meant by that number, but nobody else does. *Wass gibts? Que pasa?* Huh?

If anything, your vivid imagination makes Satan more real than God or Jesus. Why? Why were you so captivated by satanology and demonology? And why were you obsessed by the Good Guys vs. the Bad Guys to the last syllable of recorded time?

Fortunately, most people who have lived outside central North America have never become very enamored of your book, but droves of people south of Canada and north of Mexico have glommed onto it like flies to honey. Americans are a most peculiar people, in case no one ever told you that, John. We come up with some strange notions. For half a century, in the early part of the 19th century, we spawned some of the most bizarre religious lunacies history has ever been able to shake a stick at, and virtually every one of these zany notions was at least tangentially connected to some of the veiled mysteries you made more veiled in your not-unveiled Unveiling. The Jehovah Witnesses are fixated on their 144,000. The Mormons came up with their own book which is, if anything, even wilder than your book. Then there are the legions of Christians who went ga-ga over the

Scofield Bible. Holy cats, John, what a hurricane of zealous believers was born via the teachings of Messrs. Darby and Scofield! In the first congregation I served as pastor in northern Wisconsin, I ran into a whole nest of Scofield afficianados who were enraptured by pre-millennialism, post-millennialism, and a-millennialism. I, poor benighted mainline Presbyterian that I was, had never before heard of any of this stuff.

Until I encountered those elderly graduates of Mrs. Pinney's Bible class (Mrs. Pinney had been the minister's wife in that church fifty years before), I thought that a) tribulation meant a kind of a tough time for someone, b) rapture was the state of being pretty turned on by something, maybe especially by a three-lettered word, and c) a thousand years merely meant ten centuries. Little did I know that Christian fundamentalists in the 19th and 20th centuries had virtually put their own copyright on those words.

John, if nobody has yet tried to explain to you what pre-, post-, or a-millennialists are, I'm certainly not going to attempt to do so either. Suffice it to say that whatever these esoteric and eclectic ideas mean, they command vast respect among those who believe in them, and they engender fierce animosity toward anybody who is allied with the wrong camp in these titanic theological struggles. But in my admittedly – and happily – very limited association with these kinds of Christians, I conclude that they are a pretty pessimistic bunch. When the roll is called up yonder, if anybody is there, other than they themselves, it will be a damned sad day in heaven, as far as they are concerned. In fact, if people such as I somehow are allowed through the celestial back gate, the Really Righteous will likely march out the front gate in mass protest.

Through the years I have noticed that the people who are the most intrigued by your Revelation, John, are also usually the nastiest in spirit toward one another, and especially toward those of us who can't make heads or tails out of your writings, and don't try to do so either. Once again, I hasten to add that not everything you wrote is indecipherable. The first three chapters and the 21st chapter are excellent. It's all the rest that is so exasperating. And those who think they know what you are saying don't seem to know much about anything at all. They often come across as prideful ignoramuses, overconfident doofusses, illiterate nincompoops.

Not for a fleeting instant am I attempting to suggest you are like that, John. Without question you are an extremely intelligent, unusually gifted, intensely shrewd man who knew exactly what you intended when you wrote your Apocalypse. And unless I am totally mistaken (which heaven knows happens a lot!), these 22 chapters were not a bolt-from-the-blue vision from God that you simply inscribed in rapid shorthand. You had carefully thought through every number, every metaphor, every colorful image you used. None of it was spontaneously observed; all of it was cleverly plotted. And all of it was intended to be instantly understood by persecuted Christians and to be instantly dismissed as vaporous poppycock by heavy-handed Romans. Presumably that is exactly what happened. But in the intervening decades after you finished your masterpiece, the interpretive keys were lost, and your words passed into the mists of biblical uncertainty and gross misinterpretation.

Despite that, and certainly despite my great uneasiness over your Revelation, some of your words and phrases have powerfully echoed down through the centuries of Christian music and hymnody. Dozens of our most favored hymns sprout out of the rich soil of your imaginative imagery: "O for a thousand tongues to sing," "Lo, he comes with clouds descending," "Welcome happy morning," "O Jesus, Thou art standing," "Holy, holy, holy, Lord God Almighty," "Come, thou long-expected Jesus," "I love to tell the story," "Blessing and honor and glory and power," "For all the saints," "Ten thousand times ten thousand," "Jerusalem the golden," "Lord of all being, throned afar," "O holy city, seen of John" —— and the list goes on and on. Handel loved your texts; in his *Messiah* he used several of them. It was you who inspired *The Hallelujah Chorus*, and *The Hallelujah Chorus* has inspired countless millions of Christians in good times and bad ever since Georg Friedrich put his quill to paper in that marvelously manic burst of artistic energy in the middle of the 18th century. Bach loved your texts, as did Beethoven and Mozart and Brahms.

When you were writing about non-apocalyptic things, John, you were unequalled in poetic grandeur.

Christianity would be quite different had the Apocalypse not been added to the Christian canon of scripture; no one can deny that. Especially in terms of Christian musical literature, your contributions to Christian worship have been incalculable. Only a stiff-necked fool could manage to overlook that fact.

Nonetheless, John, all things considered, if had been up to me alone, knowing what I know centuries after the fact, I would have prevented the Revelation from ever seeing either the light of day or the brush of the printer's ink upon the sacred page. First of all, like so many of the other New Testament writers, you concentrated too much on Jesus and too little on God. What got into you people anyway? Did you forget who sent Jesus into the world? Didn't you recall that "the Lord" originally meant God, and only in a secondary usage did "the Lord" mean Jesus? When it becomes unclear who "the Lord" really is, "the Lord" surely is not pleased!

But of far greater consequence, the opaqueness of your words has led to far too much unsubstantiated speculation and to far too much unsupported prognostication. Too much energy has been spent anticipating events which never came to pass. The obviously errant certitude of some of the followers of the Galilean carpenter has dissuaded other more cerebral, rational people from seriously considering the validity of the Christian claims about Jesus, because they incorrectly assumed that the Christianity of the Revelation is the only Christianity there is. Over-zealous enthusiasts have a way of putting off certain types of folks. Thus, because of what you said in such a deliberately oblique manner, untold numbers of people have decided against Christianity, thinking that the Revelation is mainstream Christianity.

But it isn't, John! I'm sorry to have to say it, but it just plain isn't! It is not without great significance that your Apocalypse is at the very end of the Bible! It is on the periphery of scripture, an also-ran among the 27 books of the New Testament, and the 66 books of the whole Bible! When you wrote it, you knew what you meant, and your readers presumably knew what you meant, but for the past eighteen centuries, nobody else has truly known what you meant! And those who think they know the most seem to know the least!

It is the Law of Unintended Consequences all over again. When the canon of the New Testament was decided in the 4th and 5th centuries, the early Church never would have given the Revelation their official imprimatur, if they had foreseen what would happen because of the mystifying parts of your book. You did not intend to foment religious lunacies; of that I am certain. The early Church did not intend for Christian theology to go off on such disastrous tangents. But it happened all the same.

Well, we can all take comfort in the realization that God is the Alpha and the Omega (not Jesus, but God), and that therefore it will all come out all right in the end anyway. And whether Jesus comes back soon, or not so soon, or not at all, and whether dusty, ashen bodies shall rise up out of the ground or not, in the end God shall straighten out whatever we humans have made crooked.

John, *in illud tempore* as they say, in that time, I will surely have a lot more to explain than you will. Maybe in taking such a strong stand against your book, I will really have a lot of explaining to do. But please understand; **none of this is personal**. You are a remarkable man. And to write what you wrote at the age you wrote it is singularly astonishing. Most of us are long dead by the time we get to be your age!

For your time the Revelation was magnificently comforting, compelling, and inspiring. Ever since it has been terribly confusing, befuddling, and off-putting. But it needs clearly to be stated that that isn't your fault. That's our fault.

So, *requiescat in pace*, Ioanni. And *illegitimati non carborundum*, especially the *verbum* of this particular *illegitimatus.*

I hope to see you one day so that we can have a long chat about all this.

Another younger older man named
John

Religious Detours as a Result of Religious Devotion

Scripture – Matthew 7:21-23

Text – "On that day many will say to me, 'Lord, Lord, did we not prophesy in your name, and cast out demons in your name, and do many mighty works in your name?' And then will I declare to them, 'I never knew you; depart from me, you evildoers.'" – Matt. 7:22-23 (RSV)

THE EVANGELICAL SEIZURE OF CHRISTIANITY

The word "evangelical" has become a problematic word, a confusing word, a slippery word. Once it was virtually a synonym for "Christian." More than anything else, it now connotes a particular group of Christians, or conservative Christian theology, or highly Christocentric Christology.

Our English word "evangelical" comes from a Greek word, *euaggelion*. *Euaggelion* literally means "good news" or "good tidings." It means exactly the same thing as the old Anglo-Saxon word *Godspel*. The *Gospel* is the proclamation of the good news about God as expressed by and through Jesus Christ.

Sometimes the four Gospel writers (Matthew, Mark, Luke, and John) are called the Four Evangelists. The term suggests that each of them presents his own version of what the good news of Jesus Christ was, and is. Thus an evangelist is somebody who proclaims the Gospel of Jesus of Nazareth, and the good news thus preached is uniquely good news, because it is available only in and through Jesus.

During the Reformation, "evangelical" was a synonym for "Protestant." All Protestants were called "Evangelicals;" all Evangelicals were called "Protestants." This is not to suggest that Roman Catholics were not evangelical, but the term simply was not applied to them. Then, after the Reformation, "evangelical" came to mean "Lutheran" in most of Germany and Scandinavia, and it meant "Reformed" or "Calvinistic" in southwestern Germany, Switzerland, Holland, Scotland, and England. In northern Europe, "evangelical" is still interchangeable with

"Lutheran," and it still means "Calvinist" in parts of Switzerland and a slice of southwestern Germany. But in the Netherlands, France, Scotland, and England, Calvinists no longer call themselves "evangelicals," nor does anyone else call them that. Now the Calvinists of those countries are known either as "Reformed" or "Presbyterians."

By the opening years of the 21st century in the USA, "evangelical" is a word which seems almost to have been copyrighted by those kinds of Christians who refer to themselves, and are referred to by others, whether Christians or not, as "**evangelicals**." Thus the organization which calls itself The National Association of Evangelicals does not at all perceive itself as "The National Association of Protestants Broadly Defined;" rather it connotes "The National Association of Theologically Conservative Protestants." The National Council of Churches has been the umbrella group for liberal Protestants and others, whereas the National Association of Evangelicals is the umbrella group for denominations such as The Church of God, the Church of Christ, the various Pentecostal groups, the Christian Missionary Alliance, conservative Baptist denominations, and the like.

Nobody can control how words evolve. Words have an evolutionary existence which is almost never "fixed" for all time. Different words have different meanings through the passage of decades and centuries. To illustrate, the Greek term *hoi poloi* literally means "people of the city." In classical Greece, the *hoi poloi* were the low-class people, the poor people, those who much later would be called the proletariat. As the centuries went on, to some people "*hoi poloi*" came to mean the high-class people, the rich people, the cultured and cultivated people, the jet set, the *glitterati*, the social swells. That usage is still incorrect, but it is gathering momentum, and it shall probably win out over time. Now, if anybody uses the term *hoi poloi*, it almost needs to be explained which usage one intends, if the context in which the word is employed does not clarify the meaning.

The word "decimate" comes from Latin. In the days of the Roman legions, the Roman generals would **decimate** enemy armies or rebellious Roman legions. That is, they would kill one-tenth of the soldiers in each unit, just to show everyone that they meant business. The Latin root *dec* means "ten" or "tenth." Now, however, "to decimate" means to devastate or obliterate. Time has altered the original meaning intended by the Romans.

Or take the word "gay." For centuries **gay** connoted joy, happiness, high spirits, or, in a more obvious linguistic connection, gaiety. Today, the word gay is almost never used in that context or with that meaning. Now "gay" means "homosexual" (normally of the male variety), or else it means male homosexuality and lesbianism collectively clumped together. No songwriter in the early 2000s would ever say, "But I feel so gay/ In a melancholy way/ That it might as well be spring;" you just wouldn't say that. In the mid-20th century, yes; in the early 21st century, no. Whether we like it or not, the word "gay" now seems exclusively to connote homosexuality.

In an analogous fashion, the word "evangelical" currently seems to belong only to conservative Christians. Liberal Christians would have a hard time convincing other liberal Christians that they also are evangelical, let alone to convince conservative Christians. And yet, is not the Good News proclaimed by liberals fundamentally the same Good News as that preached by conservatives? Can the Gospel be divided? Can evangelicals truly be differentiated from one another?

Curiously, the very word "Christian" is increasingly associated with conservative Christianity, whether "Christian" is used by conservative or liberal Christians, or even by non-Christians. For instance, what is **Christian** Radio? You may be certain of this: most people of whatever theological persuasion or non-persuasion would never think of **Christian** radio as the sort of radio programming featuring Methodist, United Church of Christ, Presbyterian, Episcopal, or *Evangelical* (oops! as I was saying...) Lutheran clergy or laity. No, **Christian** radio features **evangelical** (meaning conservative) programming.

Or then there is the term "Christian music," about which elsewhere in these lengthy literary homilies I fulminate at some length. "Christian music" does not suggest compositions by J.S. Bach, Felix Mendelssohn, W.A. Mozart, Isaac Watts, or Charles Wesley; oh, no. "Christian music" doesn't even include such noted historical evangelical composers as Cecil Frances Alexander, Fannie J. Crosby, Frances Ridley Havergal, James Montgomery, and Ira Sankey. It is much, much more contemporary than those composers, and far more theologically circumscribed. Most of it is composed by people whose names would not be recognized by the kind of people who would buy a book like this, even if your very life depended on that name recognition. Are you familiar with Slavesacre or Blindside or Mark Saloman, with Third Day, P.O.D., Yolanda Adams, or Mary Mary? No? I thought not. Nor was I, until I read about them in a *USA Today* article. The vast percentage of what historically would have been called "Christian music," if they had chosen to use that terminology back then, which they didn't, is not "Christian" in the current meaning of "Christian music." To put it in deliberately pejorative terms, **good** Christian music is not **"Christian** music," and most "Christian music" is not good. I don't mean that "Christian music" is necessarily bad, and it certainly is not evil. It just isn't musically or aesthetically or thematically very good in objective, supportable terms.

The word "Christian" itself has come to mean something politically it never meant until the last decade or two. Liberal Christian politicians rarely use the word "Christian" to describe any positions they make, and with good reason. If they did, it would be misconstrued to mean **conservative** Christian, and they do not want to be identified with that. Thus, "the Christian Right" is almost synonymous with "the political right," although, thank God, there are some legitimate conservative politicians who are not conservative Christians, and some of them are not Christians at all.

Perhaps naming names will help you better understand what I am trying to say. Orrin Hatch or Tom DeLay or Trent Lott or Jesse Helms or Henry Hyde — or Jerry Falwell, Pat Robertson, or Cal Thomas — will often talk about "the Christian position" on various political issues. Note, it is never "**a** Christian position;" it is always **"the** Christian position," as though there were only one. And **The** Christian Position is **always** a particular version of a conservative, evangelical stance on such issues as abortion, prayer in schools, creationism, fetal cell research, and so on.

But why should "Christian" necessarily equate to "conservative?" Or why should "evangelical Christianity" always seem to mean "right-wing Christianity?" The Good News of Jesus Christ is good news for everyone, however it is proclaimed! Christians are Christians, whether they are on the right, the left, or in the center! Just because conservative Christians believe they are the only proper Christians does not mean that they alone **are** proper! For that matter, no Christian is truly proper, as the apostle Paul insisted. We all sin and fall short of the glory of God.

In His own time, the kind of people who most upset Jesus were those who now would be described as "evangelicals." The superreligious nearly drove Jesus round the bend. His most virulent words were reserved for them. "Woe to you, scribes and Pharisees, hypocrites!" He shouted again and again, and sometimes those who are the most evangelical are also the most hypocritical.

I realize that it isn't nice for a liberal to say things like this. But then, with as many things as I have legitimately been accused of, no one ever accused me of being nice, either. Nonetheless, these things need to be said. The greatest current danger to Christianity is not from apathetic or lukewarm liberal Christianity, although heaven knows much of liberal Christianity is far too apathetic and lukewarm. The greatest danger is from evangelical, and especially exclusivistic, conservative Christianity. Those who believe there is only one correct way of coming to God by definition have not found that way, and as long as they continue to think like that, they will **never** find it. If God insists on everybody coming to Himself by only one road and one roadmap, then nobody will ever arrive. We are all too headstrong or we get lost too easily for us ever to stay on the same path long enough to grope our way into God's presence. And so God is forced to manifest His presence among us, which is what the Bible and particularly Jesus is all about.

The rapid rise of evangelical Christianity is due, in large measure, to the flaccidity of liberal Christianity. We liberals have grown old and flabby. Liberal Christians are far more proficient at talking than doing, and we have not done much for the kingdom in the last two or three decades. At the same time, we have allowed evangelicals to seize whatever few headlines are still devoted to Christianity. If we don't take ourselves very seriously —— and we don't! ——, how can we expect anyone else to take us seriously?

Look at the giving records of the liberal denominations. The conservatives outspend us in outreach and mission projects four- or five- or ten-to-one. Money manifests itself as mission, and if the money isn't there, the mission suffers. Clearly we don't believe enough in what we say we believe, or else we would more fully turn our dollars into deeds. The denominations with the greatest gains in membership are also, without fail, the denominations with the highest percentage giving and per capita giving. Nothing succeeds like success, and today the most "evangelical" denominations are the most successful denominations.

What are the names of liberal Christians to whom journalists turn when they are writing stories about religious themes? Other than Martin Marty or Don Shriver, neither of whom is a spring chicken, can you think of any? Two generations ago, journalists would first have interviewed such princes of the pulpit as Norman Thomas, Harry Emerson Fosdick, George Buttrick, Ralph Sockman, David Read, or Harold Bosley, or theologians like Reinhold Niebuhr, Paul Tillich, or John Bennett. Among liberal Christians today there are no names with the cachet of those names. But among evangelicals there are a host of widely-recognized luminaries: Pat Robertson, Jerry Falwell, James Dobson, Billy Graham, Franklin Graham, Robert Shuller, Ben Haden, Jimmy Swaggart, Oral Roberts, Tim LaHaye. And when the journalists finish their stories, they contain the "spin" supplied by conservative Christians, not by liberal Christians.

Probably the majority of evangelical Christians do not imagine that they alone exclusively possess all the truths of the

Christian religion. But there are many evangelicals who do believe that. On the other hand, liberal Christians can act the same way. Back in the Sixties, liberals smugly assumed they **owned** the decade. As far as journalists were concerned, they did own it. Journalists contact people who will most likely be recognized by their readers or viewers, and it does not matter what theological or religious "stripe" these people might represent. That may offend the sensitivities of Christians all across the spectrum, but it has always been thus. And so, as the tide inevitably swings back and forth from liberal to conservative, pundits point in whatever direction they think the tide is flowing.

As long as human beings have existed, no doubt some humans have felt superior to others. At the current time, Christian evangelicals probably are more prone to feelings of superiority, if only because it appears that they represent the ascendant side of contemporary Christianity, not only in the USA, but around the world.

Conservative Islam also seems to be dominant over moderate or liberal Islam. The headlines scream about groups like Al Qaeda or Hamas or Hezbollah or the Islamic Brotherhood, and we hear almost nothing about the vast majority of Sunni and Shiite Muslims, who desire nothing more than peaceful co-existence with Christians, Jews, Hindus, Buddhists, and everyone else.

It is impossible accurately to quantify, but most religious people of every religion, even in this period of growing conservatism, are almost certainly moderate to relatively liberal in their outlook. Few people are able to maintain intense religious fervor over a lifetime; it simply requires too much spiritual, physical, and mental effort. Nevertheless, an increased number and percentage of evangelical and even more conservative Christians are now convinced that they represent the majority of Christians. Even though statistically they are wrong, it creates a most unpleasant situation for all other Christians.

Jesus was greatly put off by "triumphalist" believers. Throughout the Gospels He confronted them head on. Sadly, no one can be certain about what Jesus actually said and did during His ministry in first-century Judea. We all choose to believe what we want to believe about that. But it seems evident that the attitudes of the scribes, Pharisees, Sadducees, and priests regularly got under the skin of the Messiah, and He attacked them without let-up.

In the Gospels, Jesus seems to express ambivalence about the level of commitment He demanded from His followers. It is one thing to say, "He who is not with me is against me" (Mt. 12:30), and quite another to say, "He who is not against us is for us" (Mk. 9:40). "My yoke is easy and my burden is light" (Mt. 11:30) sounds a whole lot less demanding than "Whoever finds his life shall lose it" (Mt. 10:39) or "If anyone would come after me, let him deny himself and take up his cross and follow me" (Mt. 16:24). In some passages Jesus seems to promote unlimited zealotry, but in others He seems to oppose it.

Our scripture passage for this sermon quotes Jesus as saying in His Sermon on the Mount, "Not everyone who says to me, 'Lord, Lord,' shall enter the kingdom of heaven, but he who does the will of my father in heaven. On that day many will say to me, 'Lord, Lord, did we not prophesy in your name, and cast out demons in your name, and do many mighty works in your name?' And then will I declare to them, 'I never knew you; depart from me, you evildoers'" (Mt. 7:21-23).

We are familiar with these words; we know what they **say**. But what do they actually **mean**? First of all, Jesus clearly implied that we cannot just **declare** that we are His followers; we must **do** what God commands us to do. That applies to everyone, regardless of theological leanings. But, Jesus continued, even doing those things which appear to be the proper deeds of discipleship is no guarantee that anyone is therefore automatically "in." Prophesying or healing people or doing mighty works in themselves will not suffice.

So what does suffice? As the disciples asked Jesus at another location and in another context, "Then who can be saved?" Can anyone? Indeed, is it possible for anyone ever to be granted salvation?

I believe that the most authentic expression of Christian faith continuously insists that people cannot be saved by their own actions. Good deeds, no matter how good or plentiful or heartfelt or genuine, are of no avail for our salvation. Only the grace of God can save us. Further, God's grace **does** save us, all of us, or so the Church at its best has always declared.

Strangely, those Christians who best know that we are saved by grace alone, who are evangelical Christians, are also the Christians most likely to act as though they have earned God's favor through their good deeds. True, many moderate or liberal Christians also may labor under that dangerous delusion. But it is evangelicals, conservatives, and fundamentalists who are the most likely to fall into the Snare of Good Works. And they do it because, in general, their faith is stronger or more pronounced or more generously shared or even trumpeted than the faith of most other Christians.

Smug Christians are cloying Christians. They are really hard to take. Sadly, most smug Christians are conservative or evangelical Christians. Liberals don't have anything to be smug about, because most of us are so insipid in living out our Christian lives. Theologically, we know we don't have a leg to stand on, and so we don't even try to stand - - - for anything or anyone, including Almighty God. We correctly rely on grace for our salvation, but we don't rely on ourselves to do what we know we ought to do. We have, if we don't say so ourselves, excellent understanding. But far too often we also have shockingly poor performance. Evangelicals are much better than liberals at putting their faith into action. That has always been true.

But evangelicals, knowing that it is true, subconsciously may come to believe that they are more acceptable than liberals in the eyes of God. That is what Jesus saw so frequently in the most religiously devoted people of His time, and that is why He so frequently got so steamed at them. "I never knew you; depart from me, you evildoers," He said to such folk in the Sermon on the Mount.

The gap between valid discipleship and preening self-righteousness is an exceedingly fine line! It is infinitesimally narrow. Few of us have the fiery zeal of Orthodox or Hasidic Jews or fundamentalist Christians or fanatical Muslims, and most of us look like lukewarm dropouts in comparison to those kinds of people. They, by their mighty works, show themselves to be truly committed, and we, by our wobbly, wishy-washy behavior show ourselves to be dubious disciples at best.

Where can we discern the truth? If the line between healthy commitment and fanatical zeal is so narrow, most of us will naturally swing toward the side of tepid commitment, rather than run the risk of zealously making complete asses of ourselves.

Well, if the truth is told, asses of any sort are never complete asses. We are all incomplete asses. In that we should all find some consolation. Besides, if we are going to err (and we are all going to err, and often), it is better to err on the side of doing too much in our discipleship than doing too little. Conservatives might do too much, and for the wrong reasons, but liberals need never be concerned about overdoing anything. For us, "too little" usually feels like "enough," and "enough" usually feels like "too much."

* * * * * * *

So, as a Russian chap named Vladimir Ilyitch Ulanov asked in another time and context, what is to be done? Should moderate and liberal Christians continue to withdraw from the struggle with the evangelicals, letting them take the lead by taking over the primary thrust of the Christian mission to the world? Or should there be a more deliberate demarcation, a clear and present drawing of a line in the sand by both sides?

Without doubt, some evangelicals are attempting to seize the whole of Christianity for their own purposes. The most convinced among them believe that they are duty-bound to elbow the rest of us out of the field of Christian mission altogether. If they had it in their power to eliminate the kinds of individuals, churches, and denominations they think are apostate, they would do so in a heartbeat. Because they are unable to do that, they realize they must take longer to achieve their goals.

The theological war in the mainline denominations between evangelicals and moderates is illustrative of what is going on.

The battle for the soul of the Southern Baptist Convention, which has been waged for well over a decade, is another sign of the same struggle in a more traditionally conservative denomination.

Nobody is ever going to achieve total victory in these confrontations. Theological polarities have always existed in the Church, from the time of Jesus and His disciples to the present time. Differences abound, and they must be both acknowledged and accepted.

But certain leaders among the evangelicals do not want to tolerate differences, let alone acknowledge or accept them. It is in the nature of ultra-conservatism, as well as ultra-liberalism, that more moderate points of view must not be allowed. Extremists insist on extremism, and too many evangelicals in the Church have become extremists. Extremist liberals in most churches evaporated en masse about 1972, never to have been heard from again. Give them time, and they shall re-appear, wreaking their own unique brand of havoc upon the body of Christ. But for now, it is extremist conservatives who represent the greatest threat to the health of the churches.

Tragically, a few or several mainline Protestant denominations may split, yet again, over some of the theological issues which are now so fiercely brewing. Ordination of homosexuals, the marriage of homosexuals, and Christology are three matters which have dragged several denominations close to the brink of schism.

But this time, even the Roman Catholic Church seems to be teetering on the edge. The pedophile crisis among the priesthood, the perceived inflexibility of the Pope and the bishops, and the questions of married priests and female priests bespeak a major internal crisis which seems to broaden the gap from ever being successfully resolved. In Catholicism, however, it is not so much an "evangelical-moderate" battle as a "conservative-liberal" battle. The conservatives want to keep the lid on, and the liberals want to blow it off, forcing in some new, fresh, if also untested, air.

Certain issue-oriented liberals also seem willing, and perhaps eager, to split Churches over their pet concerns. The ordination or marriage of homosexuals, previously mentioned, are two such concerns. The whole matter of inclusivity is another. If these liberals are unable to "win," they are willing to allow their denominations to disintegrate. Thus their inclusivity does not include people who are deemed too conservative.

In the long run, denominational ruptures are a scandal to proper Christian faith. When they occur, a few people on the two extremes are happy, some in the middle adopt the posture of stoicism, but most thoughtful people are simply sad. Any gains that are accomplished are always overshadowed by the inevitable losses. Sometimes Christians care too much about certain matters for their own good or the good of Christ's Church. As much as we are convinced of the propriety of our positions, we still need to realize that others will have differing or even opposing views. It has always been like that, and there is no reason to suppose that it can ever be otherwise.

Then why should liberals not be willing to stick it out with the conservatives, and just allow them to take over? After all, the fundamentalists took over the Southern Baptist Convention, didn't they? And the SBC still exists, doesn't it? And aren't most of the Southern Baptist moderates still there in the Southern Baptist Convention?

For the time being, they are. But it appears likely that the Southern Baptist Convention soon shall lose several million members to a new, and as-yet undetermined, sort of Baptist grouping. Meanwhile, the Methodists, Lutherans, Presbyterians, and Episcopalians have managed thus far to avoid more schism. But the internal problems in those denominations have by no means been resolved. For the present the combatants have merely agreed to disagree.

In the Fifties and Sixties, liberals won the theological wars of those decades, and it proved disastrous. One glance at the membership trends will verify that. In the Nineties and Oughts, conservatives have come close to winning, and it has been equally disastrous in the other direction. Nobody should ever be allowed to gain an unconditional surrender in a theological war.

Instead, Christians should learn better how to call a truce when their differences threaten to obliterate one another. We should work hard at finding ways to value the people whose views we most deplore, knowing that our views are also deplored by them. We need, in an oft-used phrase, to live and let live. Christians are too death defying in their disputes; we ought, instead, to become more life affirming — especially for The Other Guys.

There is an expression which Paul used in his letter to the Galatians: "God is not mocked" (Gal. 6:7). We often use that phrase when we want to emphasize a certain point, and almost always it is a point we ourselves insist on making. Well, in the kind of theological disputes which lead to divisions within the body of Christ, God *is* mocked. He is mocked when any of us become so fixated on a doctrine, dogma, or position that we refuse to allow any serious disagreement. God is mocked when peace **or** purity **or** unity become more important singly than peace, purity, and unity together. God is mocked when the Church or **my** version of the Church or even Jesus Christ become more important to anyone than God Himself. Sadly, tragically, Christians have made a mockery of God with deadening regularity through our twenty centuries of existence. It is mockery to suggest that God cannot be mocked.

Evangelicals will not be able permanently to effect a seizure of Christianity, because nobody ever wins on a permanent basis. The inherent weakness in any form of excess, whether to the right or the left, ultimately issues in its own downfall. In the end, I suppose, God really is not mocked, because in the end God has the necessary time and patience to wait out the next crisis, and the next, and the next, and the next. Much as we might mock God, God always refuses to mock Himself.

So, liberals, moderates, and anyone else who is uneasy about current trends in Christendom: take heart. Things will get better. They always do. You may not be around to see it, but others will be there. Most important of all, God will definitely be there. He never gives up. And that is a very good thing. It is nothing short of *euaggelion*, *Godspel*, Good News.

Scripture – Mark 9:33-41

Text – But Jesus said, "Do not stop him; for no one who does a deed of power in my name will be able soon afterward to speak evil of me. Whoever is not against us is for us." – Mark 9:39-40 (NRSV)

DESTROYING RELIGION WHILE TRYING TO UPHOLD IT

Religious people are giving religion a bad name. It is not a new problem, however. It has always been a problem, as long as any religion of any sort has existed.

Zealots or extremists are more likely than normal folks to damage the very principles they want to uphold. But even calm, reasoned, reasonable, ordinary-garden-variety Christians can do considerable harm to Christianity, just by becoming over-committed in certain situations to doing what they think God or Jesus would want.

In both Mark (9:38-41) and Luke (9:49-50), there is an incident where the disciple John came to Jesus with a matter which disturbed John. He told Jesus that he had encountered someone who was casting out demons in the name of Jesus. John gave the man holy ned for doing that, and he insisted that the man cease and desist forthwith. John did this, he patiently explained to Jesus, "because he was not following us."

It all seems simple enough. Who did this stranger think he was, casting out demons in Jesus' name, if he wasn't one of the twelve? Or minimally, he should have been one of the other hangers-on who followed Jesus for short periods of time, and then went back to doing whatever it was they were doing before they joined up for what John and the other disciples may have felt was their second-rate short stint.

Without question John took what he thought was the proper course of action, given the circumstances. He wanted to protect the sanctity of what modern scholars now frequently call the

305

"Jesus Movement." No unauthorized would-be miracle worker should be out there on the streets driving out demons in the name of Jesus unless Jesus Himself had given His own explicit approval! Besides, this guy hadn't even paid his Disciples Union Local No. 433 dues in Capernaum!

Therefore John must have been very surprised, and possibly even shocked, when Jesus told John he had done the wrong thing. "Do not stop him," Jesus said to the so-called beloved disciple, "for no one who does a deed of power in my name will be able soon afterward to speak evil of me. For whoever is not against us is for us" (Mark 9:39-40).

On the face of it, John's instinct does not seem all that far off the mark. In fact, in Matthew, Jesus is quoted as saying the opposite sort of statement: "Whoever is not with me is against me, and whoever does not gather with me scatters" (Mt. 12:30). John was acting on those sentiments, not the ones which Jesus told him in response to his attempt to thwart the would-be exorcist. So which is the accurate statement, Jesus: Matthew 12:30, or Mark 9:40 (Luke 9:50)?

When I was a boy and then young man, I used to think Jesus was all of one mind about everything. He always knew exactly where He stood on every matter under heaven, and He never vacillated a millimeter from His immovable convictions. I thought that because it is what I thought I was supposed to think. But the Gospels don't give us that blissful, naïve luxury. Jesus was like all the rest of us. Sometimes He thought one thing, and sometimes He concluded the exact opposite. The two opposing statements are an example. I can imagine that Jesus said both things. But I also imagine this: "Whoever is not with me is against me" He said in a bad moment on a bad day. The versions in Mark and Luke seem much more accurate in their depiction of Jesus at His best.

In any case, although it is apparent that Jesus did not mean to tear John limb from limb, He did mean to clarify an important issue for him, and for us. It is this: regardless of our best intentions, Christians can damage or erode or undermine or even destroy Christianity by being too solicitous for what we perceive to be the wellbeing of Christianity. Our commitment to faith can eradicate faith, maybe not for us, but for others.

In mid-December, 2001, U.S. military forces in Afghanistan captured a videotape of Usama bin Laden talking to an unidentified religious leader about the September 11 terrorist attacks. Bin Laden told the sheik about hearing of the attacks in a radio broadcast very shortly after they had occurred. He then said to the sheik, "At the end of the broadcast they reported that a plane just hit the World Trade Center." To this the sheik responded, "Allah be praised!" Then bin Laden said, "After a little while, they announced that another plane had hit the World Trade Center. The brothers who heard the news were overjoyed by it."

Usama bin Laden is no doubt a very complex man, with a personality to match. No one would deny that in his own unique way, he is completely devoted to his understanding of Islam. But to the moderate Muslims of the world, who are the great majority of the Muslims of the world, Usama bin Laden is a clear and present danger to the health and the future of Islam. For fear of other Islamic militants, however, not many are going to come out and say that. Nonetheless, Mr. bin Laden and others of his ilk are doing great harm to the cause of Islam everywhere. They are greatly compromising their religion while trying fanatically to uphold it.

In the short run, or even over the course of a few or several years, violent extremists can accomplish their ends. But over the long haul, they eradicate support for the so-called principles or ideals they seek to support.

In late 2001 the FBI arrested Clayton Lee Waagner, who was one of the two anti-abortion activists who had been on the FBI Ten Most-Wanted list for four years. Mr. Waagner had threatened to kill 42 abortion clinic workers, and he said that he had staked out more than a hundred clinics in 19 states. He, and others like him, have rendered it very difficult for any woman anywhere in the US to receive a safe, legal abortion.

It would appear that Clayton Lee Waagner *et al* have accomplished exactly what they set out to do. But their excessively conservative theological agenda threatens to undercut the Roman Catholic or fundamentalist Protestant religious foundations from which they seek to operate. Moderate or liberal Roman Catholics or Protestants are not won over to extremism by extremist actions; they are repelled by them. Sadly, some moderates even become repelled by religion altogether, if religion can lead to such horrendous excesses.

I think Jesus was concerned about a little too much zeal when He ordered John not to impede the man who was performing miracles in Jesus' name, never having been authorized to do so. Jesus wanted to win converts to His approach to faith in God, and He feared that if His followers were too narrow, they would repel people instead of win them over.

Some of the strongest historic mainline Protestant denominations are severely damaging themselves over the issue of the ordination of sexually-active-or-inactive homosexuals and Lesbians. Many of the most conservative of these Protestants oppose the ordination of homosexually-oriented people altogether, particularly those of the female variety, since they oppose the ordination of all females, regardless of sexual orientation. Others, who are less conservative, reluctantly support the ordinations, female or male, so long as the homosexual individuals promise to remain celibate.

On the other side, some liberal Protestants support the ordination of celibate homosexuals. Some of the more liberal Protestants support ordination for those homosexuals who are in a loving relationship with only one person.

It is not my intention here to argue for or against the ordination of homosexuals, whether they are celibate or not. You can probably correctly guess my position on that issue anyway.

However, I very strongly want to suggest that this issue is not worth splitting any denomination over. Nevertheless, the Evangelical Lutheran Church, Presbyterian Church (USA), Protestant Episcopal Church, and the United Methodist Church all appear to be coming apart at the seams over this divisive question. Other denominations are also being hurt by the battles, but to a lesser extent. Everyone needs to realize that they can be against one another's **positions** without being against **one another**. What they need to say is this: "Whoever is not against us is for us." They are all on the same team, for heaven's sake! Must the whole team be destroyed for the sake of one particular notion of how the game should be played?

For centuries, the Church has quietly ordained homosexuals. As long as the ecclesiastical authorities had faith in the individuals they ordained, and they believed they would behave properly and with the required decorum, they quite correctly did not question their sexual orientation. But in the 20th and 21st centuries, sexual orientation has become the primary litmus test for ordination. It is absurd! God has given no one the right to destroy His Church over this contentious issue! As the dying Mercutio cried in *Romeo and Juliet*, "A plague on both your houses!" Enough, already! The best way to deal with this dispute now is to become determined not to deal with this dispute now - - - at all, in any way, shape, or form! All sides, for the good of the cause, must cease and desist from addressing this question with so much as another word for the next three or four decades. They are killing the Church while trying to shove through their version of what the Church ought to be. Let it alone! Leave it be! Lighten up!

It is a sad fact, however, that the trials and tribulations of mainline American Protestantism over the ordination of homosexuals are as nothing compared to the traumas currently being faced by the American Roman Catholic Church. Roman Catholic membership statistics are as notoriously soft as the numbers for the Southern Baptist Convention. Both denominations have actually lost millions of members in their internal squabbles, but no one has been honest enough to reflect that in accurate statistics. Trying to defend the Church the clergy, particularly the bishops, have greatly weakened the Church. There has been a widespread flight from reality into a cocoon of wishful thinking.

The most glaring and damaging example is how badly the bishops have dealt with the problem of pedophile priests over the past few decades. In his ordination, a bishop takes a vow which is not required of ordinary priests in their ordination. The bishop promises to keep in strictest confidence anything he thinks might damage the welfare of Mother Church. In the case of pedophilia among the priesthood, that has turned out to be a devastatingly short-sighted vow. Had the Church owned up to the problem in every instance at the time it happened, it would not be undergoing such a terrible public pummeling now.

People like Cardinal Law of Boston seemed to have no concept of how much they have hurt the Church by their stonewalling. Even when the shocking statistics are made public about the hundreds of millions or the billions of dollars which the Church has paid out to the victims of the pedophile priests, some of the bishops still refuse to turn over names to the civil authorities, or to discipline the priests from within.

Are they unaware that the Church simply can no longer withstand the attempts to keep the lid on this scandal? Can they not sense the terrible trauma their hesitancy is producing?

But there are other important, if less pressing, matters which are eroding the confidence of millions of Roman Catholics in their beloved Church. Nearly half the Catholics in the USA now speak Spanish. Nonetheless, the Church has done far too little to make sufficient preparations for that reality. Not wanting to offend the constituency they have had, the ones who paid the bills, increasingly they are offending half the constituency they now have. There are far, far too few priests in general, but the shortage of Spanish-speaking priests is an absolute scandal.

Or there is the question of how widely certain Roman Catholic dogmas are ignored. A dogma is defined as "that which must be believed." A *New York Times* survey showed that over half the Catholics who attend Mass weekly said they believe the bread and wine of the Eucharist are "strictly the symbolic presence of Christ." As a Protestant, I support their view — but it's OK for Protestants to say that! It isn't OK for Catholics! Further, the percentage of Catholics who use various birth control methods is little different from Protestants or any other people. And the number of Catholics who never go to confession, not even the once-annual requirement, is steadily increasing.

William J. O'Malley teaches at Fordham Prep School in the Bronx. In an article in the influential Catholic periodical *America* (9/16/00), he wrote that he has tested the indifference of Catholic students to traditional teachings in 10 high schools, 4 colleges, and about 50 workshops for catechists, on 3 continents. In a remarkably pointed statement, he said, "The strategists – who wrote the *Catechism*, forge diocesan syllabi, and X-ray tests – want indoctrination rather than conversion, young people who avoid sin rather than strive for moral integrity, thorough coverage rather than heart-to-heart engagement. They have no tolerance for ambiguity, no sense (or concern) for receptivities, no willingness to settle for high probability in faith and morals lest they hazard reassuring certitude. They want catechesis without conversion – or even apologetics."

In the fastidious response which John gave to the demoncaster-outer, Jesus saw some of the same tendencies. Jesus wanted the disciples to seek conversions among anyone who seemed ready for conversion. Jesus was not as persnickety about doctrinal purity or ecclesiastical conformity as John was. Jesus didn't really care much at all about specificity of faith, but He was greatly committed to the spontaneity of faith. He wanted faith to take root in all of us, so that eventually we could live as God intended. But He didn't give a great deal of thought to how faith might germinate. Any way was fine with Him.

Not so with most of us. We care about specifics. Most of us care a lot. And unless people believe the way we think they should believe, and believe what we think they should believe, we maybe don't care if they believe at all. In fact, we might prefer them to be unbelievers rather than to be wrong-believers. (That depends, of course, on our getting to decide what is right or wrong.)

Therefore it may be sobering to realize that Jesus did virtually nothing to uphold religion, but He did everything in His power to promote and to sustain faith. The manner in which people collectively attempt to transform their faith into institutionalized action is one definition of religion. Because Jesus' public ministry lasted only three years, He could devote no time even to suggest a bare framework for how His teachings might become institutionalized. That effort God left in the hands of Paul, Peter, others in the New Testament Church, and other post-biblical early Church leaders.

For well over nineteen centuries there has been an institutional Church, and countless Christians have done their best to uphold it. Every Christian owes them a debt of gratitude. However, through the ages some have nearly exterminated the Church by their efforts to support and maintain it.

All of us are aware of churches where internal battles have nearly killed those particular congregations. Usually it is the clergy around whom the war rages. They say things or do things with which some people take exception, and other people choose to defend them. Often they say or do things they should have known better than to say or do, but still there are those who go to the barricades to defend them.

Or it may be a congregational issue which divides a church. Should we build a new sanctuary? Should we re-locate? If so, where? Should we call this minister? Should we try to fire the organist? Should the pew cushions be muted purple, or forest green? Is it at all proper for a church to provide financial support to a home for unwed mothers, or a rehabilitation center for sex offenders?

In the life of every congregation, such matters must be dealt with. But in absolutely none of those kinds of questions does the future of the earth hang in the balance. Far too frequently people get horribly bent out of shape over minor, important, or even crucial issues. But nothing matters so much that it is worth killing a congregation or denomination over to gain a victory for any side of any cause.

"Get a life!" Jesus was saying to John. Ease up, for the love of Pete. You have other fish to fry, beloved disciple. So fry them, for frying out loud.

Christians are not supposed to hate. Nonetheless, something very close to hatred sometimes emerges when Christians clash about one thing or another. As a pastor, I have known scores of otherwise exemplary church members who never spoke to one another for years because of some flap over something or other. How can anybody care enough about anything to do their very worst because of it? How did we ever deduce that Christian faith can legitimize unchristian behavior when we strongly disagree with someone?

James Baldwin was talking about how people became very emotionally charged during the civil rights struggles of the Sixties. He said, "Hatred, which could destroy so much, never failed to destroy the man who hated, and this was an immutable law.... I imagine that one of the reasons that people cling to their hates so stubbornly is because they sense, once hate is gone, they will be forced to deal with the pain."

What a wise observation that is! Applying it to the issues religious people really care about, what do you do if your side loses, especially when you cared deeply about the issue? What if you think a terrible mistake was made, and you feel powerless to undo it? Can you become a loveable loser, or shall your become hateful in your defeat?

Or how do you treat the losers if your side wins? Can you be magnanimous, or will you be spiteful? Will you allow them to forgive you, particularly if you don't think you need to be forgiven?

It is hellish to be involved in what are perceived to be high-stakes conflicts, regardless of how it all turns out. It is devilish to be so consumed by an issue that, win or lose, it depletes or defeats or enervates you. Nonetheless, it happens every day in one or another ecclesiastical organization or agency or congregation or denomination. People are determined to protect what they believe at all costs. But in the end, they may be like the US Army commander in Viet Nam who made the infamous, ludicrous declaration: "In order to save the village, we had to destroy it." In order to save the congregation or the organization or the Church, some Christians seem convinced it is necessary to destroy it.

Reinhold Niebuhr was perhaps the most influential American theologian in the mid-20th century. In his book *The Nature and*

Destiny of Man, he said, "The worst form of intolerance is religious intolerance, in which the particular interests of the contestants hide behind religious absolutes. The worst form of self-assertion is religious self-assertion in which under the guise of contrition before God, He is claimed as the exclusive ally of our contingent self."

In another book, *The Children of Light and the Children of Darkness*, Niebuhr further addressed the bitterness which can erupt in religious disputes. "The solution requires a very high form of religious commitment. It demands that each religion, or each version of a single faith, seek to proclaim its highest insights while yet preserving *humble and contrite* recognition of the fact that all actual expressions of faith are subject to historical contingency and relativity. Such a recognition creates a spirit of tolerance and makes any religious or cultural movement hesitant to claim official validity for its form of religion or to demand an official monopoly for its cult."

Reinhold Niebuhr was as cogent about the early 21st century as he was about the mid-20th century. When we disagree with one another, we need to learn more humility. Just before the incident with John's complaint about the unauthorized exorcist, Jesus said, "Whoever wants to be first must be last of all and servant of all" (Mark 9:35). In our disagreements, we must seek truth instead of victory, a humble discussion of the issues instead of an all-powerful marshalling of our arguments.

Too many of us, laity and clergy alike, see ourselves as "company men," or, if you prefer, as "company people." We think that in order to defend the Church, we must defend our positions at all conceivable costs, lest *They* win, whoever they might be.

It was not until I retired from the active pastorate that I was able fully to comprehend how compromised I always was as an ordained "company man." There are both assets and liabilities to being a member of the clergy. From my perspective, the assets far outweigh the liabilities.

Nevertheless, there were innumerable times when I held back on what I might have said, because I did not want to offend too many people or to jeopardize the church itself by any positions I might too strongly present. (Some who have known me as a pastor might find that hard to believe, but it is true!) On the other hand, I was probably seduced far too frequently into giving proper consideration to the arguments of those who had little concern for the church as an institution when we were arguing questions that would inevitably affect the institution. There may be far more objectivity among "marginal company people" when debating company issues, but as the purported No. 1 Ecclesiastical Functionary in our particular shop, my inclination was not to give such folk much credit.

Jesus Christ is stronger than the Church of Jesus Christ, and God is stronger than Jesus Christ. Therefore, the Church's cause is not well served by those who either win or lose in a graceless fashion. The Church will keep on keeping on despite all of us, and despite our best, or worst, efforts to uphold it. And remember, "Whoever is not against us is for us." So let's all be for one another - - - even when we're against one another!

Scripture – I Corinthians 11:17-26

Text – For, in the first place, when you assemble as a church, I hear there are divisions among you, and I partly believe it, for there must be factions among you in order that those who are genuine among you may be recognized. – I Cor. 11:18-19

WHEN THE CHURCH ISN'T THE CHURCH

Everyone who has ever been a member of any church has an idea – or an ideal – of what **The** Church or **a** church is supposed to be. In this ideal Church (church) which exists between their two ears, the Church (church) is an institution in which faith is fostered and deepened. Their ideal church is a group of people who understand, appreciate, and love one another. It is a company of committed believers who band together to do the will of God in the world as they readily, eagerly, and jointly perceive His will.

And of course the church (Church) is, or should be, those things, and much, much more. The course of world history would be far bleaker were it not for the Church and the literally millions of churches which have existed for the past twenty centuries. Your life and mine has been greatly blessed because we have been affiliated with the Church of Jesus Christ and with a particular church or churches throughout much if not all our lifetime. In my experience, church people in general are wonderful folks, the kind of people in general you'd be happy for your son or daughter to bring home with them, and maybe even eventually to marry.

The problem is not the Church or churches or church people in general; it is the Church, churches, and individual Christians in particular. We have all encountered people in church from whose shoulders we would gladly have twisted their heads if it were legal or moral to do so. Some church people seem to be congenitally and consistently ornery, and are as mean as snakes. They are so obnoxious that we'd like to give them their head and their hands and their ears to play with, as my mother used to say.

316

When the church isn't the church, when Christians make huge mistakes and commit obviously grievous errors, it has terrible repercussions for people inside and outside the Church. However, it is vital at the outset of this sermon to distinguish between the church **as an institution** making mistakes and Christians **as individuals** making mistakes. Using an analogy, it is one thing to get furious at the USA because our government decides to bomb Iraq or some such cockamamie thing, but it is quite another if the President of the United States issues an order to do the bombing. In the second instance, other people, especially the analogical Iraqis, might blame the US, but it is really the President who should be blamed, and not the whole country, even though it would be American airplanes and pilots and weapons which would be used in the attack.

Just so, when the pastor of a church is involved in sexual abuse with parishioners or embezzlement or heavy-handed church politics or disregard of decisions made by authorized church boards or whatever other troubles pastors can get into, which are an unlimited legion, it is the pastor who is at fault, not the church. Nonetheless, such behavior can have devastating results in the life of a congregation.

Many, many years ago I knew a minister whom I greatly admired. He was very influential in my teenage years. A new associate minister came to the church of which he was the pastor. At first they worked together in highly productive harmony, and they both were well received by everyone. Eventually friction developed personally between the two. It may have been nothing more than jealousy on the part of both of them; I can't honestly say, because I really don't know. In any case, the two ministers arrived at the sorry place where they no longer spoke to one another privately, and they talked to each other in public only when it was absolutely necessary. Their behavior badly damaged that church. Nobody seemed to know how to straighten things out. Each man was respected so much that no one on the governing board, or the entire board itself, had the courage to tell them both to grow up. It nearly destroyed that congregation. The

317

church never fully recovered, even to this day, and the whole episode occurred over forty years ago.

I know a church which called a very controlling man as their pastor. They did not know he was such a controller, or else they would never have called him. He was unusually able, but he ran that church with an iron fist in an iron glove. People in the church either greatly admired their pastor or they felt increasingly disgusted with him. His personality began to infect the membership of the church, and many of his worst traits started to emerge in other church leaders. They began to treat one another as he treated them, which was to manipulate everyone he could manage to control.

In one sense it doesn't matter what are the particular circumstances which coalesce to keep a church from being the kind of church everyone knows it should be. Clearly it matters when it is happening, and that is the best time to prevent things from spiraling out of control. But given the fact that it has already happened in some church somewhere, what ought to be done? When the pastor has so badly botched things that there is no good solution, which less-than-good or which bad solution should be chosen? When the beloved youth advisor is discovered to have forced himself on eight different girls in the youth fellowship, how can the church then authentically be the church? When there is a vote to move the church from one location to another, and the vote is 51% for and 49% against, how can that church continue to be that church? There can be a multitude of reasons for the particular ecclesiastical failure when the church isn't the church, but what ought to be done when the church ceases acting the way we know it should act?

The church in Corinth was such a fractious outfit that Paul felt it was necessary to write them at least four times, or so say the New Testament scholars. We have only two of those epistles in the Bible, however, and they may or may not be complete in themselves. In the first Corinthian letter, Paul took the Corinthian Christians to task for their abominable behavior in conjunction with the celebration of the Lord's Supper.

Prior to addressing that issue, Paul told the Corinthians he had heard they were badly splintered. "When you assemble as a church, I hear there are divisions among you, and I partly believe it, for there must be factions among you in order that those who are genuine among you may be recognized" (I. Cor. 11:18-19). What an edifying idea that is! How can anybody tell who is right unless a bunch of people are wrong, Paul seems to be suggesting. Must churches **always** have factions? Many churches do have cliques which constantly do battle with one another, but is that an ecclesiastical necessity? Paul seems to think so!

Then Paul laced into the Corinthians for their bad manners when they got together to participate in the Lord's Supper. Remember, there were then no churches as we currently understand churches. That is, there were no church buildings, no gathering places with names etched in stone on the front façade or inscribed on lighted signs by the sidewalk or roadside. People met in homes during the first couple of centuries of the Church's existence. Thus there was no altar or communion table; there was only whatever ordinary furniture was to be found in an ordinary Greek home.

Paul wrote, "When you meet together, it is not the Lord's supper that you eat. For in eating, each one goes ahead with his own meal, and one is hungry and another drunk. What! Do you not have houses to eat and drink in? Or do you despise the church of God and humiliate those who have nothing? Shall I commend you in this? No, I will not" (I Cor. 11:20-22).

It was at that point where Paul wrote what now is often described as "the words of the institution of the holy supper of our Lord." "You confounded Corinthians obviously don't know the proper manner for celebrating communion, so I'm going to give it to you," Paul seems to imply. "You don't know how properly to be the church, so I'll tell you. If I don't, nobody else in Corinth will ever want to join you, because you come across as a gluttonous gang at a drunken orgy. Get some decorum when you worship, or get out!" A diplomat Paul was not.

Here's one of the worst results which occurs when the church isn't the church. It dissuades outsiders from going in, and it convinces many insiders to get out. When the activities of a church reach a sufficiently noxious impasse, people in go out, and people out won't come in. It has a disastrous effect on the mission of Jesus Christ in the world.

Randy Woodley is a Keetoowah Cherokee Indian who has served in ministry among Indians for twenty years. He said, "*Christianity* is a dirty word in our community, so I don't believe 'Christianity' affirms us. For the past seven years of pastoring in Nevada with traditional people, I had to learn to avoid that term. So many Indians have said to me that Christianity is a white man's religion, the white man wrote the Bible, and the white man always uses erasers. Our people are willing to follow Jesus, but not 'Christianity'" (Quoted in *Context*, Jan. 1, 2002, p.7).

There are at least two very profound insights in those words. First is the notion that white men wrote the Bible with erasers. Red man shoot straight arrow into white man with that one! We say we believe lots of things, but when we get to the very bottom of it, we may not believe these things at all. And then there is the concept that Indians (or anybody else, for that matter) are willing to follow Jesus, but not Christianity.

Retirement from the ministry has given me entirely new eyes with which to view many people outside the church – or The Church – who insist they are Christians, but they are not church members. As a card-carrying clergyman, I always questioned the viability of that declaration. Now my skepticism is waning. More and more, now that I am no longer a full-time paid parson, I am able to see that truly there are millions of people outside the churches who nevertheless are every bit as "Christian" as the Christians inside the churches. And one of the reasons many of those people are outside is that they don't approve of what goes on inside.

They have a point; they really do. Far too often the church isn't the church. If it were, it would be doing much better institutionally than it is doing. Millions of people who are on a church membership roll scarcely act like Christians even on rare occasions, and lots of people who aren't on any church's roll anywhere act like Christians almost all the time. Of course, only God knows the heart of any of us. But to the degree that we can observe Christianity being lived out in the persons of the people around us, many non-church people obviously seem to be Christians, and many church members seem obviously not to act like Christians.

For the church to be the church, all the "Christians" ought to *be* Christians. Too many Christians in the Church think that the Christians outside the Church aren't Christians. But the reverse is true as well. Too many non-church Christians think that no church members are true Christians at all. We all are too quick to judge one another, and too slow to be what we claim to be, namely, committed followers of the man from Nazareth.

"Christian Europe" isn't very Christian, if active church membership is the primary index of Christianity. Only 17% of German Roman Catholics attend church on a regular basis, which is half as many as attended a generation ago. A mere 4% of registered Protestants attend church each week. In the past thirty years, the number of church baptisms and weddings has dropped by a third. However, when one considers that registered Christians in Germany must pay 8 or 9% on top of their regular income tax to be on a church's roll, it is amazing there is not better participation. People should want to go to church just to see what is happening to their money. Heaven knows many American Christians watch church finances as though they themselves had contributed every dollar that passes into the ecclesiastical coffers. I have noticed through the years that many of the most intent church budget watchdogs are also some of the most meager stewards in the church.

A survey was taken recently among nearly a thousand British self-professed Christians. A total of 71% of those people admitted that they attend church only twice a year or so. Further, 40% of them said they think Jesus would not attend church were He now living in Britain. An astounding 43% of these British Christians believe that the church harms, rather than helps, people's openness to Christian faith. Or is that really so astounding?

A similar poll among American Christians likely would result in quite different figures. However, most of us who have spent most of our lives in the Church would probably be astonished to see how many American Christians would echo those sentiments about the Church, even though the numbers would almost certainly not be as high.

Here, beloved church member (if you are one) is the point: many people outside the Church think the Church is an impediment to Christianity, not a valuable asset. They think the Church isn't the Church, or at least not what the Church is supposed to be.

And of course they are absolutely correct. It isn't. The actual Church is a pale copy of what the ideal Church should be.

Unfortunately - - - and here is another sobering truth - - - the Church can never be ideal. That is a human, and even a divine, impossibility. As long as human beings comprise the membership of the Church, the Church all too frequently is bound to act contrary to the manner in which the Church should act. Both church members and non-members need to come to grips with that sad truth. It is juvenile nonsense to imagine that the Church fundamentally will or ought to behave exponentially better than any other human institution.

During the course of my ministry, I served three congregations as pastor, one as an assistant pastor, and four as the interim pastor. I got fired in one of the interim pastorates. For the life of me, I still don't know why. I have my suspicions, but there is nothing, no single thing or group of things, I can definitely enumerate. There were a few ultra-liberals in that church, and I think they didn't believe I was sufficiently politically-correct in my language. I speak of blacks rather than African-Americans, for example (for reasons explained elsewhere in this book), and I call God "He" with a capital-H (for reasons also explained elsewhere in this book). A few elders did not like my pastoral style. But in an interim minister, style should not be a big issue, since an interim, by definition, is short-term. Afterward, several people told me they thought whoever came to that particular church at that particular time as the interim pastor was destined to become a sheep for slaughter. If so, it was probably providential that I was the sacrificial lamb, because likely I was able to die with less mess than most other ministers, and I can probably get over the death more quickly than most.

Never once have I thought that particular church was not the church. I didn't get axed by "the church;" I was axed by a very small number of unusually mean-spirited people in that church. At least that is how I have chosen to interpret it. On the other hand, I might have been a total nincompoop, and deserved to have been fired. Other people would be far more objective about that than I am. In any case, "the church" was never the problem, from my perspective. Rather, it was a half dozen people who got the bee in their bonnet that I was a parson who, as a person, needed to be dismissed. I still don't know why, alas. Fortunately, my dismissal did not do serious damage to the congregation, even though a number of people were very upset.

In the past year in American Christianity, the question of pedophile priests has been the most horrendously painful example of what happens when the Church is not the Church. Those who view this tragedy with nothing other than deep disgust deliberately overlook some of the grave institutional concerns confronted by this sinful abuse. It is easy to attack the bishops, and without question they have often acted very improperly. But **why** did they do what they did?

In the publicity surrounding this sad saga, I learned something I had not know before, as I stated in a previous sermon. I suspect many others, including many Catholics, did not know it either. When a Roman Catholic priest is ordained as a bishop, he takes a vow before the Pope himself "to keep in confidence anything that, if revealed, would cause a scandal or harm to the Church." On the face of it, that seems to be a proper and perhaps even necessary vow. And in most instances it would be valid. But in the case of pedophile priests, it is a calamitous idea. No doubt most bishops tried to keep the lid on this problem because it would indeed cause a scandal and harm the Church. This is precisely what has happened.

But the scandal is worse, and the damage is far greater, **because** the bishops tried to hide it. If they had admitted every problem with every accused pedophile the moment they were alerted to the accusations, the Roman Catholic Church would not be suffering as it now is. Obviously, when priests sexually abuse children the Church is not the Church. But when the Church deliberately attempts to cover up these scandals, it appears callused and insensitive to an astonishing and devastating degree. Without question untold thousands of Catholics will permanently stop going to church because of the cowardly behavior of many bishops.

Quite apart from the pedophile crisis, the Church of Rome has been losing priests at an alarming rate. In 1965 there were 58,600 American priests; today there are 45,000. Yet there are millions more Catholics now than then. Further, it is estimated that 35 to 50% of all American Catholic priests are homosexuals. For those Catholics who are not opposed to homosexuality in principle, that is not a problem. For those who are opposed, "the Church is not the Church" to them, because they think it somehow should have screened out all homosexuals before they even got to seminary. And to some in the first category, any homosexual priest who is not celibate is outside the bounds of acceptable behavior, since all priests are supposed to be celibate. Sexually active homosexual priests further indicate that "the Church is not the Church" to those Catholics.

I have been amazed at the vitriol expressed by journalists who have been active Catholics in their reporting of this ongoing tragedy. Some of them seem ready to tar and feather some of the bishops and the pedophile priests, or to see them all brought up on criminal charges. When people feel that strongly, subconsciously, if not consciously, they have concluded that the Church is not the Church. How could it be, and allow such things to happen?

It was estimated that by mid-summer of 2002, the Roman Church had already paid out a billion dollars to victims of the abusing priests. That is an unthinkable amount for most denominations, but even for the Roman Catholic Church, it is a financial dislocation of gargantuan proportions. If the Church is going to be paying out that much money to the victims of abusive priests, then the Church cannot be what the Church ought to be, nor can it do what the Church ought to be doing.

Maureen Dowd would never be accused of being a journalistic milquetoast. The lady always tells it the way she sees it, and she usually sees it on the comically caustic side. On **THE** Ecclesiastical Issue of 2002, she has been ballistic. She is struck by the high percentage of homosexual priests, and seems not too pleased with that fact. She wrote, "The vow of celibacy serves as a magnet for men running away from sexual feelings they are ashamed of. And the allegedly celibate world these men enter…retards their sexual development, funneling their impulses in inappropriate directions."

Those are unusually strong words, even for Maureen Dowd. They also are very debatable words. For purposes of this sermon, however, the veracity of those allegations is not the issue. Rather it is this: Ms. Dowd, along with millions of other American Catholics, has sadly decided that in this matter, the Church simply has not been what the Church should be. It has acted shamefully, and its indifference to the victims of the abusers is beyond any rationale the bishops might seek to concoct.

Andrew Sullivan is the senior editor of the *New Republic*. In a *Time* essay, he wrote, "As a Catholic struggling to keep the faith through all this, I find myself asking: Why? Why can't (the bishops) not get the enormity of what has happened? The best I can come up with is that they are well-intentioned men who somehow cannot see what they have enabled is systematic child rape. They resist deep change claiming celibacy is not the issue. But the hierarchy's cover-up of this evil surely has something to do with celibacy." This sounds like a man who believes that the Church cannot possibly be the Church when it acts like this.

There is a growing demand among Catholics for married clergy and female clergy. The movement has been given immense impetus by the pedophile scandal. The Pope, following the deepest inclinations at the core of his being, has said there

325

will be no discussion of married or female clergy, ever, which means as long as he is Pope. And thus many more millions of Catholics come to believe that the Church just isn't the Church, if it refuses even to discuss what clearly is a major concern of untold numbers of Catholics.

The denomination I have served as a minister, the Presbyterian Church (USA), has had more than its share of denomination-damaging crises. But as on outside observer of the Catholic crisis, I have decided that an episcopally-governed Church, such as the Roman Catholic Church, has the most cumbersome form of government for dealing with the pedophile crisis, and all the ancillary issues which evolve out of it. Where a Church has a hierarchy, the hierarchy is more prone than any other kind of Church officials to try to protect the Church as an institution at all costs. In business terms, bishops are quintessentially "company men." They will do anything they can to defend "the company." They are like the board of directors. If the CEO (the Pope) has the courage to admit a mistake and set about to right the wrong, then reform will happen. But as long as the CEO stonewalls, the board of directors will also stonewall. It is the way hierarchical organizations inevitably function.

In a congregationally-governed church, a pedophile minister would be summarily fired; end of story. Even in a presbyterian-governed church, which is a representative government, such a scandal would be dealt with fairly swiftly, though not quite as quickly. But when bishops are involved, they are more likely to be concerned for the institution than for the individuals who are harmed. It is the very nature of their office. For this reason denominations with bishops are the most resistant to major or rapid changes of any sort.

Again, I am not attempting to argue for one form of church government over another. You pays your money and you takes your choice. Winston Churchill said that the worst form of government is democracy —— except for all the others. Well, the worst form of church government is episcopacy, **and** presbyterianism, **and** congregationalism. Each has its advantages and disadvantages, but the greatest disadvantage of all three is that Christians have only the three choices, with slight variations in between. But for the purposes of this sermon, in the pedophile scandal, episcopacy has conspired against the largest of all episcopal Churches, the Catholic Church, and it turns out to make that Church look as though it is not being an authentic Church. The Roman hierarchy has badly managed this terrible crisis, and Roman Catholicism is bound to pay a staggering price over the next years and decades.

I have spent far more time on the pedophile situation in Roman Catholicism than any other examples of church problems. I do not intend therefore to single out Roman Catholicism as being more culpable than other denominations or branches of Christianity. Unfortunately, their crisis is much on the minds of everyone, whether people are or are not members of the Roman Catholic or and other Church.

If we live long enough, all of us are bound to encounter situations where a denomination or a congregation gets into some serious difficulties. And when it happens, we may ruefully conclude that the church just doesn't act as we know it should act. When we find ourselves at odds with something "the church" has done or is doing, we need consciously to take four very deliberate steps.

Try to be as specific as possible in identifying the source of the problem. Almost never is "the church" or "The Church" the problem. Usually it is one or more individual church people who are the culprits, if culprits there be. More often than not, it will be a pastor or some other minister who is the prime suspect. However many scrapes lay people get the church into, the clergy account for at least ten times that number. But "the clergy" are not "the church," and it is unfair to blame the church for something that is really an issue with the clergy.

Following from that step, next try to determine whether the problem is truly a "church problem" or an "individual problem." Sam Smith can profoundly disrupt dear old St. Matthew's Methodist Church, but St. Matt's is bigger than Sam. St. Matt's may have issues with Sam, and Sam with St. Matt's, but it is crucial that St. Matt's survive, whether or not Sam stays with St. Matt's. No individual should ever be allowed to destroy a whole congregation, no matter how sincere or even correct the individual may be.

Remember that every church is comprised solely of ordinary sinners, not extraordinary saints. The extraordinary saints are all outside the Church; you need only ask them, and they will tell you it is absolutely true. Because it is only sinners who are allowed to be members of churches, their sins will emerge in predictable and sometimes very unpredictable ways. The Church is bound not to act like the Church on a periodic basis, because it is **The Church**, and The Church is a fallible, sometimes foolish, occasionally utterly foolhardy bunch of believers. The only way to avoid encountering that in the Church is to move outside the Church. But if you do that, you're totally on your own. Maybe you're strong enough to go it alone, but most people aren't. They need the companionship, fellowship, direction, and strength in numbers which are the benefits of being part of an institution.

4) When assessing the Church, especially when it is in one of its plethora of problems, try to be as fiercely realistic as possible, and try to avoid being idealistic altogether. Idealists lose their religion very quickly when they associate with a church. That is why the people outside the church often truly are much nicer and more moral than the people inside the church. Realists love the church, because – if you'll pardon the expression – it's so damned **real**. But idealists frequently despise the church, because ideal it ain't. If you intend to stay in your church or in **The** Church, then for God's sake and your own sake, get real about the church, and about every kind of cuss who is bound to be found within its membership.

When the apostle Paul heard about the behavior of the Corinthian Christians during their observance of the Lord's Supper, he knew he had a full-blown crisis that had to be confronted. Thus he tore them up one side and down the other. But then, very wisely and pastorally, he gave them an acceptable proscription for how properly to celebrate the sacrament.

Everybody knows when the Church is not the Church. But the most helpful and genuine of believers will then set about to help steer the Church back onto the correct course. Pointing out the problems is the easy part. Effecting the solutions is the hard part. God needs people to become problem-solvers. Problem-pointers He has always had more than enough of.

Musings on
Matters Ecclesiastical

Scripture – Ephesians 4:1-16

Text – And his gifts were that some should be apostles, some prophets, some evangelists, some pastors and teachers, for the equipment of the saints, for the work of ministry, for building up the body of Christ. – Ephesians 4:11-12 (RSV)

THE RAPID RISE OF CAUTIOUS CLERGY

If the apostle Paul could somehow be plucked out of heaven and gently dropped, once more in the possession of a body, onto the earth, especially in any large metropolitan area in the United States of America, he would be absolutely astonished, agog, aghast, ga-ga, thunderstruck, tongue-tied, speechless, dumb-struck, mystified, mortified, overwhelmed, disoriented, amazed, immobilized, and stupefied. He probably would be a tad non-plussed as well.

The complex Church of the 21st century would be utterly unrecognizable to the true, albeit usually the unrecognized, founder of the Christian religion. The 1st century Church in which Paul ministered was an exceedingly pale copy of what the contemporary Church has become. Even tiny congregations in the jungles of the Upper Amazon or in the remote villages of Ethiopia would be so foreign in their essence to Paul that he would never recognize them as being churches unless he was told that is what they were.

For one thing, most congregations anywhere in the world today have a building in which to worship. No church in Paul's day met in a building which the local Christians of whatever community would call "the church." "The church" meant solely the people gathered together for 1st century Christians, and that was true for Paul and every other member of the New Testament Church. "Church" simply did not mean a building. Nor would "church" connote "building" for at least two or three more generations. Not until sometime during the 2nd century did congregations begin to worship and gather in their own buildings.

332

Even at that, it was uncommon for a few centuries for most congregations to meet in specific "church" buildings.

Furthermore, Paul would be completely baffled by the organizational structure of the contemporary Church. In the 1ˢᵗ century, there were no paid clergy. A few times Paul made a rather large issue of that fact. He made his living as a tentmaker, we are told, but he lived his life as an apostle. He refused to accept any required payments for his voluntary services as an itinerant preacher and teacher, although he was not averse to receiving what today is called "a free-will offering." We know from the New Testament that certain Christians were ordained as various kinds of church leaders, but nobody was ordained into "the professional clergy," because there was then no concept of a professional clergy. Being a pastor or teacher or evangelist was not a **profession**; it was a **vocation**. Paul believed —— as most Christians have always believed —— that **God** alone *calls* people to the offices of the Church, and nobody could ever *decide* or *choose* to become an official in any church. In ordination, it is assumed, the Church (or church) confirms the vocation by God of certain people to the religious offices they fill.

Many New Testament scholars insist that the letter to the Ephesians was not written by Paul. Whether they are correct or not, let us, for purposes of moving ahead, assume he did. And even if he didn't, Paul would likely agree with nearly everything said in Ephesians. Thus he would have a clear, 1ˢᵗ century understanding of the terms used in our sermon text: apostles, prophets, evangelists, pastors, and teachers. Almost certainly some of the functions of these particular offices overlapped. That is, apostles might engage in a little prophecy or evangelism or pastoral work or teaching, and pastors might evangelize and teach, and so on. Paul being Paul, and being pretty persnickety about certain things, he would no doubt insist that only apostles could do the work of apostles, and that apostles, by definition, had to be people who had actually seen Jesus with their own, actual, eyes. (Paul claimed his apostolic rank on the basis of a vision of Jesus, which is described both in Acts 9 and II Corinthians 2. You can decide for yourself whether that validated him as an authentic apostle. In his own mind, it certainly did.)

The main point I am trying to make here is this: **In the 1ˢᵗ century, there was no concept of two different kinds of Christians, laity and clergy**. Everybody was considered to be part of the laity in Paul's time. But from the 3ʳᵈ century on, there were laity, and there were clergy. And when the clergy emerged as ordained professionals, albeit **called** ordained professionals (i.e., with a **calling**,) the clergy ran the show. And ever since, with few exceptions, the clergy have, in essence, run the show. As I have said many times in new member classes, "Folks, you have to keep your eye on the clergy. They'll try to take over everything every time."

Over the centuries there evolved a few denominations which assiduously refused to ordain clergy. In retrospect, that may have been a wise decision. Quakers don't have clergy. Well, sort of, anyway. Some of the Anabaptists don't (Brethren, Amish, Mennonites). There are Pentecostal churches without clergy, and some of the independent fundamentalists. Mormons and Jehovah Witnesses manage to survive without clergy, but then, many people would insist that the LDS and JWs are outside the boundaries of even the broadest definition or description of Christianity. (You can debate that yourself. But we have other fish to fry.)

Through Christian history, probably 95 to 99 per cent of everyone who ever officially joined any particular church has had a member of the clergy who was "in charge" of that church. Whatever might be the gifts of the clergy, they are expected, and expect, to "run the show," whether as prophet, preacher, teacher, administrator, or whatever. Oh, there is always philosophizing about "the ministry of the laity," and in most churches, the laity have varying degrees of collective or individual authority. But if a church has clergy of any variety, the day-to-day governance of the church, any kind of church, depends upon the leadership of the clergy, for better or worse.

The breadth and depth of clergy authority is determined in large part by the form of government used in particular congregations. In general, clergy in episcopal-governed churches have the most power, those in presbyterian-governed churches have more moderate power, and the clergy in congregational-governed churches have, at least theoretically, the least power. The most salient example of this gradation is that the congregation can fire the clergy in a church with congregational government, such as the Baptists, Congregationalists (United Church of Christ), many Pentecostal churches, and others. Only bishops can fire pastors in churches with bishops, and only presbyteries (a regional collection of clergy and laity acting like a "collective" bishop) can, in theory, fire a Presbyterian minister. Presbyterian congregations can engineer the dismissal of their parson, but technically they cannot directly do it themselves.

Among the Churches governed by bishops (*episkopos* is the Greek word for bishop), Roman Catholic bishops and priests likely have more raw ecclesiastical clout than any other kind of clergy. Up until the pedophile abuse scandal in the Catholic Church, it has been little short of astonishing how much clerical clout is exercised by Roman Catholic parish priests. Orthodox bishops and priests also are very autonomous. Among Protestants, Methodist bishops have the most power, followed (in order) by Lutherans, and then Episcopalians. Among those who are pastors, the authority of Presbyterian, Methodist, Lutheran, Episcopalian, and Reformed clergy is more or less equal. Baptist and Congregationalist or UCC ministers may actually have more power than the others, depending on the individual minister or church, but they also may have considerably less. Sometimes parsons in congregational-governed systems must feel as though they have no power at all. And Pentecostals also vary considerably in the power of their office.

However it is that any contemporary church operates, that methodology would be virtually unrecognizable to Paul, Peter, or any other 1st century Christian. Through the centuries, churches evolved into worship centers, counselling centers, social service agencies, political headquarters, health care dispensaries, fitness centers, day care centers for the very young and very old, arbitration agencies, music venues, sports centers, and so on. It would have been impossible for anyone to have foreseen that, when Christianity was in its infancy. Actually, it would have been impossible to forecast it only 50 or 75 years ago.

I went directly from high school to university to seminary, graduating from seminary in 1964. Less than 50% of my seminary classmates ever went into the pastorate, and less than 50% of those who became pastors remained pastors for their entire careers in the Church. In other words, although the common perception is that seminaries train people for the parish ministry, less than a quarter of my classmates stayed in parish ministry as clergy, and less than half even started out as parish clergy.

So what did the others do? A few earned doctorates and became professors. A few became military or hospital chaplains. A few became professional counsellors. A few went into some phase of social work. Some went on to graduate studies which took them out of "church work" by even the broadest definition. Some simply disappeared from the alumni office radar screen, never to be heard from again.

But what of those who stayed in parish ministry? And what of those who currently are graduating from seminaries and are going into parishes somewhere?

It is difficult to quantify or qualify what "success in ministry" means. On God's scorecard, some clergy who have always served in small and "insignificant" churches (can **any** church **ever** be considered truly insignificant?) may be infinitely more successful than other clergy who gain fame and even a fair measure of fortune as the pastors of tall-steeple churches in famous and influential cities. And on the other hand, clergy whom most people would suppose had very successful careers may get very low marks from the only One who truly knows how properly to keep score.

During the Nineties, I served for several years on the board of trustees of my seminary. I was constantly struck by the high percentage of second- and third-career people who entered the seminary, and the ever-increasing percentage of women going into various forms of ministry. This is the pattern in every seminary of every denomination as well. Although there were also second-career students in the Sixties when I was in seminary, the majority of students went directly from high school to college to seminary, as I did. What this means in the contemporary Church is that there will be fewer and fewer 35-to-40 year ministerial careers. The current number is likely to average 20 years or so. And what that means is that fewer clergy will have enough time to become wily old veterans who have, as Paul said, "fought good fight, finished the race, and kept the faith."

Being a parish pastor or associate pastor in any denomination has become a much more stressful vocation than it was a generation ago. The expectations of clergy performance are much higher, the pressures upon the clergy are much greater, and because of these factors, the possibilities of the clergy getting into serious ecclesiastical disputes are significantly increased. It is impossible to quantify what I have just said, but I am certain that a poll of long-time pastors would validate it.

Furthermore, very few students in their mid-twenties are entering seminary. In the Presbyterian Church (USA), half of the 14,000 parish clergy will retire in the next decade. And the clergy who are "coming along" are perceived by parishioners to be less able and more cautious than their older peers. Large churches are having a very hard time identifying qualified candidates to fill their pulpits. One denominational executive referred to pastors as "the cannon fodder of the Christian army." So many clergy are being attacked so often for so many things that there has been a very understandable "pulling in" among the clergy who manage to survive the assaults.

Few who are serving in ministry will provide bold leadership if they are constantly worried that they will eventually be sacrificed on an ecclesiastical altar for taking initiatives which might, or might not, succeed. There is more job security in being the coach of a major football or baseball team than in being the pastor of a major congregation which has inordinately lofty expectations of clergy success.

Some clergy failures are the result of poor clergy performance; of that there can be no doubt. But many clergy whose authority is undercut or destroyed are the victims of lay leaders in the church who see themselves as contra-clergy vigilantes. And usually such lay people are in middle-management positions in their occupational lives; they are not CEO-types. Those who are in the top management of any kind of organization clearly understand that somebody needs to be in charge, and such people who are also church leaders are willing to allow the clergy the freedom to exercise their gifts by being the primary managers of church "business." It has been my experience that the most supportive lay officers have generally had the highest positions in their employment, whereas the most thorny officers have been frustrated in mid-level positions in their work. Having felt jerked around by people who determine their salaries, they believe they are somehow entitled to jerk around the ecclesiastical factotum whose salary they think they can determine. This is clearly a generalization, but were your pastor to be honest, he/she would likely corroborate this pattern of behavior among lay leaders.

USA Today ran a cover story called "Lay Catholics are demanding more control of the church." In responding to it, a minister from Tucson wrote a letter to the editor which said the story "ran shivers down my Protestant spine. If things aren't bad enough with all the sexual abuse," he wrote, "just wait for the laity really to muck it up.... In starting several churches from scratch, I discovered early on how some people would do anything to gain 'power and control' in the church. Many of them came forward out of frustrated ego needs, not because of a 'calling.' Often those who were the least successful in 'the real world' desired the most control in 'the church world.' ...The laity is not a panacea for the Catholic Church. All one has to do is look across the street at the so-called mega-Protestant churches. They are successful because they are led by pastors and guided by a pastoral vision. On the other hand, the denominations that are in decline...have high lay participation and involvement. One is tempted to conclude, 'It's the policy, stupid!'"

Well, well, well. That disgruntled round-collar states it far more pointedly than even I would do. I think he is too confident that usually there will be strong and wise clergy leadership, and he gives strong and wise lay leadership too little credit. But in the main I agree with his primary thrust: churches that operate well and effectively usually do so because the pastor is authorized by the officers and members freely to exercise pastoral gifts. It is almost impossible for any lay people to give the kind of day-to-day leadership which a large, complex congregation requires. The clergy are academically and ecclesiastically prepared for such leadership, and they should be encouraged to provide it, rather than to be thwarted when they seek to exercise it. Lay "would-be" pastors are a thorn in the side to ordained actual pastors.

More and more, it is becoming evident that the congregation is "where it's at" in the Church. Denominations are decreasing in importance, as another of these sermons shall indicate. Duke University published an extensive study called "Pulpit and Pew." Among other things, the research project suggested that two-thirds of the clergy polled had encountered some level of conflict in their congregations in the previous two years, and 20% of them said the conflict was sufficiently "significant" or "major" that people left the congregation because of it. Furthermore, denominations tend to be disrupted by issues such as homosexuality, ordination of women, and doctrinal debates, whereas congregations become disputatious over such matters as the pastor's leadership style, priorities in spending money, and changes in the worship format. Through all these conflicts, loyalty to a denomination often erodes, while loyalty to a congregation often remains remarkably high, despite the heat of the differences of opinion.

As a "denomination" (if one may so describe it), Roman Catholicism has been in greater distress in the past year or two than any other equivalent ecclesiastical organization. The whole matter of clerical celibacy has been spotlighted by the pedophile scandals among the priesthood. Eugene Kennedy is a professor emeritus of psychology at Loyola University in Chicago. In a Religious News Service article, he was quoted as saying, "The pedophilia crisis is a result of approving seminarians whose lack of psychosexual maturity made celibacy an easy choice that was misinterpreted as solid virtue. They accepted celibacy because they had little, if any, attraction to marriage. Their lack of internal growth seeded them with a destiny terrible for them and for those whose innocence they violated."

No less a formidable figure than Pope Paul VI wondered aloud about the wisdom of celibacy. "Is it possible and appropriate nowadays to observe such an obligation? Has the time not come to break the bond linking celibacy with the priesthood in the Church?" Sadly, Paul VI did nothing to break the bond, and John Paul II is the last person in the world who will sever the sometimes unhappy and sometimes unholy connection.

But what does this specifically Roman Catholic problem have to do with the larger question of cautious clergy? Just this: the requirement of celibacy automatically weeds out countless young Catholic men who otherwise would be strong, virile priests, and it produces too many priests who are effeminate, homosexual, or asexual. By no means am I saying that even a sizeable minority of priests are like that, or that effeminate, homosexual, or asexual priests cannot be highly gifted and effective. But the very requirement of celibacy results in too many priests who turn out to be ineffective because of their uncertain sexual orientation.

I know that some readers will misinterpret what I am now am going to say, but the certainty of that fact will not prevent me from saying it: whether male or female, pastors need a sufficient amount of the internal strength and self-confidence which purportedly derives from the infusion a certain hormone produced in a certain part of the male anatomy. In other words, whether they are female or male, all pastors need, figuratively speaking, gonads. A woman whom I highly respect said approvingly of her new pastor, whom I also highly respect, "She really has _ _ _ _ _!" The statement was made with as much fervor as admiration, and I knew exactly what this woman was intending when she described her female parson.

If you are now enraged, try to calm yourself, and think about it as dispassionately as you can. Inner strength is an absolute pre-requisite in a pastor. It is impossible to function effectively without it. Obviously hormones do not literally provide that strength. But it is imperative that the kind of resolve and tenacity universally ascribed to alpha-type males is needed in anyone who is going to be the pastor of a church. Kindness, compassion, sen-sitivity, perceptivity, sympathy, and empathy also are useful secondary pastoral traits. But strength is a primary necessity. That may be a sad reality, but it is true beyond dispute.

Tragically, far too many contemporary congregations are – to use another sexually-oriented word – *emasculating* their clergy. They are turning them into ecclesiastical wimps, churchly mil-quetoasts. For fear of getting shot at, the clergy choose to do nothing that will evoke opposition. But it may mean that in the end, they just do - - - **nothing**. And doing nothing is not an option for being a useful priest or minister.

In my opinion, the clergy have little real power, at least as the world reckons power. The centurion said to Jesus, "Lord, I am not worthy to have you come under my roof; but only say the word, and my servant will be healed. For I am man under author-ity, with soldiers under me, and I say to one, 'Come,' and he comes, and to my slave, 'Do this,' and he does it" (Matt. 8:8-9). **That** is power. But if a pastor were to proclaim the last part of that, droves of parishioners would think, if not actually say, "Stick it in your ear, parson! Who are you to tell me what to do?"

Nevertheless, unless the clergy are invested with a proper imposition of power in a congregational setting, either there will be a power vacuum, which is less likely, or there will be a power struggle, which is more likely. Inevitably, however, emasculated clergy become cautious clergy, and cautious clergy are a danger to their churches, the Church, and to God.

As a by-now geezer, too often I have seen lay leaders remain silent when another lay person who is a bully tries to take over in an official board meeting. Rather than call the bully's bluff, or give him holy what-for, they allow someone whom everyone knows to be a total nincompoop to assume control in a tense situation. Sometimes the pastor is powerless to step in and confront a belligerent ignoramus unless others will join the fray. Often "being nice" is anything but a Christian virtue; sometimes it can be an unmitigated vice. Surprisingly, laity will usually take on the clergy in a heartbeat, but often they will not call one another on the carpet for anything. It is a strange form of ecclesiastical cowardice. By their silence, people will give tacit support to people who are utter asses, and when they truly feel supportive of the pastor, they may also stay silent, and thus undermine her in her hour of greatest need.

Nevertheless, there is one example of power the clergy have, and by having it, they should exercise it to the best of their ability. I am referring to **the power of the pulpit**. It is in the pulpit where the minister or priest has the most obvious and natural authority which ordination can provide. When I was growing up, I was always very active in church, and I saw my pastors in numerous roles. But it was in their role as preacher where they most influenced me. I suspect that is true of most Christians, even if many are never consciously aware of it.

The pulpit is where the pastor has the greatest effect on the greatest number of parishioners. The spoken word of the preacher can become, by the mysterious chemistry of the Almighty, the veritable word of God. Long after every pastor leaves a congregation, even long after the clergy leave this world, the echo of their words from the pulpit still rings in the minds and hearts of their parishioners in a fashion which no one can ever fully determine or predict. If the preached word is well spoken, it is bound to bear permanent fruit.

Sadly, preaching has fallen upon very hard times in far, far too many churches and among far, far too many clergy. The seminaries have soft-pedalled preaching for three or four decades. "Liturgy" is what is taught. But however much careful preparation is given to liturgy, it will be totally lifeless if it is accompanied by lifeless preaching.

Sermon subscription series and the Internet have also eroded good preaching, however good were the intentions of those who created such vehicles. Supposing they can use someone else's ideas and words, too many clergy crib too much from these outside sources. But parishioners are not fooled. They know when someone is preaching a sermon not his own. They can tell when she has taken the easy way out that week.

PreachingToday.com was launched in 2000 by *Christianity Today* magazine, an evangelical periodical. By January of 2001, 12,512 clergy subscribed. By early 2002, that number had swelled to over ***20,000***. Those numbers speak volumes about the quality and status of preaching today.

Recently there have been highly publicized instances where pastors were dismissed by their congregations when it was discovered that the preachers were using, verbatim, sermons written by someone other than themselves. The defense of these clerical offenders is that there are too many other things to do in the pastorate for them also to take the proper amount of time to prepare a sermon each week.

But there is **nothing** more important than the preparation of thoughtful, provocative, edifying sermons! For the vast majority of all the members of every congregation, the Sunday sermon is the single most influential form of ministry in which the pastor is ever engaged! All the excellence in teaching, administration, counselling, and pastoral calling will matter not a bit if the pastor is not preaching well, week in and week out!

But the sad reality is that the rapid rise of cautious clergy has resulted in cautious, tepid, timid sermons. Too few of the clergy possess a sufficient gonadal repository forcefully to address some of the issues of our time which demand a careful and courageous airing and hearing. They play it safe, and thus forfeit the most effective tool in their pastoral toolbox.

If the clergy are going to get into trouble, their preaching should be the Number One Factor for propelling the turfbuilder into the mixmaster. As Paul asked in his letter to the Romans, "But how are men to call upon him in whom they have not believed? And how are they to believe in him of whom they have never heard? And how are they to hear without a preacher? And how can men preach unless they are sent?" (Romans 10:14-15) The primary purpose of a parson is preaching!!!

Most clergy can avoid most conflicts most of the time. But for anyone called by God to the ministry in any of its varied forms, some conflicts are inevitable, sooner or later. As an outstanding and now-deceased minister friend of mine often intoned, "The purpose of leaders is to lead!" Continuously trying to stay out of trouble is guaranteed only to cause trouble. Luther said of sin, "If you must sin, then sin boldly." In like manner, if pastors must get into trouble, then they should do so boldly. Caution and timidity do no one any good when confrontation is the only possible course of action.

Ron Sider is a wonderfully forthright evangelical social activist with a terrific tell-it-like-it-is manner. In the journal *Prism* he was writing about how genuine evangelicals can face the challenge of preaching Good News about the poor to the affluent and rich. Here is how he described it:

"Evangelical leaders have four options. 1. *The radical option.* You can preach fiery sermons and get thrown out. I don't recommend it. 2. *The conformist option.* Basically, you can preach and teach what the people want to hear, throwing in an occasional word about the poor on World Hunger Sunday. 3. *The calculating option.* You resolve to lead your people into greater concern for the poor, so you calculate just how much they can take without getting really upset. You push them, but never to the point of endangering your job. At the end of the day, this is just a more sophisticated version of the conformist option, a careful assessment of what the market will bear. 4. *The Spirit-filled, costly option.* You decide you would rather have Jesus than parsonage or pulpit or presidency. You decide to lovingly, gently, clearly teach all that the Bible says about justice for the poor."

So what happens if a preacher chooses Option No. 4? Says Ron Sider, "Embracing a biblical balance of prayer and action, preaching and modeling, evangelism and social ministry, worship and mission will often lead to transformed, growing congregations. But not always. Sometimes they throw you out. But unless you are ready to risk that, it means that no matter how you rationalize it, no matter how you massage your conscience, you really worship job security more than Jesus."

My quibble with Ron Sider, of course, is that it is far more important to worship God than Jesus. But setting that aside, he has put his finger on one of the besetting sins of many contemporary clergy; they are more interested in keeping their jobs by keeping out of trouble than they are in fully serving God in the high and holy vocation to which He has called them. It is by the grace of God that some are called to be apostles, some prophets, some evangelists, some pastors and teachers. And if God calls anyone to any of these institutional offices, then He shall also provide the necessary intestinal fortitude to function effectively in the office. As they used to sing in the Church of Scotland congregation in which I served as a student assistant minister in Paisley, Scotland, in those ignorantly sexist days of auld, "Courage, brother, do not stumble/ though the way be dark as night;/ There's a star to guide the humble/ trust in God, and do the right."

No member of the clergy can do the right when the primary personal concern is to cover one's backside. Throwing caution to the winds may not usher in the kingdom of God. But we may be certain that an abundance of caution is guaranteed to prevent the kingdom from ever appearing. Clergy and laity alike: Get God, get going, and get gonads. Otherwise, get out.

Scripture – Psalm 147:1-11

Text – Praise the Lord! For it is good to sing praises to our God; for he is gracious, and a song of praise is seemly. – Psalm 147:1

"CASUAL WORSHIP" IS AN UNHOLY OXYMORON!

The last five Psalms in the Book of Psalms are sometimes called "The Songs of *Hallel*." In Hebrew the word *hallel* means "praise." Thus *Hallelejah* literally means "Praise Yah" or "Praise Yahweh." When we worship, we are praising God. Anything less than that or other than that is not really worship.

At its very core, worship is, and must be, the activity of believers who come together to praise God. Worship must never focus primarily on **us**; it always must focus essentially on **God**.

The writer of Psalm 147 declared, "Praise the Lord! For it is good to sing praises to our God; for he is gracious, and a song of praise is seemly" (147:1). Indeed, **not** to sing praises and **not** to worship God on a continuous basis is **not** seemly for those who know and love God. That is probably the primary reason why people who don't go to church are kidding themselves when they say they worship God on the golf course or in the woods or on the beach. You can **acknowledge** God in those places, but you can't **worship** Him there. We can worship God only in communion with others, and never by ourselves. Further, we can obviously **pray** by ourselves, but we cannot **worship** by ourselves.

To overstate the issue, fundamentalists and liberals have usually pointed primarily toward God in their worship, while evangelicals have tended to point toward themselves. Some of you may want to quibble or seriously quarrel with that observation, but it seems to me it is generally valid. Nevertheless, in the past four decades or so there has been a fairly widespread movement away from worship as the praise of God to worship as a vehicle for uplifting or informing or transforming people. In other words, many kinds of churches have fallen into the trap of directing the center of the worship experience toward people rather than toward God. Churches with boxy auditoriums and no symbols of any sort are implicitly declaring that **We** are in the spotlight here, not **God**. If you can't see God in the architecture, then you can't hear God in the **auditorium**. (And hey, what's wrong with calling it what it is —— or should be —— a **sanctuary**?)

Accompanying this trend, or perhaps actually leading it, is an ever-growing casualness in dress when people gather to worship. Anyone who is forty or older who has attended church regularly for a lifetime is aware that many people today do not come dressed for worship the way most people dressed for worship one or two generations ago. This is not a universal phenomenon by any means, but it is an undeniable trend in general.

Having interviewed with several churches over the past few years for interim pastor positions, I am aware that many large Presbyterian congregations have inaugurated what they call "contemporary" or "non-traditional" or "modern" services of worship. Most of those congregations also have a traditional and a non-traditional service each Sunday. A key feature of this "contemporary" worship is that it is intended to be casual in every conceivable meaning of that term.

One of the liberating factors of being a retired parson is that my wife and I are able to attend churches and services which heretofore would have been impossible for us to attend, because I was always professionally involved in worship leadership in a specific church. When we are home, we worship with a particular congregation where we feel very much a part of the congregation. The style of the ministers and the church's programs suits our theological and ecclesiastical quirks very well. But when we travel, which we do frequently, we visit a variety of churches, just to see what is going on "out there."

"Out there," worship is often the most god-awful mess you can imagine. Some churches are so casual they make this old coot's skin crawl. The clergy sometimes look as though they just came in from working underneath their old Honda on its old transmission. Whatever the clergy are supposed to look like, they

don't look like it. Some of the congregants come in the most outlandish get-ups ever to be displayed in a purported Christian
sanctuary. A few seem to have on almost nothing at all. Modesty
has vanished for many attenders at modern Divine Worship.

In a piece I received by e-mail (why do I get all this stuff?),
somebody named Kenneth L. Pierpont, about whom I know not
one thing, said, "I know this" (i.e., dressing up for church)
"requires a great effort, especially on Mom's part, but the effort
to get ready for church is itself an act of devotion. It is a part of
our worship. All the work it takes to get the family to church says
something important to our children. It tells them that the things
of God are important to us."

In most of the churches where most or all of the members are
black, people still dress well when they go to church. Although
their worship is a tad too spirited for this staid auld Scots stick-
in-the-mud, their sartorial elegance bespeaks a respect which is
rapidly declining in other churches. Some Roman Catholics and
evangelicals look as though they have just emerged from a rag-
pickers convention when they appear in the courts of the Lord.
Anyone who wears clothes which are too casual for the proper
worship of God betrays an attitude which may also be too casual
for the proper worship of God, says I. Such casualness declares a
theological carelessness, however unintentional the declaration.

Further, sometimes in these casual churches it appears as
though nobody gave any thought to what would happen as the
people are led in the worship of the Holy One of Israel. They just
"let it all hang out," and whatever happens, happens. It is spontaneity, but with a vengeance.

Caveat emptor: from here on, this sermon will have an even
higher percentage of personal opinions than most of the other sermons have had, and you need to be wary of it. I want you to know
that I realize it, but you also particularly need to keep it constantly in mind. What follows may be nothing other than the
semi-elderly grumbling of a semi-codger who pathetically
obsesses over the good old days gone by. Further, as much as I
have severely tested the far limits of liberalism in most of these

heated homilies, I am a hidebound traditionalist when it comes to the worship of Almighty God. But I'm going to attempt as clearly as I can to explain why I believe we need to re-examine the wisdom which lies behind traditional worship, by contrasting it with contemporary, casual worship.

What do I mean by "traditional worship?" I mean worship whose essence includes **dignity, beauty, holiness, sanctity, reverence, and** (this must also be included) **predictability**. The first five qualities of proper worship are fairly self-explanatory. And even if they're not, I shall not try to explain them further anyway. But the last quality, **predictability**, is crucial in contemporary worship, because it seems to be lacking in so many churches today.

Remember, worship ought primarily to be the praise of God, and in all Christian branches, with the exception of Pentecostalism, the clergy or other worship leaders should have a very clear concept of what they expect to happen during whatever period of time is set aside for worship. The very notion of a set time itself gives many Christians the bitter quivers. In black churches, for example, there is a long-standing tradition that worship begins when it begins and it ends when it ends. And that's okay — **in denominations which have that tradition, and where that tradition is widely accepted as an essential tenet of that denomination's self-understanding.** But for most mainline Protestants and also for Roman Catholics and Orthodox Christians, most people go to church with rather fixed notions of what ought to happen in church, and just how long it should take for it to happen. The clergy and others do the members no favors if they create a climate of worship which is totally spontaneous, because it in the minds of the congregants, that feels like total chaos. **And worship which is chaotic or poorly planned is not worship at all**.

The early 20th century German philosopher Rudolf Otto wrote about what he called "the sense of the numinous." That term is a description more than a definition, and it expresses the feeling we get when the choir has just lifted us to the very presence of God by singing a Bach cantata or a Handel oratorio or a

Mozart mass. It is what washes over us when a particular prayer has voiced on our behalf what heretofore we were unable to articulate for ourselves, and in its having been stated, we have found ourselves at the very throne of God. It is what comes over us when the preacher has thrown open the doors of our hearts to the only God who is God, who has shown us something from the life and teachings of Jesus which we never knew before.

Rudolf Otto also wrote about what he called the "*mysterium tremendum et fascinans.*" It is probably a mistake to translate that Latin phrase at all; maybe all of us should deduce for ourselves whatever we want it to mean. None of us can exactly define *mysterium tremendum et fascinans*, but at some point, or far better still, at many points in our lives, we have experienced it, and its soul-stirring force has transformed us.

But just what is the "it" which occurs when we sense the numinous, or when tremendous mystery and fascination take hold of our being? The **It** it is is the sudden and overpowering awareness of the presence of God. **To know God is to worship God**. No one can know God and **not** worship Him. Thus, those who do not worship God cannot really know God. They may know things about God, they may have academic access to numerous notions of God, but until we sense the numinous, until the *mysterium tremendum et fascinans* grips us, we cannot truly worship God.

That is why worship must center on God, and not on us. If we have ever encountered the God who is God, or, more precisely, if we have ever been encountered by the God who is God, our worship of that God needs to praise **Him** rather than to appeal to **us**. And the problem with far too much contemporary "worship," which is not truly worship at all, is that it centers on human beings and their needs, rather than on God and His praise.

Obviously this does not mean that every hymn must be a hymn of praise, every anthem a great *hallelu Jah*, every sermon a sanctified song of glory to God in the highest. But the **essence** of worship should focus on God and what He says to us, not on what God does for us. Worship is about us **doing** for God; it is not about God **doing** for us. But too often, in far too many churches, **we** are the focus, not **God**.

The word "worship" is an old Anglo-Saxon word which literally means "worth-ship." We worship only Him who is worthy of our worship, and that is God. Nevertheless, in churches all across the USA and elsewhere throughout the world, too often the emphasis is on anything other than God. It is about how-to, it is about self-improvement, it is even about building a better world, but all too frequently it does not connect all these ideas, worthy as they may be, with the One who alone is worthy of our worship.

One of the most glaring examples of where too many people took the wrong turn is in what has come to be called "Christian music." Christian music used to what Bach, Handel, Isaac Watts, and Charles Wesley composed, except that then it was not called "Christian music." It was music which Christians employed for a more proper worship of God. It became classical music, in the sense that it transcended whatever was merely popular. And it was used by Christians generation after generation, because it so beautifully and powerfully portrayed eternal truths about God and Jesus Christ. Anything that is classic has a timelessness about it. When we refuse to recognize the classic in anything classic, it illustrates how limited we are, and does not diminish the "classicity" of whatever is, and always will be, a classic.

"Christian music," on the other hand, deliberately mimics popular music. It deliberately abandons classic Christian musicology. Whether any "Christian music" shall become a classic remains to be seen, but there seems to be no intention in "Christian music" to compose for the ages. "Now" is the only temporal concept there is for "Christian music."

And yet, "Christian music" is the hottest selling genre in the music business. In the year 2001, 50 million "Christian" units were sold, which was an increase of 13.5% from the previous year. Other kinds of music units declined by 3% in 2001. Ble$$ed A$$urance, Jeu I$ MINE!

In one of his *Christian Century* M.E.M.Os, Martin E. Marty suggests that a couple of sermon themes might come out of all this, such as – quote – "'From what I have overheard and read, much Christian music is, let's say it, junk, exploitative, banal, guilty of helping to turn Christianity into mere entertainment for many': or 'On the other hand, it give the recording artists and companies credit for gaining and holding the ear of a generation that other Christians neglect, or fail to reach or don't even try to reach.'"

So let's give 'em credit; they do reach them. But with **what** have they been reached? With atrocious theology, insipid Christology, saccharine sentimentality, and dubious entertainment, none of which translates into proper worship. It might sound to you as though I am less than thrilled by what passes for "Christian music." I certainly hope so! If I have not made that clear, I have failed miserably in this pointed peroration. Listen to the words of this kind of music, Christian people; they say so much about what they say! "Christian music" is much more about what God can do for us than about what we can do for God. I believe "Christian music" is not only a mistake; it is actively leading millions of undiscerning folks down the primrose path into a terrible theological box-canyon, from which it is very difficult gracefully to return.

If people are fed drivel, their minds become "drivialized." And "drivialization" is what is happening in thousands of American churches where "contemporary worship" has become all the faddish rage. Just because many of those churches are rapidly growing does not mean that they have discovered the key to success for 21st century evangelism. In fact, the "good news" presented in many of those churches, particularly in the type of music that is employed, is actually very bad news. It bodes terrible ills for the future. God cannot be properly worshipped by means of bad theology, and people cannot be properly fed with insipid self-help tidbits. And yet that sad scenario is at the heart of what is happening in countless numbers of such churches. I am not engaged here in sour grapes, as some might conclude; it is bitter grapes which have filled my gall tank to overflowing.

For too long have more mature voices been silent in railing against the dangers which are inherent in what some evangelical churches are attempting to do. They are wrong in their theology, and they are wrong-headed in their approach! Not to call them to account is to do them no favors. It is not nice to them to be too nice to them. They are leading people astray as surely as did the false prophets in the time of Isaiah and Jeremiah.

The shocking truth is that most of the growth across the denominational spectrum is occurring in churches which use "contemporary worship" heavily or even exclusively. A survey of Faith Communities Today (FACT) illustrates that that sorry truth is virtually beyond dispute. Such worship is a bigger factor in rapidly growing churches than is "strictness," a term used by religious sociologist Dean Kelley. In other words, the desire for entertainment-oriented worship is even stronger than the desire for personal structure among many of the yuppies, dinks, and bobos who are streaming into the evangelical churches. In addition, many growing churches have deliberately sought to blend elements of the new worship with more traditional elements. This bastardized worship (my term, no one else's!) also appeals to undiscerning souls.

To be sure, many congregations in many mainline denominations which still follow traditional worship patterns also are growing. But not as many, and not as fast. And in those instances, it is usually the preaching of the primary pastor which attracts new members, rather than the hellzapoppin' entertaining "worship" which draws so many to the non-denominational mega-churches.

One thing is certain. Mainline churches which consciously attempt to institute "contemporary worship" as a major feature of their congregational life must be prepared to pay a major price for their decision to change. Such churches are almost bound to lose certain members, even though they will gain other new members. And sadly, those dropouts generally do not go to another church; they stop going to church altogether. The attitude of the dropouts seems to be, "If they won't worship God in the old ways in my old church, I'm not going to find a new church which worships in the old ways, because I'm too old, or crotchety, or disgusted, to conduct a proper search."

Timothy Padgett is the Miami-Caribbean bureau chief for *Time* Magazine. In an article in the Roman Catholic journal *America*, Mr. Padgett, a Roman Catholic, wrote, "(I)t is time for us (Catholics) to ask: in our four-decade-long zeal to make the Mass modern and relevant – by burying sublime Kyries under banal 'Kumbayas' – have we lost the vital 'affective side' of our own religion? Are liberal Catholics, who demand dialogue on doctrinal issues, open-minded enough to demand it of ourselves on liturgical issues?"

Timothy Padgett believes that the classic beauty of the traditional Mass has been lost in the insistence on mundane modernization. He asks, "How could it possibly hurt liberal Catholics to restore some transcendence to our worship — chiefly by rebuilding our own bond with two millennia of some of the most 'affective' religious language, music, and art ever inspired?" I agree with him, and I echo his thoughts for liberal mainline Protestants. Why do we sheepishly stand by while well-intentioned evangelical nudniks eviscerate the beauty, decorum, and transcendence of the worship of Almighty God? Why the hell don't we rise up against the trivialization of the proper praise of God? Anybody who thinks Amy Grant or James Taylor are as effective at musically presenting the Gospel of Jesus Christ as J. S. Bach or W. A. Mozart is only displaying a profoundly time-warped ignorance of what constitutes great music. What mother would feed her child trash when there is the best of food immediately at hand? So why should church leaders intentionally present junk music in worship when some of the most sublime music ever composed cries out to be sung or played to the Creator of the rolling spheres?

While I am in a fulminating mode, let me turn my fulminations to those clergy and churches who have decided that, in very fast-paced America, it is necessary to combine Christian holidays in order to accommodate the busy schedules of parishioners. A while back *The Wall Street Journal* had a lengthy cover story about this new trend. The article noted that Holy Week is when most of the doubling-up of holidays occurs. It stated that fully

30% of the 35,000 United Methodist congregations celebrate some part of Holy Week at untraditional time slots. Many of those churches, for example, have Maundy Thursday services on Tuesday of Holy Week, to avoid putting church members through the supposedly insurmountable obstacle of having to go to church on Maundy Thursday, then Good Friday, and then again on Easter. Some churches have combined Maundy Thursday and Good Friday into one service, so that people can celebrate two-for-one holidays in one sitting.

For crying out loud! As Robert Welch asked of the lamentable Sen. McCarthy, "Have you no shame?" Should mere personal convenience **ever** be the determining factor in when worship services are offered, or what particular format is therein offered, or what anybody thinks will be the most popular format that should be offered? Great day in the morning: what a fine mess **this** is! The *WSJ* article told of a congregation which had an Easter evening service, including a high-tech powerpoint presentation, for those folk who chose to sleep in Easter morning rather than to rise early to proclaim with others the greatest news the world has ever known. All this is alimentary-emulsifying and gastroenterologically-assaulting and colonically-upstopping; you might even say it is enough to make one sick. When worship is deliberately made **easy**, is it worthy of the description of **worship**?

So, to continue with the venting of my liturgical spleen, I call attention to those churches whose worship is characterized by some as "happy-clappy worship." How many times in recent years have you attended a church where there was applause during the service? Or how many churches have applause in virtually every service? Perhaps there are occasions when applause might be warranted, as when a children's choir presents an exceptionally well-sung anthem, or the adult choir sings a magnificent oratorio for almost the entire service. But the admitted fuddidudditude of this particular elderly flatulent makes it almost impossible for me to applaud anything in church with any genuine enthusiasm. I know the psalm says "O clap your hands, all ye people," but the clapping thereof was intended to be an

355

expression of praise to God, not an expression of appreciation to somebody or other for something or other that was well done. Even at that, says this irrepressible old fuddy-duddy, it is a dubious exercise for anyone to clap in church at all, even in praise of God. The sounds of our praise should emerge from our throats, says I, not from our hands smacking smartly together.

Or, to continue my tirade, there are those people who drift in only to those parts of the order of worship which suit them. They come late and leave early, or come late and leave later. One time Lois and I were in St. Patrick's Cathedral in New York City. We were astonished by the number of people who came streaming through the south transcept door just in time to receive communion and then to depart, post-haste, toward whence they initially came. Some were in jogging clothes, some in old clothes, and some in almost no clothes at all. What colossal chutzpah! I hope the wafer turned to sawdust in their mouths! Take **that**, yuh flitting wafer-snatchers, yuh!

What has happened to **dignity** in worship? Where is the **decorum**? Certainly worship that feels as stiff as a board is improper, but when casualness becomes a primary aim, when it is the deliberate intention of those in charge to dumb-down worship, or to turn it into entertainment, admittedly with no malice aforethought but also obviously with no forethought, to try to make worship feel "fun," then worship simply cannot be worship.

The Church of England, especially on state occasions, still knows how to Do It Right. When the Queen Mum died, her funeral at Westminster Abbey was telecast live all over the world. What a grand and glorious send-off for a grand and glorious lady! And how greatly was God praised on that memorable occasion! There was a palpable *mysterium trmendum et fascinans* from the beginning to the end. Worship, to be authentic, need not be stuffy, and the funeral for the Queen Mum was anything but stuffy. But authentic worship needs to promote **transcendence**. It needs to remind us of the greatness of God, and the smallness of humanity. It should not so much seek to bring God to us as to transport us to God.

If worship edifies humanity more than it magnifies divinity, it fails altogether at being true worship. You and I **need** to be brought into an awareness of the presence of the living God. We **need** to be lifted above the plane of human experience where worldly cares and earthly sorrows engulf us into that mystical place, which is not at all "spatial," where we perceive God. And when we truly see Him as He is, we will want to praise Him as we should. Worship is nothing less than God's primary means of reaching out to us, in all our sin and weakness and uncertainty and ambivalence. Through our worship of God, God casts the light of His being into the shadows of our own being, so that, *mirabile dictu*, we are able to make it through another week. Through worship, God enters the spiritual vacuum which again and again seizes control of us, and He fills us with His own fullness. When we sing the hymns and pray the prayers and hear the words preached, we are all talking to God while, at the same time, God is talking to all of us.

I am convinced that "casual worship," whatever that may connote, and however well-intentioned it is, is finally an unholy oxymoron. It is fundamentally a contradiction in terms. Nothing that is essentially worship can be deliberately casual, and nothing that is essentially casual can ever deliberately become worship. Worship is too important to be casual. Furthermore, casual worship is bound to be unholy; it cannot be anything else. Until the 21st century Church re-discovers that truth, it shall be confronted with the questions the prophet Isaiah asked so long ago: "Why do you spend your money for that which is not bread, and your labor for that which does not satisfy?" (Isaiah 55:2)

The word "liturgy" comes from a Greek root which means "work." The liturgy of the people in worship is their communal effort to come into God's presence, there properly to worship Him. Liturgy can technically happen only where, as Jesus said, there are "two or three gathered **together**." Worship is a communal experience, because it takes two or more people to make the liturgical work **work**. Liturgy doesn't **work** individually, it works only **collectively**.

But it doesn't work casually. Worship is too vital, too necessary, too transformative, for it ever to succeed in a deliberately casual manner.

And so the Book of Psalms ends as only the Psalms should end, with the Songs of Hallel. In everything we are to praise God. And if I and other fuds are a bit put off by timbrel and dance and loud-clashing cymbals because it offends our finely-honed religious sensibilities: well, we will just have to get over it. But don't push us too far. Don't take away our music. Don't attempt to substitute little ditties that are will-of-the-wisps of worship when the true masters have given us the music of the spheres. Let us attempt to find and to praise God in our worship, or let us not attempt to worship at all.

Scripture – Acts 17:16-27

Text – Now all the Athenians and the foreigners who lived there spent their time in nothing except telling or hearing something new. – Acts 17:21 (RSV)

CHRISTIANITY LITE

For the past couple of decades, there has been a growing trend toward calling certain foods or drinks "lite" whatever. Thus we have lite butter, lite cheese, lite ice cream, and lite beer, among many other lite products. Strangely, we have **diet** Coke and **diet** Pepsi, rather than lite. I suppose that happened because we had **diets** to get lighter before we had "**lite**" to get lighter, although a diet of Coke or Pepsi, in any of the many cola species, by itself is likely a dubious diet for diminishing girth.

Also for the past two or three decades, there has been a concurrent trend toward the establishment of what we might call "Christianity Lite." Christianity Lite is being offered in an increasing number of churches, both mainline Protestant and evangelical Protestant. (Roman Catholics don't go for lite in anything, except their music, which is so shamefully lite it would be better if it floated right up through the church ceiling, and into outer space, never to be heard again.) Christianity Lite is a type of Christianity which expects little, demands little, and produces little. It is all sizzle and no steak, all froth and no liquid, all talk and no action —— or at least little steak, or liquid, or action.

For growing numbers of Christians, Christianity Lite has become the religion of choice. It is pleasant and harmless, it provides luxurious fertilizer for the self, and it changes the world almost not at all. It doesn't concentrate very much on God, either.

But what, more specifically, do I mean by "Christianity Lite"? Rather than my attempting to describe the phenomenon, let me call on two noted scholars to describe it. Wade Clark Roof is one of the foremost sociologists of religion in our nation. A few years ago he wrote a book called *Spiritual Marketplace: Baby Boomers and the Remaking of American Religion.* Louis Weeks, the president of Union Theological Seminary in Richmond, Virginia, wrote a critique of the book in *The Christian Century* (Feb. 23, 2000). Dr. Weeks said, "Roof examines the process of 'traditioning' which has been turned upside down to foster innovation rather than continuity. Boomer dissatisfaction with conventional forms of piety such as Sabbath observance, their reluctance to make commitments, and the gender revolution all contributed to the overturning of traditional religious practices, though not the quest for wholeness." Then Weeks points out, "Roof argues that people today seek to be simultaneously fluid and grounded. We want the benefits of anchors without their limits."

What an excellent description of Christianity Lite! We want what we want when we want it, but we don't want any demands or burdens placed on us! Regardless of our age, whether we are Baby Boomers or not, Christianity has become essentially a smorgasbord for countless numbers of Christians. We choose this, and this, and this, and reject that, and that, and that. Christianity Lite is Designer Christianity, in which individuals create for themselves whatever suits their particular religious fancies.

Those who were born between 1964 and 1978 are called "Generation X." They are purported to be quite different from Baby Boomers (those born from 1945 to 1963), and they are light years (**lite** years?) away from those of us old geezers who made our terrestrial entrance prior to or during World War II. We are the Geezer Generation, although nobody, including ourselves, has bothered to give us that moniker.

Anyway, Lauren Winner is a Gen Xer who wrote an article for *Christian Century* (Nov. 8, 2000) called *Gen X Revisited,* which had as part of the title, *"A Return to Tradition?"*. Speaking as a Gen Xer, she characterizes her age cohort and peers as follows: "We're seekers. We meditate. We go to Sufi dancing on Tuesday nights. We read books like *Finding Your Religion: When the Faith You Grew Up with Has lost Its Meaning.* But we're famously hostile to institutions."

Obviously this is a generalization. Surely not all Gen Xers go to Sufi dancing on Tuesday nights. But it probably is generally a fair generalization. Then Ms. Winner quotes an article from *First Things* by Sarah Hinlicky who says that Xers believe in little and feel nothing but contempt for "anything that smacks of the Establishment." That is an over-generalization with which Lauren Winner has at least a quibble, if not an outright quarrel. Her thesis is that Generation X may be in the process of turning back to tradition in several areas of contemporary life, but especially in matters religious. Xers might even be less troubled by the Establishment, she avers.

Other social observers have suggested the same thing. And the tide indeed may slowly be turning. But from the observation post of this member of the Geezer Generation, it doesn't look like we have yet experienced anything close to a sea change, nor has the ebb tide even clearly made its appearance. I would like to believe that Lauren Winner is correct in what she says, but I do not yet perceive it myself.

The Willow Creek Community Church in northwest suburban Chicago is one of the most amazing stories of mega-church growth in the USA in the past twenty years. In 1994, under the leadership of Dieter Zander, it began a worship service designed specifically for Gen Xers. Baby Boomers did not like the service, and older people definitely did not appreciate it. The new ministry was called Axis. Dieter Zander left Willow Creek for San Francisco in 1998. The new Axis director, Nancy Ortberg, said, "Axis services are led by Xers fore Xers." She declares that the sound of the worship is louder, that there is "almost a club-like feel. The service is more interactive, and there is a less-polished feel" (*Christian Century*, Nov. 8, 2000).

Twice Nancy Ortberg used the word "feel." Boomers, Xers, and other Christians seem first to seek "feel" when they search for a church. "Thought" doesn't count for much; "feel" is everything to many of these folks.

Any church that deliberately attempts to appeal to a particular age group in the type of worship it offers is running the risk of pandering to popularity for its own sake. Popularity does not necessarily equate to validity. It may, but it also may not. More often than not, I think, it doesn't. Doing the popular thing is "doing in" genuine Christianity in far too much of American Christianity. It is intentional Christianity Lite, and it is a highly dubious diversion. It allows people to suppose that what feels good and sounds good *is* good. But it may also turn their minds to sawdust, and their hearts to shredded wheat.

Dieter Zander, the original founder of the Axis Ministry at the Willow Creek Church, has recently concluded that generation-specific ministry is likely a mistake. By separating a particular age group in a church into their own worship style, he says it allows a congregation to maintain the semblance of tradition in one part of the church, while dabbling in something new in another part of the church. Dieter Zander: "I think we are shooting ourselves in the foot in the long run with Gen X, Gen Y and then Gen Z services. The segmentation could kill the church."

This deliberately *au courant* behavior is the same sort of thing which the apostle Paul encountered when he went to Athens. Paul had just been chased out of Thessalonica, which was just one of the many places he managed to get thrown out of. (Such a *nudzh* was he.) He was waiting for Silas and Timothy to join him in Athens. Because they had not yet arrived, he went to the Areopagus, as any proper visitor to the Greek metropolis would properly have done. As he strolled around, he listened to various people proclaiming various things, all of which, he thought, sounded brand new and untested and positively cockamamie.

Paul's complaint with the Athenians may be your complaint with that kind of Christianity which uniquely prides itself on always being "contemporary." It is New Age Christianity that would never call itself New Age, Entertainment Christianity which would loudly proclaim it is not entertainment, Jivey Christianity which would insist that jive is not its main purpose at all. Methinks they do protest too much. They seek the New, simply because it is New. They pursue whatever is Contemporary, just because they want to be Contemporary. They eschew tradition for the mere sake of the eschewal. To be sure, tradition can become an idol, but in itself, tradition is neither good nor bad; it is how it is used that counts. Just so, contemporary worship is neither good nor bad; it is how it is used that counts.

Do people come to church because there they want to hear the **Gospel** proclaimed, or do they come to church because they like the **packaging** of what **purports** to be the Gospel? Too much of contemporary Christianity is packaging, and too little is Gospel. And anything that is primarily packaging is, be definition, Christianity Lite.

Packaging is the name of the game in much of what is claimed to be "Christian music." The lyrics to the songs may have religious themes, albeit of the syrupy, saccharine variety, but it is the music itself, the soft-rock packaging, which really sells. Listening to this music for much of the day deludes people into imagining that they are receiving the Good News of God, when in fact they are buying into popular music with a shallow religious veneer.

Some of the most successful proponents of so-called "Christian music" simply reflect the tastes of the music-purchasing public; they do not seek to bend those tastes to the far more stringent demands of the Gospel. In the journal *Perspectives* (January 2002), it was stated that the people in the evangelical music business base their "ideals and assumptions on consumer culture – individualism, materialism, personal taste, and freedom of choice…. (T)he commercialization of evangelical music is 'less a peculiar hybrid than a reasonable and natural progression….(C)onsumption, capitalism, and materialism are *necessary components* of both Christian music and materialism.'"

But all of this becomes popular because it is so *new*; right? It is so *contemporary*, so *current*, so… so… *so*.

It isn't new, really. In the Athenian Areopagus twenty centuries ago, people were spouting the same kind of stuff. And it drove Paul wild. "Men of Athens," he said ("*Athenians*," the NRSV, with political correctness, said he said), "I perceive that in every way you are very religious. For as I passed along, and observed the objects of your worship, I found an altar with this inscription, 'To an unknown god.' What therefore you worship as unknown, this I proclaim to you" (Acts 17:22-23).

Is the god who is praised by an eight-piece orchestra and five mike-caressing vocalists **God**? Can the God who is God be **known** when the musical medium is the message, or must God remain **unknown** when the **mechanics** of worship become the essential **meaning** of worship? Is it the very "liteness" of Christianity Lite which makes it so appealing, and if so, can "liteness" truly be Christianity at all?

The "with-it" Athenians reveled in whatever was new. They were religious faddists, spiritual dilettantes. Therefore, in the event that they might have missed the worship of a new deity with whom they might be unfamiliar, they fashioned an altar, with the enigmatic inscription etched into it, "To an Unknown God." They were not about to bypass the bandwagon of a new god whose acquaintance they had not yet made, but whose parade they would gladly join, once they knew it was in progress!

Patricia Leigh Brown is a reporter for the *New York Times*. In an article called "Megachurches as Minitowns," she wrote about the Community Church of Joy, which is located in Glendale, Arizona. The congregation has 12,000 members on a 187-accre piece of property. Besides its sanctuary complex, it has a school, conference center, bookstore, and mortuary. It has begun a $100 million campaign to build a housing development, hotel, convention center, skate park, and water-slide park. Its pastor has called the new development "a destination center." He proudly told the reporter, "Even the water park, which will have an Olympic-size aquatic center, will have a Christian theme, with laser shows depicting Jonah and the whale and David and Goliath. The housing development, which will not be limited to church members, will have a full-time chaplain. Though not meant to replicate Disneyland, it is a Disneyesque utopian vision with a Christian spin."

I wonder if the Community Church of Joy is not the Athenian Areopagus all over again. As Rodgers and Hammerstein might have said, "Everything's up to date in Arizona/ They've gone about as fer as they can go." But, as heavy a financial undertaking as this is, it all sounds ominously like Christianity Lite to me. What does any of that have to do with the Gospel?

In 2001, for the first time ever, the top-selling fiction and non-fiction books of the year were religious books. Tim LaHaye and Jerry B. Jenkins wrote their latest novel in the *Left Behind* series, and Bruce Wilkinson wrote *The Prayer of Jabez*. It is my opinion that Messrs. LaHaye, Jenkins, and Wilkinson are to serious and responsible biblical scholarship what Saddam Hussein is to worldwide philanthropy. And yet their books sell millions of copies for multi-millions of dollars. In the *New York Times*, reporter Martin Arnold wrote of this phenomenon, "What's happening apparently is that many of these books, no matter how airy they seem, are anchoring people to a new sort of spirituality without making them face the intellectual challenge of the liturgical. If the book is replacing the church for many, what's coming next from publishing? Something on the order of Chesterton's *St. Francis of Assisi* or Thomas Merton's *Seven Storey Mountain*? Not likely. Probably some form of *God for Dummies*."

Bravo, Martin Arnold! You said it; I didn't! Why is it that so much popular religion today is, if not anti-intellectual, then unintellectual? Why is it so feeling-oriented, and so glaringly thoughtless in orientation? If, as Paul Tillich declared half a century ago that God is the Ground of Being, why is so much of Christianity Lite so groundless? Where is God in the groundswell of religiosity? Jesus is there, in spades, but where is God? And how can Jesus truly be there if God is not there?

The kind of church which espouses Christianity Lite with fierce determination is often called a "seeker church." Seeker churches appeal especially to Baby Boomers, because both the boomers and their type of church prefer to focus on the self. Christian symbols are downplayed in seeker churches. The human body is given affirmation as the sensing, feeling aspect of the self. Hence many of these churches have spiffy new fitness centers. To their credit, seeker churches concentrate on the love and forgiveness of God rather than on God's anger and punishment. But they also tend deliberately to ignore the inevitably offensive side of the Christian Gospel, making it, in the words of George H.W. Bush, kinder and gentler.

A *New Yorker* cartoon captures the jarring disparity between the seeker Christian and the traditional Christian. A huge, muscular, smiling young man emerges from a traditional-looking church. His whole head is clean-shaven, he has on a light-colored suit which boldly highlights his physique, and he wears the *de rigeuer* t-shirt under his suit coat. With a genuinely friendly grin on his face, he reaches for the pastor's hand. The pastor, incidentally, is a stubby, stout old coot, replete with glasses and clerical grimace. The hunk says to the parson, "Nice job, Reverend, but I think I'll stick to worshipping my body."

T.H. White described the older Guinevere, who became a nun after King Arthur died, in this manner: "She became a wonderful theologian, but cared nothing for God." What a thoroughly appropriate description of Christianity Lite! We may become steeped in what we so readily call "spirituality," we may have a genuine desire to do good and to put morality into everyday practice, we may attend church or church meetings until the proverbial cows come home, but if we have no concern for God, we have totally missed what Jesus Christ and Christianity are all about. Even those who focus primarily or almost exclusively on Jesus in their understanding of Christianity understand little about either Jesus or Christianity. It is **God** whom we should seek to worship and serve, the same God whom Jesus so completely worshipped and served. Christianity is not about Christ; it is about the God whom Christ so compellingly revealed. But Christianity Lite never seems to understand that elusive truth.

The word "paradigm" has become a veritable paradigm of buzzwords. The only time I ever heard that word forty years ago was when I was in seminary. Back then, only theologians and other such odd ducks used it. Now, everybody, particularly business people, buzz para-**dig**-ms all over the place. Megachurches are new paradigms.

Seeker churches are new paradigms. Christianity Lite is also a new paradigm. Donald Miller, who teaches religion at the University of Southern California, writes about "the new paradigm church" or "the reinvented church." He says, "In the new paradigm church, most members are relatively young. The church meets in a building that has no stained glass, steeple, or pews. In fact, most of these worship spaces are either converted warehouses, theaters, or rented school auditoriums" (*Christian Century*, Dec. 22-29, 1999, p.1250).

Surely God can be worshipped anywhere. But is something fundamentally amiss when people deliberately seek to negate what might be called "sacred space"? Is it **wrong** to call the main place where most people worship a **sanctuary**? Is it right to **avoid** calling it a sanctuary? Theoretically, God can be worshipped as appropriately in an auditorium as in a sanctuary, but aren't we more likely to sense that we are worshipping Him when we call the place of worship "the sanctuary?" Can a church "be" a church to us if it is deliberately built with only a symbol-less auditorium and the building never acquires a churchy-looking sanctuary? And if the church's big room is called a "worship center" instead, what, exactly, is that? Just a big room?

I clearly realize that the "Non-Church Church Movement" is a ploy to attract the unchurched into the new paradigm churches, or whatever other moniker one chooses to describes these institutions. Nevertheless, once they are "in," what have they gotten themselves into? Certainly not into a non-institution! Non-denominational churches, especially non-denominational megachurches, are much more institutional than Messiah Lutheran, at the corner of Main and 3rd, with its 163 dedicated members, half of whom are 65 or over, will ever be.

Furthermore, precisely because so many of the new, fast-growing churches have no denominational connections, most of them spend every cent that comes into the offering plates (do they use alternative words for that ecclesiastical process as well?) right there on their own "campus," which is another new buzzword that drives us geezers to drink. There is no sense of mission to the world when the whole world is perceived to be the Community of the Living Presence, or some other such godawful name. When the focus in Christianity Lite is brazenly on the self, why should anyone worry about faraway selves in Nigeria or Nepal? To think about poor Nigerians is to cast a dark shadow over the bright light of Number One, and that we must avoid at all costs!

Christianity Lite employs constant stimulation to fill the vacuum which life inevitably creates within all of us from time to time. Emptiness is a part of existence. But Christianity Lite attempts to get around the emptiness with a cacophony of sound: the orchestra blasting away in the auditorium, the videos, the audiotapes, the happy voices, the optimistic chatter, the non-stop encouragement.

Joan Chittister, the outstanding, outspoken, occasionally delightfully outrageous nun, has important things to say about this phenomenon in her book *Illuminated Life: Monastic Wisdom for Seekers of Light.* "Silence is the lost art in a society made of noise," she says. "Radios wake us up, and timers on TVs turn off the day-full of programs long after we have gone to sleep. We have music in cars, elevators, and office waiting rooms. We have surround-sound that follows us from the living room to the kitchen to the upstairs bath. What the contemplative knows that modern society has forgotten, it seems, is that the real material of spiritual development is not in books. It is in the subject matter of the self. It is in the things we think about, in the messages we give ourselves constantly, in the civil war of the human soul that we wage daily. But until we are quiet and listen, we can never know what is really going on — even in ourselves…. Silence is, in other words, life's greatest teacher. It shows us what we have yet to become. Silence, the contemplative knows, is that place just before the voice of God."

What a marvelous insight! We need not fear the silence; we must cultivate it! We must make time for it! Too much religion of every sort seeks to drown out the silence, to obliterate it with sounds, even well-intentioned sounds. Lite religion is especially nervous around silence, and it clangs its cymbals together to a fine fare-thee-well to overcome the painful void which refuses to give us any stimulus of any sort. But, as Sister Joan insists, we cannot hear

God's voice until we hear the nothingness which precedes it, and we can never hear the nothingness if we are constantly being told something, anything, to answer questions not asked, or to pour salve on wounds which need to fester longer before any salve can take effect.

"Life is a Beach," the sly, tongue-in-cheek bumper-sticker declares, substituting one five-letter word starting with a "b" and ending with a "ch" for another such word. Well, life is — and must be — a bitch for all of us, sooner or later. Profound religion recognizes, affirms, and confronts that reality. Surface religion seeks to negate it with upbeat music and positive slogans and cheerful bonhomie.

Flannery O'Connor was a magnificently peculiar novelist who was a Roman Catholic in the South at a time when many Catholics had crosses burning on their front lawns, courtesy of the brave knights of the KKK. In a sobering statement directed to the most convinced and convicted of Christians, she said, "You shall know the truth, and the truth shall make you odd."

There are a few good features in Christianity Lite, and quite a number of bad features. But perhaps the worst is this: it takes people who already fit well into a world which abhors misfits, and it makes them fit even better. It acculturates people who are the epitome of acculturation, and it refuses ever to ask whether the culture might possibly be severely askew.

In our kind of society, people want to fit in, not to stand out. Maybe it has ever been thus in all societies. But if ever we are to know the truth, we must come to grips with the searing fact that the truth shall make us odd. Until Christianity first becomes a burden, it can never turn into a blessing. If Christianity is not heavy, it can never survive by being intentionally lite.

"Now all the Athenians and the foreigners who lived there spent their time in nothing except telling or hearing something new." And therein lies the loopy liteness.

Scripture – Judges 21:23

Text – In those days there was no king in Israel; every man did what was right in his own eyes. – Judges 21:23 (RSV)

THE DECLINE OF DENOMINATIONS AND THE ASCENDANCY OF CONGREGATIONS

Note: What you are about to read shall be much more like an essay in the sociology of religion than a sermon. For one thing, there is only one verse of scripture to which I make any allusion. But that is because there is nothing in the Bible which has any direct relevance to the theme being addressed. I refer to the text, if only briefly. Nonetheless, the issues of this barely sermonic treatise are major ones which shall strongly influence the future of Christianity and faith for the foreseeable future. They need to be pondered, because both Christendom and individual Christians shall be greatly affected by how these trends are resolved.

The Past

The first ten centuries of Christian history was characterized by a slowly growing chasm which developed between Western and Eastern Christianity. Eventually the two major branches of the Church which then existed officially split apart, never to re-connect, even to this day.

Western Christianity became centered in Rome. Eastern Christianity centered in Byzantium, which came to be called Constantinople. (The Byzantine Emperor Constantine, who was the first emperor to sanction Christianity, changed the name of the city in his own honor. A regular paragon of humility was old Constantine.) The year 1054 saw the most visible and permanent rupture between the East and West, and from that time on, the two main strands of Christian faith deliberately, and with headstrong determination, went their separate ways.

Then, over the course of the next several centuries Eastern Orthodoxy (as it came to be called) evolved into numerous "national" Churches: Greek, Russian, Georgian, Serbian, Rumanian, Ukrainian, Syrian, Egyptian (the Coptic Church), Ethiopian, and so on. Each of these Orthodox "denominations" had their own patriarchs, bishops, governmental structure, and liturgical language.

In the West, Christianity rallied around Rome, its patriarch (the bishop of Rome, a.k.a. the Pope), and the Latin language. By calling itself the **Catholic** Church, Roman Catholicism was highlighting its universality. Every Catholic church everywhere in the world was basically like every other Catholic church. The diocesan structure was the same, the doctrines and dogmas were the same, and the liturgical language, Latin, was the same.

For five centuries, from about 1000 to 1500 CE, the two branches of Christendom remained apart, Orthodoxy in the East and Catholicism in the West. And then along came that stubborn German chap, Martin Luther, and that stubborn English chap, Henry VIII, and those other stubborn chaps, Huldrich Zwingli and John Calvin and John Knox and Menno Simons and multitudinous others. From them came Lutherans, Anglicans, Swiss Reformed, Presbyterians, and Anabaptists (Mennonites). Then later, throughout the 17th century and into the 18th century, along came Baptists, Congregationalists, Disciples of Christ, Methodists, and other denominations. The 20th century saw the emergence of the Pentecostals.

All of these denominations sent missionaries hither and yon throughout the world. Those missionaries had varying degrees of success, from fantastic (Central and Southern Africa and Korea) to dismal (China, India, Pakistan, Iran, and anywhere else where Islam was already dominant). Then, in the 20th century, especially after the conclusion of World War I, Christianity started to wane in Europe, which had been its stronghold for almost two millennia. Today, dozens of nations in Africa, Asia, and Latin America have a far higher percentage of Christians in their populations than many of the nations of the European Christian heartland.

In the United States of America, there has been an uneven history of denominational dominance. To generalize, the 18th century belonged to the Presbyterians, the 19th century to the Methodists, and the 20th century to the Baptists. It has been speculated (with solid statistical evidence) that the 21st century will belong to the Pentecostals.

In none of this atrociously rapid historical summary am I trying to make any value judgments. Rather I am only pointing out what many who are career scholars (as opposed to yours truly, who is not) have said.

The major notion I want you to understand is that with the coming of the Protestant Reformation, denominationalism became the dominant factor in the unfolding of the Christian religion. Prior to that time, no one thought of "church" as being anything other than "Church," and that meant Orthodoxy in the East and Roman Catholicism in the West. But for five centuries, or one-quarter of Christian history, Christianity manifested itself through various denominational entities. No longer were there just churches; now there were Greek Orthodox churches or Catholic churches or Episcopal churches or Presbyterian churches or Methodist or Baptist or Congregational or Pentecostal churches. **THE Church** manifested itself as the Churches, those branches of Christendom with distinctive beliefs and/or structures and/or theological principles.

And all of that leads to

The Present

By the end of the 20th century, all that had started to change. And it is changing all over the world, not just in Europe or North America, where denominationalism and most denominations first emerged.

When Christianity took a foothold in such traditionally non-Christian nations as India, Japan, or Nigeria, there was no serious attempt to maintain denominational identities. Thus there is a

United Church of India, Japan, and so on. Although missionaries from various denominations in the 19th centuries established congregations in these nations, in the 20th century it became evident that where Christians were a decided minority, a denominational moniker was hindrance, not a help.

However, in those nations where Christianity became dominant (in Europe, North and South America, and Australia), denominations also are losing their influence. The "national" Churches of Europe, such as the Lutherans in Germany and Scandinavia, the Reformed in Switzerland and Holland, the Anglicans in England, and the Presbyterians in Scotland and Northern Ireland, have long since lost the majority of the populations of those Churches to other denominations or, more likely, to utter secularity. Australia has perhaps the lowest percentage of its population as active church members of all other traditionally "Christian" nations. In Europe today, an average of only 3 to 7 or 8 per cent of the people attend church on a regular basis. The percentages are not significantly higher in Catholic or Orthodox European countries, such as France, Italy, Poland, Ukraine, Greece, or any of the former Yugoslavian republics.

In the United States and Canada, the numbers are more encouraging. Nonetheless, both the percentage of church attenders and church members has been slowly dropping since the mid-20th century. The US has better numbers than Canada, but we too are dropping. And when polls are taken regarding church involvement and attendance, it is statistically undeniable that many American and Canadian Christians are simply bold-faced liars. A third to a half of respondents say they go to church regularly, but the numbers are much closer to one-sixth and one-quarter. Pagans, heathens, and believing non-attenders are truthful about their non-attendance, but church members blithely break the 9th commandment to a fine fare-thee-well. God knows they are shameless prevaricators, but they don't want anybody else to know it. And so, as it so eloquently states in the Episcopal Book of Common Prayer, "they think of themselves more highly than they ought to think." Tsk, tsk.

Accompanying this trend of a slow seepage of ecclesiastical involvement is a much more obvious trend away from denominational loyalty. With the rapid mobility of people in the post-industrial world, individuals or families tend to join a congregation they "like," one which "suits their needs," much more than one which is affiliated with the denomination in which they have been lifelong members. As a pastor associated with large churches for over thirty years, I would guesstimate that between half and two-thirds of the new members in those churches came by transferring their membership from a church of a different denomination, by re-affirmation of their faith (meaning that they had not been an active member of any church for a few years or decades), or by profession of faith (meaning they were officially joining a church for the first time as an adult). Well less than half had always been Presbyterians.

Furthermore, the greatest trend in church growth in the past twenty or thirty years has come through the establishment of non-denominational congregations, not churches which were sponsored by any particular denomination. For every new Methodist, Presbyterian, Lutheran or Baptist church, there have been two or three or five new congregations which subtly or loudly proclaimed no affiliation with any denomination.

Along with these changes there has evolved the growth of the "mega-church." A common definition of a mega-church is to say that it is a congregation in which there is an average Sunday attendance of 2000 or more people. Early mega-churches, those which emerged in the Sixties through the Eighties, tended more often to be denominationally affiliated. By now the great majority of newer mega-churches are not connected to any denomination, or they are members of non-geographical congregational clusters of loosely connected churches, such as the Vineyard churches. (As much as this non-sermon in sociological in nature, I'm not going to take time to provide further details about what many of these trends mean. If you already know, it will make sense, and if you don't know, you'll just have to trust that I am recording current ecclesiastical reality, even if you are not aware of these trends yourself.)

Referring to one part of these changes, Gene Edward Veith has some very cogent comments. He writes, "First the vogue was for local churches to drop their denominational affiliation from their name. Then came the fad of dropping the word church. The Community Assembly of God Church became first 'Community Church' and then 'The Community Family Worship Center.' Now words that so much as connote religious activities are considered too negative for the unchurched, so we have congregations that go by names such as 'The Center for Family Love.'" Then Mr. Veith gets right down to the nub of things. "Such churches are doing everything they can to eliminate anything that might make them sound like churches. Make it all like a pop concert or a TV talk show. If this is all there is, no wonder more and more Christians think they might as well stay home."

Great observations, Gene Edward Veith! When "churches" manage rapidly to grow into mega-churches by deliberately avoiding calling themselves churches, what does their growth mean? And if they aren't churches, what are they? Can there be a "churchless church?" Is it possible consciously to construct a Christian institution to replace the Church that does not automatically become part of the Church? If people say they aren't part of "The Church," but they are "church-like," can they avoid being either "church" or "Church?" Who is trying to kid whom here? If anybody is so gullible as to join a church which says it isn't a church but it is a church, then will they also be gullible enough to buy whatever cockamamie ideas are cast about in such a non-church church or church non-church? The organizing pastors of churchless churches are either too cunning for words or too deluded to be taken seriously! As the great American President-theologian said, "You can fool all of the people of the time, and some of the people all of the time, but you can't fool all of the people all of the time!"

Concurrent with the rapid growth of non-church churches is the growth of the mega-churches, as I have said. Cynthia Woolever and Deborah Bruce wrote a book called *A Field Guide to U.S. Congregations: Who's Going Where and Why*. Their research is based on answers from 300,000 worshipers in 2,000 congregations of various denominations (or non-denominations). They discovered an American church membership pattern that they describe as "50-40-10." That is, 50% of all churchgoers are involved in only 10% of American congregations. Further, 10% of all churchgoers are involved in 50% of all congregations. In other words, half of American Christians belong only to the largest churches, and half of all American churches have memberships of 75 or fewer members. We can translate these numbers into this fact: large churches shall continue to grow, and small churches shall continue to dwindle, given the unmistakable trends which are current in American Christendom.

It has been alleged that in many of the fastest-growing mega-churches, large percentages of the newest members have never been previous members of any church. Ms. Woolever and Ms. Bruce discovered that, quite to the contrary, only 7% of new members in any size or kind of church fit into that category. The vast majority of new members in every church join by letter of transfer (75%) or re-affirmation of faith (18%). Further, they state, first-time members make up only 2% of the American churchgoing population. In addition, one-third of all members of all churches have been members for fewer than five years, which suggests that there continues to be a very high degree of ecclesiastical mobility among American Christians. The two authors say that the typical person most values a congregation that is "sharing the sacrament of Holy Communion, the sermon or homilies, and traditional worship and music." (Take **that**, you pop-band-and-hokey-lyrics churches, yuh! As they say, he who marries the spirit of the times will soon find himself a widower!)

Jackson W. Carroll and Wade Clark Roof collaborated on a book called *Bridging Divided Worlds: Generational Cultures in Congregations*. They point out that many congregations deliberately choose to work with people of all ages, not trying to create generational "congregations within congregations." But some churches, especially mega-churches, intentionally attempt to divide into generational groupings, preparing various kinds of worship services and settings for each generation or sub-group. Such congregations may end up with separate constituencies who live uneasily with one another in the same building, the authors aver. Other congregations very consciously make their appeal only to one particular age group, knowingly wanting to avoid being, as the apostle Paul said, "all things to all people."

However, it is beyond Europe and North America where the most significant Christian growth is occurring, even though we in the USA suppose that the main growth is in American evangelicalism. This growth beyond the base of traditional Christianity is a fact of which most European and North American Christians are totally unaware. In 2001 David Barrett published the second edition of his monumental *World Christian Encyclopedia*. In it he stated that out of the roughly six billion people in the world today, five billion (or 85%) are what he calls "religionists." Of those, two billion are Christians, 1.18 billion are Muslims, and there are a billion Hindus.

There were 588 million Christians in 1900, and 2 billion of them in 2000. Most of that 20th century numerical growth occurred in less developed nations, despite what we might suppose. There were 83 million Christians in those countries a century ago, and now there are 1,120 million. Among denominational "families," Pentecostal and charismatic churches have seen the greatest growth in recent decades. They now account for 27.7% of worldwide Christians, says David Barrett, and their full-time workers represent 38% of the world's full-time Christian vocations.

In 1981, according to David Barrett, there were 20,800 denominations worldwide. Now there are 34,000. And **I** have the chutzpah to suggest that denominations are declining???!!!

But it is true. Most of that Pentecostal and charismatic growth is in congregations per se, and not in denominations at all. Thus, while the **number** of denominations may be increasing throughout the world, the **percentage** of Christians in non-denominational congregations is also increasing. To express it differently, fewer and fewer people are associated with more and more denominations, and more and more people are associated with no denominations whatsoever.

According to David Barrett, there is an astonishing shift going on within worldwide Christendom. Christianity is growing much faster in the Southern Hemisphere than in the Northern Hemisphere. In addition, whites are rapidly becoming a small minority of the world's Christian population. In 1900, 81% of the earth's Christians were white, but in 2000, that number had shrunk to 45%.

In his book *The New Christendom: The Coming of Global Christianity*, Prof. Philip Jenkins of Penn State University says, "At present, the most immediately apparent difference between the older and the newer churches is that the Southern Christians" (meaning the Southern Hemisphere) "are far more conservative in terms of both beliefs and moral teachings. The denominations that are triumphing all across the global South are stalwartly traditional or even reactionary by the standards of the economically advanced nations. Indeed that conservatism may go far toward explaining the common neglect of Southern Christianity in North America and Europe. Western experts rarely find the ideological tone of the new churches much to their taste."

Parenthetically, I would note that is perhaps the main reason why Pope John Paul II was so confident that his traditionalist posture for Roman Catholicism was the correct stance for him to take in his papacy. Mentally he probably gave up on European and North American Catholicism years ago. His hope was built on nothing less than Africa, South America, and Asia — and **their** righteousness. Even though hundreds or thousands of priests in those areas may have wives, and the Pope does little to discourage it, at least the laity among Southern Catholics don't practice much birth control, and they are producing little Catholics like there's no tomorrow (which there may not be, if they keep up their current level of production.)

And all of the above leads to

The Future

Where Christianity has been the strongest in the first twenty centuries of its existence (in Europe, and in nations organized and colonized by ethnic Europeans), it shall no longer be the strongest. The domination of world Christendom for the foreseeable future shall come from the Christians of the Southern Hemisphere. Blacks, Hispanics, and Orientals (to use my old-fashioned terminology) shall be calling the shots. Whites shall take the back seat. Probably there is more than a small degree of justice emerging from that reality. God never intended for Bwana to run the show anyway, even though Bwana always thought so.

In addition, Christianity in general is likely to become far more emotional, exuberant, and expressive than European or American Christianity has been. Some of us will get a severe case of the bitter quivers if we to live long enough to see that happen in a widespread fashion. Fortunately for us, most of us probably shall shuffle off this mortal coil long before **they** (the dark-skinned, conservative charismatics) take over.

Philip Jenkins postulates that by 2025, "Africa and Latin America will be in competition for the title of the most Christian region. About this date, those two regions will account for half the Christians on the planet. By 2050, only about one-fifth of the world's three billion Christians will be non-Hispanic whites." His conclusion is even more jarring, if also likely very accurate: "The difficulty is deciding just what that vast and multifaceted entity described as the Third World actually does want or believe. As Southern churches grow and mature, they will increasingly define their own interests in ways that have little to do with the preferences and parties of Americans and Europeans. We can even imagine Southern Christians taking the initiative to the extent of evangelizing the North, in the process changing many familiar aspects of belief and practice and exporting cultural traits presently found only in Africa or Latin America.... However partisan the interpretations of the new Christianity, however paternalistic, there can be no doubt that the emerging Christian world will be anchored in the Southern continents."

If Philip Jenkins is correct in what he says, and I suspect he is, then many American and European Christians may go into a deep psychological and spiritual decline as a result. Part of that decline is purely racist in nature, part is cultural, and part is theological. The traditional spiritual exuberance of Africans or Latin Americans is somewhat or even profoundly disturbing to some of us. Fortunately, none of us will be around fully to see this come to pass, if indeed it does happen as the experts predict.

Furthermore, as time goes on, and peoples and nations become more developed, they tend to adopt the values and mores of the social and theological "swells" above them. I am reminded of the disparaging line of the Presbyterian preacher in *A River Runs Through It* by Norman Maclean. The semi-autobiographical novel is set in early-20th-century Montana, and the preacher-father sniffs, "Methodists are Baptists who can read." Well, by the end of the 20th century, American Christianity belonged to the Baptists, just as by the end of the 21st century, it probably shall belong to the Pentecostals. But remember, in the 18th century Methodists were the hewers of wood and drawers of water for much of the rest of the Christian West (Britain and North America), but by the 19th century they had worked their way into the lower middle class. By the 20th century, Methodists were like Presbyterians and Episcopalians, except that their money was not quite as old or musty. Italian and Irish Catholics were severely frowned upon in the mid-19th century in the USA, but by the beginning of the 21st century, they were like "anyone else," "anyone else" being folks such as would read a book like this.

When I was in seminary in the early Sixties, the theological writers and the professors were all predicting that the world would rapidly become secularized. Most thought that was probably good, but some were fearful. The thesis proved to be almost completely wrong. Never in my lifetime has there been a higher percentage of religious people throughout the world than we have now, and never has religion — for good or ill — had more influence than it has now. This is quintessentially The Age of Religion, much more so than Will Durant or anyone else could ever have predicted. It is at once fascinating, frightening, and frustrating. But it also is true that multitudes of those religious people are not affiliated with any kind of religious group or congregation.

The two most obvious current advancements of religious inclination are Evangelical Protestantism, particularly Pentecostalism, and revived Islam, particularly of the most conservative variety. In seminary I was quite conservative. Over time I became (for **these** times anyway) quite liberal. But never in my wildest imagination would I have guessed in the mid-Sixties that in the first decade of the 21st century, religious people would become, in general, more conservative. But that is exactly what has happened. Maybe it is a reaction to the possible excesses of the kind of liberal Christianity represented by the Second Vatican Council, the World and National Councils of Churches, and social-activist mainline Protestantism on both sides of the North Atlantic.

Peter Berger, arguably the most influential sociologist of religion of the past generation, says this: "Evangelical Protestantism, I would propose, is an expression of the new global culture on the popular level; renascent Islam is definitely not, representing minimally a deliberate modification of that culture, in the form of an alternative route to global modernity, and maximally a determined opposition to 'Hellenism.'" Then, focussing specifically on Pentecostalism, Peter Berger writes, "I think there is a more important reason for seeing Pentecostalism as having a positive relation to the merging global culture, namely in its psychological and moral consequences. The most important of these is an *individualized* religiosity, pitting itself against traditional hierarchies and collectivities. Pentecostalism thus has the character of cultural dynamite, which is very reasonably feared by those who would uphold traditional culture" (Quoted from the newsletter of the Institute for Advanced Studies in Culture).

Andrew Greeley is that provocative, outlandish, brilliant, and iconoclastic Chicago priest-sociologist-novelist who regularly throws darts at the Church which ordained him and which probably has wished a thousand times it hadn't authenticated him as a priest. He and two academic colleagues very seriously suggested that one single factor mainly accounts for the rise of conservative religion all over the world, and it is that conservative religious women have had more babies than liberal religious women. They even go on to insist that three-fourths of the growth of conservative religion is explained by that unique obstetrical fact.

Holy cats! What if that is correct?

But maybe it **IS** correct - - - isn't it? Look at the number of babies in the nurseries of mainline Protestant churches or in Catholic churches compared to evangelical churches! Look at the number of babies being born to Islamic fundamentalist women or Orthodox or Hasidic Jewish women or Hindu women in the villages of India or Buddhist women in the poorest sections of southeast Asia! Go to Mea Shearim in Jerusalem, and you will be overrun by droves of very little ultra-orthodox kids, if the droves of bigger kids don't stone you to death for coming into their neighborhood! Go to Mecca, if they would allow you into Mecca, which they wouldn't, and see how many mini-Muslims are running around the streets! Visit the Pentecostal barrios of Sao Paulo or Mexico City, and visually check out the birth rate! When the rest of us are weeping and gnashing our teeth about the world being overrun by people, some of the people in the Third World and the First and Second Worlds are producing babies, seemingly with no concern for tomorrow! "Be fruitful and multiply" the Good Book says, and they are doing their part to uphold the divine decree!

And everything above leads to

A Brief Concluding Unscientific Postscript

A list of apparent ecclesiastical trends, past, present, and future:

PAST:
- Denominationalism rose to the forefront after the Protestant Reformation

- There was a progression of denominational dominance in the USA, first with the Presbyterians, then the Methodists, then the Baptists, and soon with the Pentecostals
- "Church" equated to "denomination" in the past

PRESENT:
- Church membership and attendance are dropping in Europe and North America, especially in mainline Protestant and Roman Catholic Churches
- Denominational loyalty is declining. "In those days there was no king in Israel; every man did what was right in his own eyes," as it says in the very last verse of the Book of Judges. If no central authority is recognized, no central authority is followed
- There is a rapidly growing number of non-denominational congregations
- Mega-churches represent a growing percentage of American church activity and attendance
- Increasing numbers of "houses of worship" are intentionally seeking to become "churchless-churches"
- Increasing numbers of congregations have targeted specific generational groups, almost to the exclusion of other age groupings
- There is a growing conservatism in all religions in many places throughout the world

FUTURE:
- The next several generations shall witness the most rapid growth in Christianity in the Southern Hemisphere
- Whites shall soon be a decided minority in world Christendom
- Despite earlier predictions to the contrary, there shall be a growing, not a diminishing, religiosity
- Secularity, instead of making headway, shall continue to lose ground
- Conservative religious women shall likely continue to have more babies than liberal religious women

And what shall be the results from all this? **First**, liberals, such as those who would read or affirm the thrust of this book of sermons, will have a hard time accepting these trends. Some liberals may go into a severe slump because of it. However, folks such as you and I should remember the wise old saying which originated only God knows where, "This too shall pass." Historical tendencies in the Church of Jesus Christ may take decades or centuries fully to manifest themselves. Whatever we have seen in our lifetime took many long years to come about, and whatever follows from our lifetime also will take a long, long time to work itself out. And, as Koheleth said in Ecclesiastes 3, "What has been is what will be, and what has been done is what will be done, and there is nothing new under the sun." So take heart, whoever you are. In the end, it will all work out as God intends; it really will.

That having been said, however, there are still three caveats which should be kept in mind by all Christians of every variety.

ACCOUNTABILITY: The danger of individualized, my-size-fits-only-me-and-that's-what-I-want, church-less Christianity is that there may be no real accountability to anyone, other than to myself. Protestants always ran that risk more than Catholics or Orthodox anyway. I believe that God has made us accountable first to Him, and then to one another. In human society, accountability to the self as a first priority doesn't count for much, despite what some fine-sounding philosophers have declared.

CONNECTEDNESS: If congregations, rather than denominations, represent the wave of the future, then who shall do the evangelizing on behalf of Christianity? Only very large and prosperous congregations can send out their own missionaries, but with so many of their own internal programs going on for their own members, will they choose to do it? And if they don't spread the word **abroad**, who will?

UNIVERSALITY: What becomes of the notion of "the holy catholic Church" if denominations and denominationalism

384

become marginalized or extinct as religious concepts? Can Christians perceive themselves to be part of a universal mission if they do not create and construct universal institutions to promote universality?

Not everything that is happening or shall happen is good, nor is everything bad. But it behooves all women and men of faith deeply to ponder what is happening, so that the future can be shaped by us, rather than having us apathetically shaped by it.